New York: *The Movie Lover's Guide*

New York: *THE MOVIE LOVER'S GUIDE*

THE ULTIMATE INSIDER TOUR OF MOVIE NEW YORK

RICHARD ALLEMAN

BROADWAY BOOKS
NEW YORK

An original trade paperback edition of this book was published in 1988 by Harper & Row Publishers, Inc. It is here reprinted by arrangement with Richard Alleman.

PRINTED IN THE UNITED STATES OF AMERICA

BROADWAY BOOKS and its logo, a letter B bisected on the diagonal, are trademarks of Random House, Inc.

Visit our website at www.broadwaybooks.com

First Broadway Books trade paperback edition published 2005

Book design by Caroline Cunningham

Maps by Jeffrey L. Ward

The Library of Congress has cataloged the hardcover edition as:

Alleman, Richard.
New York : the movie lover's guide : the ultimate insider tour of movie New York / Richard Alleman.— 1st Broadway Books trade pbk. ed.
    p. cm.
  Rev. ed. of: The movie lover's guide to New York.
  Includes index.
    1. Motion picture locations—New York Metropolitan Area—Guidebooks. 2. Motion picture industry—New York Metropolitan Area—Guidebooks. 3. New York Metropolitan Area—Guidebooks. 4. New York Metropolitan Area—Description and travel. I. Alleman, Richard. Movie lover's guide to New York. II. Title.

PN1995.67.N7A44   2004
791.4302'5'097471—dc22   2004054477

ISBN 0-7679-1634-4

10 9 8 7 6 5 4 3 2 1

To Bruce C. Kingsley—
for 35 years
of friendship
and for all the help
with this edition

Contents

Acknowledgments

Thanks again to Charles Conrad at Random House for green-lighting this project—and to Alison Presley for her hard work and enthusiasm in putting it all together. A special debt of gratitude to Bruce Kingsley, the consummate movie lover and budding film critic, for his invaluable help, research, and support; and to David Dedeaux for his further assistance on the research (and telephone) front. More thanks to Julianne Cho at the Mayor's Office of Film, Theater, and Broadcasting; Tomoko Kawamoto at the American Museum of the Moving Image; Paul Powers at the Department of Film and Media, MoMA; Bob Masher at the Theater Historical Society; Marc Wanamaker at Bison Archives; Tom Meyers at the Fort Lee Film Commission; Kristine Krueger at the Fairbanks Center for Motion Picture Study at the Academy of Motion Picture Arts and Sciences; Howard Mandelbaum at Photofest; Diana Biederman at 21; Audrey Davis at *Law & Order*; Louis Botto; *Playbill* magazine; Bruce Parker; Fordham University; Yonkers City Office; New 42nd Street Development Office; Edison Laboratory Historic Site; Robert Keser; Andrew Achsen; Christian Duva; Mary Ellen Rich; Thom Bowser; Pamela Grace; Arnold Himelstein; Otto Wahlberg; Stephen Ingerson. I also cannot forget many of the people who helped with the original edition: Ann Roth, Joan Micklin Silver, Pat Scott, Rochelle Slovin, Robert Koszarski, Stephen Drucker, Jessica Harris, Lisa Skelkin—and especially my dear departed friends Roy F. Barnitt Jr., Billy Reilly, and Martin J. Walsh, along with the late Tom Hanlon, Michael P. Miller, and J. Evan Miller.

Introduction

The idea for this book first came about when I was in Los Angeles in the mid-1980s researching the original edition of *Hollywood: The Movie Lover's Guide.* In my efforts to track down and document the surviving monuments of L.A.'s film past, I was constantly confronted by the fact that the real roots of the American movie industry lay not in Southern California, but in the New York metropolitan area. Practically without exception, almost every important film name and film company in early Hollywood either started off in or had strong ties to the East Coast. Someday, I remember thinking at the time, it would be interesting to take a closer look at those ties. But while I entertained the possibility of a *New York: The Movie Lover's Guide,* I feared that most of the studios and sites relevant to New York's early film history—which goes back to the 1890s—had long since been torn down.

Nevertheless, when I returned to the East Coast, my curiosity got the better of me, and I started poking around New York in search of lost movie landmarks. To my surprise, I found that there was a lot more for a movie lover to discover than I had previously surmised—early studios, movie palaces, and film locations; landmark hotels and townhouses where silent-screen idols stayed and played; superstar cemeteries; even an occasional scandal. In fact, I quickly realized that New York was crammed with as many movie sites as L.A. Only here they were less obvious, since film is just one of New York's many personalities and dimensions.

Ultimately, though, it wasn't New York's rich film past that convinced me that the time had come for a *New York: The Movie Lover's Guide;* it was its burgeoning film present. Indeed, in 1988, when the original edition came out, New York was enjoying a major comeback as a moviemaking center. Not only were historic studios like Kaufman-Astoria in Queens, which dated back to 1920, humming once again, but new studios like Silvercup, also in Queens, were coming on line to meet the growing demands of New York–based productions. Today, almost twenty years later, in the face of stiff competition from Canada, which frequently lures budget-conscious producers to its studios (despite unconvincing faux New York streets), the *real* New York City is still a major force on the film front, with movie and television production accounting for some $5 billion in the city's annual gross revenues. And not only are the studios still thriving and in many instances expanding, more are being built, such as the Brooklyn Navy Yard's brand-new Steiner Studios, which even features a back lot.

Besides new and expanded studio facilities, New York (and New Jersey) now boast a whole new crop of filmmakers—innovative directors like Kevin Smith, Todd Solondz, Darren Aronofsky, Wes Anderson, and most notable of all, Spike Lee, who has joined the ranks of urban legends Woody Allen, Sidney Lumet, and Martin Scorsese, all of whom document the local scene in their own unique fashion. And the NYC scene, constantly evolving and reinventing itself, has changed considerably since the first edition of *New York: The Movie Lover's Guide* was published. Downtown Manhattan, for example—from below Houston Street to Battery Park—was originally covered in just one chapter, but with the rise of camera-ready neighborhoods like SoHo, NoLita, and TriBeCa (where Robert De Niro has made New York film history with his Tribeca Film Center and Tribeca Film Festival), Downtown now requires two chapters. And whereas Harlem formed a relatively short section in 1988, the revised chapter on this happening Upper Manhattan neighborhood has virtually doubled in size.

And of course, since the original *Movie Lover's Guide* was written, the city has seen scores of memorable New York films shoot here. Witness *Working Girl, Wall Street, Fatal Attraction, When Harry Met Sally, Ghost, Malcolm X, GoodFellas, Donnie Brasco, Six Degress of Separation, Basquiat, Piñero, Manhattan Murder Mystery, Clockers, The Devil's Advocate, As Good as It Gets, Requiem for a Dream, 25th Hour,* and *Men in Black*—to name just a few. These and many more are featured in this new edition, which also looks at how some of New York's recent megahit TV series now rival film in the way they use the city as a location and help to define it—from *Sex and the City* and *The Sopranos* (shot entirely in New York and New Jersey) to *Friends, Seinfeld,* and *Will & Grace* (shot in Hollywood but with lots of NYC establishing and background shots). Indeed, so much has happened on the film and television scene since the first *Movie Lover's Guide* that over one-third of the material in this revised edition is brand-new.

As with the original guide, this book is designed for armchair travelers as well as for movie buffs wishing to visit the sites it documents. For those in the latter group, a numbered map precedes each chapter, but since many of these are not drawn to scale, it's a good idea to take along an additional, more detailed map, especially in the outer boroughs and New Jersey and Westchester County, where a car is also a must. Needless to say, because many of the places covered by this book are private property, movie lovers are requested to respect the privacy of tenants and owners at all times. Keeping that in mind, let's start traveling. There's a lot of ground to cover—not to mention over a hundred years of film history—on our movie lover's odyssey through America's greatest city.

—Richard Alleman

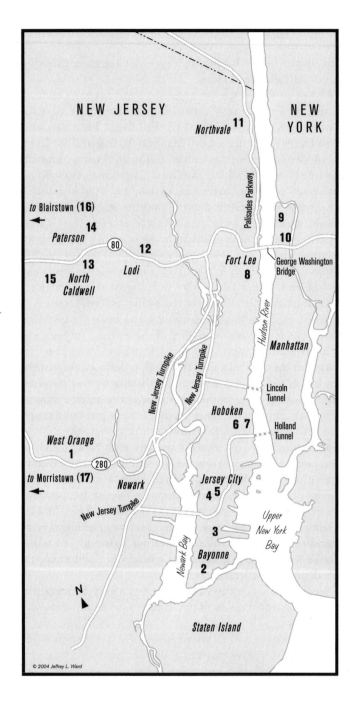

New Jersey: In the Beginning

For all intents and purposes, the motion picture as we have come to know it was born in the late 1880s some sixteen miles due west of the island of Manhattan at the Edison laboratories in West Orange, New Jersey. Recognizing that fact, we begin our movie lover's odyssey there. It wasn't just the Edison Company, however, that made New Jersey a powerful force in the early motion picture industry, because, from the very beginning, the state was home to scores of other film companies. These included long-forgotten studios with names like Centaur, Nestor, Champion, Eclair, Victor, Solax, and World—as well as many that are still familiar, like Fox, Metro, Selznick, Goldwyn, and Universal. All took advantage of New Jersey's then wide-open spaces and its pristine fields and forests for location shooting. The world's first Westerns were not done in Colorado or California—they were done in New Jersey.

Needless to say, today's New Jersey is a very different place and tracking down traces of the state's early film history can be as challenging as working on an archaeological dig. But for the intrepid movie lover who knows where to dig and what to look for, the rewards to be unearthed along the *west* bank of the Hudson River are many. These range from ancient movie studios to famous and infamous silent film locations and even to the world's first screening room.

Easier to find are the sites and locales associated with New Jersey's current big comeback on the film and television front—especially with the popularity of shows like *The Sopanos* and *Ed*. This chapter also explores this exciting new New Jersey world.

1. EDISON LABORATORY
Main Street and Lakeside Avenue, West Orange

For the movie lover, this is probably the single most important site connected with the development of the motion picture in America—if not the world—for it was here that, toward the end of the nineteenth century, Edison researchers perfected and successfully marketed a practical system for photographing and exhibiting moving images. Thomas Alva Edison is often credited as the inventor of the movies, but it is difficult to attribute this achievement to any one person since various inventors in America and abroad were experimenting with "moving pictures" at around the same time. And, indeed, even if we credit the Edison Laboratory with coming up with the first commercially viable motion pictures, it seems that Edison himself had relatively little to do with the project.

The real force behind the endeavor was Edison's assistant, an Englishman named W. K. L. Dickson who, as early as 1889, came up with a machine called the Kinetograph that showed moving pictures backed up by synchronized sound provided by an Edison phonograph. (It is said that the main reason Edison gave his go-ahead to motion picture development was because he saw the new medium as a way to further enhance—and thus further capitalize on—his already immensely successful phonograph.) The big breakthrough made by Dickson's device, however, was not the fact that it employed synchronized sound, but the incredible realism of the moving images it recorded. To achieve this, Dickson had taken advantage of George Eastman's newly invented celluloid film, which was thin, tough, and flexible. Cut into continuous 35mm strips and perforated with four holes per frame, the film was fed through the Kinetograph by means of sprockets, another key design element because these

The first mogul:
Thomas Alva Edison

regularly stopped the film for that fraction of a second needed to record the image on the frame. Today, more than a hundred years later, even with the rise of digital technology, most motion pictures still use 35mm film as well as this same basic stop-and-go sprocket mechanism.

In 1893, an improved version of this Kinetograph—redubbed the Kinetoscope and minus the synchronized phonograph—was unveiled at the Chicago World's Fair. Essentially a coin-operated peep show, the Kinetoscope was housed in a large wooden box into which the viewer peered to see a silent movie lasting less than a minute. Before long, Kinetoscope parlors started springing up all across the country, and Edison was in the motion picture business in a big way. To provide product for these Kinetoscope parlors, and later for storefront nickelodeons, where motion pictures were projected onto screens, Dickson built the world's first movie studio at the West Orange laboratory in 1893. It was really nothing more than a tar paper–covered shack with a roof that could be opened up and adjusted to let in sunlight. In addition, the bizarre structure was mounted on wheels so that it could be rotated to keep up with the sun throughout the day. The studio was dubbed the Black Maria, because it resembled the police patrol wagons of the period, which bore the same nickname.

What were the first Edison movies like? Directed by W. K. L. Dickson, they relied heavily on vaudeville and circus performers for talent—and showed snippets of everything from animal acts, exotic dancers, and Gaiety Girls to 1890s superstars like Annie Oakley and Buffalo Bill Cody. By the turn of the century, however, with the arrival of director Edwin S. Porter on the Edison scene, the company's films became longer and more sophisticated and started to tell stories. It was Porter who in 1903 directed what is considered the milestone of early story films, the eleven-minute-long *The Great Train Robbery*.

Today, one of the treats in store for the movie lover who visits the Edison Laboratory site (now a museum administered by the National Park Service) is the chance to see *The Great Train*

The first movie studio: Edison's Black Maria

Robbery on a big screen in its entirety. Several less well-known early Edison films are also shown: One features the original Little Egypt doing her famous hoochy-koochy; another is a slapstick comedy centering on a husband and wife's attempts to swat a giant fly. There's even a bizarre sketch using trick photography about a barber who removes the heads of his customers, shaves them, and then replaces them!

For movie lovers, other highlights of the Edison Laboratory site are the full-scale mock-up of the Black Maria studio, a working Kinetoscope from the 1890s, and Edison's handsome private library and study. A grand wood-paneled room with two balconied stories and a huge chandelier, the library has been left exactly as it was—down to the half-smoked cigars on the rolltop desk—when Edison died in 1931. Especially interesting is the little second-story projection booth that faces a large rolled-up screen suspended from the ceiling across the way. Edison's library, it turns out, was one of the world's first screening rooms.

While Edison's name is linked with many motion picture firsts, it is ironic how small a role his company played in the ultimate flourishing of the film industry. Immediately besieged by rival producers using what Edison considered to be pirated equipment, the Edison Company fought hard to retain supremacy in the movie business and summarily sued all competitors for patent infringement. Eventually some of these competitors became so strong that Edison stopped fighting and joined with them in 1908 to form the Motion Picture Patents Company. Effectively, this new organization was a business trust, and it was ruled illegal and dissolved in 1915. By that time, however, the competition from the outside was too strong and too innovative. The company that started it all was out of the film business by 1918. But at the West Orange laboratory, the movie lover witnessed beginnings, not endings.

As this book goes to press, the Edison Laboratory is in the final stages of a major restoration program that began in 2003. Set to reopen to visitors in mid-2005, the facility will once again offer guided and self-guided tours of its 1880s factory complex, which will now feature both Thomas Edison's private laboratory as well as his Music Room, where he auditioned singers and musicians for his

*phonograph recording business. Nearby, Glenmont, Edison's
spectacular twenty-three-room red-brick Victorian mansion, will
also be open to the public on weekends. For information, call
973–736-5050 and visit www.cr.nps.gov/nr/twhp/curriculumkit/
lessons/edison/4edison.htm.*

2. CENTAUR FILM COMPANY SITE
900 Broadway, Bayonne

Strange as it may seem, Hollywood has its roots in Bayonne,
New Jersey. In 1911 the Bayonne-based producer David Horsley
took his company of New Jersey cowboys and Indians and relocated to the small Southern California community of Hollywood. While several other East Coast film companies had
already discovered the sunshine of Los Angeles (as well as its
convenient location some 2,500 miles from the strong arm of the
Edison-led Motion Picture Patents Company trust), Horsley's
was the first to set up a permanent studio within the borders of
Hollywood proper.

But back to Bayonne, where a storefront—equipped with
bathtubs for developing film—was the Centaur Company's headquarters from 1907 to 1911. Specializing in Westerns, Centaur
came out with such provocative titles as *A Cowboy's Escapade*
(1908), *Johnny and the Indian* (1909), *Redman's Honor* (1910),
The Cowboy Preacher (1910), and *Those Jersey Cowpunchers*

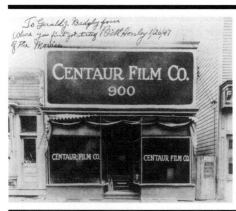

Centaur Film
Company,
Bayonne, 1908

(1910), which was a spoof on its own horse operas. When Centaur first came on the scene in 1907, unsophisticated nickelodeon audiences didn't know the difference between rural New Jersey and the wilds of Wyoming, but as directors started to shoot in the real West a few years later, a demand for more authentic locations soon arose. This prompted Centaur to move into other genres, including a series based on the *Mutt and Jeff* comic strip. It also prompted the company's 1911 move to the West Coast.

Today, the spot where Centaur once had its Bayonne headquarters is occupied by a one-story brick-fronted dentist's office. While this is not the original Centaur office building, the clapboard structures on either side of it—Vector Books and a party supply store respectively—were around in 1907. In fact, much of this section of Broadway, Bayonne's main street, is made up of little wooden buildings that, in an odd way, do not look unlike those of a small town out west.

3. THE PENINSULA AT BAYONNE HARBOR
52 Port Terminal Boulevard, Bayonne

When the U.S. Army departed from Bayonne's Military Ocean Terminal in 1999, this vast 2.5-mile-long, 430-acre port was redeveloped for civilian uses with offices, storage areas, and a cruise ship terminal. In a move to cater to New Jersey's burgeoning film industry, two of its vast warehouses were turned into soundstages for movies and television. It was in one of these that HBO shot its prison series *Oz* for several seasons and where it recently lensed the Glenn Close TV movie *Strip Search* (2003). The busy new facility has also provided soundstages for the features *A Beautiful Mind* (2002), *Two Weeks Notice* (2002), *Far from Heaven* (2002), *Eternal Sunshine of the Spotless Mind* (2004), and *The Forgotten* (2004).

4. STANLEY THEATER SITE
2932 John F. Kennedy Boulevard, Jersey City

Old-timers will remember the enormous rooftop sign that once proclaimed, "The Stanley . . . One of America's Great Theaters." And that it was. With 4,332 seats, the Stanley was one of the largest movie palaces ever built. Then there was its lobby, a spectacular space of faux-marble columns, grand staircases, cloud-painted ceilings, and glittering chandeliers. Finally, the house itself was a stunner—with walls of backlit, three-dimensional Gothic façades, including a replica of Venice's Rialto Bridge spanning the stage.

The Stanley opened its ornate brass doors back in 1928 with a mixed bill that featured a prerecorded welcome message by Norma Talmadge, a performance by the house orchestra, a stage show called *Sky Blues,* a newsreel, musical selections on the Wurlitzer organ, and eventually the film presentation, which was *The Dove,* starring the aforementioned Miss Talmadge and Gilbert Roland.

The Stanley survived as a theater for fifty years and, despite its enormous size, never suffered the ignominy of multiplexing. When it finally closed down in 1978, however, it was a prime candidate for the wrecking ball. Luckily, it escaped this fate when the Jehovah's Witnesses purchased the building in the early 1980s to use as a convention center, bringing some 5,500 volunteers to Jersey City to help with its restoration. While most preservationists applaud the saving of the Stanley, some regret that the theater's original Willy Pogany murals, which featured scantily clad Greek gods and goddesses, have been replaced by biblical scenes. Nonetheless, the good news is that the Stanley still stands, and movie lovers who wish to take a peek at it can stop by on a weekend when thousands of Jehovah's Witnesses converge on the place for meetings, religious services, and baptisms. A far cry from Norma Talmadge, Gilbert Roland, and *Sky Blues,* however.

5. LOEW'S JERSEY THEATER
54 Journal Square, Jersey City

Opened in 1929, this Journal Square landmark—boasting a wonderful baroque façade with a mechanical statue of the mounted St. George that periodically slays a dragon—was the most opulent movie palace ever built in New Jersey. Designed by the noted theatrical architectural firm of Rapp and Rapp, the dazzling gold Loew's Jersey auditorium seated 3,187 movie

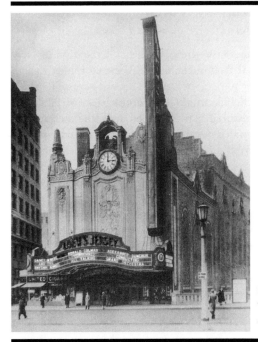

Loew's Jersey
Theater, Jersey
City, ca. 1930

lovers who had first passed under an equally dramatic three-story lobby rotunda supported by jade green columns. Although triplexed in 1974, the Jersey retained much of its original splendor right up to the day it closed its doors in the summer of 1986.

What followed were years of plans, schemes, and disputes about the theater's future—not to mention brushes with demolition. A happy ending eventually came when a preservationist group managed to get the theater de-triplexed, restored, and reopened as an entertainment and performing arts center for the Jersey City community. Today, a vital aspect of the theater's new life is its film program, which features classic films as they were meant to be shown—on the big screen.

For film program details, call 201-798-6055 and visit
www.loewsjersey.org.

6. OUR LADY OF GRACE CHURCH
400 Willow Avenue, Hoboken

It was *the* picture of 1954—an incredible collaboration of New York–based talent that brought together director Elia Kazan, screenwriter Budd Schulberg, composer Leonard Bernstein, plus a cast headed by Marlon Brando, and featuring Eva Marie Saint, Karl Malden, Lee J. Cobb, Martin Balsam, and Rod Steiger. And when Hollywood handed out the Academy Awards that year, *On the Waterfront* received no less than eight of them, including best picture, director, actor (Brando), and supporting actress (Saint). Not bad for an independent, low-budget, made–in–New York film.

Made in New York perhaps, but it was shot largely on location in Hoboken, the little town directly across the Hudson River from Greenwich Village in Lower Manhattan. In the 1950s, Hoboken, like New York City, was a thriving port, and it pro-

On the Waterfront in Hoboken: Eva Marie Saint, Marlon Brando, and Timothy Carey at Our Lady of Grace Church

vided an ideal setting for Kazan's hard-nosed look at the very real corruption that was an ugly fact of waterfront life in New York and New Jersey. (The film was based on a series of shocking newspaper articles by muckraking journalist Malcolm Johnson.) Today, the Hoboken docks and warehouses that served as backgrounds for *On the Waterfront* have been transformed into shops, offices, condos, and marinas. One important location from the film does survive, however: the Roman Catholic church where the crusading priest played by Karl Malden helped Brando's failed prizefighter-turned-longshoreman realize the forces of evil lurking in his union. For the church, Kazan chose Hoboken's historic 1874 Our Lady of Grace, a striking brick structure with a statue-studded Gothic façade and an ornate interior. Perhaps this interior was a bit too grand for Kazan, because a different, much more austere church (Hoboken's Sts. Peter and Paul at 400 Hudson Street) was used for the interior scenes.

Fans of *On the Waterfront* may also remember that a number of scenes take place in front of the church, including a touching love scene between Brando and Eva Marie Saint, where the two of them are sitting on a children's swing set. A bit of cinematic trickery was involved in these sequences as well. The shots that show Our Lady of Grace Church in the background were done in the park that's directly across the street; but when we see Brando and Saint looking out at the murky waterfront in the same scene, a different park (Stevens Park, which fronts Sts. Peter and Paul Church) was used. Films often use a combination of sites to create one location. By "cheating the location," that is, using two churches and two parks, Kazan was able to move the more photogenic Our Lady of Grace some four blocks away from where it really stood and magically reposition it . . . on the waterfront.

7. FRANK SINATRA HOUSE
841 Garden Street, Hoboken

The house where Francis Albert Sinatra was born on December 12, 1915, stood at 415 Monroe Street in Hoboken. It was demolished in 1968, and a parking lot now marks the spot. But

Sinatra fans can still check out the skinny three-story brownstone on Garden Street, where Hoboken's most famous native son spent his late teen years. Sinatra's father, Marty, was an Italian immigrant who had a string of jobs—boxer, bootlegger, saloon keeper, and fireman. Sinatra's mother, Dolly, as the world has learned from Kitty Kelley's "unauthorized" Sinatra biography, *His Way* (Bantam Books, 1986), was said to have performed illegal abortions in the basement of this same Hoboken house.

Young Sinatra, who attended Hoboken High School but never graduated, got his first break as a singer when he and three friends, appearing as the Hoboken Four, won a *Major Bowes Amateur Hour* radio show contest in 1935. This led to a tour, nightclub gigs, stints as vocalist with both Harry James's and Tommy Dorsey's bands, and by the early 1940s Sinatra had become the country's number-one teen idol.

With his great success as a singer, Sinatra was tapped by Hol-

Hoboken's favorite son: Francis Albert Sinatra

Frank Sinatra's
Hoboken home

lywood to appear in a number of fluffy 1940s musicals, but by the early 1950s, both his singing and film careers were on the downswing. Attacked by the House Un-American Activities Committee for supposed Communist affiliations, and by the press for alleged Mafia contacts, Sinatra was, as he said in a 1980s talk at the Yale Law School, "busted."

The surprise was that his acting ability, not his singing voice, brought about his comeback—notably through his Oscar-winning performance as Private Angelo Maggio in the 1953 film *From Here to Eternity*. With the roles that followed—in *The Man with the Golden Arm, Pal Joey,* and *High Society*—the kid from Hoboken wound up one of the most powerful figures in the entertainment industry.

Throughout the years, Sinatra, who died in California in 1998, had very little to do with his hometown. Among his few and far between visits were a highly publicized stop in 1947 for Frank Sinatra Day; a 1952 appearance at a benefit for the International Firefighters orchestrated by his fireman father; and a 1984 drop-by, to accompany his Hollywood pal Ronald Reagan to St. Anne's Church on the Feast of St. Anne (a holy day dedicated to pregnant women), where the president was to deliver a nationwide message against legalized abortions. Needless to say, the irony of Sinatra's presence at the event was not lost on some Hoboken old-timers who remembered what supposedly once went on in the basement of 841 Garden Street.

Today, Sinatra lovers who visit Hoboken will find, in addition to his childhood home, a pretty little park named for the singer, which was dedicated in 1998. Edging the Hudson, with great views of Manhattan, Frank Sinatra Park—off Frank Sinatra Drive—has benches, a soccer field, a launch for canoes and kayaks, and the Frank Sinatra Café, serving burgers and beer.

8. FORT LEE

Known to most New Yorkers as the town on the Jersey side of the George Washington Bridge (and to movie audiences as the suburb that was home to Rosanna Arquette in *Desperately Seeking Susan* and Ray Liotta in *Goodfellas*), Fort Lee is a booming community of upscale condos, corporate headquarters, hotels, and some of the highest commercial real estate prices in the Northeast. It wasn't always like this. At the beginning of the century, Fort Lee was a rural village surrounded by green hills, forests, and farms, with the added geographic distinction of being bounded by the dramatic Palisades cliffs and the Hudson River. Despite the fact that Fort Lee was easy to get to from Upper Manhattan via ferry boat (the George Washington Bridge wasn't built until 1931), the town was worlds away from the big city on the other side of the Hudson, and this fact was not lost on early film directors, who quickly came to see Fort Lee as the ultimate rural "location."

One of the first directors to discover Fort Lee was Edwin S. Porter, who in 1907 (working out of Edison's Manhattan studio at 41 East Twenty-first Street) used the towering cliffs of Fort Lee's Palisades for the exteriors of *Rescued from the Eagle's Nest*, a melodramatic yarn about a baby kidnapped by an eagle. In the film, the role of the mountaineer who saves the baby was

Fort Lee romance: Tallulah Bankhead and Tom Moore in *Thirty a Week*, 1918

played by a young actor named D. W. Griffith. A year later, Griffith would move to the other side of the camera to become a director at Biograph, and in this new role, he would often return to shoot in Fort Lee. Among Griffith's most important Fort Lee films are *The Curtain Pole* (1908), a slapstick comedy starring Mack Sennett before he, too, became an important director/producer; *The Lonely Villa* (1909), featuring Mary Pickford in her first performance on screen; *The Battle* (1911), in which Griffith developed many of the photographic techniques that he would later employ in his landmark *The Birth of a Nation;* and *The New York Hat* (1912), with its all-star cast including Pickford and Sennett, as well as Lionel Barrymore, Mae Marsh, and Lillian and Dorothy Gish in a story written by a fifteen-year-old schoolgirl from San Diego named Anita Loos.

Besides the scenic variety that Fort Lee offered as a location, the town provided an even more important commodity to the rapidly growing film industry—low-cost real estate—and soon a number of companies had built studios within its borders. The first company to set up shop in Fort Lee was the Champion Film

Company, opening on Fifth Street in 1909. Since Champion, which specialized in East Coast Westerns, was not a member of the Edison-led Motion Picture Patents Company, its Fort Lee facility was in constant danger of being closed down by this all-powerful trust of supposedly "legitimate" film producers. For this reason, Champion built its studio partially below ground level in order to disguise the fact that the building had a high ceiling and was actually a moviemaking installation.

Ironically, this little 1909 building is the only one of Fort Lee's many early movie studio structures that survives. Used today as a printing plant, it sits where Fifth Street comes to a dead end just beyond Washington Avenue. Across the street—actually more of an alleyway—from the Champion site, the house at 2486 Fifth Street was frequently used as a location in early Westerns.

The great flourishing of Fort Lee's film industry was from 1914 to 1919. By then, the Motion Picture Patents Company was no longer a force to be reckoned with (it was declared illegal in 1915), the feature-length film had become the staple of the movie business, and practically every major, and a number of minor, film companies had some kind of Fort Lee operation. Some of the more memorable Fort Lee movie names—Goldwyn, Selznick, Fox, Paramount, Universal, and Metro (the company that would become the first M of MGM)—are still household words. Other Fort Lee studios—Solax, Eclair, Victor, and Lincoln—are known only to hard-core film buffs and historians.

The scope of the moviemaking that went on in Fort Lee during its five-year heyday is astounding. For epics like Fox's 1918 *Les Misérables,* nineteenth-century Paris was re-created on some sixty acres of nearby farmland, and most of the townspeople were recruited for the film's cast of five thousand extras. It's also interesting to note that many famous films, which the world automatically assumes were produced in Hollywood, were actually done in Fort Lee. An example is Fox's *A Fool There Was* (1915), the vehicle that launched a Cincinnati tailor's daughter named Theodosia Goodman as the country's sultriest siren. (Wisely, Fox changed her name to Theda Bara.) It was also in Fort Lee, not Hollywood, that Mack Sennett made several entries in his Fatty (Arbuckle) and Mabel (Normand) series.

Alas, for all that went on in Fort Lee (some historians have calculated that Fort Lee in its heyday was responsible for 50 percent of all the feature films produced in the United States), the end came quickly. With the country's involvement in World War I, the government made it difficult for eastern movie studios to secure the coal they needed to heat their plants and, as a result, many companies headed to the warm West. A postwar economic slump further enhanced Southern California's hold on the film industry, since budget-conscious companies realized that it was just too expensive to have bicoastal production operations. Forced to choose between coasts, producers went with winter-free Southern California, and Fort Lee was finished.

Even sadder than Fort Lee's sudden demise as a film capital is the fact that almost nothing remains to remind the world of the city's glorious moviemaking years. Other than the print shop on Fifth Street that once was the city's first film studio, intrepid movie lovers will have to search hard for any tangible evidence of Fort Lee's movie history. But the city is waking up to its film

Fort Lee epic: *Les Misérables*, 1918

history, so the pale-blue clapboard house over at 2423 First Street, for example, now finally has a plaque that indicates that it was once an establishment called Rambo's Hotel. A popular hangout for film folk who ferried over from Manhattan to work in Fort Lee back in the 1910s, Rambo's also furnished an exterior for many made–in–Fort Lee features.

Another vestige of that same era was a big Victorian house a block away at 2405 Hammet Avenue, which once belonged to America's most famous theatrical family, the Fabulous Barrymores. All three Barrymore children—Ethel, John, and Lionel—worked in silent films on the East Coast, and some of those were made at Fort Lee. Unfortunately, the house was demolished in 2000 after a much-publicized battle waged by local preservationists to save it. Out of the defeat came a new appreciation by many Fort Lee citizens of the city's film legacy—and this translated into support for a film commission as well as a museum, which is now at 1588 Palisades Avenue and which has permanent displays of film stills and other historic movie memorabilia.

In addition to visiting the museum, movie lovers coming to Fort Lee will find several sites of interest on Main Street, which was once lined with so many studios that it was known as Studio Row. Although none of the actual buildings remain, recently the Film Commission dedicated plaques to mark particularly historic spots. The intersection of Main and Linwood Avenue, for example, has been renamed Theda Bara Way, in honor of the great silent-screen vamp who once made pictures at the Fox Studios, which were on the western side of the corner. Three more plaques (with photos and descriptions) can be found nearby in Constitution Park, also on Linwood Avenue, where Fox, American Eclair, and World all had studios. It was on this site that the Marx Brothers made their first film, *Humor Risk,* in 1922. Meanwhile, the town's newest plaque can be found at the entrance to the Food Emporium at 3000 Lemoine Avenue, adjacent to Fort Lee High School; it commemorates the first woman film director, the French-born Alice Guy-Blaché, who built and ran Solax Studios on this site from 1912 through World War I.

Granted, plaques go only so far in commemorating the days when a small New Jersey town played a major role in the history of the American motion picture industry—but for a long time there weren't even any of those. Another heartening development is the Film Commission's Cliffhanger Film Festival, held twice a year, which focuses on classic and often rare New Jersey–made films. Given the fact that some screenings are held at the restored Loew's Jersey Theater (see item 5) in nearby Jersey City, the festival does its best to bring back the grand old days.

The Fort Lee Museum is open weekends from 12 noon to 4 p.m. For information on both the museum and on Fort Lee's Cliffhanger Film Festivals, call 201-592-3663 and visit www.fortleefilm.org.

9. "PEARL WHITE MEMORIAL CLIFF"
Palisades Interstate Park, Coytesville

To the moviegoers of the early twentieth century, the term cliffhanger was likely to bring up the image of a hero or heroine confronting some life-threatening situation—from being tied to the railroad tracks with the train approaching to actually hanging from a cliff—at the end of an episode of one of the numerous serial films that swept the country between 1910 and World War I.

Of all the serial sirens who hung from cliffs in silent-film days,

Cliff-hanger: Pearl White atop the Palisades for *The House of Hate*, 1918

the actress who reigned as Queen of the Cliff-hangers was Pearl White. She starred not only in the legendary *Perils of Pauline* but also in a string of other serials with such titles as *The Exploits of Elaine, The Iron Claw, The Fatal Ring, The House of Hate,* and *Black Secret.* Most of Pearl's films were produced by Jersey City–based Pathé Studios with the financial backing of newspaper magnate William Randolph Hearst, who bolstered the circulation of his papers by running the serial in print at the same time as it appeared on screen.

When Pearl White needed a cliff to hang from, Coytesville's Palisades provided some of the steepest of any on the East Coast, with one that was a particular favorite of early moviemakers. Large and flat enough to accommodate several actors as well as a cameraman, it also jutted out a good 250 feet above the Hudson River in an especially dramatic—and photogenic—fashion. Today, this cliff of cliffs is unchanged, except that the George Washington Bridge now looms to the south.

Pearl White's cliff is not easy to find and should be visited only by the most intrepid of movie lovers. To reach the site, drive (a car is a must) north from the George Washington Bridge along the Palisades Interstate Parkway about two miles to the first gas station on the right. Pull in, park, and then backtrack south by foot for about ten minutes along the path until you reach a large clearing in the park. Continue walking south beyond the clearing for another hundred feet or so. Off to the left, you'll find a grass-covered step that leads to the cliff, as well as to a glorious view of the George Washington Bridge, the Hudson River, and Upper Manhattan. Be very careful, however, because it's very steep, very dangerous!

10. GEORGE WASHINGTON BRIDGE
Fort Lee

Almost a mile long, this sleek silver suspension bridge spanning the Hudson River between Fort Lee and Upper Manhattan was considered the "most beautiful bridge in the world" by the Swiss architect Le Corbusier. Since the George Washington Bridge is a relative newcomer on the New York City bridge scene (it was completed in 1931), it has never had the same landmark appeal to filmmakers as, say, the Brooklyn Bridge, which is almost half a century older. Still, the George Washington Bridge has been featured in a number of famous films, and for some reason, it has often spelled trouble!

A classic case in point is *Ball of Fire,* the 1942 comedy from Samuel Goldwyn that has Barbara Stanwyck, a gangster's moll named Sugarpuss O'Shea, hiding from the police in a Manhattan mansion inhabited by eight unmarried professors who've been cooped up together for nine years revising an encyclopedia. When one of them, the ultra-shy Bertram Potts (played by Gary Cooper), falls for, and instantly proposes to, Sugarpuss, she agrees to a marriage in New Jersey as a ploy to get herself out of Manhattan and safely into the arms of her underworld boyfriend. Cut to: Stanwyck and the now top-hatted professors gliding across the George Washington Bridge in a glamorous touring car en route to the bogus wedding. Warned by her boyfriend that the bridge will be "swarming with cops," Stanwyck has a very close call when the professor driving the car (he's the worst driver on earth!) rear-ends another vehicle at the toll booth. After a very dicey couple of moments, Stanwyck charms her way through the police, only to encounter real trouble later when she realizes that she's in love with Professor Potts ("He looks like a giraffe and I love 'im") and not her mobster man.

Another dreadful driver, Woody Allen, also has a rough go of it crossing the George Washington Bridge in *Manhattan Murder Mystery* (1996), as he and Diane Keaton pursue the neighbor they assume has murdered his wife. Allen obsesses about having an accident and is particularly afraid of hitting a school bus. When Keaton points out to him that it's night, Allen replies, "But what about night school?"

In *How to Marry a Millionaire* (1953), Fred Clark and Betty Grable also have some tense moments crossing the George Washington Bridge when returning from what the very married Mr. Clark had hoped would be an amorous adventure at his lodge in Maine with the very available Miss Grable. The Maine odyssey has turned out to be a disaster for Clark, however. Not only did Grable wind up catching the measles, she also fell for a handsome forest ranger, Rory Calhoun. Despite the fact that Clark has struck out with Grable, he still takes great pains to keep the trip secret from his wife and business associates. In fact, he boasts to Betty of his cleverness in returning to the city via New Jersey ("On this side of the river, no one knows me"). It's therefore quite a surprise when his 1953 Lincoln is met by sirens, police, and ultimately congratulations as he crosses the George Washington Bridge. It is, it seems, "George Washington Bridge Week," and Clark's car is the fifty millionth vehicle to cross the span.

On a decidedly darker note, the 1948 made–in–New York film noir *Force of Evil* also features a George Washington Bridge sequence. A depressing tale of the New York numbers game, the film stars John Garfield as a lawyer trying to get the numbers legalized, while his brother is hopelessly caught up in the illegal side of the racket. At the end of the film, Garfield finds his murdered brother's body ("like some dirty rag that nobody wants") floating by the rocks alongside the Little Red Lighthouse under the George Washington Bridge. More recently the lighthouse figures in the harrowing climax of the 2003 Jane Campion–directed Meg Ryan thriller *In the Cut*. But to say too much more would give away the ending.

As for good times, the bridge has had a few. Back on the New Jersey side, for example, it's at a carnival held under the magical span that David Moscow makes a wish to be a grown-up—and gets it, becoming Tom Hanks for most of the rest of the 1998 film *Big*. And who can forget that archetypal GWB moment when the Ricardos and the Mertzes cross the bridge in Ricky's brand-new 1955 Pontiac convertible at the beginning of their legendary journey from Manhattan to California in *I Love Lucy*?

11. STUCKEYBOWL
199 Paris Avenue, Northvale

Formerly known as Country Club Bowling, this abandoned New Jersey bowling alley with its orange-and-aqua color scheme and its vintage vinyl furnishings serves as the central location for the four-year run (2000–2004) of the NBC series *Ed*. Starring Tom Cavanagh as a New York lawyer (Ed Stevens) who had returned to his hometown (Stuckeyville) to start a new life after losing his job and his wife in the Big Apple, *Ed* focused on Stevens's new career as a bowling alley owner/legal adviser. For the series, the old Country Club Bowling location was extensively redone by removing twenty of the original thirty-six lanes to provide space for production offices as well as soundstages. Meanwhile, Northvale and the surrounding towns of Montclair, Ridgewood, Westwood, and Hillsdale were used for other Stuckeyville locations. For series star Tom Cavanagh, who called *Ed* "the best bowling-alley–romance–legal show on the air," a bonus to filming at the Northvale location was that he and cast members could bowl a couple of frames during lunch.

12. SATIN DOLLS
230 State Route 17 South, Lodi

Featuring topless pole dancers in G-strings, this classic road-house is where Tony Soprano and his buddies chill out from the rigors of a life of crime. A real-life location off Route 17, Satin Dolls (Bada Bing on *The Sopranos*) is a bunker of a building that features girls, beer, and biker nights.

For information, call 201-845-6494.

Satin Dolls: better known as Bada Bing in *The Sopranos*

Lambert's Castle, Paterson

13. LAMBERT'S CASTLE
Valley Road, Paterson

With its thick stone walls and its crenellated turrets and towers, Lambert's Castle (originally called Belle Vista) was the fantasy residence of nineteenth-century industrialist Catholina Lambert, the town's most important silk manufacturer. Built in 1892 and furnished lavishly with an eclectic mix of European and Asian antiques, the castle was an exercise in the nouveau riche ostentation typical of the times.

The visual power of the place was not lost on early filmmakers, and the Edison Manufacturing Company (Thomas Edison was a close friend of Lambert) is reported to have used the castle as a background for some of its productions. D. W. Griffith also used the castle as a location and, in 1910, shot a medieval adventure there titled *The Call to Arms,* starring a young actor named Mack Sennett. Sennett, of course, would soon become a director/producer and achieve world fame with his Keystone comedies.

Today, Lambert's Castle is the headquarters of the Passaic County Historical Society and is open to the public as a museum.

Besides exploring this strange structure with its Victorian Gothic interior of ornate twisted columns and sculpted plaster of Paris walls, there is an additional reason for movie lovers to visit this site. Just below the castle, on the flat grassy area between Route 80 and the hillside on which the property stands, the tracks of the Lackawanna Railroad once ran. Although there is still some debate among film historians on the subject, it is believed that many of the train sequences of the landmark 1903 film, *The Great Train Robbery,* were shot right down there. Important for being the first American film to tell a dramatic story in a sophisticated, cinematic way—with cross cuts, multiple locations, carefully choreographed action and chase scenes, and a large cast of actors and extras—*The Great Train Robbery* was also the first Western.

The grounds of Lambert's Castle are open daily, from dawn to dusk. The castle itself is open Wednesday through Sunday from 1 to 4 p.m. A nominal admission fee for adults includes a docent-guided tour. For information, call 973–247–0085 and visit www.lambertcastle.com.

The first Western: *The Great Train Robbery,* 1903

Niagara in New Jersey: Great Falls, Paterson

14. GREAT FALLS
McBride Avenue, Paterson

One of the little-known wonders of northern New Jersey, Paterson's Great Falls are a thundering mini-version of Niagara. First exploited by our country's original secretary of the treasury, Alexander Hamilton, the falls were harnessed to provide water power for the budding industrial city Hamilton helped establish at Paterson in 1791.

Toward the end of the nineteenth century, the falls were exploited in a different way by a pair of early filmmakers named Albert E. Smith and J. Stuart Blackton. Both English immigrants, the two were part of a vaudeville act called the International Novelty Company. The novelty was that they had an Edison projector and showed films as part of their routine. Quickly realizing that it would be both cheaper and more satisfying to produce their own films rather than to buy them from Edison, Smith and Blackton figured out how to convert their projector into a camera, and they were off and running as moviemakers. At first they shot street life, parades, prizefights—literally anything that moved. By 1897, they were ready to take on something really big, and decided to capture the power and majesty of Niagara Falls on film. But when they discovered that there were some pretty spectacular falls just twenty miles away in New Jersey, Smith and Blackton saved both time and money by hopping over to Paterson, where they shot the Great Falls and passed them off to the world as Niagara. According to Smith's autobiography, the film was shown all over the eastern United States and no one ever challenged its authenticity. The Vitagraph Hoax of 1897 may well have been the birth of serious special effects.

Today, Paterson's Great Falls form the centerpiece of the town's National Historic Landmark District, a fascinating area of museums, shops, and restored nineteenth-century mills and factories. The falls are also still used as a film location, most notably in an early episode of *The Sopranos,* as the spot where mobster Mickey Palmice threw a drug dealer to his death.

15. THE SOPRANO FAMILY HOME
16 Aspen Drive, North Caldwell

A long, tree-edged driveway leads to this grand modern mansion with the big doorway and the distinctive bowed picture windows on either side. Like most of the homes in this upscale

Suburban splendor: *The Sopranos* family home

Family portrait:
the Sopranos
at their front door

Essex County community, this one has the standard-issue pool and barbecue-ready patio in back. On television, this is the home of Tony and Carmela Soprano and their kids, Meadow and A.J. To his upper-middle-class neighbors, Tony runs a waste-management business, but to the millions of viewers who have made HBO's *The Sopranos* one of recent history's most popular nighttime television series ever, Tony has other business interests.

In real life, the Soprano mansion belongs to New Jersey builder Victor Recchia and his wife, Patricia. The Recchias don't appreciate gawkers on Aspen Drive, however, and have done their utmost to keep the exact address of their home out of print. Their quest for privacy did not keep them from making available a complete set of blueprints of their $3.5 million, 6,000-square-foot property, just in case some serious *Sopranos* fan wanted to build a Soprano home of their own. The cost of the plans—recently available on CD-ROM at www.sopranohomedesign.com—was $699.

16. CAMP NO BE BO SCO
11 Sand Point Road, Route 818

Just south of the historic west Jersey hamlet of Blairstown, this Boy Scout camp, which dates back to the 1920s, was Camp Crystal Lake in the original *Friday the 13th* (1980). A scary little tale of a homicidal child named Jason set on avenging his drowning many years earlier, this classic slasher film was inspired by the success of John Carpenter's ultra-low-budget *Halloween* two years earlier. Much like its cash-cow inspiration, *Friday the 13th* went on to spawn sequel after sequel after sequel. Playing a lead role in the 1980 original was a young Kevin Bacon. Another cast member was veteran TV actress and game show panelist Betsy Palmer as the monstrous Jason's mother. Like Camp No Be Bo Sco, Palmer went on to appear in several of the film's eight (and counting) sequels.

17. MORRISTOWN

One of north Jersey's most beautiful and historic small towns, Morristown was founded in the early 1700s and harbored Gen. George Washington and his troops in the harsh winters of 1779 and 1780 during the War of Independence. With its leafy streets and clapboard colonial houses, Morristown is a popular bedroom community for executives with offices in Manhattan, thirty-nine miles east. This proximity to Manhattan also makes Morristown a popular spot with New York location managers looking for a motion-picture-perfect East Coast hamlet for TV commercials, print ads, and the occasional feature.

In the screen adaptation of *New York Times* columnist Anna Quindlen's autobiographical novel *One True Thing*, 11 Farragut Place provided the idyllic college-town colonial home for professor William Hurt and wife Meryl Streep and their children Renée Zellweger and Tom Everett Scott. Documenting a mother's brave battle with cancer and her daughter's own coming to terms with her family, the 1998 film shot several weeks in Morristown as well as at Riverside Cemetery in nearby Clinton for the inevitable funeral sequence. Ms. Streep, by the way, grew up in the nearby New Jersey town of Bernardsville, where she appeared in

Oklahoma her senior year at the local high school. The actress has frequently quipped that the reason she does so many exotic accents in film is because her own nasal New Jersey twang is so boring.

In addition to *One True Thing,* Morristown can also be seen in *Firstborn* (1984), *Ed's Next Move* (1996), and *The Emperor's Club* (2002).

Midtown Manhattan: Archetypal NYC

The movie lover's Midtown Manhattan represents New York at its busiest, its most intense, its most exciting. This is the New York of landmark skyscrapers, legendary department stores, historic grand hotels, glamorous restaurants and nightclubs. Possibly the only place on earth with so much power, energy, and screen appeal concentrated in such a small space, Midtown is ultimately the hunk of New York that many people think of as "New York." One of the reasons that the images of Midtown are so powerfully embedded in our collective consciousness may well be because the area has been immortalized by so many films—especially films made in Hollywood, which needed only the right music and a couple of dramatic process shots of the Empire State Building or Rockefeller Center to establish their New York settings. Herewith, then, a look at this awesome part of town—focusing both on its screen presence over the years as well as on the dynamic (and occasionally scandalous!) roles that many of its famed hotels, restaurants, clubs, and office towers have played in the lives of the movers and shakers of the motion picture business. For the movie lover, indeed for the rest of the world, Midtown is not only archetypal New York, it's the center of the earth.

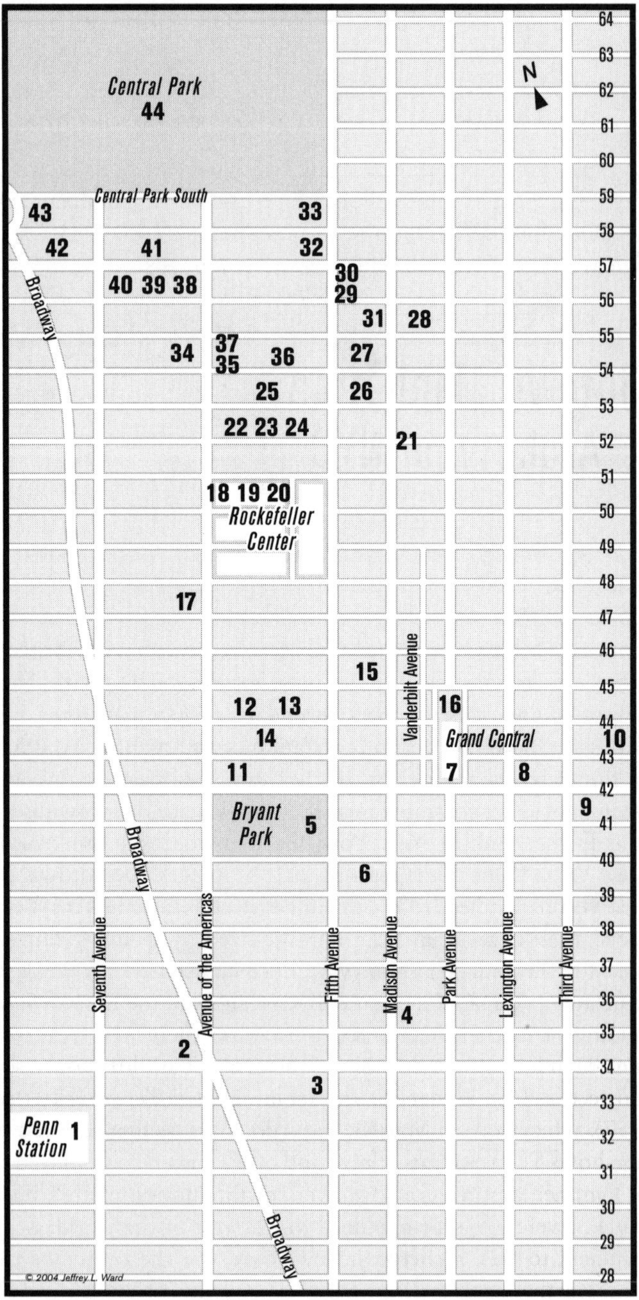

Central Park
44
Central Park South
N
64
63
62
61
60
59
58
57
56
55
54
53
52
51
50
49
48
47
46
45
44
43
42
41
40
39
38
37
36
35
34
33
32
31
30
29
28
43
33
42
41
32
Broadway
40 39 38
30
29
31
28
34
37
35
36
27
25
26
22 23 24
21
18 19 20
Rockefeller
Center
17
15
Vanderbilt Avenue
12
13
16
14
Grand Central
10
11
7
8
9
Bryant
Park
5
Broadway
6
Seventh Avenue
Avenue of the Americas
Fifth Avenue
Madison Avenue
Park Avenue
Lexington Avenue
Third Avenue
4
2
3
Penn
Station
1
Broadway
© 2004 Jeffrey L. Ward

1. PENNSYLVANIA STATION
Seventh and Eighth Avenues between 31st and 34th Streets

One of the greatest things about film is the way it can document certain landmarks for all time. A case in point is New York City's original Pennsylvania Station, a grand colonnaded Roman temple of a building—actually modeled on Rome's Baths of Caracalla—that was equally impressive inside with its spectacular waiting room and iron-and-glass train shed. Built in 1910, the station bit the dust in 1963, to be replaced by a massive but not terribly exciting modern hulk that combined an office tower, Madison Square Garden, and a low-ceilinged subterranean train station. So to check out the original, it's necessary to check out a few videos or DVDs. Start with *Applause,* a 1929 early talkie made in New York by director Rouben Mamoulian and starring the legendary torch singer Helen Morgan as an aging vaudevillian. In the Penn Station sequence Morgan meets her daughter, whom she's shipped off to a convent to spare her the realities of her tough showbiz life, amid crowds of commuters. Fast-forward to 1945 and Vincente Minnelli's *The Clock,* in which his then wife Judy Garland meets and falls for a soldier on a forty-eight-hour leave (Robert Walker) at Penn Station, where Walker rescues Garland's shoe, which has gotten caught in an escalator. Although the station scene is highly realistic, Minnelli had the capable MGM art department do up the whole thing in Culver City. But for Hitchcock's 1951 adaptation of Patricia Highsmith's novel *Strangers on a Train,* the director used the real station for a scene that has police following Farley Granger, who's the prime suspect in the murder of his estranged wife, which was actually committed by a stranger (Robert Walker) he met on a train. Penn Station was also one of the New York locations used by director Billy Wilder for the infamous *The Seven Year Itch* (1957), which starred Marilyn Monroe. The opening shot of the film shows Penn Station in all its skylit glory at rush hour on a hot summer day, as Tom Ewell puts his family on a train to Maine. Ewell will stay behind in Manhattan and return to his apartment to find Marilyn as his new neighbor.

As for the current Penn Station, it has made relatively few

screen appearances, since New York boasts a much more popular and spectacular train-station location in Grand Central. Still, movie lovers can catch today's Penn Station in *Clockers* (1995), *Hurricane Streets* (1997), and *A Perfect Murder* (1998). In the last, Viggo Mortensen tries to escape with $400,000 on an Amtrak overnighter to Montreal. A maniacal Michael Douglas foils his plan, however.

Meanwhile, if all goes according to plan, a third Penn Station will soon rise within what was the former U.S. Post Office Building. Standing directly across Eighth Avenue from the current Penn Station/Madison Square Garden, the old post office structure is another neoclassical affair with an enormous staircase leading to a colonnaded arcade. It went up in 1913, four years after the original Penn Station, and was designed in the image of its neighbor. Thus, when it opens in 2006, New York's new Penn Station will look and feel much more like the original. Good news for travelers, filmmakers, and movie lovers.

2. MACY'S
Herald Square

"The world's largest store" boasts over 2 million square feet of floor space and reportedly employs as many as ten thousand salespeople! For the movie lover, the significance of Macy's has less to do with retailing statistics than with a very important event that took place over a century ago in the building that once stood on the mammoth department store's Herald Square site. That building—demolished at the beginning of the twentieth century to make way for Macy's—was a theater called Koster and Bials Music Hall, and it was there that, on April 23, 1896, Thomas Edison publicly unveiled the Vitascope, a magical machine that *projected* lifelike moving images on a twenty-foot screen set in a huge gilded frame. There were many oohs and aahs at Koster and Bials that famous evening as the audience saw a group of seconds-long snippets of such things as a prizefight, dancing girls, and "Venice, showing gondolas." One of these little films, titled *Sea Waves*, depicted rough surf and crashing breakers and is said to have caused a bit of a stir among the spectators in the front rows. The magic, and ultimately the power, of motion pictures was clear right from the start.

The first picture show: Koster and Bials Music Hall, 1890s

About ten years after the debut of motion pictures on the Macy's site, Edison's top director, Edwin S. Porter, shot an important early story film using the newly erected department store as a location. The film, titled *Kleptomaniacs,* told the parallel stories of two women, one rich, the other poor, who get caught shoplifting at a big department store—and pointed out the disparities between the ways society treats the rich and the poor. The wealthy woman is let off and considered an unfortunate victim of kleptomania, whereas the other woman is arrested and ruthlessly hauled off to jail. Clearly, the movies had come a long way in ten years.

Forty years after *Kleptomaniacs,* Macy's had come a long way, too, when it was given a starring role in Twentieth Century–Fox's 1947 Christmas classic, *Miracle on 34th Street,* which pits an eccentric Macy's Santa Claus against a bah-humbug toy department head. Besides a number of exteriors shot at Macy's, the film also includes footage of the store's famed once-a-year media event, the Macy's Thanksgiving Day Parade. The parade turned up again in the lackluster 1994 remake of *Miracle,* which although still set in New York, was shot largely in Chicago. Since Macy's refused to be associated with the remake, the store's name was changed to the fictitious CF Cole's, with Chicago's famous Art Institute serving as the faux store's exterior.

Back in Manhattan, other films that have immortalized the real Macy's have been the George Cukor–directed made–in–New York screwball comedy *It Should Happen to You* (1954), where a newly famous Judy Holliday is mobbed by autograph hounds while shopping for sheets; *Auntie Mame* (1958), which finds Rosalind Russell, as the madcap Mame, trying to sell roller skates at Macy's at Christmastime; *Love with the Proper Stranger* (1963), where Natalie Wood works in the pet department and where her love Steve McQueen draws quite a crowd outside the store when he plays bagpipes at the end of the film wearing a "Better Wed Than Dead" sign; *The Group* (1966), in which Kay Strong, played by Joanna Pettet, rises up the retail

Natalie Wood, John Payne, and Macy's Thanksgiving Day Parade in *Miracle on 34th Street*, 1947

ladder as a Macy's executive, only to find that corporate success doesn't necessarily mean happiness; and *Radio Days* (1987), where Little Joe (who grows up to be Woody Allen) is treated to a chemistry set in the toy department in the 1940s.

3. EMPIRE STATE BUILDING
350 Fifth Avenue

Of all New York's landmarks, none is as closely associated in the popular imagination with one single film as is the Empire State Building with the legendary monster movie *King Kong*. When RKO released the picture in 1933, the Empire State Building was barely two years old, but it had already made history as the world's tallest building. Soaring 1,250 feet into the air, this sleek sandstone-and-steel structure stunned the world with its 102 stories, 87 elevators, 2 observation decks, and special mooring for airships. Despite the impressiveness of its statistics, the Empire State Building bombed when it first opened—the Depression was in full swing and few firms were able to afford its offices. *King Kong,* on the other hand, was a big box-office success and helped fill RKO's coffers for decades. In 1981, however, the tables were turned when the now booming Empire State Building decided to celebrate the great ape's fiftieth birthday by flying an eight-story-tall nylon balloon version of King Kong from its observation tower. Alas, the aging superstar had a rather rough time of it. No one could get him blown up properly; he kept springing leaks; and finally he had to be taken down when high winds threatened to blow away his half-inflated hulk. The whole fiasco became the subject of ridicule in the newspapers and on the radio. The real King Kong, by the way, was an eighteen-inch-tall, fur-covered jointed metal skeleton designed by a pioneer in puppet animation techniques named Willis O'Brien.

Besides *King Kong,* the Empire State Building has been used in countless other films. Not only does its towering presence announce that we are definitely in the greatest city on earth, its eighty-sixth-floor observation deck—usually re-created on a soundstage in Hollywood—has traditionally provided one of the screen's most romantic rendezvous points. Think of all those *Love Affair*s in which it's played a pivotal role—from the 1939

Metropolitan monsters; King Kong and the Empire State Building

Charles Boyer–Irene Dunne original to the 1957 Cary Grant–Deborah Kerr remake (*An Affair to Remember*) to the 1994 Annette Bening–Warren Beatty version. The observation deck has also been immortalized in *The Clock* (1945), *On the Town* (1949), *The Moon Is Blue* (1953), and *Sleepless in Seattle* (1993), where long-distance lovers Tom Hanks and Meg Ryan finally come face-to-face high above Manhattan. For *Sleepless*, the building's exterior and lobby shots were the real thing, but the deck was a set in Seattle.

On a less romantic note, the Empire State Building's distinctive spire takes on a much different significance in the 1991 film *Piñero*, which documents the rise and fall of drug-addicted avant-garde Puerto Rican playwright Miguel Piñero. As the playwright, played by Benjamin Bratt of *Law & Order* fame, becomes increasingly undermined by his demons, the spire, at first so glamorous and seductive, comes to look ominously like a hypodermic needle.

Movie lovers wishing to visit the Empire State Building can do so any day of the week between 9:30 a.m. and 11:30 p.m. For

information and prices, call 212-736-3100. In addition to the romantic observation deck, it's possible to take an elevator to the circular, glassed-in observatory on the 102nd story. Visit www.esbnyc.com.

4. MORGAN COURT
211 Madison Avenue

In architectural circles, an ultrathin high-rise is known as a sliver—and in 1993, this thirty-three-foot-wide, thirty-two-story Murray Hill apartment building provided housing for Sharon Stone as well as the name of the movie she starred in. In *Sliver,* the address of the building is given incorrectly—a frequent ploy of moviemakers to confuse location spotters—as 113 East 38th Street. To further complicate matters, the entrance used in the film was a much more photogenic and camera-friendly faux-glass affair created just for the film out of the sliver's rear entrance on 36th Street.

Morgan Court, the "sliver" of an apartment building used in *Sliver,* 1993

The New York Public Library

5. NEW YORK PUBLIC LIBRARY
455 Fifth Avenue

One of the city's most impressive Beaux Arts buildings, this 1911 masterpiece is especially known for the two gigantic marble lions that guard its grand staircase. In a long-forgotten 1935 Claudette Colbert film, the library steps provide the regular popcorn-munching spot for Colbert and her buddy Fred MacMurray; the scenes involved a combination of Hollywood studio sets and real NYC footage. The same was true when the library appeared in Vincente Minnelli's *The Clock* (1945), during Judy Garland and Robert Walker's forty-eight-hour whirlwind visit to Manhattan before soldier-on-leave Walker has to report back to the base . . . and again in MGM's *On the Town* (1949). The library can also be seen in the original *Ghostbusters* (1984), as the site of a ghost-busting operation that involved ridding the place of a phantom librarian who was causing trouble in the stacks. In the remake of *The Thomas Crown Affair* (2000), the library masqueraded as the grand foyer of the Metropolitan Museum of Art, which re-fused to allow any part of its property to be used in a film that involved an art heist. In *Spider-Man* (2002), the library was the dramatic backdrop for the scene where Tobey "Spider-Man" Maguire is dropped off by his uncle (Cliff Robertson), who is later shot and killed by carjackers at the same landmark Midtown location.

Behind the library is Bryant Park, a beautifully landscaped space with gravel walkways, folding garden chairs, and park benches. The park looks positively Parisian in *Manhattan Murder Mystery* (1993), when amateur sleuth Diane Keaton reports on her latest caper to her husband, Woody Allen, in front of the park's gushing fountain. Bryant Park is also the site of one of New York City's most glittering biannual events—Fashion Week—which sees top designers parade their latest frocks in fashion shows within huge tents; the scene is well documented in *Unzipped* (1995), an insider's look at the wacky world of fashion designer Isaac Mizrahi, who lately has become a bit player in Woody Allen's stable, having appeared in *Celebrity* (1998), *Small Time Crooks* (2000), and *Hollywood Ending* (2002).

Visit www.nypl.org.

Diane Keaton and Woody Allen at the Bryant Park fountain in *Manhattan Murder Mystery,* 1993

6. DYLAN HOTEL
52 East 41st Street

For some six months in 2002, this chic boutique hotel was much in the news as the site of pop-star Britney Spears's Nyla restaurant. Like many rising celebrities such as Jennifer Lopez, who is the principal backer of the popular Pasadena eatery Madre's, Spears was attracted by the restaurant business to further cement her celebrity and further enrich her coffers. She was not as lucky as Lopez, however, for Nyla seems to have been cursed from the get-go, with some five hundred fans jeering Spears on the establishment's rain-soaked opening night, when the diva arrived ninety minutes late and shot inside without even a wave to the crowd. As the months went on, Nyla was plagued with hygiene violations, morale problems among its staff, and serious financial issues. Six months after its opening, Spears severed her connection with the place, after which she was sued by a group of creditors who claimed the celebrity eatery owed them some $44,000. Nyla closed soon thereafter, but despite its failure, it nonetheless lasted somewhat longer than Spears's January 2004 wedding to hometown pal Jason Allen Alexander, which was annulled a mere fifty-five hours after it took place. For the nuptials, held at Las Vegas's Little White Wedding Chapel, the bride wore torn jeans and a baseball cap.

7. GRAND CENTRAL TERMINAL
89 East 42nd Street

Back in the glory days of Hollywood, during the 1930s and 1940s, if you were heading from New York to the West Coast, chances were Grand Central Terminal was where you would have begun your journey. And the train that you would have taken was the legendary *Twentieth Century Limited*, which traveled overnight to Chicago, where passengers would then board the *Super Chief* for the rest of their westward trek. The *Twentieth Century* left Grand Central every evening at around six o'clock from track 34, where a red carpet would be rolled out for departing passengers. Making their way down that carpet might have been Marlene Dietrich or Joan Crawford, with two or three redcaps in tow to handle their voluminous baggage. Both stars, according to former Grand Central redcap Oswald S. Throne, were good tippers, as was Mae West, who not only traveled with lots of luggage, but with five or six male "escorts" as well!

Alas, times and travel styles have changed. The *Twentieth Century* bit the dust in the mid-1960s, and Grand Central, which once was home to a number of other glamorous, long-distance trains, caters mostly to commuters these days. Still, Grand Central's glorious 1913 Beaux Arts terminal building—with its massive marble staircase, seventy-five-foot-high windows, and twinkling-star-studded ceiling—remains one of New York City's most dramatic public spaces. Grand Central is also a triumph of preservation. In the 1970s, it narrowly escaped "radical alterations" planned by developers who wanted to build a high-rise office building on top of it. Thanks to the commitment of concerned citizens—including the late Jacqueline Kennedy Onassis, who organized a grassroots campaign to ensure its landmark

NYC super station: Grand Central

status—this didn't happen, and it has since been magnificently restored.

Over the years, Grand Central (or Hollywood facsimiles thereof) has appeared in many movies. In 1934, the landmark station was the final location for *Twentieth Century,* the Columbia Pictures comedy about a Broadway producer (John Barrymore) and his protégée (Carole Lombard), much of which takes place aboard the train of the same name, and all of which was shot in Hollywood. Meanwhile, old-movie lovers can spot MGM's version of Grand Central in *Going Hollywood* (1933) and *The Thin Man Goes Home* (1944). In the latter, Asta breaks loose in the terminal at rush hour and a very hungover Nick Charles (William Powell) has one hell of a time retrieving the pooch.

By the 1950s, however, going on location had become the rage. Thus, when Cary Grant needed to make a fast escape from New York City aboard the *Twentieth Century,* in *North by Northwest* (1959), director Alfred Hitchcock shot the sequence at night inside the real station. In 1965, director John Frankenheimer also used the real thing when he shot the opening sequence of the thriller *Seconds* at Grand Central, which tells the story of an aging businessman (John Randolph) who gets a new lease on life (and into big trouble) after plastic surgery that turns him into Rock Hudson. Other thrillers to use the dramatic terminal to great effect have been *A Stranger Is Watching* (1982), in which a psychopath holds a mother and child captive in a secret Grand Central cavern; Peter Yates's *The House on Carroll Street* (1988), which lensed its spectacular climax on location at the station; and *A Shock to the System* (1990), which shows businessman-commuter Michael Caine morphing into a murderer after a younger coworker beats him out of a promotion.

Another famous Grand Central commuter was Richard Gere, who rode Metro North from Westchester to his job in Manhattan in *Unfaithful* (2002), whereas his wife Diane Lane traveled the same route (later in the day) to hook up with her hot young stud in Downtown Manhattan. Gere and Lane came to Grand Central under decidedly different circumstances in Francis Ford Coppola's *The Cotton Club* (1984), when at the end of the film Gere gets the gangster's girlfriend (Lane), and the two of them take off for Hollywood aboard the *Twentieth Century Limited*. One of the most romantic Grand Central moments ever, however, is in *The Fisher King* (1991), when Robin Williams and Amanda Plummer magically turn the whole place into a glittering ballroom.

Other notable films to use Grand Central include *Midnight Run* (1988), *Loose Cannons* (1990), *Carlito's Way* (1993), *Hackers* (1995), *One Fine Day* (1996), *Extreme Measures* (1996), *Conspiracy Theory* (1997), and *Tadpole* (2003). And finally, a trio of films with great fake Grand Central sequences: *Beneath the Planet of the Apes* (1970), which featured a well art-directed, postapocalyptic Grand Central; the original *Superman* (1978), where the spectacular scenes of archvillain Lex Luthor's fantastic subterranean Grand Central palazzo were all done on a soundstage at a London movie studio; and Sergio Leone's saga of Jewish gangsters, *Once Upon a Time in America* (1984), whose Grand Central scenes were actually shot at Paris's Gare du Nord, proving that one good *gare* deserves another.

Besides serving as an important movie location, Grand Central once had a CBS television studio on one of its upper stories, and the early dramatic series *Man Against Crime*, starring Ralph Bellamy, was broadcast live from here between 1949 and 1952. Sponsored by Camel cigarettes, the program always showed the good guys smoking, and never allowed its bad guys a single puff! Today, the old CBS studio is now a tennis club that charges over $100 an hour for a court.

Movie lovers who want to see Grand Central Terminal close-up— the building is loaded with intriguing nooks, crannies, catwalks, and a glamorous, relatively new food court—can take the walking tour sponsored by the Municipal Art Society that is given every Wednesday at 12:30 p.m. The tour meets in front of the main information kiosk on the Main Concourse—and it's free, although donations are appreciated. All aboard!

Visit www.grandcentralterminal.com.

Divine Deco: Chrysler
Building

8. CHRYSLER BUILDING
405 Lexington Avenue

It must be one of New York City movie director Sidney Lumet's
favorite skyscrapers because in *The Wiz,* when Diana Ross and
Michael Jackson ease on down the road into Lumet's fantasy ver-
sion of Manhattan as the Emerald City of Oz, no less than five
Chrysler Buildings pop up on the horizon—and not one Empire
State Building! Woody Allen, who once said, "There are very few
modern skyscrapers that I like," nevertheless includes the 1931
Chrysler Building on the itinerary of the architectural tour of
Manhattan that Sam Waterston gives in Allen's *Hannah and Her
Sisters*—whereas the Empire State Building is noticeably absent.
And when Dustin Hoffman points out major Manhattan land-

marks to his son in Robert Benton's *Kramer vs. Kramer,* the Chrysler Building tops the list.

More recently, in *Two Weeks Notice* (2002), Hugh Grant and Sandra Bullock circle the building in a helicopter, while Grant tells of the famous rivalry in the late 1920s between the Chrysler Building's architect William Van Allen and his former partner H. Craig Severence to build the world's tallest building. (Severence, who was working on the Manhattan Company Building at 40 Wall Street, lost—and both men were overshadowed a few years later when the Empire State Building made its debut.) And when Ridley Scott wants to symbolize Manhattan at its most glamorous in *Someone to Watch Over Me,* he dazzles us with nighttime views of this glorious 1930s high-rise. What is it about the Chrysler Building that's so appealing? Its six-story Art Deco spire? Its huge chrome gargoyles (one of which provides the steely opening image for the 1990 film version of Tom Wolfe's *The Bonfire of the Vanities*), which were designed to look like 1931 Chrysler hood ornaments? Or simply the fact that there will never be another building quite like this one?

The Chrysler Building's meatiest film role may well have been in a campy made-in-Manhattan monster movie called *Q,* about a gigantic mythological bird that comes to life and flies about zapping hard hats, window washers, penthouse sunbathers, and various other high-level New Yorkers. The creature's nest? You guessed it . . . the spire of the Chrysler Building. With its inane plot and over-the-top performances by Michael Moriarty, David Carradine, Candy Clarke, and Richard Roundtree, *Q* is a treat not just for cult-film buffs, but for architecture lovers too, because it features lots of shots of the Chrysler Building's sleek lobby of Moroccan marble and stainless steel and also provides rare close-up glimpses of the skyscraper's distinctive spire from every conceivable angle.

9. THE NEWS BUILDING
220 East 42nd Street

Christopher Reeve and Margot Kidder stopped traffic back in 1977 when they emerged from the lobby of the then Daily News Building, during the filming of *Superman.* In this big-budget movie version of the famous comic strip, the landmark 1930 of-

Margot Kidder/Lois Lane in the *Daily News/Daily Planet* lobby for *Superman,* 1978

fice building of a great metropolitan newspaper, the *Daily News,* doubled as the headquarters for the legendary *Daily Planet.* Especially striking, both in the *Superman* film and in real life, is the twelve-foot globe that revolves under a spectacular black-glass cupola in the lobby of the building, which is now simply the News Building, since the *Daily News* relocated to West 33rd Street in the 1990s. Movie lovers may also recall the thrilling helicopter crash that supposedly took place on the roof of the Daily Planet Building, leaving Lois Lane/Margot Kidder dangling from the side of the structure. Those sequences were a triumph of special effects—not location shooting.

10. SCREEN GEMS STUDIOS
222 East 44th Street

Unlike Hollywood, where most of the film and TV facilities are concentrated in large studio buildings and complexes, New York constantly surprises with its many small studios dotted across the city. A case in point is this CBS-run soundstage, currently home to the soap opera *The Guiding Light.* Among the New York actors who performed on this venerable soap early in their careers are Kevin Bacon, Sarah Michelle Gellar, Allison Janney, Mira Sorvino, and JoBeth Williams.

Visit www.screengemsstudios.com.

11. HBO
1100 Avenue of the Americas

The daring cable network that frequently leaves the big television networks in the dust—with sophisticated, edgy, and frequently sexually explicit series like *Sex and the City, Six Feet Under,* and *The Sopranos*—has its New York City base here. Besides TV series, HBO is known for its award-winning TV movies, mini-series, and docudramas. Among them are *Band of Brothers, And the Band Played On, Barbarians at the Gate, Gotti, Truman, Gia, Citizen Cohn, Winchell,* and *Angels in America.*

Visit www.hbo.com.

12. ALGONQUIN HOTEL
59 West 44th Street

A hotel that is a literary landmark, the Algonquin will always be linked to an irreverent group of Manhattan intellectuals, known as the Round Table, who hung out in its Oak Room and later in its Rose Room in the 1920s and 1930s. The crew included critics Alexander Woollcott and Robert Benchley, playwright George S. Kaufman, essayist and short-story writer Dorothy Parker, humorist Ring Lardner, actress Tallulah Bankhead, and *New Yorker* editor Harold Ross (who is said to have put together the magazine at the hotel rather than in its offices across the street). Although most of the Round Table held the movies, and especially Hollywood, in disdain, many of them eventually developed pretty strong ties with the film industry when the studios offered one of the best sources of employment for writers during the Depression. Of the elite Algonquin group, Dorothy Parker wound up spending the most time in Hollywood, where she worked on the screenplays for such classic films as David O. Selznick's 1937 *A Star Is Born* (for which she shared an Oscar with her coauthor husband Alan Campbell) and Hitchcock's 1944 espionage thriller *Saboteur.*

It was also in 1944 that Hollywood immortalized the Algonquin's Rose Room with Otto Preminger's quirky murder mystery *Laura,* featuring a scene set in the historic dining room where the Round Table held forth. *Laura's* Rose Room, of course, was a facsimile created on a soundstage at Twentieth

Century–Fox, but when director Alan Rudolph immortalized the Round Table in his 1994 *Mrs. Parker and the Vicious Circle*, although the film was mainly shot in Montreal for budgetary reasons, the real Algonquin was one of the few New York City locations used for the picture. Jennifer Jason Leigh played Parker, with Peter Gallagher as her handsome husband Alan Campbell; other Round Table members were Campbell Scott as Robert Benchley, Matthew Broderick as Charles MacArthur, and Sam Robards as Harold Ross.

Another film that featured the Algonquin playing itself was *9½ Weeks*, where it was one of the spots where Mickey Rourke and Kim Basinger engaged in kinky sex in the 1986 Adrian Lyne feature. Five years earlier the hotel had been the scene of an amusing literary-sexual encounter in George Cukor's *Rich and Famous*. In the film, neurotic writer Jacqueline Bisset is giving a tour of the Algonquin, along with a history of the Round Table, to a much younger man she has just picked up and is about to escort up to her room.

The Algonquin Hotel's legendary Rose Room

This was all a far cry from a century ago, when it was in the Algonquin's lobby—a cozy clutter of Victorian armchairs, sofas, and coffee tables—that Douglas Fairbanks first wooed Mary Pickford back in the 1910s. Fairbanks, who kept a suite at the Algonquin from 1907 to 1915, was the first of many film stars who thought of the Algonquin as home. Other legendary habitués were Audrey Hepburn, Billy Wilder, Sir Laurence Olivier, Yves Montand, and Melina Mercouri—all of whom loved the Algonquin for its proximity to the theater district, its lobby so perfect for cocktails and/or a proper British tea, its chandelier-hung dining room that serves old-fashioned hotel food like chicken pot pie and calf's liver with bacon. Happily, despite the current rage for minimalist hotels, here at the Algonquin, very little has changed.

Visit www.algonquinhotel.com.

13. HOTEL IROQUOIS
49 West 44th Street

Not nearly as historic or fashionable as its next-door neighbor, the Algonquin, the Iroquois can nonetheless claim a young actor named James Dean as a former resident. This was during the dawn of his New York career back in the early 1950s, when the only acting job he could manage to find was as a guinea pig testing out the wacky stunts for the producers of the popular TV game show *Beat the Clock*. At the Iroquois, Dean occupied room number 802, which he shared with fellow actor William Bast. In those days, both guys, if they were meeting someone they deemed important, would arrange to see them next door in the lobby of the Algonquin. Today, the same ploy is no longer necessary, because the Iroquois has been considerably spiffed up since its James Dean days.

Visit www.iroquoisny.com.

14. ROYALTON HOTEL
44 West 44th Street

One of Manhattan's hippest hostelries, the Royalton debuted in 1988 as the brainchild of ex–Studio 54 ex-cons Ian Schrager and Steve Rubell. With the help of über-designer Philippe Starck, they took over an aging hotel on West 44th Street and made it the last word in minimal decor and maximum profile. Immediately the stars of New York publishing flocked to its restaurant—*Vanity Fair*'s Tina Brown, *Vogue*'s Anna Wintour, and the late fashion doyenne of the *New York Times* Carrie Donovan. The supermodels all hung out here, too—Linda, Christy, Cindy—in the days when they reigned on the covers of all the major fashion magazines before being dethroned by beautiful young movie stars. The hotel was also used for premiere parties for such films as *This Boy's Life* (1993), which brought Leonardo DiCaprio to the hotel for the first of many visits and interviews over the years. Today, the Royalton is still a happening place to stay and play, but the initial buzz is decidedly more muffled. Still, when the 2001 Tom Cruise film *Vanilla Sky,* set in the publishing world, needed an appropriately insider location for a hotel scene, they went with the Royalton.

Visit www.ianschragerhotels.com.

15. SCREEN ACTORS GUILD
360 Madison Avenue

Like most professionals, movie actors have a labor union. The twelfth floor of this Madison Avenue high-rise is headquarters for the New York City offices of the Screen Actors Guild (SAG). Out of a total of 118,000 members nationwide, some 29,000 actors belong to SAG in the New York metropolitan area. For a day's work in a theatrical film, the 2004 SAG minimum base rate was $678 for a day (featured) player and $115 for an extra. But before you think of rushing into the film business, be advised that 80 to 85 percent of SAG's New York members make under $9,000 a year from their screen appearances.

Visit www.sag.org.

16. METROPOLITAN LIFE BUILDING
200 Park Avenue

One of New York's first precast concrete skyscrapers, this Park Avenue landmark sparked a great deal of controversy when it came on the scene in 1963, since it blocked views up and down Manhattan's most elite street. The work of legendary Bauhaus architect Walter Gropius, who collaborated with various other architects on the project, it was named the Pan Am Building for the once grand, now defunct airline that was headquartered here for almost twenty-five years. The structure's stunning marble lobby, with its dramatic public art works and floating escalator banks, was featured in the 1968 film *No Way to Treat a Lady,* where serial-killer Rod Steiger uses the marble phone banks in the lobby to phone police headquarters, outraged that a strangulation victim has been attributed to him when it was the work of a copycat. Other 1960 films that took advantage of the then new building's cachet include *On a Clear Day You Can See Forever* (1970), where Yves Montand sings "Come Back to Me" to a distant Barbra Streisand from the rooftop of the sixty-five-story building in the Vincente Minnelli–directed musical; and *Coogan's Bluff* (1968), which has western sheriff Clint Eastwood arriving in NYC in a helicopter that lands atop the Pan Am Building's famous heliport, which enabled travelers to hop from JFK to Midtown Manhattan in a matter of minutes. In 1977, however, those days came to an end when a helicopter flipped over and its rotors broke off, killing four people on the roof—including porn film director Michael Findlay, known for classics like *Wet and Wild* (1976) and *The Curse of Her Flesh* (1968)—and one person on the ground.

More recently, the former Pan Am Building—complete with its old sign—turns up in *Catch Me If You Can.* In the film, which is set in the 1960s, con man Leonardo DiCaprio, in his efforts to impersonate an airline pilot, phones Pan Am from a booth outside the building to find out who supplies their uniforms.

17. NEWS CORP. BUILDING
1211 Avenue of the Americas

In 1985, Australian publishing mogul Rupert Murdoch went shopping for a movie company to add to his growing portfolio of U.S. media acquisitions. He bought the venerable studio Twentieth Century–Fox and for a while in the early 1990s even ran it himself, when then CEO Barry Diller resigned. Today, Murdoch's News Corp. empire includes not only the Fox movie division but Fox News, HarperCollins publishers, the *New York Post*, the *London Times*, and the Sky cable network—and that's just the beginning. Murdoch's prime New York base of operations is here on Sixth Avenue, where the hyper-fit septuagenarian recently built a large gym to encourage his staff to be as healthy as he is. *Vanity Fair* put Murdoch at the very top of its 2003 list of the fifty most important media people in America; in 2004 he fell to the number-two spot.

Visit www.newscorp.com.

18 RADIO CITY MUSIC HALL
1260 Avenue of the Americas

It advertised 6,200 seats, but the total has always been closer to 5,960. Still, when Radio City Music Hall opened in 1932 as part of New York's futuristic Rockefeller Center complex, it was the largest indoor theater in the world. And today it still is. Everything about Radio City Music Hall is outsized—from its sixty-foot-high foyer to its two-ton chandeliers (the largest in the world) to its Wurlitzer organ (the mightiest on earth, with fifty-six separate sets of pipes).

While many people assume that this great Art Deco theater started out as a movie palace, Radio City Music Hall was actually planned for spectacular stage shows, whereas the now de-funct Center Theater on the next block was to have been Rockefeller Center's main venue for films. When the Music Hall's six-hour opening-night program bombed, however, the enormous theater quickly turned to the formula that would spell its success for the next three decades: a thirty-minute stage show

Postcard view of Radio City Music Hall stage

combined with a first-run family movie. More than just a commercial success, Radio City Music Hall—with its high-kicking Rockettes, spectacular Christmas and Easter pageants, and top-notch movies—became an entertainment landmark of New York City, a must on every visitor's list of things to see and do.

Not only has it played a role as an important site for the New York premieres of more than six hundred films like *Mr. Smith Goes to Washington* (1939), *An American in Paris* (1951), and *Singin' in the Rain* (1952), the hall has also wound up being featured in a number of films including *The Godfather* (1972), *Annie* (1982), *Radio Days* (1987), and Alfred Hitchcock's *Saboteur* (1942), in which Robert Cummings runs across a Hollywood mock-up of the Radio City stage while a film is being shown. Since a gunfight is taking place on screen, the audience at first doesn't realize that a real gun is being fired at Cummings in the theater.

Radio City's glory days ended in the 1960s. For one thing, the studios had started mass-releasing films by then, making it next to impossible for Radio City still to boast first-runs. Also, America's tastes had changed. Family films were out of fashion in the 1960s and 1970s, and the Rockettes kicking up their heels were considered high camp, not mass entertainment. By 1978, Radio City was losing millions of dollars a year, and the Rockefeller

Group, its parent company, decided to close it down. A white elephant, the grand Art Deco entertainment palace was earmarked for demolition. Happily, a citizens group managed to get the interior of the Music Hall declared a historic landmark and management set about finding new uses for the mega-auditorium.

And so, these days, Radio City Music Hall hosts everyone and everything from rock and pop stars and groups (Madonna, Sting, the Rolling Stones, Grateful Dead, Bette Midler, Liza Minnelli, Tina Turner, Janet Jackson, Celine Dion, Whitney Houston, Stevie Wonder) to trade shows and awards shows (the Tony Awards, MTV Music Awards, ESPY Awards) to TV specials and its own classic Christmas and Easter extravaganzas. And, while movies no longer play a major role in Radio City's life, special screenings still go on here from time to time, such as the New York premieres of Disney's *The Lion King* (1994) and the 1983 New York first showing of the restored version of the Judy Garland/James Mason *A Star Is Born,* which featured the "lost" twenty-four minutes that had been cut from the film by Jack Warner back in 1954. Radio City is also where Francis Ford Coppola first unveiled his reconstructed version of Abel Gance's 1927 silent-screen epic *Napoleon* before New York audiences. The music for the revived film was composed by Coppola's father, Carmine.

Movie lovers can experience the splendor of the Radio City Music Hall either by attending a performance or by taking an hour-long backstage tour of the place. Tours are given daily at frequent intervals; they depart from the Main Lobby. Call 212-247-4777 and ask for the Tour Desk, or visit www.radiocity.com.

19. ROCKEFELLER CENTER
48th to 52nd Streets between Fifth and Sixth Avenues

It makes for one hell of an establishing shot: a long pan down the seventy stories of the RCA Building to the gigantic gilded statue of Prometheus backed by a row of fluttering flags and spurting jets of water. Hold on the statue, then pull back and angle down to reveal a huge outdoor café—or, if it's winter, an ice skating rink. Pull back farther to include a long courtyard studded with a series of lavishly planted mini-gardens. Or do the whole sequence in reverse. Rockefeller Center, which the American Institute of Architects' *AIA Guide to New York City* calls "an island of architectural excellence . . . the greatest urban complex of the twentieth century," is so beautifully laid out, so well proportioned, so *perfect* that it's hard to make it look anything less than extraordinary, no matter how you shoot it. Used in the movies, a shot of Rockefeller Center—as in *Nothing Sacred* (1937), *How to Marry a Millionaire* (1953), or *Manhattan* (1979)—establishes New York at its best: a perfectly balanced combination of power, glamor, and humanity.

Add the skating rink—especially when backed by the most renowned Christmas tree in America—and we see Midtown Manhattan at its most romantic in films such as *Desk Set* (1957), *Sunday in New York* (1963), *40 Carats* (1973), *Home Alone 2* (1992), and *Autumn in New York* (2000). Or focus on the forecourt of the center's Atlas Building at 630 Fifth Avenue—with its dramatic statue of the Greek god Atlas holding the world on his shoulders—and you enhance the already powerful image of this serious office building, which has been used as the talent agency

On the Town at Rockefeller Center: Frank Sinatra, Jules Munshin, Gene Kelly, 1949

that could change violinist John Garfield's life in the 1947 Joan Crawford melodrama *Humoresque*; the magical spot where has-been journalist Bruce Willis is given the tip for a sensational story that will jump-start his sagging career in the 1990 film version of Tom Wolfe's blockbuster novel *The Bonfire of the Vanities*; and the newspaper where Gregory Peck has gone undercover to do his big story on anti-Semitism in Elia Kazan's *Gentleman's Agreement* (1947). Especially memorable in this film is the scene where Peck, echoing his own emotional state, explains the burden Atlas is shouldering to his young son. On the other hand, in *Hercules in New York* (1970), Arnold Schwarzenegger (under the stage name of Arnold Strong), in the title role, not only knows who Atlas is, but says the statue is not a good representation of his fellow muscleman.

Besides the many films that use Rockefeller Center as background, two recent features have focused on a unique aspect of its history. When Rockefeller Center was being built, the famous Mexican artist Diego Rivera was commissioned to do the murals in the then RCA (now GE) Building at 30 Rockefeller Plaza. But when it was discovered the left-wing Rivera had included and refused to delete a likeness of Lenin, hypercapitalist John D. Rockefeller fired Rivera and brought in artist José Maria Sert to do a whole new set of paintings. The incident is referenced both in *The Cradle Will Rock* (1999), Tim Robbins's homage to left-wing New York of the 1930s, and in *Frida* (2002), a biopic produced by and starring Salma Hayek as Rivera's artist wife, Frida Kahlo. In the film Edward Norton plays Rockefeller and Alfred Molina is Rivera.

Conceived and founded by John D. Rockefeller, the twelve high-, middle-, and low-rise buildings that comprised the original Rockefeller Center were built between 1930 and 1940. The centerpiece of the complex is the seventy-story GE Building (formerly the RCA Building). When Rockefeller first envisioned his urban center in the 1920s, his plan was to provide a new home for the Metropolitan Opera House (it was on Broadway at 38th Street at the time) to be surrounded by office, retail, entertainment, and dining facilities. When the Depression hit in 1929, the Met decided that it couldn't afford to move, so Rockefeller and his advisers decided to build an office tower instead of an opera house. At the same time, the Radio Corporation of America and its subsidiary, the National Broadcasting Company, were among the few companies in the country that were prospering despite the Depression. Looking for a corporate headquarters to suit their growing needs and power, RCA/NBC found a classy home at Rockefeller Center and became the principal tenant of the handsome skyscraper at 30 Rockefeller Plaza, which opened in 1933 bearing the RCA name (which was changed to GE in the 1980s, reflecting RCA/NBC's new owner General Electric).

For the radio and television lover, 30 Rockefeller Plaza—which still houses NBC's principal New York radio and TV studios—is one of the most historic sites in the country connected with these media. Television literally came of age here beginning in 1935, when NBC started broadcasting two programs a week from studio 3H. These first telecasts consisted of plays, comedians, scenes from opera, cooking demonstrations (limited to salads because the intense heat from the then necessary ultra-high-powered TV lights made stovetop cooking unthinkable), and even live transmissions from the streets of New York thanks to a mobile unit that went into operation in 1937. Despite these experiments, it wasn't until after World War II that TV really got off the ground. Then, too, NBC was at the forefront of the medium with such programs as *Kraft Television Theatre* (1947), *Howdy Doody* (1947), the John Cameron Swayze–anchored *Camel News Caravan* (1947), *Meet the Press* (1947), and Milton Berle's *Texaco Star Theatre* (1948)—most of which were televised from Radio City.

In 1952, NBC took a bold step in early-morning programming by introducing a two-hour show that mixed news, interviews, and entertainment features. The host of NBC's new *Today* show was a laid-back gentleman named Dave Garroway and one of his sidekicks was a chimpanzee named J. Fred Muggs. Instead of using a studio in 30 Rockefeller Plaza, however, the *Today* show was done live from a spacious Rockefeller Center showroom with street-to-ceiling picture windows on the south side of West 49th Street just west of Rockefeller Plaza. Passersby pressed their noses up against the glass to watch the live TV production going on inside, and at various times each morning the camera was turned on the gawkers. Soon *Today* not only became a hit television show, it became a major New York City tourist attraction. In the 1960s, *Today* revamped its studios, and its old 49th Street base was turned into a bank. In 1994, however, *Today* not only returned to a street-level studio at 10 Rockefeller Plaza, it started shooting out on the plaza itself—and sign-carrying spectators line up well before dawn in hopes of prime places and possible close-ups.

For TV lovers, an early-morning visit to the *Today* show can be followed by the fifty-five-minute NBC Studio Tour. Among the attractions of this behind-the-scenes look at Radio City are studio 8H, the *Saturday Night Live* auditorium as well as the site of such classic early TV shows as *Your Hit Parade, What's My Line,* and the *Kraft Television Theatre.* The tour also takes television lovers to Studio 6A, where *Late Night with Conan O'Brien* is taped, and lets them participate in the NBC Experience, where, among other interactive displays, they can be interviewed by Jay Leno or Conan O'Brien on video. And, if they're lucky, NBC Studio Tour guests might also catch glimpses of the real Conan as well as other current NBC celebrities such as Katie Couric, Matt Lauer, and Tom Brokaw, who all work in the building.

The NBC Studio Tour is currently given daily at fifteen-minute intervals. Tours leave from the NBC Tour Desk on the main floor of 30 Rockefeller Plaza; admission is currently $17.75 for adults, $15 for seniors and children from six to sixteen. No one under six. Call 212-664-3700. To buy tickets online, go to http://nbc-television-studio-tour.visit-new-york-city.com.

20. THE RAINBOW ROOM
49 West 49th Street

With its glorious views, its revolving dance floor, and its stunning Art Deco interiors, Rockefeller Center's sixty-fifth-story Rainbow Room was the last word in New York City nightlife when it opened in 1934. Over the years, as supper clubs went in and out of fashion, the magnificent venue has had various incarnations, the most recent being the classy cabaret nightclub Rainbow and Stars, which featured such legends as Liza Minnelli and the late Rosemary Clooney. Currently open for dinner and dancing just one evening a week (usually Fridays), the old Rainbow Room space is now managed by the chic Venetian Cipriani organization, which also runs the posh Rainbow Grill restaurant in the space's former Promenade Bar. Meanwhile, movie lovers can also catch the Rainbow Room in all its glory in *The Prince of Tides* (1991), where Barbra Streisand dances with Nick Nolte; *Six Degrees of Separation* (1993), where Will Smith dances with Eric Thall (and is asked to leave); and *Sleepless in Seattle* (1993), where Meg Ryan breaks her engagement to Bill Pullman.

For information and reservations, call 212-632-5100; visit www.cipriani.com/rainbowroom.html.

21. CBS BUILDING
485 Madison Avenue

In the beginning there was NBC . . . and only NBC. Then, in 1927, a new radio network called the Columbia Phonograph Broadcasting System came along to challenge the National Broadcasting Corporation's monopoly of the airwaves. The new network had a rough go of it initially. When its owners, the Columbia Phonograph Record Company, backed out, a young cigar magnate named William S. Paley stepped in, shortened the network's name to the Columbia Broadcasting System, and perked up its credit rating by getting powerful Paramount Pictures to come in on the deal. Thus it was with great pride and much fanfare that, in the autumn of 1929, Mr. Paley cut the ribbon for CBS's headquarters in the brand-new Columbia Broadcasting Building at the corner of Madison Avenue and 52nd Street.

CBS occupied the top five floors of the impressive new twenty-four-story structure and had fifteen studios on the premises; these ranged from tiny chambers to an auditorium large enough to hold 250 performers. Some of the studios were equipped with glassed-off, soundproof balconies to accommodate spectators for early radio shows, and one studio was set up for what everyone knew was coming sooner or later: television. Indeed, many important early experiments in television took place in the CBS Building in the 1930s. In those days performers had to wear garish makeup, and the primitive camera, with its high-powered spotlight, practically blinded the actors after just a couple of seconds in front of it.

But it was radio that was responsible for CBS's great success in the 1930s and 1940s. As the country's number-two network, CBS devoted most of its energies to its radio programming in order to catch up with top-ranked NBC. Meanwhile, NBC was so convinced that television was just around the corner that it let its radio division slide as it moved full speed ahead on the development of TV. Thus, by the end of the 1930s, CBS—with a strong news division that included pros like Edward R. Murrow and Eric Sevareid, and equally impressive dramatic programming that featured the talents of Orson Welles and Archibald MacLeish—was a force to be reckoned with. When World War II erupted and further delayed the coming of television, CBS's position in the industry was made even stronger.

CBS and Mr. Paley stayed at 485 Madison Avenue for thirty-six years. When the network moved into its current headquarters at 52nd Street and the Avenue of the Americas in 1965, it was Mr. Paley who, in the tradition of ships' captains, was the last person to leave 485 Madison Avenue. Paley died in 1990.

22. BLACK ROCK
51 West 52nd Street

Known as Black Rock, this thirty-eight-story Eero Saarinen–designed skyscraper of Canadian black granite has been the corporate headquarters of CBS since 1965. No longer an independent company, CBS is currently part of the massive media conglomerate Viacom, which also counts Paramount Pictures, MTV, Showtime, and VH1 among its family members. Viacom paid a cool $40.6 billion to acquire CBS in 1995.

In 1977, Black Rock was featured in the film *Exorcist II: The Heretic*. In this lame follow-up to the famous supernatural thriller, the formerly possessed Regan MacNeil (Linda Blair) is now living in New York in her actress mother's posh penthouse, which supposedly is in Black Rock. Director John Boorman used this high-up location for numerous vertigo-inducing terrace scenes.

23. MUSEUM OF TELEVISION AND RADIO
25 West 52nd Street

The brainchild of CBS founding father, the late William S. Paley, the Museum of Television and Radio was founded in 1976 as the Museum of Broadcasting. The first institution to be dedicated exclusively to the preservation, cataloguing, and showcasing of radio and television *art,* the museum has accumulated over 100,000 television and radio programs in its archives. Open to media scholars and fans alike, the museum provides custom-built private viewing consoles where individuals can screen the titles they have requested from the museum's computerized database.

Besides providing an opportunity for individuals to explore radio/TV history firsthand, the museum has a program of TV and video screenings, which it presents in two theaters and two screening rooms. These can be anything from an examination of James Dean's career in early television to *Sex and the City* marathons to "Sound and Vision: David Bowie on Television." A sign of the museum's success is the fact that it opened a Beverly Hills branch in 1996.

The Museum of Television and Radio is open Tuesdays to Sundays, from 12 noon to 6 p.m. Suggested contributions: $10.00 for adults; $8.00 for students/senior citizens; $5.00 for children under thirteen. Call 212-621-6800 or visit www.mtr.org.

24. 21 CLUB
21 West 52nd Street

When Karen Richards, wife of playwright Lloyd Richards, has a lunch date with Margo Channing, Broadway's reigning leading lady, in *All About Eve,* the setting is naturally the 21 Club. And when Karen arrives at 21, whom should she bump into but Addison DeWitt, the all-powerful newspaper columnist, who just happens to have the up-and-coming Broadway actress Eve Harrington in tow!

In the days of *All About Eve* (the early 1950s), 21 was one of *the* places in New York for the rich and the famous to break bread together. It still is. Here, on any given day, you're likely to find a

Top table at 21:
Burt Lancaster and
Tony Curtis in
*Sweet Smell
of Success,* 1957

cast of characters that might include Donald Trump, Hugh Jackman, Julianne Moore, Chris O'Donnell, Brooke Shields and Chris Henchy, and Hillary Swank and Chad Lowe. You may not find critic Rex Reed at 21, however, since he was once barred from the dining room for not having a tie. "But this is Bill Blass," Reed is reported to have protested, referring to his dapper sports coat. Still, he flunked the stringent 21 dress test and was refused entry.

In a city that is constantly changing, 21 adheres to its traditions—from dress codes to not tolerating customers who insult waiters to ejecting patrons who've had too much to drink (allowing them to return the next day if they're sober) to not "selling" choice tables. Indeed, for many, 21 has served as a club, a place where they could go anytime and always count on finding a warm welcome and no surprises. It was no doubt this strong sense of continuity that attracted Humphrey Bogart to 21, and today his table—number 30 in the downstairs bar—is still known as Bogie's Corner, indicated by a sign hanging nearby. Upstairs, in the main dining room, Joan Crawford always had the table just to the left of the entrance.

It may come as a surprise to some that this bastion of Manhattan luxury started out as an expensive speakeasy. Founded in 1930 by Jack Kriendler and Charlie Berns, 21 was then equipped with an elaborate security/screening system, secret cellars that concealed some five thousand cases of liquor, and a James Bond–like bar that could automatically dispose of all the booze on the premises in the event of an unexpected visit from the feds. In those days, the block of 52nd Street between Fifth and Sixth Avenues was one of the city's liveliest spots, noted for its speakeasys, restaurants, and nightclubs. Today, the same block is wall-to-wall office towers. The sole survivor from the street's glory days is the cluster of three brownstone townhouses that together form 21. With its wrought-iron grill, old-fashioned lanterns, two American flags, and row of cast-iron jockey statues out front, 21—despite occasional changes in ownership—remains a monument to a glamorous New York that once was and that, inside 21 at least, lives on.

The restaurant also lives on in other films besides *All About Eve*. In *Written on the Wind* (1956), directed by "women's picture" maven Douglas Sirk, 21 was the spot where Rock Hudson and Robert Stack began their rivalry for Lauren Bacall, and in *Sweet Smell of Success* (1957), when press agent Tony Curtis and jaded newspaper columnist Burt Lancaster exit 21, they see a drunk being thrown out of a nearby bar—to which Lancaster responds with: "I love this dirty town." A popular power-lunch spot in real life and reel life, 21 saw Michael Douglas as that ultimate 1980s corporate animal Gordon Gecko lunching with his protégé Charlie Sheen in *Wall Street* (1987), whereas Whoopi Goldberg does a meeting here with Eli Wallach, Lainie Kazan, and Timothy Daly in *The Associate* (1996). The restaurant also provides festive dining in *Metropolitan* (1990), *Manhattan Murder Mystery* (1993), and *One Fine Day* (1996).

Call 212-582-7200; visit www.21club.com.

25. MUSEUM OF MODERN ART
11 West 53rd Street

In addition to its trove of van Goghs, Picassos, Monets, and Mondrians, the Museum of Modern Art—after its recent two-year, $850-million redo—counts among its treasures important works by De Mille, Chaplin, Griffith, Porter, Stiller, and Méliès. In fact, MoMA has some twenty thousand films in its archives spanning the medium's history from late-nineteenth-century silents to twenty-first-century video art.

Believing that film was "the only great art peculiar to the twentieth century," former MoMA director Alfred H. Barr Jr. established the Department of Film at the Museum of Modern Art in 1935, and immediately sent curator Iris Barry on a special mission to Hollywood to drum up support for his innovative undertaking. There, at a party given by Mary Pickford and Douglas Fairbanks at Pickfair, their lavish Beverly Hills estate, Miss Barry met industry heavyweights like Samuel Goldwyn, Harold Lloyd, Harry Warner, Harry Cohn, Ernst Lubitsch, Mervyn LeRoy, Walt Disney, Jesse Lasky, and Mack Sennett. Returning to New York with what the *Los Angeles Times* reported to be "more than a million feet" of film, Miss Barry had the beginnings of MoMA's collection. But one old-timer who was not as forthcoming as many of his Hollywood colleagues was D. W. Griffith, who refused to donate his own films to the museum, reportedly saying that nothing could convince him that films had anything to do with art. Ultimately MoMA enlisted the aid of Griffith's friend and former star actress, Lillian Gish, who eventually persuaded him to hand over to history his collection of films, music, still photographs, and papers. It seems, however, that it was the lure of the tax write-off that was really responsible for Griffith's change of heart.

For the movie lover, the best thing about MoMA's film collection is that it is constantly on view. The museum has two theaters—one with 460 seats, the other with 217—which together are used to present some two dozen screenings a week. The Department of Film and Media–MoMA also cosponsors, with the Film Society of Lincoln Center, the New Directors/New Films festival, which is held every year in March/April. In addition to showing films, the Department of Film and Media–MoMA maintains a library of film books, screenplays, reviews, publicity material, and four million stills that is an important research center for students, authors, and historians.

By far the most important activity of the Department of Film and Media–MoMA is its work in film preservation. A frightening fact is that, of all the feature films made before 1952, half have disappeared entirely; of those produced before 1930, only a quarter survive, since the nitrate stock on which they were shot eventually self-destructs. Newer motion pictures, especially those shot on color-negative film during from the 1950s to the 1970s, are endangered too because the dyes in their negatives are un-stable. As a result, many important classics from these decades—*Rebel Without a Cause* (1955), *Tom Jones* (1963)—have faded or are fading fast. Despite the fact that tremendous amounts of money are needed to transfer older movies onto newer, more sta-ble film stock, MoMA perseveres in its noble goal of preserving the modern era's unique art form.

Screenings by the Department of Film and Media–MoMA are presented free to MoMA members and are open to the general public for a modest admission charge. For information, call 212-708-9480, or visit www.moma.org.

26. SAMUEL PALEY PLAZA
3 East 53rd Street

Built in 1967 by CBS founder William S. Paley in honor of his father, Samuel Paley Plaza is a pleasant little park with tables, chairs, trees, and a waterfall. A popular place in warm weather for Manhattanites and tourists to have light lunches or snacks,

Stork Club stars: Henry Fonda, Joan Crawford, Ruth Warrick, Peggy Ann Garner, Walter Winchell, and Dana Andrews in *Daisy Kenyon,* 1947

the park stands on the site of what was once one of New York City's most fashionable watering holes: Sherman Billingsley's famous Stork Club. Always crammed with celebrities, the Stork Club was the favorite hangout of columnist Walter Winchell, who kept the rest of the country informed of its glamorous goings-on.

The most exclusive place to be seated at the Stork Club was in the small Cub Room, which owner Billingsley reserved for stars (many of whose portraits graced the walls) and socialites. The rest of the world had to make do with a table in the main dining room, which had a large dance floor and nonstop music. In both rooms, and at the long bar, Billingsley ran a tight ship. His strictly enforced house rules included refusing admittance to unescorted women at night, although they could turn up for lunch or at cocktail hour; also, any customer who started a fight was permanently barred from the premises.

So great was the fame of the Stork Club that Billingsley was contracted by the *Encyclopaedia Britannica* to write its first entry on nightclubs. In addition, the club was immortalized in the movies, notably in Hitchcock's made–in–New York *The Wrong Man* (1957), with star Henry Fonda in the role of a Stork Club bass player, and in Otto Preminger's *Daisy Kenyon* (1947), where columnists Walter Winchell and Leonard Lyons play themselves in a dramatic Stork Club sequence toward the end of the film. The club closed in 1965, made a brief comeback on Central Park South in the 1970s, and now lives on on video and DVD.

27. SHERATON ST. REGIS HOTEL
2 East 55th Street

Built by Col. John Jacob Astor, this was the tallest (eighteen stories) and most luxurious hotel New York had ever seen when it went up in 1904. Public rooms were decorated with the finest European furnishings; china was by Royal Worcester, Royal Minton, and Sèvres. There was marble everywhere—in stairways, corridors, even in the basement engine and boiler rooms! Many guest rooms came with their own Steinway pianos, and all were equipped with such then unheard-of innovations as auto-

The St. Regis, 1987

matic vacuum-cleaning systems and individual thermostats to control the temperature and humidity of the rooms.

With all its amenities, the St. Regis attracted quite a few glamorous guests over the years—from Humphrey Bogart (it was Bogie's favorite Manhattan hotel) to Marilyn Monroe, who stayed at 2 East 55th Street when she came to town in 1954 to do location shooting for *The Seven Year Itch*. Her marriage to Joe DiMaggio was in serious trouble at the time, but matters got a lot worse the evening she shot the infamous scene on Lexington Avenue in which her skirt gets blown up by the air from a passing subway train. Supposedly, the fight that followed between Monroe and DiMaggio in their St. Regis suite was so intense that it woke up the whole floor.

Three decades later, the characters played by Michael Caine and Barbara Hershey in *Hannah and Her Sisters* get along much better in their St. Regis room, which they use as a trysting place in the 1986 Woody Allen film. Hotel sources point out that only the hotel's handsome Beaux Arts façade was used in the film, and that the interior of the suite shown on screen was decidedly less grand than a real St. Regis room. Woody made up for the slight when he returned to the hotel the next year to shoot *Radio Days,* which featured the St. Regis's King Cole dining room as the elegant 1940s nightclub where a blond Mia Farrow works as a cigarette girl. The same bar saw Goldie Hawn, playing an actress in *The First Wives Club* (1996), try to drown her sorrows in alcohol after being told she was too old for a role.

More recently, both Woody Allen and Michael Caine returned to the St. Regis: Allen for his 2003 film *Anything Else* and Caine for *Miss Congeniality* (2000), where he lunched at the hotel's ultra-posh Lespinasse restaurant with detective Sandra Bullock and discussed how she would infiltrate a beauty contest. The only place movie lovers will find Lespinasse these days is in the film, however, since it was one of the first big-ticket restaurants to fold after 9/11. Movie lovers can also spot the St. Regis in *Taxi Driver* (1976), where the landmark provides one of the few beautiful images in Martin Scorsese's otherwise relentlessly depressing view of Manhattan.

Visit www.starwood.com/stregis/index.html.

28. FRIARS CLUB
57 East 55th Street

This English Renaissance townhouse in Midtown Manhattan has, since 1956, served as headquarters for one of the most famous private clubs in America—the Friars. Among its officers have been: Frank Sinatra, head abbot; Milton Berle, abbot emeritus; Sammy Davis Jr., bard; Tom Jones, knight; Paul Anka, herald; Alan King, monitor; Howard Cosell, historian; Henny Youngman, squire. Founded in 1904 by a group of New York theatrical press agents in order to separate the legitimate members of their profession from the numerous frauds who misrepresented themselves to producers in order to gain free admittance to the theater, the Friars eventually evolved simply into a club for members of the theatrical profession. If movie lovers can wangle an invitation to the Friars' 55th Street "monastery," they will find a dining room and Round the World Bar (named for former abbot Mike Todd's 1956 film, *Around the World in Eighty Days*) on the first floor, the Milton Berle Room and Joe E. Lewis Bar on the second, the Ed Sullivan Reading Room and Frank Sinatra TV-Viewing Room on the third, a billiards room and barber shop on the fourth, a health club on the fifth, and a solarium and golf practice net on the roof.

World-famous for their celebrity roasts, the Friars over the years have so honored Jack Benny, Bob Hope, George Jessel, Dean Martin and Jerry Lewis, Ed Sullivan, Perry Como, Dinah

Midtown monastery:
Friars Club

Shore, Garry Moore, Johnny Carson, Burt Reynolds, Barbra Streisand, Tom Jones, Carol Burnett, Cary Grant, Elizabeth Taylor, George Burns, George Raft, Lucille Ball, Sid Caesar, Whoopi Goldberg, Billy Crystal, Bruce Willis, Kelsey Grammer, Danny Aiello, Drew Carey, and Rob Reiner. For many years, these roasts were stag affairs, and the jokes and language went well beyond being X-rated. In 1983, comedian Phyllis Diller made show-business history when, disguised as a man, she crashed a Friars roast for Sid Caesar. Phyllis, who even used the men's room at the Sheraton Centre Hotel on Seventh Avenue, where the event was held, managed to get through the whole affair without being discovered. Said Phyllis of the proceedings: "It was the funniest, dirtiest thing I ever heard in my life. Of course, I had already heard this language before, because I once ran into a truck." In 1988, Liza Minnelli made more history when she was the first woman invited to become a full-fledged Friar.

Visit www.friarsclub.org.

29. TRUMP TOWER
725 Fifth Avenue

One of big-ego real-estate mogul Donald Trump's many Manhattan monuments, this mirror-glass tower has offices and a six-story atrium with waterfall on its lower floors, and ultraposh apartments higher up. Of all its apartments, none is more lavish than that of the Donald himself, which takes over the top four floors of the building. In the movies, the same flat was home to Trump-like property developer Alexander Cullen, played by Craig T. Nelson, in *The Devil's Advocate* (1997), and both Trump's apartment and Trump himself appeared in the 1987 miniseries *I'll Take Manhattan,* based on the Judith Krantz pop novel. The Trump Tower rooftop was also one of Tobey Maguire's *Spider-Man* high-rise haunts in the 2002 film. But it and its owner have really come into their own with the 2003 debut of the reality TV show *The Apprentice,* which features lots of the carrot-haired exec on location at his glitzy Fifth Avenue lair.

Tower of power:
Trump Tower

In addition to the Donald, others famous Trump Tower denizens have included Sophia Loren, Pia Zadora, Johnny Carson, Steven Spielberg, Paul Anka, Martina Navratilova, Andrew Lloyd Webber, Susan Saint James, and the original *King Kong* star, the late Fay Wray.

30. TIFFANY & CO.
727 Fifth Avenue

"Don't you just love it? Nothing bad can ever happen to you in a place like this." Thus spoke Audrey Hepburn as Holly Golightly, the ultimate Manhattan free spirit, in the 1961 Paramount version of Truman Capote's best-selling novella *Breakfast at Tiffany's*. For the film, which was directed by Blake Edwards, at the time known mainly as the creator of the *Peter Gunn* and *Mr. Lucky* TV series, a number of New York City locations were used, including exteriors and interiors of the legendary Tiffany & Co. jewelers. Tracing its roots back to 1837 (and its current Fifth Avenue location to 1940), Tiffany's made certain that the Sunday shooting of the film went smoothly by stationing forty of its own security guards and salespeople around the store to keep an eye on the millions and millions of dollars' worth of sparkling merchandise. In the scene that was done inside the store, Audrey Hepburn and George Peppard shock an uppity Tiffany's salesman by asking to see something in the $10 range. (Says Audrey/Holly: "I think it's tacky to wear diamonds before I'm forty.") The salesman winds up showing the pair a sterling silver telephone dialer for $6.75—which they decline.

At the end of the 1960s, Tiffany's appeared briefly in a very different kind of film, John Schlesinger's gritty *Midnight Cowboy,* in a scene where hustler John Voight sees the disparity between the glittering storefront and the homeless man lying in the gutter in front of it. Cut to 1993, when Tiffany's is again the venue for some serious shopping in *Sleepless in Seattle,* as Meg Ryan and her ill-starred fiancé Bill Pullman pick out a china pattern, and in *Sweet Home Alabama* (2002), there's a memorable Tiffany's moment when Reese Witherspoon's boyfriend Patrick Dempsey leads her into a dark room, which turns out to be the diamond department in Tiffany's. Minutes later he is on his knee proposing. She says yes.

Window-shopping:
Audrey Hepburn at
Tiffany in *Breakfast at
Tiffany's*, 1961

Meanwhile, across the street at 718 Fifth Avenue, Tiffany's chief rival Harry Winston has also made some romantic screen appearances, notably in Woody Allen's *Everyone Says I Love You* (1999), when Edward Norton goes shopping at the famous jewelry store for an engagement ring for Drew Barrymore and the "My Baby Just Cares for Me" musical number ensues. Jennifer Lopez also "borrows" a diamond necklace from Winston's to wear to the ball in *Maid in Manhattan* (2003). And, of course, both stores have their praises sung by Marilyn Monroe in her classic "Diamonds Are a Girl's Best Friend" turn in *Gentlemen Prefer Blondes* (1953), a number that Madonna famously ripped off some forty years later in her *Material Girl* video.

Visit www.tiffany.com.

31. SONY BUILDING
550 Madison Avenue

When it debuted in 1984, this hulking Philip Johnson–designed skycraper was headquarters for AT&T. Drawing mixed reviews for its retro Chippendale-style cornice and praise for its spacious enclosed public plaza, the building was taken over by the Japanese electronics giant Sony in 1992 and now bears its name. A major player in the movie business, Sony bought the historic MGM lot in Culver City (Los Angeles) to headquarter its Sony Pictures division, which now also includes Columbia-TriStar. Recently, too, it made a bid for MGM itself. For movie lovers, a visit to Sony's New York base of operations offers the chance to check out the Sony Wonder Technology Lab, an interactive museum, where among many attractions, it offers the chance to shoot and edit your own video.

Visit www.sonywondertechlab.com.

Sony Pictures Building

32. BERGDORF GOODMAN
754 Fifth Avenue

She was queen of the thrift shops, a kooky creature of vintage feather boas and antique *schmatas*. It made good copy for a while, but once twenty-two-year-old Barbra Streisand was well on the road to superstardom via *Funny Girl* on Broadway, platinum record albums, and a $5 million TV deal, it was time to clean up the act. Which is just what La Streisand did in the spring of 1965 on network TV in an elaborate nine-minute musical production number of "Second Hand Rose" in which she donned hundreds of thousands of dollars' worth of glamorous high-fashion ensembles as part of her *My Name Is Barbra* special. The setting for this extraordinary media event was nothing less than New York City's most exclusive department store, Bergdorf Goodman, and, besides furnishing the location, Bergdorf's also supplied the outfits, including fabulous furs by the store's famous resident fur designer, Emeric Partos, and hats by its not-so-well-known (yet!) in-house milliner, a young southern gent named Halston.

Not to be outdone by all the clothes and designers, Miss Streisand offered her own fashion tips to readers of the *New York Times* in a special on-the-set interview. Proving just how far she had come in the fashion department, Streisand had this to say on (1) boas: "A boa can be a great look if it's kept simple, like with gray flannel and a hairdo very tight and slim. Curls and boas don't go." (2) Furs: "I used to hate mink but now I appreciate it for its solidity. . . . Lynx sheds. . . . I have Russian broadtail—it's the most beautiful fur—but terribly perishable and I can hardly wear it because it's so cold. . . . I'm mad for fisher." (3) Fashion philosophy: "I like simple elegance, neat. I'd rather change my jewelry and have a few things and wear them all the time. A person is more important than clothes. A dress should fade out of sight, but greatly." One wonders if that's what she had in mind when she turned up at the 1969 Academy Awards in a see-through pants suit.

Besides appearing in the Streisand TV special, Bergdorf's is also featured in the forgettable 1979 Ali MacGraw–Alan King film *Just Tell Me What You Want*, in a scene where the two stars get into a violent argument that spills out onto the street, and more memorably in *Arthur* (1981), where Liza Minnelli goes on a shoplifting spree. Look for the store, too, in Ridley Scott's *Someone to Watch Over Me* (1987), *Married to the Mob* (1988), and *Maid in Manhattan* (2003).

Visit www.bergdorfgoodman.com.

33. PLAZA HOTEL
Fifth Avenue at 59th Street

When it opened in 1907, it billed itself as nothing less than "the world's most luxurious hotel." A mounmental eighteen-story French château, the Plaza was designed by Henry J. Hardenbergh, the architect who had been responsible for New York City's fabled Dakota apartment building on Central Park West some twenty-three years earlier.

Of all Manhattan's hotels, the Plaza is the city's undisputed superstar as far as movies are concerned, and it's no wonder since, in addition to being one of New York City's most historic and handsome buildings, the Plaza enjoys an eminently photogenic setting. Not only does it have a fabulous fountain in its front yard, it has Central Park across the street and an ever-present lineup of horse-drawn carriages nearby to complete the postcard-pretty picture. The list of films, television shows, commercials, and print ads that have used the Plaza as a background is enormous. Among the more recent features are *Hollywood Ending* (2002), *Life or Something Like It* (2002), *It Could Happen to You* (the 1994 Nicolas Cage–Bridget Fonda remake), *Metropolitan* (1990), *Big Business* (1988), *Crocodile Dundee* (1986), *Brewster's Millions* (1985), *The Cotton Club* (1984), *Annie* (1983), *Arthur* (1981), *Prince of the City* (1980), *King of the Gypsies* (1978), *Love at First Bite* (1978), *The Rose* (1978), *Network* (1976), *The Front* (1976), *The Great Gatsby* (1974), *The Way We Were* (1973), *40 Carats* (1973), *Puzzle of a Downfall Child* (1970), and *Funny Girl* (1968).

And then, of course, there's *Plaza Suite,* the 1971 film version of the 1960s Neil Simon play that's set entirely in Suite 719 of the hotel. Four years earlier, the Plaza featured in another Neil

Dashing Cary Grant dashes through the Plaza's lobby in *North by Northwest*, 1959

Simon Broadway success turned Hollywood film, as the hotel where Jane Fonda honeymooned with Robert Redford in *Barefoot in the Park*. Further back in time, Hitchcock's classic *North by Northwest* (1959) features a dramatic Plaza sequence in which Cary Grant is kidnapped from the hotel's lobby. Before that, Twentieth Century–Fox booked Plaza rooms for the three out-of-town star couples vying for a plum New York City job in *Women's World* (1954) and, when *Ma and Pa Kettle Go to Town* in Universal's 1950 film, guess where they stay?

Other famous Plaza residents include Christopher Walken, who operated a drug ring out of his Plaza suite in *King of New York* (1990); Macaulay Culkin, who had the good sense to check in here when separated (yet again) from his parents in *Home Alone 2: Lost in New York* (1992); and Kate Hudson, as the archetypal rock groupie Penny Lane, who OD'd at the Plaza in the 2000 film *Almost Famous*.

Returning to the distant past, back in 1930, an early New York–made talkie called *No Limit* starred the famous silent-screen actress Clara Bow, and also featured the Plaza. A decade before that, Norma Talmadge's *By Right of Passage* had a major sequence done on location at an actual charity ball being held at the Plaza. Playing a small role in this film was an actress friend of Miss Talmadge's who later became a major Hollywood columnist: Hedda Hopper. The script for *By Right of Passage* was by Anita Loos, and the Plaza party that the film documented was hosted by the famed Elsa Maxwell.

Speaking of Plaza parties, one of the most spectacular ever to be staged at the hotel took place on Monday, November 28, 1966. The event was the gala Black and White Ball hosted by writer Truman Capote for *Washington Post/Newsweek* publisher Katharine Graham. The cream of Hollywood, Broadway, Washington, and New York City society turned up, and among the movie people on the guest list were Frank Sinatra and his then wife, Mia Farrow (who twisted the night away with Bennett Cerf's son, Christopher), Claudette Colbert (who sat at an "exceedingly popular" table, according to the *New York Times*), Candice Bergen, the Sammy Davis Jrs., Marlene Dietrich (a no-show), Greta Garbo (also a no-show), the Henry Fondas, the Walter Matthaus, the Vincente Minnellis, the Gregory Pecks, Jennifer Jones, the Billy Wilders, and Darryl Zanuck. Men wore black dinner jackets and black masks, women turned up in black or white dresses and white masks. During the evening, Mr. Capote, whose *Breakfast at Tiffany's* and *In Cold Blood* were turned into major movies, and who appeared in Neil Simon's 1979 film, *Murder by Death*, spent a lot of time alone at the back of the ballroom just watching and delighting in his creation. At the time, Capote said that the black-and-white theme for his evening was inspired by Cecil Beaton's costumes for the Ascot scenes in *My Fair Lady*. But movie lovers may wonder if Mr. Capote wasn't also influenced by party-guest Vincente Minnelli's spectacular black-and-white ball sequence in *An American in Paris*. Asked why he chose the Plaza for his gala, his answer was simple: "I think it's the only really beautiful ballroom left in the United States."

Thirty-five years later, the Plaza was the site of another showbiz extravaganza, the 2000 wedding of then fifty-six-year-old Michael Douglas and thirty-one-year-old Welsh movie actress Catherine Zeta-Jones. Having sold the exclusive photography rights to the British celebrity magazine *OK!* for over $1 million (with the money supposedly targeted to pay for the education of the son the couple had already brought into the world), the Zeta-Jones–Douglases and *OK!* were somewhat miffed when *OK!*'s chief rival *Hello!* came out with its own unauthorized special

Superstar hotel:
The Plaza

edition documenting the celebrity nuptials. *OK!* and the Zeta-Jones–Douglases sued the offending publication and later were awarded another couple of million, at which time the Academy Award–winning actress reportedly quipped that to her and Michael a million dollars wasn't all that much money. Later, courts overturned the initial ruling. Was it something she said?

Besides being in the movies—and the headlines—the hotel is perhaps best known for a six-year-old resident named Eloise, who drove her tricycle relentlessly up and down the corridors, poured water down the mail chutes, and made room service crazy with orders for peanut butter and jelly sandwiches. Created first as a character for a nightclub act and later mass-marketed through a series of charming books, Eloise was the brainchild of actress/entertainer/MGM musical coach Kay Thompson. Today, the Plaza remembers Eloise with a portrait that hangs on a marble wall just beyond the Palm Court.

Visit www.theplazahotel.com.

34. ZIEGFELD THEATER
141 West 54th Street

Opened in 1969, the Ziegfeld is the last major non-multiplex movie house built in New York. Architecturally uninspired, the exterior of the theater is a gigantic 1960s white-brick box that sits on West 54th Street across from the Burlington Industries Building, which occupies the site of the old Ziegfeld Theater, built in 1927 to showcase the lavish spectacles of Florenz Ziegfeld.

Still boasting some of the best projection and multiphonic sound systems in town, the 1,200-seat house (the city's second-largest single-screen movie house after the 1,500-seat Loew's Astor Plaza at 44th Street and Broadway) is frequently used for studio premieres and screenings—especially for epics like *Star Wars, The Lord of the Rings, Chicago,* and HBO's six-hour *Angels in America.* The Ziegfeld was also where Woody Allen staged that star-studded, rain-drenched grand opening of *The Liquidator,* which movie lovers will remember as the film-within-a-film starring Melanie Griffith in *Celebrity* (1998).

35. WARWICK HOTEL
65 West 54th Street

The money behind this thirty-three-story hotel, built in 1926, was that of newspaper heavyweight and sometime film producer William Randolph Hearst. When Hearst and his Hollywood-star mistress, Marion Davies, came to Manhattan in the late 1920s, they often called the Warwick home. In 1927, Marion, who was known for her unpretentious personality and her lavish Hollywood parties, played havoc with the New York social scene when Charles Lindbergh—who had just returned from his triumphant solo flight across the Atlantic—chose to attend a bash at Marion's Warwick suite over a much more prestigious party at the Vanderbilt mansion on Fifth Avenue. According to her autobiography. *The Times We Had* (Bobbs-Merrill, 1975), Mayor Jimmy Walker sent a special emissary to try to convince Marion to call off her party. She refused, however, and left the decision of which party he wanted to attend up to Mr. Lindbergh, who passed on the Vanderbilt affair and spent most of the evening sitting on the floor of Marion's Warwick suite playing the guitar. Of her social coup, Marion simply said: "It was a nice intimate little party."

One of the guests at Marion's Lindbergh party was Carole Lombard, who is said to have returned to the Warwick a decade later in the company of Clark Gable. Although they were not married (to each other) at the time, they soon would be. In the 1960s, the Warwick's most famous celebrity guests were four young men from England called the Beatles who were in New York to make their live U.S. TV debut on *The Ed Sullivan Show,* broadcast from a CBS studio just a few blocks away. In the 1970s and 1980s, Cary Grant was a frequent guest at the lavish Warwick suite maintained by the Fabergé cosmetic empire, which was headquartered across the street at 1345 Avenue of the Americas and for whom Grant was a celebrity spokesman.

The hotel can be seen on screen in Woody Allen's 2003 *Anything Else* and in *American Splendor* (2003), which documents the life of comic book author Harvey Pekar, as the place where he and his wife stay whenever they come to town to be guests on *The Late Show with David Letterman*. Letterman frequently booked Pekar because he was so "off the wall."

Visit www.warwickhotelny.com.

36. MANOLO BLAHNIK
31 West 54th Street

With spike-heeled, often backless numbers costing from $300 to $3,000, this is where those *Sex and the City* gals—especially Carrie—found the most important items in their wardrobes: shoes! Manolo Blahnik, the Spaniard behind the shoes, was born in the Canary Islands in 1943, where as a young boy he read his mother's *Vogue* magazines. In 1971, after having studied art, architecture, and literature in Geneva and Paris, Blahnik came to the United States with his portfolio and was encouraged by the legendary *Vogue* editor Diana Vreeland. It was another, fast-becoming-legendary *Vogue* editor, Anna Wintour, however, who really put Blahnik on the map in the late-1980s, when she featured him almost exclusively on her own size 8½s as well as in the pages of her magazine. At the same time, *Sex and the City* creator Candace Bushnell was a frequent contributor to the magazine, where supposedly the Big character in *Sex and the City* was based on *Vogue* publisher Ronald Galotti. All in the family?

37. MGM BUILDING SITE
1350 Avenue of the Americas

Currently the Men's Apparel Building, this glass and white-marble skyscraper debuted in the late 1960s as the MGM Building and was the New York headquarters of the historic Hollywood studio Metro-Goldwyn-Mayer, responsible for giving the world some of the greatest films of all time. The victim of corporate takeovers, mismanagement, and time, MGM is now a shadow of its former self. Indeed, throughout the 1990s, the MGM name was more associated with theme parks and hotels, such as the MGM Grand in Las Vegas, than with moviemaking. Today, however, MGM is again picking up steam as a producing

Faye Dunaway triumphant in *Network,* 1976

organization, and it still has offices in the New York building that once bore its name—although if a recent takeover bid by Sony Pictures goes through, that could change. For the moment, however, movie lovers who visit the building can spot the company's Leo the Lion logo, which still graces the façade. Movie lovers can also see the former MGM Building in the 1976 MGM/United Artists film *Network,* Paddy Chayefsky's Oscar-winning send-up of the television industry, where it played the role of the fictional United Broadcasting System.

38. METROPOLITAN TOWER
146 West 57th Street

In Terry Gilliam's *The Fisher King* (1991), Jeff Bridges is a troubled former radio host, obsessed with the notion that his advice may have caused a murder before he finds redemption through his association with a mysterious street person played by Robin Williams. In the film Williams lives in the boiler room of a Manhattan office building whereas Bridges calls this striking knife-edged black-glass Midtown high-rise home.

39. RUSSIAN TEA ROOM SITE
150 West 57th Street

Remember the scene in *Tootsie* (1980) when Dustin Hoffman shocks his agent (played by the film's director, Sydney Pollack) by turning up for their Russian Tea Room lunch in drag? And remember how, in the same scene, a producer just happens to drop by the table to say hello? That's the way it used to be at the Russian Tea Room. Practically next door to Carnegie Hall, this glitzy Russian restaurant, until it closed in 2002, a casualty of both 9/11 and a wildly expensive redo by celebrity restaurateur Warner LeRoy, who died in 2001, was one of New York City's highest-visibility watering holes for show business agents, stars, and studio executives, who did deals while noshing on blinis, blintzes, and borscht. Besides *Tootsie,* the Russian Tea Room was featured in *The Turning Point* (1977), *Unfaithfully Yours* (1984), and *Manhattan* (1980), in a memorable scene where Woody Allen takes his son to lunch there, only to have the maître d' request that he put on a house jacket over his T-shirt before he can be seated.

About the same time that Allen was having trouble with his wardrobe, the Russian Tea Room employed a budding pop singer in its coat-check room. Back then her name was Madonna Louise Veronica Ciccone.

40. CARNEGIE HALL
57th Street and Seventh Avenue

Although most people think of it as a cathedral of classical music, for Judy Garland fans Carnegie Hall will always bring to mind the historic evening of April 23, 1961, when Judy once again rose from near oblivion and dazzled New Yorkers and the New York critics with her incredible performing prowess. The evening turned out to be a milestone in Miss Garland's recording and concert careers since the two-record album of the performance, *Judy at Carnegie Hall,* was the most successful she ever made.

Judy's Carnegie Hall triumph came almost seventy years to the day after the legendary concert hall opened its doors. Built by industrialist Andrew Carnegie in 1891, this great Victorian structure on West 57th Street has presented practically every major musician of the last 115 years at some time or other. A tough survivor, Carnegie Hall was slated for demolition in the late 1950s and was to have been replaced by a garish red-porcelain-faced office building. Led by violinist Isaac Stern, New Yorkers fought hard to save the historic concert hall and ultimately were triumphant. In 1986, a $50 million renovation of Carnegie Hall further assured its continued presence on the city's cultural scene.

Throughout its history, Carnegie Hall has not only provided a stage for great talents, it has provided homes for some of them too. Built over and around the concert hall are the Carnegie Hall Studios, 140 apartments that have housed such names as Leonard Bernstein, Isadora Duncan, John Barrymore, Paddy Chayefsky, Bobby Short, and Marlon Brando. Back in the 1920s, a Spaniard named Angel Cansino gave dance classes at his Carnegie Hall studio. One of his students was his brother's daughter, Rita, who would become one of Hollywood's biggest stars two decades later as Rita Hayworth. Over the years, too, Carnegie Hall has turned up in more than a few films set in New

Carnegie Hall, ca. 1910

York—from both the 1948 and the 1984 versions of *Unfaithfully Yours* (the first starring Rex Harrison, the second with Dudley Moore, in the role of a conductor who suspects his wife of cheating on him) to 1964's *The World of Henry Orient* (in which a pretentious concert pianist played by Peter Sellers is the object of the obsessive adoration of two teenaged girls). In 1999, an especially good year for the hall, Carnegie Hall appeared in three films: *Man on the Moon,* with Jim Carrey as Andy Kaufman doing his stand-up act here; *Music of the Heart,* where Meryl Streep proves to her East Harlem violin students that practice-practice-practice really *can* get you to Carnegie Hall; and Wim Wenders's documentary *Buena Vista Social Club.*

Carnegie Hall's most famous screen appearance, however, was its title role in the 1947 film *Carnegie Hall,* which brought together world-class musicians like Lily Pons, Risë Stevens, Artur Rubinstein, Jan Peerce, Ezio Pinza, Jascha Heifetz, Fritz Reiner, Leopold Stokowski, the New York Philharmonic Orchestra, and even jazz trumpeter Harry James in a dreadful story about a cleaning woman who becomes a concert promoter. Despite the plot, the musical numbers sound great. Recently, Carnegie Hall was much in the news when it looked as though one of its famous former tenants, the New York Philharmonic Orchestra, which spent seventy years there before going to Avery Fisher Hall in Lincoln Center in 1962, would be returning to Carnegie. The deal fell through, however.

Visit www.carnegiehall.org.

41. ANITA LOOS APARTMENT BUILDING
171 West 57th Street

She got her start in the movies in 1912 when, as a teenager in San Diego, she sent an unsolicited scenario to D. W. Griffith at the Biograph Studios in New York. Griffith bought the story for $25, turned it into a movie called *The New York Hat* with Mary Pickford and Lionel Barrymore, and encouraged the young woman to keep the scenarios coming. The rise of Anita Loos as one of silent films' top scenarists and title writers was practically a story out of one of her own movies. Loos's greatest success came in 1925; it was not through a screenplay, however, but with her novel *Gentlemen Prefer Blondes,* which has since been adapted and readapted for both stage and screen. The most famous screen adaptation was Twentieth Century–Fox's lavish 1953 musical starring Marilyn Monroe as Loos's lovable blond gold digger Lorelei Lee. From the 1940s until her death in 1980 at the age of ninety-three, Anita Loos lived on the corner of Seventh Avenue and 57th Street.

42. THE OSBORNE APARTMENTS
205 West 57th Street

Completed in 1885, some six years before its neighbor, Carnegie Hall, went up across the street, the Osborne is one of Manhattan's oldest apartment buildings. In contrast to its serious brownstone exterior, the eleven-story structure boasts a lobby of extraordinary fantasy with matched marble floors, sculpted ceilings, gold-accented mosaics, and all sorts of carved columns and intriguing niches. The apartments at the Osborne are pretty fantastic too, and feature rooms with fifteen-foot ceilings, big bay windows, and tiny secret staircases that lead up or down to cozy bedrooms or sitting rooms. Among the many celebrities who have lived at the Osborne are café-society singer/pianist Bobby Short (featured in Woody Allen's *Hannah and Her Sisters*), fashion designer Fernando Sanchez, humorist Fran Lebowitz, actors Imogene Coca, Shirley Booth, Lynn Redgrave, Clifton Webb, and Gig Young.

Mr. Young's time at the Osborne ended in tragic headlines on October 19, 1978, when police discovered the bodies of the Oscar-winning (*They Shoot Horses, Don't They?,* 1969) movie star and his wife of three weeks, German-born Kim Schmidt, inside the couple's Osborne apartment. According to the police, the sixty-year-old Young—who had a history of alcoholism and who had made only five pictures in the ten years since his Oscar win—had shot his thirty-one-year-old wife and then turned the gun on himself. Young's last film, released posthumously, was titled *The Game of Death*.

43. SUPERMAN BUILDING
240 Central Park South

What did reporter Lois Lane and actress Sylvia Miles have in common? The same Central Park South address. In the movie *Superman,* Ms. Lane somehow manages—on her *Daily Planet* salary—to live in an enormous penthouse atop this classy 1941 brick high-rise. In real life, Ms. Miles said that her apartment was so small that she reduced her whole life to "a wardrobe trunk with a view."

The same building was the location for the climax of Elia Kazan's *A Face in the Crowd* (1957), a cautionary tale of celebrity that starred Andy Griffith as a hobo–turned–TV star. At the end of the film, Griffith, whose flash-in-the-pan success winds up taking its toll on his psyche, freaks out on (and may well jump out of) a high floor at 240 Central Park South.

44. CENTRAL PARK

The city's own great outdoors, this 840-acre preserve of hills, meadows, fields, and lakes was designed in the 1850s by the noted team of Frederick Law Olmsted and Calvert Vaux and has attracted filmmakers from D. W. Griffith to Woody Allen. In the early days of silent pictures, the park was less often used as a New York City landmark than simply as a convenient place to shoot sequences that called for rural settings. In some instances, too, it was called on to double for an exotic "foreign" location. D. W. Griffith, for example, cleverly turned the area around Central Park's ornate Bethesda Fountain into an Italian piazza for a photoplay that supposedly took place in Florence. As filmmaking became more sophisticated, and as stories set in New York became a staple of the industry, Central Park—with its unique vistas of pastoral countryside juxtaposed with a dramatic backdrop of metropolitan high-rises—became a staple of the New York film.

More than just a pretty background, Central Park is often used by directors when the plot or mood of the film calls for a romantic, away-from-the-harsh-world-of-the-city interlude. Consider Jane Fonda and Rod Taylor rowing on Central Park Lake in *Sunday in New York* (1964); Barbra Streisand and Robert Redford doing likewise a decade later in *The Way We Were* (1973); a dying Ali MacGraw watching hubby Ryan O'Neal skate for the two of them on the Wollman Rink in *Love Story* (1970); John Cusack and Kate Beckinsale having eyes only for each other on the same ice rink in *Serendipity* (2001); sophisticated newscaster Sigourney Weaver and janitor William Hurt overlooking their different backgrounds on the bank of Central Park Lake in Peter Yates's *Eyewitness* (1981); Hugh Jackman proving that chivalry is alive and well when he spirits Meg Ryan across the park on horseback in pursuit of a purse-snatcher in *Kate and Leopold* (2001); and hotel maid Jennifer Lopez and her young son strolling with Ralph Fiennes in *Maid in Manhattan* (2002)—Fiennes, in this modern-day update of the Cinderella story, doesn't realize that Lopez, whom he fancies, works at his hotel.

Of all the park's romantic possibilities, perhaps none is more magical than a spin in one of its horse-drawn carriages. Over the years, these have transported everyone from Will Smith and Eric Thall in *Six Degrees of Separation* (1993) to Rock Hudson and Doris Day in *Pillow Talk* (1959) to Fred Astaire and Cyd Charisse in *The Band Wagon* (1953) for the "Dancing in the Dark" production number. In this instance, however, it's Central Park according to Cedric Gibbons, the famed MGM art director. Gibbons also re-created the park, specifically the seal tank at its zoo, for Judy Garland and Robert Walker as the young lovers in Vincente Minnelli's *The Clock* (1945). And while on the subject of Hollywood studio versions of the park, does anyone remember Universal's 1948 *Up in Central Park,* one of Deanna Durbin's last films? On the other hand, the real Central Park was used that same year as the romantic, indeed otherworldly setting for Joseph Cotten's encounter with the elusive Jennie (Jennifer Jones) in David O. Selznick's classic *Portrait of Jennie.*

Aside from pure romance, filmmakers often use the park to express simply the sheer joy and freedom that New York City can sometimes embody. In the spectacular opening production number of MGM's *On the Town* (1949), for example, Frank Sinatra, Gene Kelly, and Jules Munshin, as three sailors with just a day to take in the city, spend part of it cycling in Central Park.

Close encounter in Central Park: Joseph Cotten and Jennifer Jones in
Portrait of Jennie, 1948

There are also wonderful park sequences in *The World of Henry Orient* (1964), where its two schoolgirl heroines celebrate their newfound friendship by romping across rocks and bridges. Other great romps include the entire cast of *Godspell* (1973) splish-splashing in the Bethesda Fountain; Michelle Pfeiffer and George Clooney doing likewise some two decades later in *One Fine Day* (1996); Ted Danson, Steve Guttenberg, and Tom Selleck frisbee-throwing (and getting women's phone numbers) in *Three Men and a Baby* (1987); and Edward Norton and Drew Barrymore singing and dancing in the "Just You, Just Me" production number in Woody Allen's *Everyone Says I Love You* (1996).

Of all the New York directors to take advantage of the park's scenic possibilities, perhaps none has used it more often than Mr. Allen. *Crimes and Misdemeanors* (1989), the "Oedipus Wrecks" segment of *New York Stories* (1989), *Mighty Aphrodite* (1995), *Deconstructing Harry* (1997), *Hollywood Ending* (2002), and *Anything Else* (2003) all use the park. Indeed, it's hard to find a Woody Allen film that *doesn't* have a Central Park interlude.

Sometimes these are sheer bliss, as in *Annie Hall* (1977), when Allen and Diane Keaton share the delights of people-watching at the Bethesda Fountain. Other times, the park provides a contrapuntal backdrop for more serious stuff—such as Allen contemplating the meaning of life while walking on the jogging path alongside the park's Jacqueline Kennedy Onassis Reservoir in *Hannah and Her Sisters* (1986)—or Kenneth Branagh clearing the air with Judy Davis on the park's Gapstow Bridge regarding his wish to divorce her in *Celebrity* (1998).

Traditionally Central Park has always provided a good neutral place for an important conversation, often a revelation, in films—whether it's Tyrone Power as musician Eddy Duchin telling his son Peter that he is dying, while on the swings of the Heckscher Playground, in *The Eddy Duchin Story* (1955), or Jack Nicholson and Art Garfunkel doing some serious reminiscing by that same ice rink in *Carnal Knowledge* (1971), or Dustin Hoffman, on the Central Park Mall, telling his son that he has to live with his mother in *Kramer vs. Kramer* (1979), or IRA operative Natascha McElhone, at the Wollman Rink, giving further instructions to Brad Pitt on his missile-running-mission in *The Devil's Own* (1997), or Jennifer Aniston confiding to her gay roommate Paul Rudd that she's expecting a baby, while sitting by the model sailboat pond, in *The Object of My Affection* (1998). And, of course, everyone remembers Zero Mostel and Gene Wilder discussing their exciting new Broadway show *Springtime for Hitler* over lunch by the carousel in *The Producers* (1968).

Arguably, the film that made the most extensive and creative use of Central Park as a location was the 1980 movie version of the famous 1960s Broadway musical *Hair*. Turning the park into a fantasy world inhabited by 1960s love children, director Milos Forman creates an idyllic place, totally devoid of muggers, where friendly policemen ride dancing horses and where people swim nude in the lake as casually as they would on a secluded Greek island. More recently director Mike Nichols also turned the park into a magical place in his 2003 screen adaptation of playwright Tony Kushner's *Angels in America*. In both the play and the film, the Bethesda Fountain—with its angel statue—is an especially important location. In the opening of the film we see the statue come to life, whereas at the end it provides a symbol of hope for a confused country and world.

For a documentary look at Central Park and its denizens as they were in the early 1950s, two Judy Holliday vehicles that George Cukor shot on location feature long opening Central Park sequences. In *The Marrying Kind* (1952), Holliday meets her husband Aldo Ray near the Fifth Avenue and 59th Street entrance and plays cat and mouse in several locations, whereas in *It Should Happen to You* (1954), we find a young Jack Lemmon (in his film debut) taking pictures around Bethesda Fountain for a documentary film he is making. In a matter of seconds he meets Holliday and their paths keep crossing, as we are treated to a black-and-white tour of the park as the two get acquainted.

Although the majority of Central Park's screen appearances show it off as one of New York's loveliest locations, sometimes it can be a dangerous place. George Peppard is stalked here in *Breakfast at Tiffany's* (1961); hotel-less Jack Lemmon and Sandy Dennis spend a scary night in the Rambles in *The Out-of-Towners* (1970); and the park's northern reaches embody a no-man's-land of crime and fear in *Across 110th Street* (1972). It's also in Central Park where Dustin Hoffman meets his nemesis, a sadistic Nazi played by Sir Laurence Olivier, on a catwalk above the reservoir in *Marathon Man* (1976) and where Meryl Streep has to contend with a kinky killer out to trap her amid the Rambles in *Still of the Night* (1979). Movie lovers will remember, too, that Mel Gibson's son is kidnapped at the Bethesda Fountain in *Ransom* (1996) and Jeffrey Jones meets a grisly end while jogging along the reservoir in *The Devil's Advocate* (1997).

The park's connections with show business go beyond its importance as a film location. With its Delacorte outdoor theater under the direction of the New York Shakespeare Festival, the park is the site of live theatrical productions each summer, which feature big stars. Arguably the most stellar ensemble to perform at the Delacorte was made up of Meryl Streep, Kevin Kline, Philip Seymour Hoffman, Christopher Walken, Natalie Portman, John Goodman, and Marcia Gay Harden—who did Chekhov's *The Seagull* in the park in the summer of 2002, directed by Mike Nichols no less. It was at the Delacorte, too, where Michelle Pfeiffer tried her hand at Shakespeare, with decidedly uneven results, as Olivia in *Twelfth Night* in 1989. She would have better luck—and reviews—when she did Titania in Michael Hoffman's 1999 film of *A Midsummer Night's Dream*.

Meanwhile, Central Park's ninety-acre Great Lawn is often used for free outdoor concerts that often feature big stars and attract huge audiences. Legendary concert appearances include Barbra Streisand, who famously lit up a joint in 1967, and Diana Ross, who valiantly persevered one rainy evening in 1983, until lightning, gale-force winds, and wayward hair extensions forced her to call the whole thing off. Music lovers will also want to check out Strawberry Fields, the teardrop-shaped grove that's a memorial to the late John Lennon, who was murdered on December 8, 1980, in front of his nearby apartment building, the Dakota, on West 72nd Street and Central Park West. The memorial was donated by the late Beatle's wife Yoko Ono.

Visit www.centralpark.org.

Broadway: That's Entertainment!

Times Square, 42nd Street, Broadway—just the mention of these magical names elicits images of glittering marquees, glamorous opening nights, show-stopping musical numbers. The entertainment capital of the world, New York's Broadway theater district is hallowed ground for movie lovers. First of all, it was on Broadway stages that the careers of some of our greatest film stars—Mary Pickford, Bette Davis, Joan Crawford, Rudolph Valentino, Humphrey Bogart, Barbra Streisand, Robert Redford—were launched. It was also on and off Broadway that the glorious age of the movie palace flourished in New York during the 1920s, 1930s, and 1940s. But while movie lovers can still attend many of Broadway's legitimate theaters and futuristic new multiplexes, most of its historic "cathedrals of the motion picture"—such as the Roxy, the Paramount, Loew's State, the Strand, the Rivoli, and the Capitol—are gone.

Be that as it may, the last decade has seen the rise of a spectacular new Times Square—boasting some of the world's most amazing electronic and fiber-optic signs and enormous digital outdoor movie screens. In addition, an important component of this revitalized entertainment district has been the restoration of many of its formerly derelict theaters. This is especially true

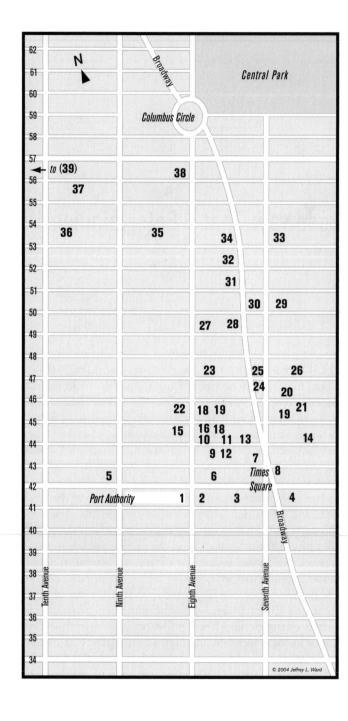

Times Square trilogy (left to right): Times Building, Paramount Building, and Astor Hotel, ca. 1930

of 42nd Street between Broadway and Eighth Avenue, which a mere fifteen years ago was a no-man's-land of drug pushers, porno movie houses, and sex shops. Now the marquees of the New Amsterdam, the New Victory, Ford Center for the Performing Arts (formerly the New Apollo and Lyric theaters), and Empire burn bright. To be sure, some purists feel the area—with its Disney Store and new Madame Tussauds Wax Museum—has become too squeaky-clean touristy and has lost its integrity. That's debatable—but one thing Times Square definitely hasn't lost is its star quality.

Besides historic theaters and futuristic billboards, movie lovers will also find that this part of town encompasses an often overlooked world of soundstages, recording studios, and production offices centered in the 40s and 50s west of Eighth Avenue. Here, filmmaking has gone on since the days of silent pictures, and while many of the historic studios in this part of town are no longer affiliated with Twentieth Century–Fox, Warner Bros., or Paramount, as they once were, they are still turning out features, television series, and commercials. This is where Hollywood on the Hudson gets down to business.

1. PORT AUTHORITY BUS TERMINAL
West 40th to 42nd Streets between Eighth and Ninth Avenues

Said to be the largest and busiest bus terminal in the world, this massive multilevel space—all escalators, garish neon lighting, and dubious denizens—Port Authority, as it is known to New Yorkers and New Jerseyites, was built in 1950 and remodeled and enlarged several times since. The least glamorous way to enter the Big Apple both in reality and on-screen, Port Authority has provided a decidedly gritty New York City welcome for ex-con Sean Connery in Sidney Lumet's *The Anderson Tapes* (1971) and for the mysterious title character, played by Rosanna Arquette, in Susan Seidelman's *Desperately Seeking Susan* (1985). The bus terminal has also appeared in *Angie* (1994), *One True Thing* (1998), and *Igby Goes Down* (2002). To see what the place looked like when it was new, *The Marrying Kind*, a 1952 Judy Holliday comedy directed by George Cukor, shows Holliday and her daughter leaving from Port Authority to see her husband, Aldo Ray, who is in a sanitarium near Brewster. On the trip the bus breaks down, which means that when they arrive they have just enough time to say hello, then board the last bus back to New York.

An integral part of the Port Authority experience is a trip through the Lincoln Tunnel, which feeds directly into the bus station. Another decidedly unglamorous New York landmark, the tunnel—almost 100 feet below the Hudson River—links New York and New Jersey. Originally built in 1937, it now consists of three separate tubes, each over a mile long. The tunnel appears in most of the aforementioned films—and it has recently been immortalized in the opening credits of the hit HBO series *The Sopranos*. The tunnel was also featured in the 2003 feature *Elf*, in a scene where Santa's helper Will Ferrell travels the tube on foot via its pedestrian walkway in his quest to find his birth father.

Adaptive reuse: 1912
Empire theater as a
twenty-five-screen
multiplex

2. AMC EMPIRE 25
234 West 42nd Street

The 42nd Street Development Corporation achieved a minor miracle in 1998, when it moved the 1912 façade of the historic Empire Theater 170 feet west on 42nd Street to form the new entrance for the city's largest multiplex—the twenty-five-screen AMC Empire. When the theater first opened it was a legit house called the Eltinge in honor of its frequent headliner Julian Eltinge, who was the town's top female impersonator at the time. In the 1930s, the Eltinge started showing films and eventually was renamed the Empire Theater. Historian Louis Botto reports that the Empire was famous for having three different sizes of seats—small, regular, and extra-large. And for film buffs who remember the Empire Theater from the famous 1948 film *A Double Life,* where Ronald Colman plays an actor/producer who gets a bit carried away in the role of *Othello,* that the Empire Theater stood at Broadway and 40th Street and was torn down in 1953.

Meanwhile, serious film buffs will be interested in yet another historic theater, the Liberty, which currently stands awaiting renovation hidden behind a fast-food court just up the block from the AMC Empire. The Liberty also began its life as a legit house, and managed to survive into the 1980s showing action and porno films. Its importance in film history, however, has to do with an event back in March 1915, when the theater hosted the official East Coast opening of a movie that represented a milestone in the art of filmmaking. So much money, effort, and time had gone into this epic production that a full-fledged Broadway theater was leased for its premiere and its promoters charged the then unheard-of price of $2 for a reserved ticket. The film was D. W. Griffith's *The Birth of a Nation*, and it ran for eleven months at the Liberty. Highly controversial owing to its decidedly racist look at the post–Civil War South, the film was protested by the NAACP as well as by a number of other groups that tried to block its exhibition. The fact that Griffith's film aroused so much feeling was ultimately one of the reasons for its landmark status in film-history books, for *The Birth of a Nation* proved just how powerful the medium of film could be if used to its full potential.

The Birth of a Nation also proved that movies could make really big money—especially at $2 a head. One of those who profited greatly from *The Birth of a Nation* was a former junk dealer from Massachusetts named Louis B. Mayer. Having gone from junk to running movie theaters, Mayer managed to tie up the New England distribution rights to Griffith's landmark film and made a fortune on the deal and became one of the industry's most important players—especially a decade later when he ran Metro-Goldwyn-Mayer studios in Hollywood.

3. NEW AMSTERDAM THEATER
214 West 42nd Street

Originally built for vaudeville producers Marc Klaw and A. L. Erlanger in 1903, the beautiful Art Nouveau New Amsterdam was taken over in 1913 by the great Florenz Ziegfeld as a site for his famous Follies. Practically every one of the next fourteen years, Ziegfeld came out with a new edition of his spectacular stage show at the New Amsterdam, and he would unleash on the world talents like Fanny Brice, Eddie Cantor, Will Rogers, W. C. Fields, Fred Astaire, Jack Benny, Bob Hope, Paulette Goddard, Mae Murray, Marion Davies, and Ziegfeld Follies queen Marilyn Miller.

While Ziegfeld's Follies flourished downstairs at the New Am-

sterdam, its rooftop nightclub—the New Amsterdam Roof—
pulled in la crème de la crème of New York society, who came to
see Ziegfeld stars in a glamorous cabaret setting. Later, when
Prohibition killed the New Amsterdam Roof, the place led a varied life as a conventional theater, radio studio, rehearsal hall,
and TV studio. Radio buffs may remember it as home of the
WOR Mutual Theater in the late 1930s–early 1940s, when it
was broadcasting the chilling series *The Shadow,* which once
starred Orson Welles.

Ziegfeld departed from the New Amsterdam's main theater
in 1927. It spent the next ten years as a Broadway house, was
converted into a movie palace in 1937, and continued to show
films until 1983. After that, the crumbling theater stood vacant
for over ten years until the Walt Disney Company, by that time
a major Broadway player with the success of its *Beauty and the
Beast* musical adapted from its 1991 animated feature, signed
a lease in 1995 to restore the New Amsterdam and operate it
as a Broadway house. After two years of painstaking restoration by Disney's innovative Imagineering division, the theater
reopened and soon was home to another Disney animated hit–
turned–Broadway smash: *The Lion King,* one of the most successful musicals of all time.

The Disney touch:
restored interior of New
Amsterdam Theater

Before Disney entered the picture, the abandoned New Amsterdam was used in several films, notably the 1988 Sam Elliott–Peter Weller urban action thriller *Shakedown,* and Louis Malle's avant-garde *Vanya on 42nd Street* (1993), as the theater where Wallace Shawn, Julianne Moore, and company rehearse and perform a modern-dress version of Chekhov's *Uncle Vanya.* To see the New Amsterdam—and Times Square—in its heyday, movie lovers should also check out the 1929 made–in–New York talkie, *Glorifying the American Girl,* which has a location sequence that documents an opening night at the theater with wonderful shots of Florenz Ziegfeld, Billie Burke, financier Otto Kahn, and Mayor Jimmy Walker. The theater's most famous film appearance, however, was fashioned at Hollywood's MGM dream factory—that is, the 1941 musical extravaganza *Ziegfeld Girl,* where showgirls Judy Garland, Hedy Lamarr, and Lana Turner stumble into fame, fortune, and misfortune respectively.

Disney offers guided tours of the New Amsterdam; for information, visit www.newyorkled.com/timessquare.htm.

4. KNICKERBOCKER BUILDING
152 West 42nd Street

Erected in 1902 and restored in 2003, this Times Square office building still stuns with its wrought-iron balconies, sculpted cornices, and elegant mansard roofs. Originally built as Col. John Jacob Astor's famed Knickerbocker Hotel, for twenty years this was one of Broadway's most fashionable places to stay and to play. Offering great luxury, the Knickerbocker had a glorious dining room with a marble floor and a ceiling modeled after one in Napoleon's palace at Fontainebleau in France. For its mirrored café, the artist Frederic Remington provided an Indian battle scene, and for the hotel's oak-paneled barroom Astor commissioned Maxfield Parrish's *Old King Cole and His Fiddlers Three,* which today hangs in the King Cole Bar of another of Astor's hotels, the St. Regis at Fifth Avenue and 55th Street.

The services at the Knickerbocker more than matched its lavish decor. For businesspeople who arrived without baggage, the hotel provided pajamas, combs, and brushes at no extra charge.

Knickerbocker Hotel
building, 1987

And if a guest had an unexpected formal function to attend, the Knickerbocker had a full array of tuxedos and accessories in a wide range of sizes. Again, there was no charge.

One of the hotel's most famous erstwhile residents was the great showman George M. Cohan. Known more as a vaudevillian, playwright, and songwriter, Cohan constantly appeared in films from the late 1910s through the early 1930s and also saw a number of his plays become films in which he did not appear, such as *Little Nellie Kelly* (1940), which starred Judy Garland. He will be best remembered by movie lovers through James Cagney's portrayal of him in Warner's 1942 musical *Yankee Doodle Dandy*.

Another of the Knickerbocker's former residents was the famous opera singer Enrico Caruso; he not only held forth on the stage of the old Metropolitan Opera a few blocks away at Broadway and 38th Street, but also appeared in two films for Adolph Zukor's Famous Players Film Company in 1918. Despite his great fame, an opera singer in a silent picture didn't make it with the public, and after Caruso's first Famous Players film, *My Cousin,* flopped at the box office, his second was never released.

The Knickerbocker Hotel didn't fare much better; in 1920 it shut down and was converted into the office building that it remains today. Its demise was blamed on Prohibition.

5. MANHATTAN PLAZA
400 West 43rd Street

A unique experiment in subsidized housing, Manhattan Plaza is the first and only luxury apartment complex where the majority of tenants are working show-business people who, during lean periods, are required to pay only 30 percent of their gross earnings in rent. At the same time, the building's star residents have to come up with the same big bucks that most Manhattanites are forced to pay for the privilege of living in the Big Apple. Among its former celebrity denizens have been Angela Lansbury, Jane Alexander, Helen Hayes, and Tennessee Williams.

How did Manhattan Plaza come about? Definitely *not* through the beneficence of some stagestruck real estate developer. Originally, the building was to have been yet another high-rent highrise. However, as Manhattan Plaza was nearing completion in 1976, New York City's real estate picture was decidedly different than it is today, and the developers were having a hard time luring high-income tenants to their project's dicey Hell's Kitchen location between Ninth and Tenth Avenues. It was then that the subsidy plan was devised by the City of New York in order to salvage the money that the city had invested in the building. Today, thanks largely to Manhattan Plaza, the neighborhood now abounds with restaurants, shops, and off-Broadway theaters. In 2004, however, the building was sold, putting the unique subsidy plan in jeopardy. Needless to say, many tenants are fighting hard to hold on to their apartments and their low rents.

6. CLUB NEW YORK SITE
252 West 43rd Street

In late 1999, this Times Square disco found itself very much in the news when two of its highest-profile patrons, rap mogul/fashion designer/actor Sean Combs (aka Puff Daddy, P-Diddy, Sean Puffy Combs), his then gal-pal Jennifer Lopez, and his bodyguard were involved in a shooting in which three people were injured. Combs, Lopez, the bodyguard, and a rapper friend all fled the club and were later arrested. Lopez was released the same night with no charges. And after indictments, press conferences, suits, countersuits, a courtroom trial, and a little legal help from O.J. Simpson lawyer Johnnie Cochran, Combs and his bodyguard were acquitted. Club New York, by the way, closed down in late 2003.

7. PARAMOUNT BUILDING
1501 Broadway

This thirty-five-story Times Square pyramid—crowned by a Deco clock tower and a gigantic glass globe—is one of the greatest monuments to early moviemaking still standing in Manhattan. Erected in 1926, 1501 Broadway made its debut as the Paramount Building, the man behind it being Paramount Pictures' Adolph Zukor, the mogul who founded the Famous Players Film Company back in 1912 and then went on to head one of the world's most powerful studios.

The dramatic mountain of a building that Zukor erected for his company on Times Square not only housed Paramount offices but was also home to the glorious Paramount Theater. Designed by architects Rapp and Rapp, the Paramount had three lobbies, including a great hall punctuated at one end by an extraordinary marble staircase modeled after the one at the Paris Opera, plus a myriad of special public rooms that ranged from a tea gallery to a ladies' smoking lounge to a music room where a string orchestra played chamber music for customers waiting for seats. To keep track of the theater's 3,900 seats, 150 ushers had a special electronic signal system that told of vacancies in the vast auditorium.

Paramount Theater, 1927

Throughout the years, the Paramount became just as famous for the headliners that studded its live stage shows as for the movies it presented. Of the performers associated with the Paramount, none is more legendary than Frank Sinatra, whose appearances at the theater in the early 1940s brought out the droves of squealing teenaged girls who helped turn Sinatra into a superstar, although much of the hysteria seems to have been a carefully orchestrated publicity stunt in which a press agent not only distributed free tickets to pack the Paramount, but even coached some young audience members on how and when to squeal during the performance.

The Paramount bit the dust in the 1950s. Hollowed out rather than knocked down, the space that the theater took up in the Paramount Building was then "filled in" with offices. In the 1990s, however, the World Wrestling Entertainment company erected a replica of the theater's famous marquee as an entrance for the wrestling arena it had installed inside. Meanwhile, Paramount, the company that started it all, is now a part of the Viacom media conglomerate, which currently has its offices next door in the high-rise at 1515 Broadway.

Home base for *Good Morning America:* Times Square Studios

8. TIMES SQUARE STUDIOS
Broadway and 43rd Street

In 1999, the Walt Disney Company, as part of its continuing efforts to spruce up Times Square, opened this high-tech TV studio with huge windows overlooking the bustling crossroads below. The studios were built expressly for ABC's *Good Morning America* (ABC is owned by Disney), and they enabled the show to go out onto the street, as its biggest rival, the *Today* show, had been doing since 1994. Today, in addition to providing a home for *GMA*, the futuristic facility is also used by *20/20* as well as by non-ABC productions.

Visit http://site.yahoo.com/timessquarestudios/.

9. ST. JAMES THEATER
246 West 44th Street

It was just like in the movies. It was 1954, and the show was *The Pajama Game* at the St. James. The star dancer, Carol Haney, broke her leg not long after opening night, and the chorus girl had to fill in for her. A big movie producer—Hal Wallis—was in the audience, and he was so taken by the twenty-year-old understudy's performance that he offered her a movie contract. And that's how Shirley MacLaine went to Hollywood.

In addition to giving the world Shirley MacLaine, the St.

James can also boast at least one former usherette who became a movie star: Lauren Bacall, who worked at the theater in the early 1940s in order to make ends meet during her starving-actress days in Manhattan.

Around the same time, in 1943, the St. James hosted a musical no one expected to be a hit—Rodgers and Hammerstein's *Oklahoma!* Of special interest to movie lovers may be the fact that the director of this landmark musical comedy (notable because it featured songs and ballet numbers integral to the story line) was film director Rouben Mamoulian, whose classic movies include *Applause*, a 1929 New York sound film (available on video and DVD) about the world of burlesque; *Dr. Jekyll and Mr. Hyde* (1932), with Fredric March; *Song of Songs* (1933), starring Marlene Dietrich; Garbo's *Queen Christina* (1933); *Becky Sharp* (1935), the first feature film to use three-strip Technicolor; and *Silk Stockings* (1957), with Fred Astaire and Cyd Charisse.

Among its other important Broadway productions, the St. James also housed *The King and I* (1951), *Li'l Abner* (1956), *Flower Drum Song* (1958), *Hello, Dolly!* (1964), and Mel Brooks's history-making *The Producers* (2002). Based on the hilarious 1968 nonmusical film, the show won a record number of Tonys (twelve) and charged a record top ticket price of $100. If that wasn't enough, *The Producers* also created a new Broadway concept, setting aside a limited number of particularly good VIP seats at $480 a pop—in other words, legitimate tickets at scalper prices. Talk about producers!

10. MAJESTIC THEATER
245 West 44th Street

In Billy's Wilder's moving 1960 film *The Apartment,* promotion-minded Jack Lemmon lets his boss use his apartment for his extracurricular amorous activities. In love with the company secretary played by Shirley MacLaine, Lemmon stands in front of the Majestic waiting for MacLaine, who seems to have stood him up for a date to the town's current hottest show, *The Music Man.* While he paces back and forth, little does Lemmon know that she is in his very own apartment with his boss. If the film were redone at any time between 1988 and the present, the show on the marquee at the Majestic would be *The Phantom of the Opera,* which is on its way to outpacing *Cats* as the longest-running musical in Broadway history.

11. BROADHURST THEATER
235 West 44th Street

This is the theater that really put Humphrey Bogart on the map. Despite the fact the Bogart had acted in theater *and* films since the early 1920s, his career was, at best, mediocre when he was signed to do the part of a gangster in Robert E. Sherwood's *The Petrified Forest,* which opened at the Broadhurst on January 7, 1935. Being cast as a tough guy was something new for Bogart, who had usually played ineffectual second leads both on stage and on screen. *The Petrified Forest* was to change all that, espe-

Bogart at the Broadhurst: *The Petrified Forest,* 1935

cially when Bogart re-created his Broadway role in the Warner Bros. film version of the play. In typical Hollywood fashion, however, Bogart almost missed out on the film because Warner Bros. really wanted its resident gangster, Edward G. Robinson, to do the part. Ultimately they wanted *The Petrified Forest*'s other star, Leslie Howard, even more than Robinson, because Howard told the studio that he wouldn't do his role unless Bogart was cast. Bogie got the part and quickly became the toughest guy on the Warner lot.

Another Hollywood legend of the 1940s got a big career boost via the Broadhurst stage. The show was a 1939 revue, *The Streets of Paris,* that featured comics Bud Abbott and Lou Costello, dancers Gower (Champion) and Jeanne Tyler, and a host of other performers. The real star of the show, however, was a Latin bombshell named Carmen Miranda, who went on to parade her fruit-laden headdresses and her fiery temperament through a string of Twentieth Century–Fox films with Latin locales and titles such as *Down Argentine Way* (1940), *That Night in Rio* (1941), and *Weekend in Havana* (1941). Appropriately, Miss Miranda's Portuguese father ran a wholesale fruit operation in Brazil!

The Broadhurst also saw Rosalind Russell triumph as *Auntie Mame* from 1956 to 1958, before she did the same thing in the Warner Bros. film version in 1959. It was also this theater where Woody Allen's *Play It Again, Sam* ran; the 1969 comedy starred Allen as well as the actress who would go on to be a major leading lady in both his on- and off-screen life: Diane Keaton. It's also not every day that Superman meets superstar on stage, but it happened at the Broadhurst in 1976, when Christopher Reeve and Katharine Hepburn costarred in the comedy *A Matter of Gravity*.

One of the theater's biggest 1990s hits was another of that growing phenomenon: the big Broadway musical based on a small nonmusical feature film. In this case, it was *Kiss of the Spider Woman*. It was also in the 1990s that the Broadhurst wound up as a location in the quirky film *Being John Malkovich* (1999) when Catherine Keener has a rendezvous with Malkovich in a dressing room. But was it really Malkovich?

12. SARDI'S
234 West 44th Street

What Hollywood's old Brown Derby restaurant on Vine Street was to the movie industry, Sardi's on West 44th Street continues to be for the Broadway theater in Manhattan. Once described as "the club, mess hall, lounge, post office, saloon, and marketplace of the people of the theater," Sardi's was founded in 1921 by Vincent Sardi, an Italian immigrant who started his New York restaurant career as a waiter. In 1921, Sardi and his wife opened their original restaurant at 248 West 44th Street, several doors away from its current location, to which it moved in 1927 to make way for the St. James Theater. From the start, the warm, family atmosphere that the Sardis brought to the theater district appealed to show folk. What also appealed was the generosity that Vincent Sardi showed toward many performers during their lean periods "between engagements." Supposedly, James Cagney, in his struggling days, frequently dined at Sardi's on

On location at Sardi's: Rod Steiger in *No Way to Treat a Lady,* 1968

credit. By the same token, Sardi's became known as a place where the famous could go and be assured that their privacy would be respected. In the 1940s, when she had left Hollywood, and every journalist on earth wanted to interview her, Greta Garbo could dine at Sardi's in relative seclusion.

Today Sardi's no longer provides handouts to out-of-work actors, but it is still a place where some of New York's most celebrated theater and movie people gather. Usually Sardi's is a celebrity-spotter's dream; but even when there are no heavyweights in the place, movie lovers will still find themselves surrounded by some of the biggest names in show business, because their autographed caricatures hang on every available inch of wall space. Muppets fans may remember how Kermit the Frog sneaked a picture of himself onto Sardi's wall and waited at a table for fellow diners to recognize him in *The Muppets Take Manhattan* (1984). Other films to feature Sardi's sequences include Martin Scorsese's 1983 *The King of Comedy*, where smalltime comic Robert De Niro dines with talk-show star Jerry Lewis, and *No Way to Treat a Lady* (1968), the campy thriller with Rod Steiger playing an actor/producer/serial killer. In the Sardi's scene, which features a cameo appearance by Vincent Sardi, Steiger asks for a phone to be brought to his table and calls police headquarters to taunt the detective in charge of investigating the serial killings. In that romantic pre–cell phone age, many restaurants had telephone jacks at all the "important" tables.

Visit www.sardis.com.

13. SHUBERT THEATER
225 West 44th Street

She had been branded "box-office poison" in 1938 by the president of the Independent Theater Owners of America because her pictures didn't make money. She wanted desperately to play Scarlett O'Hara in *Gone With the Wind,* but David O. Selznick wouldn't give it to her. When asked why, the famous Hollywood producer told Katharine Hepburn, "Because, my dear, I can't see Rhett Butler chasing you for twelve years." And so, when playwright Philip Barry approached her about a play he was writing with her in mind for the lead, Miss Hepburn, fed up with Holly-

wood, consented to do the role of headstrong heiress Tracy
Lord in *The Philadelphia Story*. In addition, together with her
good pal at the time, millionaire aviator/movie mogul Howard
Hughes, she put up half of the money needed to produce Barry's
play. It was a wise move on Kate's part. *The Philadelphia Story*
opened at the Shubert Theater on March 28, 1939, and was a
critical and financial smash hit. It not only bolstered Hepburn's
sagging career, it made her a wealthy woman—especially after
she and Hughes sold the screen rights to MGM, a deal that gave
her the starring role in the picture, opposite Jimmy Stewart and
Cary Grant, as well as a lucrative long-term contract with the
studio.

Movie lovers may also be interested in knowing that it was
at the Shubert Theater that Barbara (she hadn't yet dropped
the second *a*) Streisand made her Broadway debut (and stole
the show) in *I Can Get It for You Wholesale* in 1962. Playing the role of a secretary named Miss Marmelstein, Barbra also
stole the heart of the show's leading man, Elliott Gould, whom
she married in 1964. While doing *Wholesale,* she reportedly got
bored in her small role and asked various other female members of the cast to switch parts with her for a performance or
two. Needless to say, the other actresses declined her offers. She
also chewed gum onstage, which irked the stage manager enor-
mously. On the gum-chewing business, Streisand had this to say
in an interview: "Listen, what does gum in your mouth matter
if you're doing your job?"

In 1974, the Shubert saw Patti and Maxene Andrews, the two
surviving members of the Andrews Sisters, the legendary singing
trio of the 1940s, headline a campy Hollywood Canteen–ish
musical called *Over Here*. Two of the boys in the chorus of the
show went on to film fame: John Travolta and Treat Williams.
The following year, the Shubert Theater welcomed producer
Joseph Papp's *A Chorus Line*. The show kept on rolling until
April 1990, when it closed after 6,137 performances. The 1988
Richard Attenborough–directed film version of *A Chorus Line*
got decidedly mixed reviews and was a box-office bomb. And
while most of all those Broadway musicals inspired by films have
been big hits on Broadway, *Big*, which opened at the Shubert in
1996, proved the exception.

14. BELASCO THEATER
111 West 44th Street

In one of Woody Allen's funnier films in the last decade, *Bullets Over Broadway* (1994) had John Cusack trying unsuccessfully to get his play, *God of Our Fathers,* staged. Things changed when he got the backing of a local mobster who, it turned out, wanted a say in the casting. Thus Cusack got his show on at the Belasco, but with his backer's no-talent girlfriend (Jennifer Tilly) in a leading role. In 2002, the Belasco was again featured on screen, as playwright Gwyneth Paltrow paces outside the theater while a show of hers is premiering inside in *The Royal Tenenbaums.*

The 1907 theater is named for the flamboyant early-twentieth-century actor-director-producer David Belasco. Nicknamed "the bishop of Broadway," because of his penchant for dressing in ecclesiastical garb, Belasco is said to haunt the place, especially on opening nights, when his ghost has been spotted sitting alone in a box dressed to kill.

15. MARTIN BECK THEATER
302 West 45th Street

She was riding high in 1933. She had received rave notices for her performance in *Morning Glory,* and her work in the not-yet-released *Little Women* was the talk of Hollywood. Indeed, at twenty-four, Katharine Hepburn could do no wrong. And so, instead of making another picture, the impetuous young actress decided to do a Broadway show. A British play called *The Lake* was chosen for her by the bright young director Jed Harris. Unfortunately, it was a terrible play—and Katharine Hepburn was dreadful in it. So dreadful that Dorothy Parker wrote of Hepburn's performance the famous, "she ran the gamut of emotions from A to B." *The Lake* played the Martin Beck Theater for about seven weeks, after which a somewhat humbled Miss Hepburn escaped to Europe. Ironically, the day she set sail, she was comforted by the news that she had just won an Academy Award for *Morning Glory.*

Practically a half century later, another legendary Hollywood

Broadway flop: Katharine Hepburn in *The Lake*, 1933

star tried her luck at the Martin Beck and, much to the surprise of both audiences and critics, Elizabeth Taylor turned in a creditable performance in her Broadway debut in the role of Regina Giddens in the 1981 revival of Lillian Hellman's *The Little Foxes*. But when Miss Taylor returned to Broadway the following year in what the world expected to be one of the major theatrical events of the twentieth century—Taylor starring with her ex-husband Richard Burton in Noël Coward's *Private Lives*—she did not fare as well. *Private Lives,* which played the Lunt-Fontanne Theatre on West 46th Street, was a critical and commercial disaster. Indeed, toward the end of the run, when many of the people in the audience were there on discount tickets, Taylor's diamonds were more talked about than her performance. Liz never returned to Broadway.

In 1995, Carol Burnett, who over the years had starred in various Broadway productions, returned to Broadway in a dreadful farce called *Moon Over Buffalo* at the Martin Beck, which even Miss Burnett's prodigious comic talents could not salvage. Far better than the show was the 1997 documentary *Moon Over Broadway*, made by D. A. Pennebaker and Chris Hedges, which eavesdropped on the rehearsals, out-of-town tryouts, and considerable backstage dramas involved with bringing this turkey to the Great White Way. The Martin Beck recently changed its name to the Al Hirschfeld Theater, in honor of the famous Broadway caricaturist.

16. JOHN GOLDEN THEATER
252 West 45th Street

Does anybody remember the play *Aged in Wood,* by the famous Broadway playwright Lloyd Richards? It ran at the Golden in 1949. It starred the legendary Broadway actress Margo Channing, and it was during the run of *Aged in Wood* that Miss Channing befriended a shy young fan from San Francisco who briefly became her girl Friday. Soon, however, Eve Harrington managed not only to sabotage Margo Channing's career, but her friends and love life as well. By now, movie lovers will realize that *Aged in Wood* was not a real drama, but the play in the film *All About Eve,* which starred Bette Davis as Margo and Anne Baxter as Eve. Few people realize that the Golden Theater was also in the film—but if you watch carefully, and if you know your theater-district geography, it's easy to figure out that the Golden is definitely the Broadway house—with the Royale and the Booth theaters visible just up the street beyond it—that was used for *All About Eve*'s second-unit exteriors.

Now, fasten your seat belts for an even more esoteric bit of *All About Eve* trivia. What show was playing next door at the Royale Theater while *Aged in Wood* was at the Golden? Answer: *The Devil's Disciple,* starring Maurice Evans, which actually *was* playing at the Royale in 1949.

17. IMPERIAL THEATER
249 West 45th Street

In the 1959 Douglas Sirk tearjerker *Imitation of Life,* Lana Turner stars as Lora Meredith, a single mother down on her luck until she gets a big break and becomes one of Broadway's leading comedic actresses. Unhappy with her lightweight roles, Lana/Lora longs for meatier subject matter. Her dramatic debut is here at the Imperial Theater in *No Greater Lady.* The irony is that the 1,650-seat Imperial has traditionally been known as one of Broadway's best musical-comedy venues. Over the years it's hosted such legendary hits as *Oliver!, Fiddler on the Roof, Cabaret, Pippin, Dreamgirls,* and *Chess.*

18. ROYALE THEATER
242 West 45th Street

It was a bizarre bit of casting: a blond, blue-eyed, all-American young man from Indiana in the role of a homosexual North African houseboy named Bachir. But that's the part that James Dean played in a dramatization of André Gide's novel *The Immoralist,* which opened at the Royale Theater on February 1, 1954. After constant battles during out-of-town tryouts with the play's director, Daniel Mann, Dean further antagonized his director on opening night by lifting up his native robe and curtsying to the Royale audience during his curtain call. Mr. Mann was not amused by Jimmy's jest—nor by the fact that he announced the same night that he was leaving the show in two weeks to do a film in Hollywood. Unbeknownst to anyone, during previews of *The Immoralist,* Elia Kazan had secretly approached Jimmy and given him a screen test for *East of Eden.* Despite his abrupt departure from the cast, Dean nonetheless won a Theater World Award as a "promising newcomer" of the 1953–54 season on the basis of his stage performance at the Royale.

The following season, a British musical opened at the Royale on September 30, springing another amazingly talented newcomer onto the Broadway stage. The show was *The Boy Friend,* and its magnificent young star was Julie Andrews, who would go on to dazzle New York audiences as Eliza Doolittle in *My Fair*

Lady before achieving superstardom in Hollywood (but not in the film version of *My Fair Lady,* which went to Audrey Hepburn). Another Royale production of interest to movie lovers is the 1961 debut of Tennessee Williams's *The Night of the Iguana,* which brought Bette Davis back to the Broadway stage just before the *What Ever Happened to Baby Jane?* (1962) phase of her film career.

In May 1988, the Royale saw the stage debut of pop star and sometimes film actress Madonna, who played a secretary in David Mamet's *Speed-the-Plow.* The diva got mixed reviews, but the house was packed with celebrities every night and the street was mobbed by fans and paparazzi. When Madonna tried her luck on the London stage in the summer of 2003, in an Australian play called *Up for Grabs,* which was specially rewritten and reset in the United States for her, she got some of the worst reviews in the history of the theater. Nonetheless, the show was still the hottest ticket in town.

19. LYCEUM THEATER
149 West 45th Street

New York's oldest surviving theater that is still being used for legitimate productions, the Lyceum, with its ornate façade of sculpted limestone punctuated by five fat fluted columns and three huge arched windows, is also one of the city's most handsome houses. Built in 1903 by a then famous theatrical producer, Daniel Frohman, the Lyceum contained Frohman's living quarters above the second balcony, and he frequently made use of a special secret window that looked down on the stage to phone directions to his cast and crews! Today Frohman's former Lyceum apartment houses the archives of the Shubert Theater Organization.

On July 12, 1912, the Lyceum hosted a very important event in motion-picture history, when a private screening was held there of a revolutionary European film version of *Queen Elizabeth* starring the great French actress Sarah Bernhardt. The film was revolutionary because it lasted for a then unheard-of fifty minutes and because it featured a major actress instead of one of the anonymous beauties that populated most early movies. The

Sarah Bernhardt on-screen: *Queen Elizabeth*, 1912

American rights to *Queen Elizabeth* had just been purchased by a little man named Adolph Zukor, who planned both to market *Queen Elizabeth* in America and to set up a company that would film famous stage stars in famous plays. Which is where the Lyceum comes into the story—since producer Daniel Frohman was one of the partners that Zukor had recruited for his bold venture. Frohman would be particularly valuable to the new Famous Players Film Company (one of the companies that eventually formed Paramount Pictures) because he would supply the stars, the plays, and the theatrical clout to get Famous Players' pictures off the ground.

Soon, through films like *His Neighbor's Wife* with Lillie Langtry, *The Prisoner of Zenda* with Jakes K. Hackett, and *The Count of Monte Cristo* with James O'Neill (Eugene O'Neill's father), the new Famous Players Film Company primed the public's taste for their trademark "Bigger and Better Pictures." And when this happened, not only did appearing on-screen lose its stigma for stage stars, but other American producers jumped on the bandwagon and began coming out with longer films. In a matter of months, short films, which had been the staple of the American motion-picture industry for the first fifteen years of its existence, went out of fashion, and the "feature craze" began. For film historians, it began at the Lyceum.

Another beginning at the Lyceum was that of the film career of Bette Davis, who was discovered in 1930 by an executive from Universal while she was in a play there called *The Solid South*. Davis went directly from the Lyceum stage to Hollywood to appear in *Bad Sister* (1931), in which she played the good sister. Actually, this was not the first time that Bette had been discovered on Broadway. The year before she had been seen in a play called *Broken Dishes* at the Ritz Theater and was given a screen test by the Samuel Goldwyn Company in New York. When Sam Goldwyn saw Bette's test, he is quoted as having said: "Who did this to me?"

Bette Davis on Broadway—with Duncan Penwarden in *Broken Dishes,* 1929

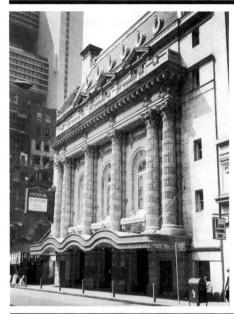

Lyceum Theater

Movie lovers can see the ornate Lyceum lobby in the 1947 theatrical thriller *A Double Life,* starring Ronald Colman as an actor who takes his *Othello* a little too seriously. The theater is also where Tom Ripley (Matt Damon) works as a projectionist before leaving for Italy and a new identity and life in *The Talented Mr. Ripley* (1999). The Julia Roberts 2003 vehicle *Mona Lisa Smile* also has a Lyceum sequence.

20. CHURCH OF ST. MARY THE VIRGIN
145 West 46th Street

Beautifully restored in the 1990s, this French Gothic–style church is actually an Episcopal house of worship. Noted for its high-church liturgy and incense-infused rituals, the church is nicknamed Smoky Mary's. Popular with theater folk, St. Mary's has also turned up in several New York movies: In *Changing Lanes* (2002), it's the site of Ben Affleck's AA meeting, whereas in Woody Allen's *Small Time Crooks* (2000), its elegant Old World chapel doubles for a church in Venice, Italy, where posh Hugh Grant has taken nouveau riche New Yorker Tracey Ullman for a bit of high culture. At a concert in the chapel, Ullman annoys everyone by chatting on her cell phone.

21. HIGH SCHOOL OF PERFORMING ARTS SITE
120 West 46th Street

Liza Minnelli went here, as did Al Pacino, Eartha Kitt, Diahann Carroll, Michelle Lee, Dom DeLuise, and Melissa Manchester. Ultimately, however, New York City's High School of the Performing Arts will be remembered less for the famous show folk it has trained than for the famous film that it inspired: *Fame*. While *Fame* was shot entirely in New York, one city location that never saw any action during the filming was the High School of the Performing Arts! At the time (1979), the board of education refused to allow the school to be used because it didn't approve of the profanity, sex, or recreational drug use called for by the script. In fact, it looked at one point as though *Fame*

Fame on West 46th Street, 1979

might have to find a high school in another city. That's when the Mayor's Office of Film, Theater, and Broadcasting stepped in and came up with the abandoned (and now demolished) Haaren High building on Tenth Avenue and 59th Street—no longer under board of ed control—for the location.

Meanwhile, the real High School of Performing Arts closed down in 1984, when the board of education merged it with New York City's High School of Music and Art to become the La Guardia High School on Amsterdam Avenue, behind Lincoln Center. Performing Arts' former West 46th Street home is now the Jacqueline Kennedy Onassis High School, specializing in training students for careers in international business and government.

22. JOE ALLEN
326 West 46th Street

Opened in 1965 by a former actor named Joe Allen, this unpretentious brick-walled pub/restaurant has been one of Broadway's top hangouts for working actors for four decades. An egalitarian place, Joe Allen is popular with kids in the chorus as well as with superstars like Elizabeth Taylor, who could usually be found dining on Joe Allen's famous chili after the curtain came down on her Broadway debut run in *The Little Foxes* in 1981. Joe Allen is also known for its burgers (currently $10), barbecued ribs, meat loaf, calves' liver, steak, and pan-fried chicken—all served in a room plastered with posters of such famous flops as *Moose Murders,* which brought 1940s/1950s TV star Eve Arden to Broadway for about ten minutes in 1983, to *Phantom of the Opera* Michael Crawford's 2003 bomb *Dance of the Vampires.* Many customers request to be seated next to their favorite flop.

Movie lovers can find Joe Allen clones in Paris, London, and Miami. The original New York venue was featured in the 1968 film *No Way to Treat a Lady,* where detective George Segal comes here following a lead in his search for serial killer Rod Steiger. When a drag queen regular leaves with a strange-looking older woman, Segal realizes something's not quite right, but not before a murder is committed. Woody Allen also used the restaurant for a scene in his 2004 *Melinda and Melinda.* And getting back to bombs, Joe Allen's was a location for Al Pacino's straight-to-video *People I Know* (2001), which looked at the life of notorious New York PR flack Bobby Zarem.

Visit www.joeallenrestaurant.com.

23. ETHEL BARRYMORE THEATER
243 West 47th Street

Built in 1928 and named for the then reigning queen of the American theater, Ethel Barrymore, this historic house, with the distinctive neon sign on its marquee, was recently the site of the monster hit play *A Woman to Love* by one of the country's most successful playwrights, Erika Barry. The play, which is based on an older woman's falling in love with her daughter's sixty-three-year-old boyfriend, is decidedly autobiographical. And for anyone reading this, the play was never really on Broadway at the Barrymore or anywhere else. But it was in the movies—as the fictional drama in the 2003 Nancy Meyers film *Something's Got to Give,* which won a Golden Globe for Diane Keaton as the playwright in love with Jack Nicholson.

A few real dramas at the Barrymore that may interest movie lovers include Clare Boothe Luce's 1936 celebration of bitchery, *The Women,* which became a classic 1939 George Cukor film; Tennessee Williams's landmark *A Streetcar Named Desire,* which opened in 1947 and made Marlon Brando a star; and a 1992 revival of the same Williams play, which brought movie stars Jessica Lange and Alec Baldwin to Broadway.

24. PALACE THEATER
1564 Broadway

The gold plaque backstage reads: "This was the dressing room of Judy Garland who set the all-time long-run record October 16, 1951, to February 24, 1952, at the RKO–Palace Theatre." For Garland fans, the Palace is not just where Judy started her concert career in the United States, it is the sacred spot where she proved that her talent was far greater than anyone had previously imagined. Fed by a live audience, Garland in person went beyond anything she had ever done on film. Ultimately, the legend of Judy Garland was not born on the MGM soundstages, but on the stage of the Palace Theater.

The idea of having Judy play the Palace was that of producer Sid Luft, who eventually became her third husband. Down on her luck, Judy had been suspended by MGM in June 1950 for not showing up for the shooting of *The Barclays of Broadway*. Then, two days later, there had been a much publicized suicide attempt in which she tried to slash her throat. As far as Hollywood studio executives were concerned, Judy Garland was no longer bankable. Unable to work in America, Judy wound up doing a series of concerts in England in 1951. They were highly successful, but on her return to America the only jobs her agents were able to line up for her were some radio guest shots. Clearly, drastic measures needed to be taken in order to show Hollywood—and America—the talent that had taken England by storm. And for Sid Luft, the Palace was the ticket.

Judy at the Palace was very much a case of being in the right place at the right time. In 1951, the great Temple of Vaudeville, which opened in 1913, and which had seen headliners like Sophie Tucker, Eddie Cantor, the Marx Brothers, Kate Smith, Fred Astaire, W. C. Fields, Fanny Brice, and Ethel Merman in its halcyon days, was a tattered remnant of its former self. Vaudeville was finished, and the theater had gone from a policy of stage show–plus–movie to just showing films—and not first-runs. Luft's plan was to get RKO (which owned the theater) to refurbish the historic house for what would be not just Judy's U.S. concert debut, but the return of "two-a-day" vaudeville to the Palace. And so it came to pass that Judy Garland, backed up by comedian Alan King, acrobats, and various other variety acts, did two shows a day at the Palace for nineteen weeks in 1951–52.

Of her opening night, her biographer Gerold Frank writes in *Judy* (Harper & Row, 1975) that it "was the biggest night Times Square had known since D-Day." Of her performance, in which she not only sang but re-created several classic production numbers from her films ("Get Happy" from *Summer Stock*, "A Couple of Swells" from *Easter Parade*), one reviewer called it "the most fantastic one-hour solo performance in theater history." For her fans, seeing her on the Palace stage represented her triumph over Hollywood, over the suicide attempts, the bad press, the drugs, and the bad times. But the euphoria didn't last long. Three weeks into the run, Judy collapsed onstage and had to be taken to a hospital. Diagnosed as suffering from "nervous exhaustion," she returned to the Palace five nights later and was welcomed back with practically as much enthusiasm and acclaim as on opening night. Only Judy could make a comeback within a comeback. It was the first of many, many more. The pattern, like the legend, was born at the Palace.

Judy was followed at the Palace by more Hollywood names: Betty Hutton, Danny Kaye, Jerry Lewis, then Judy herself returned in 1956—again to rave reviews. But a year later, the theater reverted to showing movies, and it wasn't until 1965 that it was refurbished and went legit once again. Its first production was Bob Fosse's *Sweet Charity,* starring Gwen Verdon. Its second production was—guess who?—Judy Garland, this time with her three children—Liza Minnelli, Lorna and Joey Luft—as part of the act. Besides Judy Garland, another Hollywood great who has had more than just a casual association with the Palace is Lauren Bacall. In 1970 she starred at the Palace in *Applause,* the musical version of *All About Eve,* and won a Tony Award for her performance. (In a clever bit of replacement casting, Anne Baxter, who had played the role of Eve Harrington in the film *All About Eve*, took over the role of Margo Channing in *Applause* when Bacall left to do the show in London.) In 1981, Bacall returned to the Palace as the star of *Woman of the Year,* the Broadway musical version of the classic Spencer Tracy–Katharine Hepburn film. Again, Bacall won a Tony for her performance in a Broadway musical based on a Hollywood dramatic film. And in another clever bit of replacement casting, Raquel Welch took over the role when Bacall went on vacation for a couple of weeks toward the end of the run. Raquel, to everyone's surprise, got wonderful reviews from the New York critics. Supposedly, the person least pleased with Raquel's notices was Miss Bacall who, when she returned to the Palace, is reported to have sulked in her dressing room.

In 1994, theater history was again made at the Palace when Walt Disney took Broadway by storm with a lavish live musical version of its recent animated hit *Beauty and the Beast.* The show ran at the Palace for five years before transferring to the nearby Lunt-Fontanne, but Disney quickly returned in 2000 with another innovative musical, *Aïda,* the Elton John–Tim Rice version of the Verdi opera.

25. I. MILLER BUILDING
Northeast corner of 47th Street and Broadway

"The Show Folks Shoe Shop Dedicated to Beauty in Footwear." So says the inscription on the 47th Street side of this little two-story building on Broadway, which was once a branch of the I. Miller Shoe Company that specialized in dance and theater footwear. Today, Times Square tourists eat pizza and drink beer at TGIF, where they used to try on shoes, but if movie lovers look up when they pass the old I. Miller building along West 47th Street, they will be treated to a wonderful gallery of statues immortalizing famous women in show business. Fashioned by A. Stirling Calder—father of mobile-maven Alexander Calder—the star statues include Mary Pickford, Ethel Barrymore, diva Rosa Ponselle, and *Ziegfeld Follies* headliner Marilyn Miller.

Star statues at I. Miller Building

While movie lovers may not realize that Miss Miller appeared in a few early sound films, they will remember the 1949 Warner Bros. film version of her life, *Look for the Silver Lining*, which starred June Haver. They may also remember Judy Garland's cameo performance as Miss Miller in MGM's 1946 film version of Jerome Kern's life, *Till the Clouds Roll By*, in which Judy sang "Who?" and "Look for the Silver Lining."

26. CORT THEATER
138 West 48th Street

Known as a "lucky house" because of the many long runs that played here early in its history, the Cort opened in 1912 with Laurette Taylor starring in *Peg o' My Heart*, which ran for two years. One of its medium runs was *The Jazz Singer*, which played 315 performances between 1925 and 1926, starred George Jessel, and was quickly turned into the world's first commercially successful motion picture with sound (starring Al Jolson—not George Jessel).

Other Cort productions of interest to movie lovers may be the 1949 revival of Swedish playwright August Strindberg's *The Father*, which featured the Broadway debut of a beautiful young actress from Philadelphia named Grace Kelly, and the three-night (not so lucky?) run of a play called *See the Jaguar* in 1952, which nonetheless put James Dean on a Broadway stage for the first time.

In 1955, a teenager from Brooklyn made her way across the East River to Manhattan and the Cort Theater to see *The Diary of Anne Frank*, which was a big hit at the time. It was Barbra Streisand's first time in a Broadway theater . . . but not her last. Between 1969 and 1973, the Cort had a stint as a TV studio, during which time *The Merv Griffin Show* was the theater's principal tenant.

In 1997, the Cort hosted the hottest show in town, a transplant of British playwright David Hare's *The Blue Room*, which featured movie star Nicole Kidman playing a number of different roles, one involving partial nudity. Miss Kidman went to great pains in interviews to point out that she was wearing a body stocking, but many who saw the show weren't quite so sure.

Broadway debut:
Grace Kelly
(with Mady Christians)
in *The Father,* 1949

27. ST. MALACHY'S CHURCH AND ACTORS CHAPEL
239 West 49th Street

In the heart of the theater district, St. Malachy's is a Roman Catholic church with a separate Actors Chapel where show folk can escape the crazy world of making rounds and/or actually working in theater and films in New York.

In August 1926, St. Malachy's was the scene of the world's most famous show-business funeral—that of Rudolph Valentino. It began with his untimely death from a bleeding ulcer and peritonitis at New York Polyclinic Hospital on Monday, August 23. It continued at Frank Campbell's Funeral Church, which at the time was on Broadway at 66th Street. At Campbell's, there were mobs of mourners, special police patrols, and all sorts of rumors. These ranged from speculation that Valentino had been murdered, to stories that a wax dummy and not Valentino's body was on display at Campbell's, in case someone in the unruly crowd tried to desecrate the corpse.

Amid all the rumors and pandemonium, one thing was certain: United Artists, the studio behind Valentino's most recent pictures, was going to make the most of the situation. Hollywood had learned from the premature deaths of other 1920s superstars like Barbara La Marr and Wallace Reid that the public forgot quickly. So this time, they would do things right. Valentino's would be the most carefully orchestrated—and well-publicized—star funeral in the history of the movie business.

Plans called for the body to lie in state at Campbell's for a full week, after which a funeral Mass would be said at St. Malachy's on Monday, August 30. This posed one small problem, however, because Valentino had been twice divorced and therefore, in the eyes of the Catholic Church, which doesn't recognize divorce, he was not entitled to a Catholic burial. But where there's a will, there's a way—both in Hollywood *and* in Rome—and it was later decided that since both of Valentino's marriages had been contracted in civil courts, and not in Catholic churches, both were invalid. Thus, the "bachelor" star was entitled to a full High Requiem send-off.

Rudolph Valentino

The St. Malachy's funeral was quite a spectacle. Shopkeepers and apartment dwellers on 49th Street charged outsiders to view the proceedings from their fire escapes and rooftops. Indeed, it seemed more like a premiere than a funeral as cheers from the crowds greeted arriving stars like Gloria Swanson, Douglas Fairbanks, George Jessel, Hope Hampton, and Marilyn Miller. The featured attraction, naturally, was Valentino, whose rose-bedecked coffin was followed by such close friends as Norma and Constance Talmadge, Mary Pickford, and Pola Negri, the Polish-born star who claimed to be Valentino's last lover and whose dramatic performance as mourner extraordinaire—complete with frequent faintings and designer widow's weeds—was the subject of much publicity.

After the church services, it was back to Frank Campbell's again, where the body remained for another two days (special permission had to be obtained from the commissioner of health for the body to stay aboveground for so long) in order for Valentino's brother, who was en route from Italy, to pay his last respects. With the arrival of the actor's brother, the show continued with a five-day train journey to Los Angeles, where there was yet another star-studded funeral at the Church of the Good Shepherd in Beverly Hills. Finally, a good two weeks after his death, Valentino was laid to rest in crypt number 1205 of the Cathedral Mausoleum at the Hollywood Memorial Park (now Hollywood Forever) Cemetery.

The two-week funeral festival was a great success, by the way. United Artists couldn't make enough prints of Valentino's two latest films, *The Eagle* and *The Son of the Sheik,* to satisfy the demands of exhibitors. In fact, much to the studio's delight, Valentino was raking in more money in death than he had in life. Which just goes to prove that with the right publicity campaign, a dead legend can be worth more than a live superstar.

It was also at St. Malachy's that, on June 3, 1929, Joan Crawford married Douglas Fairbanks Jr.

Visit www.stmalachyschurch.org.

28. BRILL BUILDING
1619 Broadway

Welcome to Tin Pan Alley. New York's historic headquarters for music publicists, arrangers, and booking agents, the Brill Building was once the nerve center of the nation's songwriting business. Today, aside from a few exceptions like Charing Cross Music and Paul Simon, who have offices here, the building is no longer the exclusive domain of the music industry in New York, just as New York is no longer the force it once was in the music business. Indeed the days when songwriters made the rounds of the Brill's offices and hung out in the Turf restaurant (now the Colony music store) on its ground floor are gone.

The Brill Building—with its gleaming brass entrance and lobby of more brass, plus mirrors and marble—is still a classy structure, and it has been featured in two classic made–in–New York motion pictures: *The House on 92nd Street* (1945) and *Sweet Smell of*

Tin Pan Alley central:
Brill Building

Success (1957). In the first, the Brill doubled as a talent agency; in the second, it was supposedly Burt Lancaster's apartment house. More recently, the site also inspired and was used in writer-director Allison Anders's 1996 film *Grace of My Heart,* which chronicled the life of a 1960s female songwriter (Illeana Douglas) in the mold of Brill Building alumna Carole King. The Brill Building also pops up in numerous Woody Allen films, including *Broadway Danny Rose* (1983), *Hollywood Ending* (2002), and *Anything Else* (2003). The building gets its name, by the way, not from anybody in show business, but from the Brill brothers, who were the haberdashers who originally built and occupied the place, then just two stories, in 1929. In 1933, major alterations brought more stories and more glamorous tenants.

29. ROXY THEATER SITE
Northeast corner of 50th Street and Seventh Avenue

It was the "Cathedral of the Motion Picture," the ultimate movie palace—the one and only Roxy Theater. When it opened on March 11, 1927, the publicity blurbs boasted: "We cannot find adjectives and superlatives strong enough to describe the thousand-and-one wonders and innovations of the Roxy, truly the most sumptuous and stupendous theater ever erected." And that it was, with 5,920 seats, six box offices, a five-story grand foyer and rotunda, ushers in black tie, dazzling Baroque decor, lounges, smoking rooms, hospital rooms, plus three organ consoles, twenty-one-bell cathedral chimes, a resident symphony orchestra of 110 musicians and four conductors, a chorus of one hundred voices, and a ballet company of fifty dancers.

The Roxy not only marked the apogee of the Age of the Movie Palace, it represented the high point in the career of S. L. Rothapfel, the famous theater entrepreneur whose nickname, Roxy, was immortalized by this great new entertainment establishment. The premiere attraction at the Roxy was *The Love of Sunya,* a made–in–New York film that had been produced by, and also starred, la Marquise de la Falaise de la Coudraye; to millions of movie lovers la Marquise was better known as good old Gloria Swanson. Swanson, in her autobiography, *Swanson*

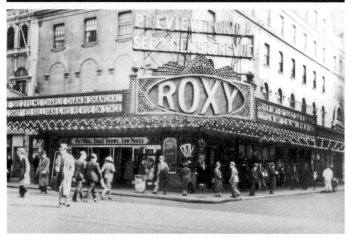

Roxy Theater, ca. 1935

on Swanson (Random House, 1980), had this to say of the glamorous 1927 premiere of the Roxy and of her film:

> When we pulled up under the marquee and got out of the car, a tremendous roar went up. In the blinding glare of a double row of klieg lights trained on the shiny new building, I turned and waved, and before I could turn back again and enter the theater, an unstoppable wave of people surged forward and almost knocked us over. In spite of the efforts of the police, we had to fight our way into the lobby in order not to be crushed against the closed doors and walls.
>
> Inside the monumental foyer, in front of an inclined bank of red and white carnations that spelled out his name, Roxy stood with his family, being photographed with celebrities. Henri [Swanson's husband, the marquis] and I joined them to kiss and shake hands with the people we knew in a steady blaze of flash powder. Roxy had pulled out all the stops. The parade of notables included four U.S. senators, three U.S. generals, three consul generals, two borough presidents, the governor of New Jersey, and the minister of Lithuania, as well as Adolph Ochs, Mrs. Otto Kahn, and Mr. and Mrs. Jimmy Walker. The crowd almost broke down the doors when Char-

lie Chaplin tried to sneak in unnoticed, and they went wild again when they recognized Harold Lloyd and his wife. We stood there for twenty minutes and greeted an endless stream of people with engraved invitations: the Shuberts, Irving Berlin, Lois Wilson, Sport Ward, Hope Hampton, Tommy Meighan, Joe Schenck, Walter Wanger, Will Hays—even Jesse Lasky. Then we all took our seats down front in the great auditorium, and the show began.

The show at the Roxy would go on for over three decades, and Swanson would be on hand for the theater's demolition in 1960, just as she had been for its gala opening in 1927. For the sad event, Gloria turned up in a black evening sheath and a feather boa to bid farewell not only to a theater, but to an era. Today, an electronics store as well as the glass-and-marble American Management Association Building occupy the famous corner where the Roxy once stood. There ought to be a plaque—but there isn't. Movie lovers can, however, get a glimpse of the Roxy in the film *The Naked City* (1948), which uses the theater's foyer for several sequences.

30. CADILLAC WINTER GARDEN THEATER
1634 Broadway

In 1911, the year it opened, the Winter Garden featured Al Jolson—the actor who would revolutionize the motion-picture industry with his sound success in *The Jazz Singer* some fifteen years later—in a musical called *Vera Violetta*. Also in the cast was a comedian who would go on to be a major force in the movies with her sexually explicit screen antics in the 1930s. Her name was Mae West.

Another major Hollywood name to appear on the Winter Garden stage early in his career was an Italian immigrant who made up half of a dance team called Glass and Di Valentina. At the time, the dancer had already changed his last name from Guglielmi to Di Valentina, but things wouldn't really click for him until he settled on Rudolph Valentino. An equally famous Hollywood name change also played the Winter Garden before heading to California. The show was a lavish revue called *The Passing Show of 1924* and one of the gals in the chorus was a sexy lady from San Antonio named Lucille Le Sueur. When MGM spotted her on Broadway and signed her to a contract, the studio conducted a nationwide contest to find a suitable name for their new starlet. The winning name: Joan Crawford.

Speaking of Hollywood, in 1928 Warner Bros. took over the Winter Garden and made it a showplace for the company's new Vitaphone talking pictures, which held forth at the theater through 1933—when it was featured in Warner's *Gold Diggers of 1933*. The place subsequently went legit again and from 1935 to 1940 employed Vincente Minnelli as its "revue master," during a period when the theater specialized in producing dazzling musical extravaganzas in memory of the late Florenz Ziegfeld. Besides directing these spectacles, Minnelli, who had previously been art director at Radio City Music Hall, also designed the sets and costumes. Some of the future film stars who appeared in Minnelli's Winter Garden productions were Eve Arden, Ethel Waters, Eleanor Powell, and Bob Hope.

Besides serving as a springboard for Hollywood talent, the Winter Garden has also been a place for film stars to stage their Broadway comebacks. Two cases in point: Rosalind Russell, who brought new life to her career when she took Broadway by storm in *Wonderful Town* in 1953, and Angela Lansbury, whose film roles had dwindled to playing the world's bitchiest women (as in *The Manchurian Candidate* and *The World of Henry Orient*), became a talent to reckon with after she scored a knockout on the Winter Garden stage in 1966 with *Mame*.

And of course, there is Barbra Streisand, who starred at the Winter Garden as Fanny Brice—the legendary comedian who had frequently played that theater in her heyday—in *Funny Girl*. Streisand went direct from the Winter Garden to Hollywood to star in, and win an Oscar for, the film version of *Funny Girl*. Since then, she has never returned to Broadway. But even bigger than Barbra was *Cats,* which opened at the Winter Garden in 1982 and closed eighteen years later, making it the longest running play in Broadway history, logging 7,485 performances. After a year of cleaning up after all those kitty-cats, the theater reopened with a new musical from ABBA called *Mamma Mia* and a new name—the Cadillac Winter Garden—reflecting its posh new corporate sponsor.

31. MARK HELLINGER THEATER/TIMES SQUARE CHURCH
237 West 51st Street

Opened in 1930 as a Warner Bros. movie palace, this theater-turned-church was originally called the Hollywood. The theater's architect/designer was the noted Thomas W. Lamb and his spectacular interior of sweeping staircases, ornate columns, and exotic balconies is still one of the most flamboyant of any legit house on Broadway. For the first two decades of its life, the Hollywood kept changing its name as well as its format, switching back and forth from films to stage shows to films. During one of its legit periods, the 1939 *George White's Scandals* had the late Ann Miller tapping on Broadway for the first time. The trooper would be back on the same stage of what was now the Mark Hellinger forty years later in one of the theater's biggest hits, *Sugar Babies* (1979), which costarred Mickey Rooney and ran for 1,208 performances—not one of which did Ann miss.

As successful as the *Sugar Babies* run was, it was not the Mark Hellinger's longest. That honor is still held by *My Fair Lady,* which starred Rex Harrison and Julie Andrews in the original cast and ran for 2,717 performances between 1956 and 1962. After *My Fair Lady,* the Hellinger saw two Hollywood legends grace its stage in the late 1960s: Marlene Dietrich, who in 1968 based her one-woman show, which had been a smash hit the year before at the Lunt-Fontanne on West 46th Street, at the Hellinger, and Katharine Hepburn, who made her Broadway musical-comedy debut as the revolutionary French fashion designer Coco Chanel, in Alan Jay Lerner and André Previn's 1969 *Coco.*

During a dark period in 1985, the Mark Hellinger was taken over by director Richard Attenborough and turned into a movie studio. The project was the long-awaited film version of the supersmash Broadway hit *A Chorus Line,* which was shot entirely at the Mark Hellinger. A critical disaster, the film quickly faded from view, as did the Mark Hellinger, which has been the Times Square Church since 1989.

Visit www.timessquarechurch.org.

32. BROADWAY THEATER
1681 Broadway

Opened in 1924 with Douglas Fairbanks starring in *The Thief of Baghdad,* this 1,765-seat theater spent the first years of its life as a motion picture/vaudeville palace known as the Colony. For movie lovers, a premiere of monumental importance took place at the Colony on November 18, 1928. The film ran barely eight minutes, but its impact is still being felt around the world and its star is probably the most famous of any screen personality in history. The title of the little movie was *Steamboat Willie,* and it unleashed a mouse named Mickey upon the world. Also in the cast were Minnie Mouse and a villain named Pete. While it was Mickey Mouse who brought fame and fortune to Walt Disney, this was not Disney's first cartoon character or cartoon series. In 1924, in partnership with his brother Roy, Disney came out with the *Alice in Cartoonland* shorts, which were followed by *Oswald the Rabbit.* But neither Alice nor Oswald was a match for the mouse that took off and soared from the Colony movie screen back in 1928.

In 1930, the Colony changed its name to the Broadway, when it became a legit house for a few years. Then, in the mid-1930s, it went back to running films, went legit again in 1940, and—except for a brief stint showing Cinerama wide-wide-wide-screen flicks in the 1950s—has remained so ever since. Because of its vast stage and large seating capacity, the Broadway is often used for musicals. Among its top productions over the years have been *Gypsy* (1959), which starred Ethel Merman; Andrew Lloyd Webber and Tim Rice's *Evita* (1979), the musical—which became a Madonna movie in 1996—based on the legendary Argentine dictator-superstar, Eva Perón; *Les Misérables* (1987), followed by *Miss Saigon* in 1991, which ran for a record-breaking ten years. Most recently, after the success of his 2001 film *Moulin Rouge,* with Nicole Kidman and Ewan McGregor, Australian director Baz Luhrmann turned to full-out opera with his redo of *La Bohème,* which had a run—in French with supertitles—at the Broadway in 2003.

33. STAGE DELICATESSEN
834 Seventh Avenue

A popular Broadway nosh-spot since 1937, the Stage—with its blintzes, matzo ball soup, and massive sandwiches—is a throwback to a different culinary world in these days of low-fat, low-carb fad dining. For filmmakers—like Woody Allen, who used it in his 2003 *Anything Else*—a Stage dining sequence shows New York at its no-nonsense best. Not a place for a glamorous evening, it's more of a drop-in spot, such as when jaded soap opera star Kevin Kline invites the ingenue of the moment to have a bite at the Stage after a hard day of taping in *Soapdish* (1991). It's also where Sandra Bullock and her Brit boss Hugh Grant go for a taste of New York in *Two Weeks Notice* (2002). The nearby Carnegie Deli just up the street at 854 Seventh Avenue offers a similar menu and filmmakers a similar ambience. Its most memorable screen appearance was as a hangout for old comics in Woody Allen's 1984 *Broadway Danny Rose*.

Visit www.stagedeli.com.

34. ED SULLIVAN THEATER
1697 Broadway

The Ed Sullivan opened its arched Gothic doors in 1927 as Hammerstein's Theater and featured a film–plus–variety show format. Four years later, the house went legit and hosted Broadway productions. Then in 1934, showman Billy Rose took over the place for his lavish musical stage shows. Two years after that, CBS stepped in and Hammerstein's became the CBS Radio Playhouse. The theater's grandest era began in the early 1950s, when CBS brought in bright lights, built camera runways, and used what it now called Studio 50 for some of its most famous television variety shows, including the *Jackie Gleason Show,* the *Garry Moore Show* (which gave Carol Burnett her prime-time boost), and, of course, the show to which the theater now owes its name, the *Ed Sullivan Show* (originally called *Ed Sullivan's Toast of the Town*). Still a vital part of NYC's TV scene, the theater was used to tape the *Kate & Allie* sitcom before a live au-

David Letterman's Broadway home: Ed Sullivan Theater

dience in the 1970s—but its current main claim to fame is the fact that it's been home to *The Late Show with David Letterman* since 1993. In 2002, ABC made a bid to lure Letterman away from his CBS roost, offering him megabucks in a deal that would have had him replace veteran ABC newsman Ted Koppel's *Night Line*. The negotiations were top secret, but whatever ABC offered, CBS topped them. Indeed, it was reported at the time that Letterman's new deal with the network was worth some $71 million a year for him and his production company.

The Ed Sullivan Theater is a historic site not only because of all the stars who have appeared on its stage, but also because of the legendary acting school—Lee and Paula Strasberg's Actors Studio—that once occupied the fourteenth floor of the building. It was here that unknowns like Shelley Winters, Marlon Brando, James Dean, Eli Wallach, Rod Steiger, and Kim Stanley learned their craft. It was also here that one very well-known film star— Marilyn Monroe—came to perfect hers. Although she started off studying privately with Lee Strasberg, she eventually joined the group class. Remembering one of Marilyn's early scenes, the late Kim Stanley said, "We were taught never to clap at the Actors Studio—it was like a church—and it was the first time I'd ever heard applause there." Of Miss Monroe's talent, Lee Strasberg once observed: "I have worked with hundreds and hundreds of actors and actresses, and there are only two that stand out way above the rest. Number one is Marlon Brando, and the second is Marilyn Monroe." The Actors Studio was at 1697 Broadway between 1948 and 1955; today it is located at 432 West 44th Street.

35. STUDIO 54
254 West 54th Street

Formerly a CBS TV studio, Studio 54 came on the NYC nightlife scene on April 16, 1977. The brainchild of Long Island restaurateurs Steve Rubell and Ian Schrager, the club was the ultimate disco in an era when disco fever ran rampant. While Schrager handled the back-of-house business, Rubell was always out front carefully handpicking who got inside the ultraexclusive enclave. The result was a hip mix of celebrities like Liza Minnelli, Halston, Bianca Jagger, and Andy Warhol plus a corps of buffed and beautiful gay party boys. By the end of the decade, however, the club, still as popular as ever, ran into big trouble when fifty federal agents raided the place, tipped off by reports of drugs and unreported cash. Rubell and Schrager were arrested and eventually did jail time for tax evasion. By the time they got out, the party that was the hedonistic 1970s was over, and a new reality in the form of a killer disease called AIDS made the 1980s a much less festive, much more frightening decade. Indeed, Rubell himself died of AIDS in 1989, shortly after he and Schrager had founded a string of chic boutique hotels like the Royalton and Paramount.

On the film front, *54* (1998) tells some of the famous nightclub's story, with Mike Myers as Steve Rubell. Shot mainly in Toronto, the film used the real Studio 54 exterior. The club is also featured in Spike Lee's 1970s period piece *Summer of Sam* (1999), where John Leguizamo and his girlfriend Mira Sorvino are turned away at the velvet ropes of the trendy spot. Studio 54 was also used in *I Shot Andy Warhol* (1996). Now home to New York City's Roundabout Theatre company, Studio 54 has hosted theatrical productions such as the revival of John Kander and Fred Ebb's *Cabaret* and more recently Stephen Sondheim's *Assassins*.

36. SONY MUSIC STUDIOS
460 West 54th Street

Now Sony Music's NYC base, this historic studio building was known as the Fox Stage for decades, since it was originally part of Twentieth Century–Fox's New York operations. From the 1950s to the 1970s, Fox dropped out of the picture, but the studio continued in the picture business in a big way, becoming one of the busiest rental stages in New York. Among the many features shot at 460 West 54th Street were *On the Waterfront* (1954), *Middle of the Night* (1959), *Fail Safe* (1964), *The Pawnbroker* (1964), *The Group* (1966), *The Owl and the Pussycat* (1970), *Where's Poppa?* (1970), *Shaft* (1971), and *The Exorcist* (1974). During the shooting of the last film, which dealt with a young girl's possession by the devil, all sorts of strange goings-on

Twentieth Century–Fox soundstage, Tenth Avenue and 54th Street

were reported on the old Fox Stage—from film that didn't develop properly to a fire and other hard-to-account-for accidents. Since then, some industry insiders now refer to the place as the *Exorcist* studio.

In addition to feature films, 460 West 54th Street also counts *Inner Sanctum, The Reporter,* and *I Spy* among the TV series that have been filmed here. Today, in addition to recording studios, the Sony facility uses the building's historic soundstages to shoot music videos. Movie lovers who visit the site should check out the murals on the 53rd Street side of the facility, which depict recording and video sessions.

37. WILLIAM FOX STUDIOS SITE
444 West 56th Street

Now a New York City high school specializing in environmental studies, this big brick building was where movie mogul William Fox kept watch over his impressive empire during most of the 1920s. Fox, who was brought to America as an infant by his Hungarian immigrant parents, grew up in poverty on New York City's Lower East Side. Dropping out of school at the age of eleven, he slaved in the garment industry for much of his youth. In 1903, at the age of twenty-four, he spent his life savings of $1,660 to buy a 146-seat movie theater in Brooklyn. When this venture earned him some $50,000 over the next five years, Fox reinvested the money into more movie houses and eventually got into the production side of the industry as well. At the height of his power in the late 1920s, Fox had assets valued at $300 million, which included studios in Los Angeles and New York, plus over fifteen hundred movie theaters across the country.

But 1929 was a bad year for William Fox. On March 3 of that year, he was poised to become the most powerful man in the movie business when he finalized a deal to purchase the controlling interest in his principal competitor, Loew's Inc. This maneuver would have given Fox all of Loew's theaters as well as their production arm, MGM Studios. But Fox had gone too far, and the U.S. government stepped in and prevented the transaction from going through. Then, as Fox was fighting the government decision, he was seriously injured in an automobile accident that laid him up for three months. To make a bad situation even worse, along came the stock market crash, which had a devastating effect on the William Fox Company. One of the ways the company's other directors dealt with its serious financial troubles was to ease William Fox out of the business. In fact, by 1934, when the Fox organization had joined with Twentieth Century Pictures to form Twentieth Century–Fox, William Fox was no longer in the corporate picture.

Even without Fox, his New York offices stayed under Twentieth Century–Fox control until the 1970s, when John Jay College of Criminal Justice took over the property. When they exited the building in the 1990s, the New York City Department of Education moved in and converted it into a high school.

38. HEARST MAGAZINE BUILDING
959 Eighth Avenue

His empire was vast and encompassed newspapers, motion-picture studios, hotels, real estate, and magazines. His taste was extravagant, especially when it came to architecture and design. His California homes—a fantastic castle on 50,000 acres in the north, and a 118-room beach "cottage" in the south—back in the 1920s and 1930s were playgrounds for the biggest names in Hollywood, all of whom flocked to the parties and weekends frequently staged at these fabulous places by his movie-star mistress, Marion Davies. At Eighth Avenue, between 56th and 57th streets in Manhattan, stands a smaller, but no less extravagant monument to William Randolph Hearst's sense of style: the Hearst Magazine Building, a massive fortress extravagantly decorated with columns, statues, and balustrades that remind one of the Jugendstil buildings of turn-of-the-century Vienna.

Created to house the magazine division of Hearst's empire, this spectacular 1928 structure was the work of Joseph Urban, a man less well known as an architect than as a set and costume designer. Urban went from decorating Florenz Ziegfeld's Follies to becoming artistic director of the Metropolitan Opera as well as a famous art director for early movies. One of Urban's landmark films was the 1921 production of *Enchantment,* which is believed to have been the first American film to use Modernist sets. Not surprisingly, the producer of *Enchantment* was William

Art director as architect: Joseph Urban's Hearst Magazine Building, 1987

Randolph Hearst, and the star of the film was Marion Davies. On designing for films, Urban had this to say to *Photoplay* in 1920: "The motion picture offers incomparably the greatest field to any creative artist of brush or blueprint today. It is the art of the twentieth century and perhaps the greatest art of modern times. It is all so young, so fresh, so untried. It is like an unknown ocean stretching out before a modern Columbus." During the 1920s, Urban would design some twenty-five films for Hearst. While many of these are lost, Urban's work can still be appreciated at 959 Eighth Avenue. The six-story building, by the way, was originally intended to have another seven stories rise above it. In 2003, work was finally started on an addition—a futuristic glass tower designed by the eminent British architect Sir Norman Foster. Whether Urban would have approved is anybody's guess.

Visit www.hearstcorp.com/tower.

39. CBS BROADCAST CENTER
524 West 57th Street

Spanning most of the south side of 57th Street between Tenth and Eleventh Avenues, this giant broadcasting complex has housed CBS's main radio and television studios since 1953. The *CBS Evening News, 60 Minutes, 48 Hours,* and *Living It Up!* are all done here. Until recently *Politically Incorrect* was head-quartered here—as was, until late 1999, the indomitable soap opera *As the World Turns* (which is now shot at the old Vita-graph studio in Brooklyn).

Once upon a time in the late-1960s, some eight soap operas were broadcast from CBS's West 57th Street facility, and the building reigned as the city's premier "soap factory." Produc-tions at the time included *Search for Tomorrow, The Secret Storm, The Edge of Night, The Guiding Light,* and *Dark Shad-ows*. During those heady days when West 57th Street was crank-ing out soaps the way Hollywood studios once cranked out pictures, Anita Loos and Helen Hayes visited the CBS Broadcast Center for their book *Twice Over Lightly* (Harcourt Brace Jo-vanovich, 1972), which chronicled the two ladies' madcap sight-seeing adventures through New York. At CBS, they discovered that the main studio building had formerly been a milk process-ing plant and that it had inherited quite a few flies from its pre-vious life. The flies, it seems, were especially troublesome on early soap sets, and many a scene had been stolen by an errant insect landing on an actor's nose. According to Loos and Hayes, the situation had gotten so bad that production assistants armed with fly swatters from Hammacher Schlemmer were needed to stand guard during shootings.

Today, most of the flies have abandoned West 57th Street—as have the soap operas.

The Upper East Side:
Beverly Hills East

What becomes a legend most? Often an Upper East Side address. Throughout the last century, this chic, ultraexclusive part of Manhattan—with its solid apartment buildings, discreet hotels, and lavish townhouses—has been home to some of the biggest names in the movies. Times have changed, however, since today's hot new celebs prefer to hang their Prada in the much cooler neighborhoods of Chelsea, the West Village, SoHo, and TriBeCa. But for anyone interested in Old Hollywood, a visit to the Upper East Side provides a chance to check out the Manhattan digs that legends like Garbo, Gish, Hepburn, Loy, Swanson, Dietrich, Crawford, and Monroe ultimately preferred to Southern California's sunshine. Among the numerous other treats awaiting movie lovers on the Upper East Side are Woody Allen's favorite restaurant, the most sought-after couturier of the stars, the secret location of *The House on 92nd Street,* and the world's most celebrated funeral parlor.

1. TWENTIETH CENTURY GARAGE
320 East 48th Street

This is no ordinary parking garage. For movie lovers, this brick fortress with the distinctive neon sign was once the site of the Norma Talmadge Film Company. Named for one of the bright-

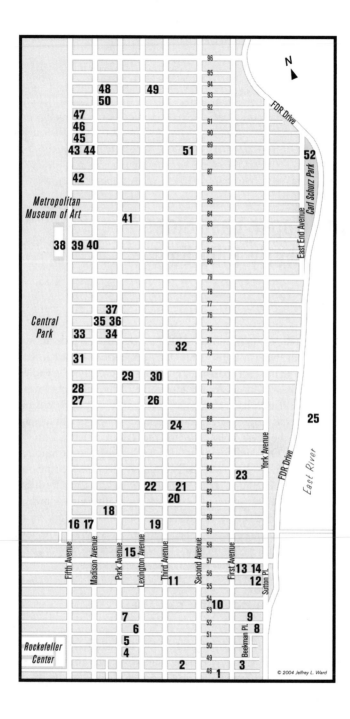

N

FDR Drive

Carl Schurz Park

East End Avenue

48
50
49
47
46
45
43 44
51
52
42

Metropolitan
Museum of Art

41

38 39 40

Central
Park

37
35 36
33 34
32
31
29 30
28
27 26
24
25
York Avenue
FDR Drive
East River
22 21
20
23
18
16 17
19

Fifth Avenue
Madison Avenue
Park Avenue
Lexington Avenue
Third Avenue
Second Avenue
First Avenue
Sutton Pl.

15
13 14
12
11
10
7
6
9
5
8
4
Beekman Pl.
Rockefeller
Center
2
3
1

© 2004 Jeffrey L. Ward

est stars in silent pictures, the studio was controlled by producer Joe Schenck, who was Miss Talmadge's husband as well as her mentor. In addition, Schenck also guided the careers of Norma's famous sister, Constance, and had comics Fatty Arbuckle and Buster Keaton under contract too. At any one time, all four of these legendary performers might be shooting films on the four floors of the Norma Talmadge Studios, which writer Anita Loos, who worked on scenarios for Schenck, described as "as lively as a Keystone farce."

By the 1930s, the Norma Talmadge Studio had become the De Forrest Photo Films Company, and both of the Talmadge sisters had retired from films. Norma, who never lost her Brooklyn accent, bombed in the couple of sound pictures that she made. Divorced from Schenck in 1927, she stayed briefly on the edge of the limelight by marrying comedian George Jessel in 1931. Constance, on the other hand, was wise enough to retire from the screen without uttering a word.

The career of Joe Schenck was another story. In 1933 he formed the Twentieth Century Picture Corporation with Darryl Zanuck. Two years later, Twentieth Century merged with William Fox to become Twentieth Century–Fox, where Schenck remained a major mogul for the next two decades and where he was especially helpful in getting the career of a beautiful young contract player named Marilyn Monroe off the ground. Schenck died in Hollywood in 1961.

Today there is no Joe Schenck building to remember this influential producer's New York beginnings. There is, however, the Twentieth Century Garage, which bears the same name as one of his major ventures.

2. TURTLE BAY GARDENS
48th and 49th Streets between Second and Third Avenues

A very special place to live, Turtle Bay Gardens is made up of the blocks of townhouses on 48th and 49th streets between Second and Third avenues. What makes them special is the fact that each house not only has its own private garden in back, but all share a large communal garden as well. For movie lovers, the most

Katharine Hepburn's
Turtle Bay townhouse

famous resident of this charmed Manhattan neighborhood was the late Katharine Hepburn, who lived in the same four-story brownstone with the black wrought-iron gates and white-curtained windows at 244 East 49th Street for over half a century.

Over the years, Miss Hepburn had a number of famous neighbors. Composer Stephen Sondheim was next door at number 246 and writer Garson Kanin and his writer/actress wife Ruth Gordon once lived on the same block. They were best of friends until Mr. Kanin wrote *Tracy and Hepburn* in 1971, a literary endeavor that the very private Kate is said not to have appreciated. The headstrong Miss Hepburn was not a woman to be crossed. A case in point concerns a burglar who, in the late 1930s, broke into her Turtle Bay house while she was napping and was about to make off with a $5,000 necklace that her man-friend at the time, Howard Hughes, had given her. Waking up in the knick of time, Hepburn bellowed at the thief: "What are you doing here?" She then chased him into the street, where he hopped into a getaway car—without the necklace.

Hepburn died in 2003 at her other longtime residence, her family summer home in Old Saybrook, Connecticut.

Visit www.turtlebay-nyc.org.

3. UNITED NATIONS PLAZA APARTMENTS
860 and 870 United Nations Plaza

Around the corner from the low-rise townhouses and apartments of Beekman Place, the twin glass skyscrapers of the United Nations Plaza Apartments at 49th Street and First Avenue, just north of the United Nations, offer not only luxurious housing but extraordinary floor-to-ceiling views of the city. Built in 1966, the U.N. Plaza instantly attracted a number of celebrities to its posh pads. Among its star tenants over the last two decades have been Johnny Carson (during *The Tonight Show*'s Manhattan days), the late Truman Capote ("living on *Cold Blood* money," is the way Helen Hayes once put it), Cliff Robertson and Dina Merrill (before they split), Mickey Rooney (who sublet here during his triumphant Broadway run in *Sugar Babies*), the late producer David Susskind, tennis star Vitas Gerulaitis, photographer/film director Gordon Parks (*Shaft*), Academy Award–winning director Michael Cimino (*The Deer Hunter*), TV host Hugh Downs, and the late Sen. Robert Kennedy.

4. ST. BARTHOLOMEW'S CHURCH
109 East 50th Street at Park Avenue

This exotic neo-Byzantine Episcopal house of worship—with a columned Romanesque entrance salvaged from the church's former 24th Street location—strikes a handsome pose on Park Avenue. Indeed, even though it's used only as background, it's still easy to spot in such recent films as *Maid in Manhattan* (2003), *Catch Me If You Can* (2002), and *Serendipity* (2001). It plays much meatier roles in two earlier films, however. Ironically, each

St. Bartholomew's
Church

involves a wedding that doesn't come off. In *Arthur* (1981), Dudley Moore jilts Jill Eikenberry at the St. Bart's altar, whereas fifteen years later Steve Guttenberg does the same thing to bride-from-hell Jane Sibbett (featured on *Friends* as Ross's ex-wife) in favor of Kirstie Alley in *It Takes Two* (1995). Movie lovers may wish to make a special visit to pay their respects to silent-screen star and former St. Bart's member Lillian Gish, whose ashes are buried here in a basement chapel alongside those of her actress sister, Dorothy, and stage mother, Mary. Lillian Gish, who died in 1993, also had an impressive stage and post-silent-film career, making her final screen appearance at the age of ninety-one (or ninety-four, if we are to believe the dates—1893–1993—incised on her crypt), opposite Bette Davis and Ann Sothern, in *The Whales of August* (1987). Today, an anonymous admirer sends flowers to the Gish crypt every year on her birthday, October 14.

Visit www.stbarts.org.

5. WALDORF-ASTORIA HOTEL
301 Park Avenue

One of the world's grandest Art Deco structures, Park Avenue's monumental Waldorf-Astoria went up in 1931 as a replacement for the original Waldorf-Astoria, which had been at 34th Street and Fifth Avenue and was demolished to make way for the Empire State Building. With 2,200 rooms when it opened (the number has since been reduced to 1,800), the new Waldorf was the largest hotel in the world, and over the years it would host practically every major VIP on earth—from heads of state to heads of studios. The hotel's presidential suite is world-famous and, unlike the presidential suites of many hotels, has actually put up every U.S. president since Franklin D. Roosevelt.

Of all the Waldorf's accommodations, by far the most fashionable for non–chief executives are the 113 apartments that comprise the legendary Waldorf Towers. Literally a hotel within a hotel, the Towers has its own private entrance on East 50th Street, its own concierges, its own discreet style. Among the Towers' most celebrated long-term tenants have been the Duke and Duchess of Windsor, Richard Nixon, Henry Kissinger, Cole

Working girl: Jennifer Lopez at the Waldorf in *Maid in Manhattan*, 2003

Porter, Gregory Peck, Frank Sinatra, and Marilyn Monroe, who had a four-room apartment here in 1955 after she fled Hollywood stardom for the life of an acting student in New York.

While the Waldorf, with its twin Deco towers and its sleek Moderne lines, is extremely impressive from the outside, the interior of the hotel is the real showstopper. The lavish lobby is a dream of mahogany-paneled walls, marble floors and columns, monumental urns, streamlined sconces and chandeliers. Stepping inside this dramatic space is like walking into a glamorous 1930s Hollywood movie. Hard-core movie lovers may, in fact, remember a 1940s film from MGM that took advantage of the Waldorf's Deco dazzle. A postwar take on the studio's classic early talkie, *Grand Hotel,* MGM's *Weekend at the Waldorf* (1945) had an incredible lineup of stars that included Ginger Rogers, Lana Turner, Walter Pidgeon, Van Johnson, Keenan Wynn, Robert Benchley, and even Xavier Cugat. Although the film received mixed reviews, most critics cited the fine performance turned in by the Waldorf. Indeed, if the film does little else, it provides a fascinating behind-the-scenes glimpse at the workings of a great hotel, with second-unit sequences filmed in such rarely visited areas as the garage, the massive telephone switchboard, the in-hotel police station, the secretarial pool, and the kennels. *Weekend at the Waldorf* is also a triumph of MGM art direction, because it is practically impossible to tell which scenes have been shot by the second-unit crew on location and which were done at the MGM studios in Culver City, where much of the Waldorf's splendor was painstakingly re-created.

In more recent years, the grand ballrooms and luxurious suites of the Waldorf have been featured in such films as *The Out-of-Towners*—the Waldorf is where Sandy Dennis and Jack Lemmon *should* have stayed in the wacky 1970 Neil Simon story about all the things that can go wrong on a visit to the Big Apple; *Rich and Famous* (1981), the George Cukor film in which best-selling novelist Candice Bergen rents a whole floor; *Scent of a Woman* (1992), where blind veteran Al Pacino chooses the best hotel in town for what he expects to be his final fling in the Big Apple; *The Royal Tenenbaums* (2002), as the Lindbergh Palace Hotel, which estranged Tenenbaum family scion Royal (Gene Hackman) calls home, until he's thrown out; *Serendipity* (2001), where John Cusack and Kate Beckinsale play a kind of Russian roulette with their budding romance at the elevator banks, leaving it to Cupid to determine if they end up on the same floor; and *Maid in Manhattan* (2003), as the fictional Beresford Hotel, in a modern-day Cinderella story of Latino maid Jennifer Lopez looking after the lavish suite of celebrity politician Ralph Fiennes. While many exteriors and interiors were done at the hotel, the suite was reproduced at Astoria Studios in Queens.

The hotel can also be seen in *The Great Gatsby* (1974), *My Favorite Year* (1982), *Six Weeks* (1982), *Broadway Danny Rose* (1983), *Hannah and Her Sisters* (1986), *Coming to America* (1988), *Crimes and Misdemeanors* (1989), *The Godfather III* (1990), and *Analyze This* (1999).

Visit www.waldorf.com.

6. TRANS LUX THEATER SITE
Lexington Avenue at 52nd Street

The Trans Lux was a neighborhood movie house that stood at 586 Lexington Avenue from 1940 until the late 1970s. One hot September evening in 1954, Hollywood director Billy Wilder brought a film crew to the Trans Lux to shoot an exterior for *The Seven Year Itch*. More important, Wilder also unleashed the film's superstar, Marilyn Monroe, on the streets of Manhattan. Alerted to the event by studio publicity people, the press was on hand en masse to document the filming, and they were joined by a couple of thousand spectators. In the scene, Marilyn and her downstairs neighbor, Tom Ewell, are coming out of the Trans Lux, having just seen *The Creature from the Black Lagoon*. Marilyn liked the film, but "just felt so sorry for the Creature at the end." Then, along comes the Lexington Avenue IRT and up goes Marilyn's billowy white skirt. "Oh, do you feel the breeze from the subway?" she coos to her costar. "Isn't it delicious?"

Meanwhile, the crowd cheered and shouted, "Higher, higher!" as the country's number-one sex goddess showed her panties—to all of Lexington Avenue. One visitor definitely not amused by the proceedings, however, was Joe DiMaggio, Marilyn's husband of barely nine months. Having already found life with a superstar

Street theater: Marilyn filming *The Seven Year Itch* on Lexington Avenue, 1954

to be no picnic, DiMaggio viewed Marilyn's Lexington Avenue antics as the final straw. Back in Hollywood, less than a month after the incident in New York, the DiMaggios filed for divorce. Ironically, much of the scene that wrecked the marriage had to be reshot on the Twentieth Century–Fox lot.

Today, movie lovers will find a gigantic office building on the northwest corner of Lexington Avenue and 52nd Street, where the Trans Lux once stood, but the Marilyn Monroe memorial subway grating remains.

7. SEAGRAM BUILDING
373 Park Avenue

An amazing collaboration between two of the world's greatest architects at the time—Ludwig Mies van der Rohe and Philip Johnson—this bronze and bronze-colored-glass landmark broke all the architectural and real estate rules by being set far back from Park Avenue to allow for a spacious pedestrian plaza and two large fountains. Inside, the building featured a glittering window-walled Four Seasons restaurant, with tables set around a central fountain. The restaurant—as well as its adjacent Four Seasons Grill—is still one of New York's top power lunch and romantic dinner venues. When it opened in 1959, the glamorous new building was instantly called on by director Jean Negulesco to use as Fabian Publishers in his movie about women working in the glamorous world of publishing—*The Best of Everything*. In the film Hope Lange goes to work at the Seagram Building for bitchy boss Joan Crawford, in one of her many comeback roles. The impressive thirty-eight-story structure would also come back to the screen frequently, usually in the role of a high-powered office building: Diane Keaton worked here in *Baby Boom* (1987), for example, as did Michael J. Fox in *Life with Mickey* (1993);

Seagram Building

Bill Murray in *Scrooged* (1988), where it was the IBC Network; and Nicolas Cage in *The Family Man* (2000). In Woody Allen's 1998 *Celebrity*, the Seagram plaza was the site of a fabulous film shoot featuring Melanie Griffith as the star and Winona Ryder as an extra. The building was also used in the Douglas family ego fest *It Runs in the Family* (2003), originally titled *Smack in the Kisser*.

8. THE CAMPANILE
450 East 52nd Street

She was the world's most public private person. Even though she had not made a film since 1941, Greta Garbo still fascinated the press, the masses, even the precious few who were permitted to be her friends right up until her death in 1990 at the age of eighty-four. Dressed in floppy hat, long trench coat, and trademark dark-dark glasses, she prowled about Manhattan, darting in and out of doorways, peeking at shop windows, occasionally

Queen of 52nd Street:
glorious Garbo

attending a film at the Plaza Theater on East 58th Street. For most of that time she lived in a seven-room apartment in the Campanile, a small 1920s brick building with Gothic arches and leaded-glass windows on the cul-de-sac where 52nd Street meets the East River. While Garbo's neighbors over the years included such notables as Alexander Woollcott (Dorothy Parker dubbed the building "Wit's End"), Rex Harrison, Henry and Clare Boothe Luce, by far her most interesting fellow tenants were the Russian couturier Valentina and her millionaire husband George Schlee.

In an arrangement straight out of neighbor Noël Coward's play *Design for Living,* Garbo had an intense personal relationship with Mr. Schlee from the mid-1940s until his death in 1964. He was not only her financial adviser, he was her escort, her confidant, and often her traveling companion. All the while, Schlee remained married to Valentina, who not only made Garbo's clothes but sometimes accompanied Schlee and the former movie actress on social outings. The whole arrangement was eminently civilized but fell apart rather abruptly when Schlee was stricken with a fatal heart attack while staying at the Crillon Hotel in Paris, where he and Garbo had adjoining suites. When Garbo discovered that Schlee was dead, she reportedly ran from the hotel and left Valentina to deal with the messy details involved with death in a foreign country. Garbo's irresponsible behavior is said to have so angered Valentina that she made it clear that she didn't want the actress to attend her husband's funeral. The two remained neighbors at 450 East 52nd Street for years thereafter but reportedly never again exchanged a word.

When Garbo died, although she hadn't worked for almost half a century, she left an estate of some $200 million, thanks in large part to her clever investments, especially in property (she is said to have owned much of Rodeo Drive in Beverly Hills at one time). Visitors to her native Sweden can see a room of her East 52nd Street flat on display next to the men's room in the basement of the PUB department store, where the original superstar once worked as a hat model and salesgirl. They can also visit beautiful Skogskyrkogården Cemetery in southern Stockholm, where Garbo's ashes were interred in 1999 near the graves of her parents.

9. RIVER HOUSE
435 East 52nd Street

Protected by an ornate iron gate that opens onto a formal drive-way, River House is one of the fashionable East Side's most prestigious addresses. Besides great privacy and security, the building also provides its residents with such luxuries as squash and tennis courts, a swimming pool, a ballroom, and, in the days before the FDR Drive skirted the East River, River House even had its own private boat dock. Like many Manhattan apartment buildings, River House is a cooperative, which means that its tenants own shares in the building and have a say in its affairs via an elected board of directors. Since the board at River House has traditionally been a conservative lot, the building is sometimes better known for the people who have been refused apartments than for those who actually reside here.

Among the former group, celebrity fashion designer (and former actress) Gloria Vanderbilt had a rough go of it at River House in 1980, when the board denied her an apartment, reportedly because her finances weren't up to River House standards. The multimillionaire then sued River House, alleging that the real reason she had been refused the apartment was because she enjoyed a close friendship with black cabaret singer Bobby Short. River House denied that racism had entered into its decision, but did acknowledge that it thought Miss Vanderbilt's high profile in Manhattan society would bring "unwelcome publicity" to the building. Little Gloria eventually dropped the suit, and was happy at last when she found friendlier digs up on Gracie Square.

Among the celebrities that *did* meet River House standards were former Secretary of State Henry Kissinger and his wife Nancy; actress/author/diplomat Clare Boothe Luce, whose play *The Women* was turned into MGM's all-star movie of the same name in 1939; director Joshua Logan of *Mr. Roberts, Picnic, Bus Stop, Sayonara,* and *South Pacific* fame; and, reportedly, Charlie Chaplin.

10. NEIGHBORHOOD PLAYHOUSE SCHOOL OF THEATER
340 East 54th Street

In 1915 the Neighborhood Playhouse was established as an amateur theater group on Manhattan's Lower East Side. It was one of many projects in the Henry Street Settlement's fight to improve the lot of slum dwellers. Although the original Neighborhood Playhouse closed in 1928, the acting school that grew out of it has flourished ever since. Located in a handsome double townhouse on the Upper East Side since 1948, the Neighborhood Playhouse School of Theater counts among its famous former students Gregory Peck, Tyrone Power, Diane Keaton, Robert Duvall, Lorne Greene, Elizabeth Ashley, Eli Wallach, Anne Jackson, Keir Dullea, James Caan, Joanne Woodward, Jeff Goldblum, Griffin Dunne, Tammy Grimes, Efrem Zimbalist Jr., Dabney Coleman, Brenda Vaccaro, Suzanne Pleshette, Darren McGavin, Patrick O'Neal, Pamela Bellwood, Mary Steenburgen, Lee Grant, and director Sydney Pollack. For many years, besides its star students, the school was noted for its legendary acting teacher, the late Sanford Meisner, whose techniques are currently very much in vogue both in the United States and the United Kingdom.

Visit www.the-neiplay.org.

11. P. J. CLARKE'S
913 Third Avenue

Third Avenue today is a busy boulevard that shows off some of Manhattan's sleekest skyscrapers. It's a far cry from the *old* Third Avenue with its low-rise brick tenement buildings and low-lit neighborhood pubs, all in the shadow of the overhead tracks of the famous Third Avenue El. One of the few vestiges of the old Third Avenue is a two-story brick building on the northeast corner of 55th Street that still houses P. J. Clarke's bar. Founded in the early twentieth century by an Irish immigrant bartender named Patrick J. Clarke, this archetypal New York neighborhood pub, P. J.'s—with its tin ceiling, beveled mirrors, and wood-paneled walls hung with sports photos—is a casual place for a business lunch or a happy-hour cocktail. There are many legends surrounding P. J. Clarke's. It was here that Buddy Holly proposed to Maria Elena Santiago, whom he later married. It's also said that Johnny Mercer wrote his famous hit song "One for My Baby" on a napkin while sitting at the bar. And when the late Richard Harris, a regular whenever he was in New York, showed up and asked for "the usual," the bartender simply lined up six double vodkas.

But for movie lovers, P.J.'s is of particular interest because it served as Nat's Bar in Billy Wilder's classic 1945 film about alcoholism, *The Lost Weekend*. Or so the legend goes. In reality, none of the footage shot at the bar could be used because of the noise of the El running overhead, so the bar was re-created on a Paramount soundstage in Hollywood. What Wilder couldn't duplicate in Hollywood, however, was the long sequence in *The Lost Weekend* where a desperate Ray Milland staggers up Third Avenue trying to pawn his typewriter. Shooting early in the mornings, Wilder, cameraman John Seitz, and Milland spent two weeks and covered sixty-five blocks of Third Avenue sidewalks

Third Avenue classic: P. J. Clarke's

Ray Milland shooting *The Lost Weekend* on Third Avenue, 1945

working on this famous scene in which Milland can't find an open pawnshop because it's Yom Kippur, the holiest day of the Jewish religious calendar. For Milland the shooting was particularly grueling, and he was reported to have been "muscle sore, chest-foundered, and swaybacked" by the time it was over. In fact, when the company returned to Hollywood, Milland was in such bad shape that they had to shoot around him for three days until he got rid of the limp he had developed from pounding the Third Avenue pavements with typewriter in hand. But ultimately it was worth the pain, because Milland won an Academy Award for his performance in *The Lost Weekend*.

As for P. J. Clarke's, it has weathered several brushes with the wrecker's ball, the most recent being in early 2002, when the legendary bar closed down. Happily, a syndicate of heavy-hitter investors—including actor Timothy Hutton and high-profile New York Yankees owner George Steinbrenner—took it over, restored it, and reopened it a year later.

Visit www.pjclarkes.com.

Sutton Place sirens: Marilyn Monroe, Betty Grable, and Lauren Bacall
with Cameron Mitchell in *How to Marry a Millionaire*, 1953

12. *HOW TO MARRY A MILLIONAIRE* APARTMENT
36 Sutton Place South

They were three of the most glamorous gold diggers ever to
go prospecting in Manhattan—Lauren Bacall, Betty Grable, and
Marilyn Monroe—and their ensemble aim was quite simple:
Each wanted to tap into the life of the richest man she could
find. To do this, they needed a base of operations that would fit
their decidedly upscale aspirations. Or, as Bacall bellowed early
on in the film: "To catch a mouse, you use a mousetrap . . . to
catch a bear, you use a bear trap." The three beauties found
the ideal bear trap in a palatial penthouse that was available for
sublet on posh Sutton Place. It cost $1,000 a month—a lot of
money back in 1953—but it had bedrooms and terraces for
days, and it came completely furnished. The furniture, however,
didn't last long as the gals started selling it off piece by piece
when they discovered that marrying a millionaire was not the
easy task they had thought it would be. The luxury apartment

building used as an exterior for this classic CinemaScope comedy from Twentieth Century–Fox still looks exactly as it did in the film.

13. LILLIAN GISH APARTMENT
430 East 57th Street

For over half a century, this basic-brick Sutton Place apartment building was Lillian Gish's Manhattan home. An extraordinary woman whose film career began in 1912 with D. W. Griffith's *An Unseen Enemy,* Lillian Gish appeared in such landmark silent pictures as *The Birth of a Nation* (1915), *Intolerance* (1916), *Way Down East* (1920), *Orphans of the Storm* (1922), and *The Scarlet Letter* (1925). When her film career slowed down in the 1930s, it was not, as it was for many of her contemporaries, on account of the talkies, but rather because Hollywood's taste in heroines had changed, and virtuous virgins like Miss Gish were

Lillian Gish in *The Birth of a Nation*, 1915

no longer in fashion. The actress dealt with this turn of events by concentrating on the Broadway stage, where she had a string of successes in classical roles. Her film career was far from over, however, for she went on to triumph as a character actress in a number of films in the late 1940s and 1950s, from David O. Selznick's *Duel in the Sun* (1947) and *Portrait of Jennie* (1948) to United Artists' *Night of the Hunter* (1955). And La Gish went on and on. Witness her roles in *A Wedding* (1978), *Sweet Liberty* (1986), and *The Whales of August* (1987). The actress, who died in 1993 at the age of ninety-nine—although she only admitted to ninety-six—once said she liked living in the Sutton Place area because "it is like a village where everyone knows you."

14. MARILYN MONROE APARTMENT
444 East 57th Street

If you wanted to reach Marilyn Monroe in the late 1950s, you had only to look in the Manhattan telephone directory under "Marilyn Monroe Productions Inc., 444 E. 57 . . . PL 9–5353." Marilyn moved into 444 with her third husband, playwright Arthur Miller, in 1956, and when she died some six years later

Marilyn Monroe and Arthur Miller's apartment building

in Hollywood, she still held a lease on the same Sutton Place apartment. In fact, when she made her final visit to the city in June 1962 to sing "Happy Birthday" to President John F. Kennedy at Madison Square Garden, she stayed at 444—although some sources reported that she spent at least part of the evening at the Carlyle Hotel, where the president was staying *without* Jackie.

Marilyn's East 57th Street apartment was on the thirteenth floor and had a lovely view of the East River. During the good times of her marriage to Miller, she played housewife and delighted in making breakfast and midmorning coffee for her writer husband. Marilyn also played decorator and did the whole place in white. Indeed, when she flew to California to make *Some Like It Hot* in 1958, Marilyn insisted that her suite at the Bel-Air Hotel be decorated in white to match her Manhattan home.

By early 1961, however, Marilyn's New York apartment was showing the strains of her personal and professional troubles. Now divorced from Miller and a veteran of stays in several mental hospitals, Marilyn had become a semi-recluse, and her secretary reported that her once-posh pad was "filthy, dirty, and depressing, with dog stains all over the carpets." According to her hairdresser, George Masters, Marilyn was "living on caviar, champagne, and hard-boiled eggs. She could let herself look like an old bag for two weeks. She'd smell sometimes, and never comb her hair for weeks. That's why it would take nine hours to get her ready and re-create Marilyn Monroe."

It was during this desperate period of her life that Marilyn is said to have come close to committing suicide by jumping out of her living room window. The reason for her extreme panic at the time was because she had read that Clark Gable's wife had blamed "the King's" recent death on the delays and tensions caused by Marilyn's erratic behavior while shooting *The Misfits*. Marilyn didn't jump, however, supposedly because she recognized a woman on the sidewalk below her. It was also around this time that Marilyn finally gave up on New York—the city that had held so much promise for her when she arrived in late 1954—and decided to go back to where she came from: Hollywood. A year later, she would give up on Hollywood, too.

15. RITZ TOWERS
Park Avenue at 57th Street

Among media mogul and early film producer William Randolph Hearst's many real estate holdings in Manhattan was the posh Ritz Towers apartment hotel, a beautiful 1920s building exotically ornamented with cornices, balustrades, finials, and obelisks. It was here that Hearst and his movie-star mistress, Marion Davies, kept a lavish suite that they often used when they were in New York in the 1930s. While most people these days think of Miss Davies's film career as little more than a plaything for Hearst, the truth of the matter is that Marion was an extremely successful film comedian who made quite a lot of money from her pictures and through her own shrewd investments. In fact, in 1937, she saved Hearst from bankruptcy by coming up with a cool million of her own money. The two were staying at the Ritz Towers at the time, and Marion spent a full day selling off her jewelry and mortgaging her real estate to produce the cash to bail out her buddy.

A decade later, another movie celebrity who resided at the Ritz Towers was Greta Garbo. Her quarters were not nearly so grand as those of her landlords, Davies and Hearst, however. The late photographer and designer Cecil Beaton, who claims to have had a love affair with Garbo in the late 1940s, writes in his autobiography, *Memoirs of the 40s* (McGraw-Hill, 1972), that Garbo at the Ritz "lived like a monk with little except a toothbrush, a piece of soap, and a jar of face cream." The affair ended when Beaton had to return to work in England. He wanted Garbo to accompany him, but the great star refused his offer, saying, "You see how difficult and neurotic I am. I am impossible to get on with." Nevertheless, the two remained friends—until, of course, Beaton published his book in 1973.

16. SHERRY-NETHERLAND HOTEL
781 Fifth Avenue

According to columnist Earl Wilson, the late Spencer Tracy reportedly once shocked the residents of this discreet hotel by turning up in the lobby smashed and stark naked, in search of a drink. Better-behaved Hollywood residents of the Sherry-

Netherland have included Diana Ross, Pia Zadora, and Danny Kaye, all of whom have owned luxurious apartments here.

The hotel was used extensively in one segment of 1989's *New York Stories,* a three-films-in-one opus directed by Martin Scorsese, Francis Ford Coppola, and Woody Allen. In the Coppola segment *Life Without Zoe,* the title character is a young girl left to her own devices and adventures by her superrich but always off-somewhere parents. The screenplay, by Coppola's then twenty-year-old daughter Sofia, was trashed by some critics at the time. Fifteen years later, Ms. Coppola would have the last laugh when her screenplay for *Lost in Translation* (2003) won her an Academy Award. The apartment used in *Life Without Zoe* was her father's Sherry-Netherland pad at the time.

Visit http://sherrynetherland.com.

17. THE COPACABANA SITE
10 East 60th Street

Immortalized in the Barry Manilow song "Lola" (about a Copa chorus girl), which later inspired the 1985 Emmy Award–winning television movie called *Copacabana,* New York City's Copacabana reigned as one of the town's most glamorous night spots from its opening in 1940 until well into the 1950s. Among the star performers who headlined here were Ella Fitzgerald, Sid Caesar, Frank Sinatra, Tony Bennett, Sammy Davis Jr., Nat King Cole, Jimmy Durante, and a couple of comics named Dean Martin and Jerry Lewis who, in 1949, broke all Copa records when they took in $68,543 in one week. Four years before that, it took Lena Horne to break the Copa's color barrier, when she became the first black entertainer to perform in the club's posh downstairs room. It was a bittersweet achievement, however: While the Copa allowed Miss Horne to perform, they refused to let blacks into the audience. This resulted in picket lines and protests and caused much grief for the star. Although she honored her contract and completed her run, from then on she made sure that all future nightclub contracts contained a clause barring racial discrimination at the door. The next time she played the Copa, African Americans were part of the audience.

Movie lovers may be interested to learn that June Allyson was

MONTE PROSER'S
COPACABANA
NEW YORK
MINIMUM CHARGE
(Per Person)
Weekdays & Sundays - $3.00
Sat., Hol. & Hol. Eves. - $4.50

Copacabana postcard, ca. 1950

once a Copa girl, as were Joanne Dru and Janice Rule. Movie lovers may also remember a 1947 bomb of a picture called *Copacabana,* in which Groucho Marx (with neither his mustache nor his brothers) played an agent who tried to double his commission by booking his client (Carmen Miranda) into the same New York City nightclub as two separate acts (a veiled chanteuse and a Latin spitfire)!

Well past its prime by the late 1960s, the Copa closed down in 1973, but has had various comebacks and incarnations since—including several gigs playing itself in the movies. In the 1990 Martin Scorsese film *Goodfellas,* the Copa turns up as the 1960s hotspot where Ray Liotta impresses wife-to-be Lorraine Bracco by avoiding the queue and taking her in through the kitchen, dropping numerous $20 tips along the way, before being shown a front table to catch Henny Youngman's act. Later the club shows up again when the film's merry band of mobsters come by with their girlfriends in tow on a Friday night (Saturday night was for wives). The Copa also appeared in Brian De Palma's 1993 thriller *Carlito's Way* as the club where Sean Penn, as a lawyer flying on cocaine, talks a little too much about a plan to spring a client from prison.

Today the old Copa space is now home to the sleek minimalist restaurant Nicole's, part of smart London fashion designer Nicole Farhi's New York flagship store.

18. CHRIST UNITED METHODIST CHURCH
Park Avenue at 60th Street

It was a fashionable affair, the marriage of socialite Frances Seymour Brokaw of 646 Park Avenue to Mr. Henry Jaynes Fonda of Hollywood, California. The ceremony took place on September 16, 1936, at Park Avenue's ultra-Waspy Christ United Methodist Church, and in his autobiography Mr. Fonda says of the event: "I don't know if I was ready for that kind of fancy dress wedding. They got me into a black coat with swallowtails, a pair of striped pants, an ascot around my neck, and a high silk hat on my head. Shit! I thought any minute the director would yell, 'Roll 'em! Action!' "

Henry Fonda had met Frances Brokaw earlier that year in London, where he had been shooting *Wings of the Morning*. It was love at first sight, followed by a whirlwind courtship carried on in Berlin, Budapest, and Paris, and culminating in matrimony on Park Avenue. There was no honeymoon, since Fonda was scheduled to start a picture in Hollywood the next day. But while all had been idyllic in Europe and New York, the couple ran into problems in California. For one thing, Frances Fonda never really fit into the town where her husband made his living and could never settle for being just another Hollywood housewife. Despite their problems, the Brokaw-Fonda union endured and produced two children: Jane Seymour Fonda, born on December 21, 1937, and Peter Henry Fonda, born February 23, 1940. As time went on, however, Mrs. Fonda's inability to cope with life in L.A. became more pronounced and she was plagued with hypochondriacal illnesses that put her out of commission for longer and longer periods of time. Even the family's move to the East Coast (when Fonda was starring in *Mr. Roberts* on Broadway in 1948) didn't help. In fact things got worse, and by 1949 Frances Fonda was spending more time in institutions than out of them. At the same time, her husband had met another woman—Susan Blanchard—and had asked his wife for a divorce. Mrs. Fonda granted this freely, even wished her husband good luck. But it was she who needed the luck. In April 1950, Frances Seymour Fonda ended her life, cutting her throat with a razor blade that she had smuggled into the sanitarium where she had been confined for several months. The funeral, in contrast to the glittering wedding fourteen years earlier, took place at a funeral home in upstate New York with only Henry Fonda and his mother-in-law Sophie Seymour in attendance.

19. BLOOMINGDALE'S
1000 Third Avenue

A landmark of conspicuous consumption on the Upper East Side, Bloomingdale's has naturally found its way into more than a few made-in-Manhattan movies. Notable Bloomie's on-screen

Retail romance: Kate Beckinsale and John Cusack at Bloomingdale's in *Serendipity*

shopping sprees include Diane Keaton and Michael Murphy's perfume-counter encounter in Woody Allen's *Manhattan* (1979), and the sequence in Paul Mazursky's *Moscow on the Hudson* (1984) in which the Russian musician played by Robin Williams defects to the West, smack in the middle of this bastion of capitalism. It's here, too, where mermaid-in-Manhattan Darryl Hannah's high-pitched voice breaks TV sets when she tries to tell Tom Hanks her name in *Splash* (1984), and where Barbra Streisand has lunch with her movie-mom Lauren Bacall in *The Mirror Has Two Faces* (1996), and where star-crossed lovers John Cusack and Kate Beckinsale meet at the glove counter in *Serendipity* (2001). Meanwhile, outside the Art Deco department store, a soap opera actress named Dorothy (Dustin Hoffman) fought for a taxicab in a most unladylike way in Sidney Lumet's *Tootsie* (1982).

Visit www. bloomingdales.com.

20. MONTGOMERY CLIFT TOWNHOUSE
217 East 61st Street

The star of *The Search* (1948), *Red River* (1948), *The Heiress* (1949), *A Place in the Sun* (1951), *From Here to Eternity* (1953), *Raintree County* (1957), *Suddenly, Last Summer* (1959), *The Misfits* (1961), and *Freud* (1962) lived in this four-story townhouse on East 61st Street from 1960 until his death at the age of forty-five in 1966. The home—which Teddy Roosevelt had given to his daughter, Alice Roosevelt Longworth, as a wedding present—had a sixty-foot living room, four bedrooms, six baths, six fireplaces, and a big garden in back. Despite these sumptuous surroundings, Clift's final years were far from happy ones. In constant pain from the injuries he had sustained in a near-fatal automobile accident in Hollywood in 1957, the star was hooked on drugs as well as plagued by a host of other health problems that ranged from premature cataracts and hypothyroidism to alcoholism and insomnia. Clift was also obsessed with the loss of his leading-man good looks and with the knowledge that both of his costars in *The Misfits,* Marilyn Monroe and Clark Gable, had recently died. Believing that bad things come in threes, he spent the early 1960s waiting to be the next to go.

Montgomery Clift townhouse

Sick, drugged, and drunk much of the time, Clift fell in with a sex-and-drugs crowd, and his East 61st Street abode was often the scene of some wild goings-on. Eventually when things had gotten so out of hand that Clift reportedly would try to solicit male sex partners by calling down to passersby from his upstairs window, his family and doctor hired a full-time male companion to care for the fast-fading superstar. On July 27, 1966, the light from that star faded completely.

Soon after his death, Clift's townhouse was sold by his sister with the stipulation that the new owners put up a plaque in the front of the building to read: "Montgomery Clift lived here in 1960–1966." The buyers did as they had been asked, but became so bothered by Clift cultists hanging around the building that they planted a bush in front of the plaque to hide it. Today, movie lovers passing by the former Clift townhouse will find that the plaque has disappeared totally.

21. TALLULAH BANKHEAD TOWNHOUSE
230 East 62nd Street

She made "Dah-ling" a fashionable form of address long be-fore the Gabors came on the scene. She drank heavily, smoked six packs of cigarettes a day, went to bed with both men and women, was renowned for her bawdy stories, and yet, through-out it all, Tallulah Bankhead was one great lady. She moved into this handsome East 62nd Street townhouse in the late 1950s,

Tallulah's townhouse

when her longtime home in the suburban community of Bedford Village had become too difficult for her to handle. Indeed, the lush life that Tallulah had led for four decades was starting to catch up with her by the time she hit the Upper East Side. Despite face and bust lifts, her looks had gone, and her career was reduced to summer stock and occasional guest shots on TV and radio. When she was home, her favorite pastime was a game of bridge that would last into the wee hours of the morning and during which much alcohol would be consumed. She also liked baseball, and could often be found at the Polo Grounds cheering for the New York Giants.

Although Tallulah Bankhead was not a movie star per se, she made films throughout her long career in show business. In fact, when she arrived in Manhattan as a stagestruck fifteen-year-old in 1918, among her very first acting jobs were roles in two silent films, *When Men Betray* and *Thirty a Week,* both shot in nearby Fort Lee, New Jersey. It wasn't until 1931, however, that Tallulah's motion-picture career began in earnest. Having become a great star of the London stage in the 1920s, the glamorous expatriate was wooed back to her native land with a lucrative movie contract from Paramount, which planned to market her as a second Marlene Dietrich. Back in New York, Tallulah quickly made three films at Paramount's Astoria studio. Despite the fact they weren't successful, the studio sent her to Hollywood, where she made three more pictures. But these, too, were disappointing at the box office, and she eventually returned to New York and to the Broadway stage, where she enjoyed a busy career for the next two decades. Among her legendary stage performances were as Regina Giddens in Lillian Hellman's *The Little Foxes* in 1939 (a role that Bette Davis later played in the film version) and her portrayal of Sabina the maid in Thornton Wilder's *The Skin of Our Teeth,* which won her a New York Drama Critics Circle Award in 1942.

A year later, just when everyone least suspected it, the unpredictable Tallulah returned to motion pictures and scored the coup of her career in Alfred Hitchcock's *Lifeboat,* winning the New York Film Critics Award for Best Actress of 1944 for her performance as a mink-coated reporter. During the film, Hitchcock kept getting complaints that Tallulah was not wearing un-

Paramount pretty:
Tallulah Bankhead,
ca. 1931

derwear—to which he famously replied: "I don't know if this is a matter for the costume department or the hairdresser." Despite her newfound film success, Tallulah was not so lucky with *A Royal Scandal,* which she made the following year, and once again she gave up on the medium in favor of radio, further forays onto Broadway, and lots of touring.

Always known for her outrageous behavior, Bankhead hardly mellowed with age. When she guested as the Ricardos' new neighbor in Connecticut on *I Love Lucy* in the late 1950s, she showed up with quite a few cocktails under her belt at rehearsal. This did not amuse no-nonsense Lucille Ball, and when Bankhead peeled off her trousers—no one quite knows why—in a meeting after Vivian Vance admired them, Ball wanted to fire her. She was talked out of it, however—and Bankhead's performance was flawless when they filmed the show before a live audience, whereas Ball supposedly blew her lines. Bankhead's final screen appearances were as the Black Widow in two episodes of the

1960s *Batman* series and as star of the 1965 British horror film *Die, Die, My Darling*. At a screening of the latter, no doubt again after a couple of cocktails, she vociferously apologized to the audience throughout the film for looking so terrible on-screen. She died in New York in 1968.

22. THE MELROSE HOTEL
140 East 63rd Street

Smack in the middle of the East 60s, this was one of the world's most fashionable boardinghouses when it opened in 1927 as the Barbizon Hotel for Women. Although its rooms were small and spartan simple, the twenty-seven-story hotel provided extras like a huge swimming pool and health club, a library with a full-time librarian, plus all sorts of club and game rooms. The hotel also had a strict policy regarding the opposite sex: Men were not admitted beyond the second-floor Recital Room. The Barbizon Hotel for Women was thus a place where protective parents could send their daughters and feel relatively untroubled about

Barbizon (now Melrose) Hotel, 1987

their whereabouts in the big city. Judy Garland and Vincente Minnelli, for example, knew teenaged Liza was in good hands when she made the Barbizon her New York nest during the making-the-rounds period of her career. Nor did the John Kellys of Philadelphia have to worry too much about their daughter Grace falling in with the wrong crowd as long as she was at the Barbizon. Ditto for the Bergens of Beverly Hills when their sweet Candy dropped out of the University of Pennsylvania for the bright lights and big bucks of a Manhattan modeling career. The Leachmans, those lumber barons of Des Moines, could breathe easier with little Cloris based at the Barbizon when she came to New York to try her wings on Broadway after having been a runner-up in the Miss America pageant. The poet Sylvia Plath, whose tragic life was portrayed by Gwyneth Paltrow in *Sylvia* (2003), was another Barbizon alumna. The hotel also lists Joan Crawford as a former famous occupant, but Joan's Broadway chorus-girl career had ended before the Barbizon was built, and it is hard to imagine Joan "the movie star" as a Barbizon girl.

The Barbizon Hotel for Women flourished for close to forty years, but toward the end of the 1960s, the sexual revolution as well as a decline in the hotel's physical plant caused it to lose much of its former cachet. Nonetheless, it was still a beautiful building—with its tapestry-brickwork façade, its gargoyles and columned balconies—and after being restored in the 1980s, it has flourished as a full-service hotel . . . for both sexes.

Visit www.melrosehotelnewyork.com.

23. MYRNA LOY APARTMENT
425 East 63rd Street

Bubbly, witty, fast-talking Nora Charles of *The Thin Man* will go down in film history as one of the movies' most sophisticated New York ladies. For several decades before her death in 1993, the great star who created her on screen lived—appropriately—on the Upper East Side. The surprise was that Myrna Loy was born way out west (in Montana) and grew up in Southern California. A fierce activist, Loy temporarily abandoned her film career during World War II to

Class act: Myrna Loy
with William Powell in
The Thin Man, 1934

work full-time for the Red Cross. In her NYC years she was a U.S.
representative to UNESCO. She never won an Academy Award but
was given an honorary Oscar in 1991.

24. BARBRA STREISAND APARTMENT
1157 Third Avenue

Early on in her journey to superstardom—and a long, long way
from Beverly Hills and Malibu, where she would eventually own
considerable property—Barbra Streisand lived in an apartment
above Oscar's Salt of the Sea Restaurant. The year was 1962, she
was twenty-one, and this was the first apartment she'd ever had
on her own. The neighborhood wasn't bad, but it seems that the
apartment reeked of fish from the restaurant downstairs, and
predictably, so did much of Streisand's wardrobe. Fish or no fish,
Barbra eventually reeled in her *I Can Get It for You Wholesale*
leading man, Elliott Gould, who wound up sharing the Third
Avenue pad with the lady who would be his wife. Here the two
had romantic meals that they ate off of a sewing machine in the

living room because, according to Mr. Gould, "a big rat named Oscar lived in the kitchen." Although Barbra didn't seem to mind her hovel, her managers Marty Erlichman and Marty Bregman did. And when they decided that their client needed a major makeover in order to prepare her for the big time that lay ahead, one of their top priorities was to move Barbra and Elliott to less odorific quarters.

Today, the fish restaurant is gone but the little walkup Streisand shared with Gould has somehow managed to survive amid the massive co-ops and condos that have swallowed up much of upper Third Avenue.

25. MR. AND MRS. RICKY RICARDO APARTMENT
623 East 68th Street

He was a Cuban band leader, and she was the wackiest of wives. Together they lived in apartment 3D of a Manhattan apartment house managed by their neighbors and good friends, Fred and Ethel Mertz. When the Ricardos had a son, Little Ricky, in 1953,

Leaving Manhattan: Lucy, Ricky, and the Mertzes pack up the Pontiac

the family moved to a larger apartment (3B) in the same building. Later, as was true of many Manhattan couples with young children in the 1950s, the Ricardos abandoned the city and headed for the suburbs. In their case, they settled in Greenwich, Connecticut. The Mertzes followed them and became their good neighbors in the country, just as they had been in the city. But by 1959 there were rumors that the real-life marriage behind the Ricardo TV marriage was on the rocks, and by 1960 *I Love Lucy* was off the air. Television hasn't been the same since.

P.S. The Ricardo apartment building is extremely hard to find. In fact, it's impossible to find, since the six hundred block of East 68th Street would probably be smack in the middle of the East River! The best place, therefore, to check out the Manhattan residence of Lucy, Ricky, Fred, and Ethel is on one of the many reruns of their classic sitcom.

26. *DRESSED TO KILL* OFFICE
162 East 70th Street

In Brian De Palma's bloody little 1980 horror film, *Dressed to Kill,* Michael Caine plays a mild-mannered Manhattan psychiatrist named Dr. Robert Elliot, who practices out of a posh office in the basement of this Upper East Side brownstone. Despite the fashionable address, movie lovers would do well to think twice before going into therapy with Dr. Elliot. Ask Angie Dickinson.

27. JOAN CRAWFORD APARTMENT
2 East 70th Street

She was not just one of Hollywood's greatest stars, she was one of its toughest survivors. When she was dropped by MGM in 1943, Crawford quickly resurfaced at Warner Bros., with whom she won an Oscar for her performance in *Mildred Pierce* in 1945. When her career was again on the downswing in the mid-1950s, she made a brilliant move with her marriage to Pepsi-Cola tycoon Al Steele. Indeed, for the first time in her life, she had hitched up with a man who could support her, instead of the other way around. With her new husband, Joan moved from Los Angeles to New York and quickly set to finding an apartment that would befit a movie star married to a captain of industry. Two East 70th Street was the chosen address, and here the Steeles secured not one but two apartments which they then turned into a massive duplex. Joan's adopted daughter, Christina, describes the flat in great detail in her now legendary look at her mother's life, *Mommie Dearest* (Morrow, 1978)—from the plastic flowers and plants to the plastic-covered furniture to the fact that no one was allowed to wear shoes beyond the entrance hall because "Mother didn't want those white rugs soiled."

Despite those plastic covers on the furniture, Joan and Al lived lavishly on East 70th Street—but not wisely. The apartment had cost close to $1 million to redo, which Steele had financed by borrowing against his future salary at Pepsi-Cola. Thus, when Steele died unexpectedly of a heart attack in 1959, Joan was left with massive debts. Once again, her survivor's instinct kicked in. She not only moved to less grand quarters at 150 East 69th Street, she turned her token membership on the board of directors of Pepsi-Cola into a lucrative full-time occupation. (Movie lovers will remember the scene in the Pepsi boardroom from the

Selling herself:
Joan with 1962
autobiography

film of *Mommie Dearest* in which Joan, played by Faye Dunaway, delivers the famous line: "Don't fuck with me, fellas!")

Joan also made a smart move in 1961, when director Robert Aldrich approached her about doing a film version of a creepy novel called *What Ever Happened to Baby Jane?* Seeing the potential box-office appeal of the vehicle, Crawford persuaded Aldrich to cast her archrival Bette Davis in the title role. But whereas Bette went for $60,000 up front plus 5 percent of the film's profits, crafty Crawford settled for a mere $30,000 salary against a whopping 15 percent of the gross. The film was a runaway hit, and Joan wound up making over $1 million on the deal. This, coupled with her Pepsi-Cola cash, set her up for the rest of her life.

28. POLA NEGRI APARTMENT
907 Fifth Avenue

Once a famous silent-screen star, Pola Negri was a Polish-born actress who came to Hollywood via her fame in German movies. While her exotic on-screen persona sold tickets in the 1920s, she—and her heavy Polish accent—didn't survive the talkies, and she spent most of the 1930s in Europe, until World War II broke out.

Pola Negri's place in film history is sometimes traceable less to her films than her being the self-proclaimed last lover of Rudolph Valentino. Her "grief" at the time of Valentino's death was legendary. Producer Walter Wanger supposedly said of Pola's train journey to the Valentino funeral that "she fainted all the way from Hollywood to Kansas City and then laid down on the job—but promised her press agent to come through with some really big swoons in Chicago and carry it right through to Rudy's bier in New York."

In the early 1940s, when Pola returned to the United States after her European sojourn, people were talking about a romantic involvement that she was rumored to have had with another famous personality—Adolf Hitler. Pola denied the allegations but was never able to pick up her American acting career. In the 1950s, she resided in Manhattan at 907 Fifth Avenue. Neighbors reported that a great portrait of Valentino hung in a prominent place in her foyer. By the end of the decade, she had moved into the San Antonio mansion of oil heiress Margaret West. When

Miss West died in 1963, she willed Pola her jewelry and lifetime use of her Texas house. When Pola died in 1987, she was still living in Texas.

29. *MIDNIGHT COWBOY* APARTMENT
114 East 72nd Street

Movie lovers will remember how Sylvia Miles slipped John Voight past the doorman of 114 East 72nd Street after she had picked up the young Texan outside on the street in *Midnight Cowboy*. At the time of their encounter Miss Miles was walking her poodle and having a hard time getting the animal to "Do it for Mama!" Miles received an Oscar nomination for her brief appearance as the trashy, over-the-hill East Side matron in the film; Voight also got an Academy Award nomination for his work and was judged best actor of 1969 by the New York Film Critics.

30. *BREAKFAST AT TIFFANY'S* APARTMENT
171 East 71st Street

Supposedly it was a tiny apartment in the East 70s, but for those who know New York, the enormous pad—complete with zebra-skin rugs on the floor—that Paramount art directors designed for Holly Golightly (Audrey Hepburn) in Truman Capote's *Breakfast at Tiffany's* could exist in only one place: on a Hollywood

Breakfast at Tiffany's block

soundstage. When *Breakfast at Tiffany's* came to New York City to shoot exteriors, however, reality won out over fantasy, and a real East 70s townhouse was chosen to represent Holly's apartment building. Wedged between an identical (save for the striped awnings) townhouse on the left and a distinctive stone building with Gothic arches on the right, this backlot-beautiful location looks much the same today as it did in 1961, when it was immortalized in *Breakfast at Tiffany's*.

31. GLORIA SWANSON APARTMENT
920 Fifth Avenue

She was born in Chicago, made a name for herself in Hollywood, and became a countess in France, but ultimately, for Gloria Swanson, New York was home. In fact, in the 1920s, when the bulk of feature-film production was deserting the East Coast for California, Swanson went from West to East, and made some of her major 1920s movies in New York City.

Straphanger Swanson: *Manhandled*, 1924

Actually, with the exception of her magnificent comeback as aging silent-movie star Norma Desmond in *Sunset Boulevard* (1950), Swanson virtually retired from the screen in 1934 and was involved in a variety of New York City–based ventures throughout the 1940s. These ranged from her own cosmetics company to a business that backed inventors to starring in road shows of Broadway plays. In 1948 Swanson broke new ground in show business when she hosted one of the world's first weekly hourlong television talk shows. Broadcast by WPIX in New York, this pioneering venture in TV programming featured a set that duplicated Swanson's Fifth Avenue apartment, and the format—a mix of celebrity interviews, public-service segments, and cooking demonstrations—was not unlike many of the morning shows that are now televised all across the country.

In 1970, at the age of seventy-two, Swanson had yet another career triumph when she replaced Eileen Heckart in *Butterflies Are Free* on Broadway. During the run of the show the indomitable Swanson drove herself to and from the theater in her own little yellow Toyota. Home then, as it had been for several decades in New York, was a spacious apartment at 920 Fifth Avenue. Married to her sixth husband, writer William Dufty, Swanson was at the same New York address when she died in 1981.

32. CARRIE BRADSHAW RESIDENCE
245 East 73rd Street

From 1998 to 2004, this was the official address of the columnist Carrie Bradshaw (Sarah Jessica Parker), who chronicled her Manhattan adventures in the *New York Star*. Like many New Yorkers, Carrie started off renting, but when the building went co-op she purchased her flat. Thanks to HBO, millions of people all over the world have followed Ms. Bradshaw's life and loves in the series *Sex and the City*. Although she has ostensibly lived at the above address (which doesn't exist) throughout most of her seven-year stint on TV, five different locations have been used to represent the exterior of her building.

33. WOODY ALLEN APARTMENT
930 Fifth Avenue

A one-man film industry, Woody Allen produces, directs, writes, and usually stars in movies that, more likely than not, are set in New York City. Prolific (he comes out with about a film a year), and acclaimed even by the Hollywood establishment (witness *Annie Hall*'s and *Hannah and Her Sisters*' Oscars), Allen reportedly likes to work in New York because he feels "serene in the knowledge that, if I want to, I can always go home and get a sweater." From 1969 to the 1990s, Woody kept his woolies in a large duplex apartment at 930 Fifth Avenue. He currently lives with his wife, Soon-Yi Previn, the adopted daughter of Allen's former partner Mia Farrow (with whom he has two adopted children and one biological child), in a large townhouse a little farther uptown.

34. SHERMAN McCOY APARTMENT
800 Park Avenue

It was one of the great literary successes of the 1980s—Tom Wolfe's scathing look at greed and social inequity in modern-day Manhattan in *The Bonfire of the Vanities*. But the 1990 movie version of the Wolfe super-seller was one of that decade's biggest bombs, grossing barely $16 million of its $47 million budget. In fact, the Brian De Palma–directed film was such a disaster the whole debacle was chronicled in author Julie Salamon's book *The Devil's Candy* (Houghton Mifflin, 1991). In the film the protagonist Sherman McCoy (Tom Hanks) and his wife Judy (Kim Cattrall in her brunette, pre–*Sex and the City* days) lived in this posh Park Avenue building at 78th Street.

35. CARLYLE HOTEL
35 East 76th Street

One of Manhattan's chicest and most discreet hotels, the Carlyle has catered to the rich and famous for decades. Among its regulars have been Elizabeth Taylor, Robert Evans, Steve Martin, Paul Newman and Joanne Woodward, and Warren Beatty (who is said to have been a lousy tipper). In the early 1960s, the Carlyle was where President John F. Kennedy liked to stay, and it is reported that Marilyn Monroe was a frequent, often incognito, visitor to his suite when Mrs. Kennedy was not accompanying him.

Besides its elegant rooms, suites, and cooperative apartments, the Carlyle is also known for the glittering Cafe Carlyle, where Bobby Short sings sophisticated songs. It was here that Woody Allen had a less-than-satisfying date with Dianne Wiest in *Hannah and Her Sisters* (1986) and wound up uttering the ultimate put-down: "You don't deserve Cole Porter!"

In 2002, Allen returned to the Carlyle to shoot a scene for *Hollywood Ending*. Before that, the hotel doubled as the European hostelry where heiress Glenn Close meets her future husband, Jeremy Irons, in *Reversal of Fortune* (1990). The hotel was also the site of the lavish penthouse where media mogul Anthony Hopkins lived in *Meet Joe Black* (1998) and where Brad Pitt, as Death, pays him an unwelcome visit.

Visit www.thecarlyle.com.

36. VERA WANG BRIDAL SALON
991 Madison Avenue

A former fashion assistant at *Vogue* magazine, Vera Wang has become the most successful creator of wedding gowns in the world. Although she has branched out into couture for other occasions—such as the Academy Awards ceremonies—Wang is still the star designer on the celebrity and socialite nuptials circuit. In 2003, during the off-again, on-again, off-again, etc. engagement of Jennifer Lopez and Ben Affleck, Wang was commissioned by J. Lo to run up a little $20,000 number for what was then expected to be the wedding of the year. But then, since Wang would get so much publicity from the Bennifer event, the star wangled a freebie dress. When J. Lo canceled the big wedding in favor of a smaller affair and then when the whole thing was called off, Wang got a lot of publicity, but not the kind she expected. Wang kept to an official "no comment" regarding the dresscapade—but insiders say we shouldn't expect to see Lopez wearing Wang at any upcoming awards ceremonies.

The story continued when the notoriously penny-pinching actor Kevin Costner tried to talk Wang into letting his fiancée Christine Baumgartner wear the dress for free at their upcoming wedding in exchange for publicity. Wang supposedly said she'd give them the dress if they paid her $5,000 for alterations. Costner agreed, but Baumgartner reportedly balked at the idea of getting married in J.Lo's cast-off frock. Meanwhile one thing is certain: Ms. Wang has certainly gotten her fair share of publicity.

37. *SIX DEGREES OF SEPARATION* APARTMENT
860 Fifth Avenue

They were the perfect Upper East Side couple. He was the well-known art dealer J. Flanders Kittridge and his wife, Ouisa, was attractive, witty, and frequently very useful in schmoozing with the prospective buyers of Flan's multimillion-dollar paintings. When actor Sidney Poitier's son Paul, a friend of the Kittridge kids at Harvard, winds up on their doorstep one evening in need of a place to stay, Flan and Ouisa at first think it's a hoot—not to mention wonderful dinner-table conversation. When it turns out that Paul is actually a con man, they still dine out on the experience, but Ouisa, ultimately, is profoundly moved and changed to discover the "six degrees of separation" that bind all human beings together. The Fifth Avenue apartment of Flan (Donald Sutherland) and Ouisa (Stockard Channing) where the faux Poitier (Will Smith) shatters their serenity in the 1993 film version of John Guare's play *Six Degrees of Separation* was here at 860 Fifth, although for most of the interiors another building—1049 Fifth Avenue—was used. Guare's story was based on a real event, and the playwright was unsuccessfully sued by the young man who claimed Guare had stolen his story.

38. METROPOLITAN MUSEUM OF ART
Fifth Avenue at 81st Street

It was one of the greatest, longest, and kinkiest seduction scenes ever: Angie Dickinson in the Metropolitan Museum of Art playing cat and mouse with a mysterious man in dark glasses. After many minutes of cruising among the Impressionists and Post-

Impressionists, the two finally make more than eye contact. The film is *Dressed to Kill* (1980), Brian De Palma's homage to Hitchcock, and for those who haven't seen it, we won't divulge what happens. What we will divulge is that while the famous *Dressed to Kill* seduction scene seems to take place in the Metropolitan Museum of Art, the truth of the matter is that the museum would allow De Palma to do only exteriors on its property. For the interiors, therefore, the director had to head down to his hometown—Philadelphia—where the Museum of Fine Arts, that columned Greek temple that looked so sensational in the original *Rocky*, opened its doors and its galleries to the *Dressed to Kill* crew.

In 1966, the Philadelphia Museum of Fine Arts did the same thing for a long sequence in Barbra Streisand's television special *Color Me Barbra*. Again, the Met had been the producers' first choice for a location, but again the institution refused to allow a film crew—even Barbra Streisand's—to shoot among its treasures. Indeed, if you're a film crew, it's never been easy to get in-

The Met according to MGM: Robert Walker and Judy Garland at the Egyptian galleries in *The Clock,* 1945

side the Met. In the quirky 1990 film *All the Vermeers in New York,* the exterior of the museum was used but the galleries are those of the nearby Whitney—and the Vermeers, needless to say, are copies. For the 1999 remake of *The Thomas Crown Affair,* the Met would hear nothing of a major art heist being shot on its premises, so the interiors were done some forty blocks down Fifth Avenue at the New York Public Library. For Woody Allen's *Everyone Says I Love You* (1996), the Met posed no problem, since the scene where Edward Norton and Drew Barrymore break out in song takes place at the fountain *in front* of the museum. On the other hand, back in 1944, when Vincente Minnelli wanted to stage a sequence in the Met's Egyptian galleries for *The Clock,* which starred his wife, Judy Garland, and Robert Walker, all the director needed to do was to make his wishes known to MGM's art department, and, voilà, the Met was re-created for Minnelli on a soundstage. And while those exteriors of the Metropolitan in *The Clock* are authentic, Judy and Bob never had to set foot out of Culver City to appear to be on the steps of the great New York museum. It was all done through the magic of the "process shot," i.e., rear projection.

These days, however, the Met does permit filming within one wing of its property: the dramatic, glassed-in Temple of Dendur pavilion, a vast space that houses a restored Egyptian Temple surrounded by fountains. Frequently rented out for major-league receptions and parties in New York (and a major moneymaker for the museum), Dendur has also provided the setting for gala sequences in many Manhattan movies. Among them: *Six Degrees of Separation* (1993), *Changing Lanes* (2002), *Maid in Manhattan* (2003), and *A Perfect Murder* (1998). In this last film, which starred Gwyneth Paltrow and Michael Douglas and which used hundreds of extras for the Dendur do, some of the Screen Actors Guild extras were angered and complained to their union when a few of Douglas's friends, whom he had invited to take part in the shoot, were placed closer to the camera than the SAG actors. The Temple of Dendur was also used as background in a walking-and-talking shot with Meg Ryan and Billy Crystal in *When Harry Met Sally* (1989).

Visit www.metmuseum.org.

39. STANHOPE HOTEL
995 Fifth Avenue

It was at this classy Upper East Side hotel that Carrie Brad-shaw (Sarah Jessica Parker) stayed when her handyman-of-the-moment Aidan Shaw (John Corbett) was redoing the floors of her nearby apartment in *Sex and the City.* To mark the visit, the Stanhope now features a *Sex and the City* cocktail, a Cosmopolitan-like concoction of cranberry juice, vodka, and Alizé Red Passion.

Both Parker and Anne Heche, who played a lawyer staying at the Stanhope in *Return to Paradise* (1998), were model Stanhope guests. The same cannot be said of the bad-boy actor played by Leonardo DiCaprio in Woody Allen's *Celebrity* (1998), who trashes his Stanhope room. (Shades of Johnny Depp, who in 1994 trashed his $2,200-a-night presidential suite at the Stan-hope's neighboring Mark Hotel. Though he offered to pay for the damages, the young star was forcibly ejected from the prem-ises and his accommodation for the night was subsequently pro-vided by the City of New York. Indeed, he was taken to three different jail cells that night—and was overwhelmed by female cops at each location.) Meanwhile, the Stanhope can also be seen in *Igby Goes Down* (2002), when the misunderstood Igby (Kieran Culkin) interrupts his mom's, Susan Sarandon's, lunch in the hotel's dining room, which has a stunning view of the Met-ropolitan Museum.

Visit www.stanhopepark.hyatt.com.

40. FRANK E. CAMPBELL FUNERAL HOME
1076 Madison Avenue

The setting for the final production number in the careers of many a superstar, the Frank E. Campbell funeral home has been in the business of stylish send-offs since the 1890s. Constantly in the news when it hosted Rudolph Valentino's last rites in 1926, Campbell's was then on the West Side of Manhattan at Broad-way and 66th Street. In its present East Side location since 1937, Campbell's has buried, from its Madison Avenue chapel, such celebrities as Tommy Dorsey, Gertrude Lawrence, Ezio Pinza, John Garfield, Montgomery Clift, Judy Holliday, Joan Crawford, James Cagney, Jacqueline Kennedy Onassis, Douglas Fairbanks Jr., rapper Christopher Wallace (Notorious B.I.G.), and Cuban superstar singer Celia Cruz, whose street-mobbed funeral rivaled Valentino's. (Movie lovers may also remember Campbell's as the bizarre setting for the "Enjoy yourself, it's later than you think" production number in Woody Allen's 1996 urban musical *Everyone Says I Love You*.)

The funeral to end all funerals was the production Campbell's staged for Judy Garland's final farewell appearance in June 1969. Some 22,000 faithful fans, many of whom had lined up at the funeral home even before the plane bearing her body from London had touched down at John F. Kennedy Airport, filed past Judy's glass-topped, blue-velvet-lined casket for over twenty-four hours. Many carried portable record and tape players that echoed Garland's greatest hits as they waited to see their idol one last time.

Since Judy's husband, Mickey Deans, the thirty-three-year-old former manager of New York's trendy Arthur discothèque, was reportedly too distraught to deal with the historic circumstances that enveloped him, Judy's daughter Liza Minnelli handled most of the funeral arrangements, with the help of her godmother, entertainer Kay Thompson. Wanting to keep everything upbeat, Liza insisted that Campbell's be decorated with yellow (Judy's favorite color) and white flowers, and ordered everyone invited to the private funeral service to wear "anything but black." There were, of course, problems. Makeup, for one. It seems that Judy had requested in her will that Gene Hills, her old MGM makeup man, do her final face. Hills, however, was in charge of Eva Gabor's makeup for the TV series *Green Acres,* and Eva refused to let him off the show. Then there was the problem of the color of the casket. Liza wanted it white but Campbell's didn't have a white one readily available. To the rescue came Kay Thompson, who suggested spray-painting the mahogany number that the funeral parlor had come up with.

The trickiest point of all had to do with cremation. Judy had requested it, and Liza wanted to adhere to her mother's wishes. But Judy's ex-husband Sid Luft, and their two children, Lorna and Joey, were against it. In the end, the Lufts prevailed. Sid Luft also felt that Judy should be buried in Hollywood, but on this point it was Liza who won out and saw to it that her mother was laid to rest on the East Coast at Ferncliff Cemetery in New York's Westchester County. According to Liza, Judy loathed Hollywood.

The service itself brought out Mickey Rooney, Ray Bolger, Lauren Bacall, Jack Benny, Cary Grant, Katharine Hepburn, Burt Lancaster, Dean Martin, Lana Turner, Freddie Bartholomew, Otto Preminger, and comedian Alan King. King, who had warmed up audiences for Judy's triumphant run at the Palace Theater back in 1951, reportedly joked to Liza at the beginning of the service, "This is the first time that your mom was ever on time for a performance." The rites were officiated by the same Catholic priest who had married Judy and Mickey Deans (her fifth husband) in London six months earlier. The hightlight of the ceremony, however, was the eulogy delivered by Judy's *A Star Is Born* costar, James Mason. (Mickey Rooney was considered for this role, but it was felt that he was too upset by Judy's passing to handle the assignment.) The final touching moment was when the whole congregation sang *The Battle Hymn of the Republic*—the song that Judy had sung on her TV show in November 1963 when the whole nation was mourning the untimely death of President John F. Kennedy. And then, amid both laughter and tears, it was over. There was no applause, however, and no calls for more. This time Judy was not coming back for an encore.

Visit www.frankecampbell.com.

41. MARLENE DIETRICH APARTMENT
993 Park Avenue

For close to three decades, Marlene kept, and often resided in, a four-room apartment in this serious thirteen-story Park Avenue building at 84th Street across from St. Ignatius Loyola Church. Among her many treasures here was a photo of her great friend Ernest Hemingway, which sat for years on a Sheraton table in her living room and bore the inscription: "To Marlene, if she still loves me or if she doesn't—Papa." Dietrich also had amassed an

Dietrich at legendary
nightclub El Morocco
with French actor
Jean Gabin

impressive art collection that was displayed throughout her
apartment and included paintings by Chagall, Cézanne, Corot,
Delacroix, Picasso, and Utrillo.

A *hausfrau* at heart, the ultraglamorous Marlene was frequently known to get down on her hands and knees with a wash
bucket and scrub her own floors. She was also known to play
telephone tricks, and often screened phone calls by pretending
to be the maid. Sometimes the maid charade went even further.
New York actor and die-hard Dietrich fan Martin J. Walsh
recalls the time in the early 1970s that he gained admittance to
993 Park to deliver a bouquet for her birthday. After ringing the
legendary lady's doorbell (apartment 12E), Walsh was told by a
high-pitched voice that "Miss Deetrish" was not in. When Walsh
announced his gift, the door was cracked open, a famous arm
appeared and snatched the posies, and the door was closed
again.

In the mid-1970s, Marlene, after a series of disastrous onstage accidents, moved permanently to a posh but small apartment at 12 avenue Montaigne in Paris, where her "maid"

continued to screen all calls. Dietrich's last on-screen appearance was in *Just a Gigolo* (1979), which starred David Bowie and featured Marlene as the proprietor of a ballroom where German war widows paid to dance with young gentlemen. After that, she lived as a virtual recluse in her Paris apartment, which Maximilian Schell re-created in a film studio for his Academy Award–winning documentary on Dietrich's life and career, *Marlene* (1985). Dietrich, who remained the master of her image right up to the end, speaks throughout the film, but refused to allow Schell to photograph her or her apartment for the project.

Dietrich died in Paris in 1992 at the age of ninety-one. She is buried in her native Berlin.

42. *BUTTERFIELD 8* APARTMENT
1050 Fifth Avenue

Elizabeth Taylor won her first Oscar for her role as a high-class call girl in the 1960 film *Butterfield 8*. While her acting is dodgy at best, Taylor deserved an Academy Award for the opening se-

Cozy at El Morocco: *Butterfield 8* buddies Eddie Fisher and Elizabeth Taylor, ca. 1961

quence of the film in which she wakes up alone in the very married Laurence Harvey's flashy New York apartment. For a good ten minutes, we are treated to Liz primping, smoking, putting on her makeup, and eventually coming across the $250 Harvey has left her along with the note "Is that enough?" Furious, Liz leaves the money and writes a reply on the mirror in lipstick: "No sale!" But before she storms out, she nicks a nifty little mink from the closet of Harvey's absent wife (Dina Merrill). The Harvey apartment building was called the Sandringham in the film and its address was given as 1038 Fifth Avenue, although the real building is on the northeast corner of 86th Street at number 1050.

As bad as Liz is in most of the film, the worst-acting award in this soap opera should go to Eddie Fisher, in the role of Liz's best friend Steve. It was a bit of nepotistic casting, since Taylor had recently married Fisher, having stolen him from Debbie Reynolds. *Butterfield 8,* based on a John O'Hara novel, could also win a worst-dialogue award; at one point Liz, whose character is named Gloria Wandrous, introduces herself as "Gloria—as in Sic Transit."

43. *RANSOM* APARTMENT
1067 Fifth Avenue

Superwealthy airline executive Tom Mullen (Mel Gibson) and his beautiful wife, Kate (René Russo), live an enviable upper-class life in this Upper East Side building just steps from the Guggenheim Museum—until their young son is kidnapped and held for $2 million ransom. When the initial drop is botched and the kidnappers subsequently up the ante, Type-A Gibson decides to go after the criminals himself in the 1996 Ron Howard thriller *Ransom.* Gibson and Russo's posh Manhattan pad overlooked the Central Park Reservoir, which is now named for its most famous jogger, the late Jacqueline Kennedy Onassis, who lived a few blocks away at 1040 Fifth Avenue. Meanwhile, *Ransom* was based on the 1956 Glenn Ford film *Death Wish*—not to be confused with the five Charles Bronson thrillers that co-opted that same title from 1974 to 1994.

44. SOLOMON R. GUGGENHEIM MUSEUM
1071 Fifth Avenue

Frank Lloyd Wright's 1959 museum is one of New York City's most spectacular architectural wonders. A seemingly endless gallery that spirals up or down—depending on how you visit it— around a great round atrium, the space is a delight to experience, even if the art is sometimes less than stellar. For filmmakers, the Guggenheim is too good to be true. Woody Allen first featured it in *Manhattan* (1979), as the trendy Manhattan museum where he first meets Diane Keaton. Allen then returned to the Guggenheim for *Everyone Says I Love You* (1996) and *Small Time Crooks* (2000). Although Alfred Hitchcock never used the Frank Lloyd Wright landmark, it has had its Hitchcockian moments—notably in director Ridley Scott's stylish 1987 thriller *Someone to Watch over Me,* where a thug who has threatened Mimi Rogers in the ladies' room is pursued round the curlicue museum by detective Tom Berenger. More fantastic is the sequence in *Men in Black* (1997), where Will Smith chases an alien, disguised as a human,

Frank Lloyd Wright wonder: Solomon R. Guggenheim Museum

who climbs up the exterior wall of the museum. Smith races up the ramp to see the human/alien fall off the roof onto Fifth Avenue. The Guggenheim also turns up in *She-Devil* (1989), as the glamorous spot where successful romance novelist Meryl Streep first meets frumpy Roseanne Barr Arnold and sets her sights on Roseanne's dapper husband, Ed Begley Jr. Messing with Roseanne turns out not to be a good idea, however. When first asked what attracted her to her unsympathetic role in the film, Streep replied, "I've always wanted to be a glamour-puss."

Visit www.guggenheim.org.

45. CHURCH OF THE HEAVENLY REST
2 East 90th Street

This austere Gothic church on upper Fifth Avenue will be of interest to movie lovers since it is here where the ashes of the great

Church of the Heavenly Rest

film star Gloria Swanson, who lived twenty blocks down Fifth Avenue, are interred. Swanson was born in Chicago in 1897 of Swedish-Italian parents and died in Manhattan in 1983.

Visit www.heavenlyrest.org.

46. CARNEGIE MANSION
2 East 91st Street

A survivor from the days when Fifth Avenue was noted for its grand private homes rather than its imposing apartment buildings, the sixty-four-room Carnegie Mansion was built in 1898 by industrialist Andrew Carnegie. Home to Carnegie's widow until her death in 1946, the place was later used by Columbia University, and today is the headquarters of the Cooper-Hewitt National Design Museum, which focuses on architectural, decorative, and industrial design. Movie lovers may recall the elegant Georgian building from its many roles in features as well as in made-for-television films and miniseries: *Daddy Long Legs* (1955), as playboy Fred Astaire's mansion; *Marathon Man*

Carnegie Mansion

(1976), as the Russian embassy; *The Next Man* (1976), as the Saudi Arabian embassy; *Arthur* (1981), as Dudley Moore's grandmother's home; *The Two Mrs. Grenvilles* (1986), as the Grenville mansion; and *Working Girl* (1988), as the site of the Trask wedding, which Harrison Ford and Melanie Griffith crash. The location has also appeared in *The Anderson Tapes* (1972), *Godspell* (1973), *Jumpin' Jack Flash* (1986), *84 Charing Cross Road* (1986), Sidney Sheldon's *Master of the Game* (1987), and Judith Krantz's *I'll Take Manhattan* (1987).

Visit http://ndm.si.edu.

47. CONVENT OF THE SACRED HEART
1 East 91st Street

Like the Carnegie Mansion (now the Cooper-Hewitt National Design Museum) across the street, this great Fifth Avenue palazzo was originally built for a millionaire. In this case, the man was New York banker and patron of the arts Otto Khan, who moved into what was one of the largest private homes ever built in Manhattan—complete with dramatic arched carriageway—in 1918. Today, besides being the site of a Catholic girls school, the grand mansion is often used as a film location. One of the most interesting of its appearances was for the Trask wedding sequence in *Working Girl* (1988), in which the Kahn/Convent property provided the interiors while the neighboring Carnegie Mansion/Design Museum was used for the exteriors. On its own, the Convent of the Sacred Heart can be seen in *The Anderson Tapes* (1972), where it was the object of Sean Connery's criminal intentions, and in *A Perfect Murder* (1998), as the lavish digs shared by Gwyneth Paltrow and Michael Douglas.

Visit www.cshnyc.org.

48. *THE HOUSE ON 92ND STREET* HOUSE
53 East 93rd Street

Elsa Gowns was the name of Elsa Gebhardt's dress shop on the north side of 92nd Street, near the corner of Madison Avenue, in Twentieth Century–Fox's landmark 1945 spy thriller, *The House*

Leo G. Carroll and Signe Hasso in *The House on 92nd Street*, 1945

on 92nd Street. In this riveting, action-packed tale of Nazi agents operating in New York City during World War II, Elsa Gowns is actually a front for the Fifth Column. Based on an actual FBI case and shot entirely on location, *The House on 92nd Street* told its dramatic story in a realistic, documentary way, a style that the film's producer, Louis de Rochemont, had perfected as creator of the March of Time newsreel series. Writing in the *New York Times,* film critic Bosley Crowther said at the time that *The House on 92nd Street* proved that "realism can be entertaining, too." Of course, even in the most realistic of films, there's always a trick or two, and in *The House on 92nd Street,* one of the tricks was that the house used in the film was actually on *93rd* Street! Today, the famous movie mansion no longer stands, although its identical twin—the Alamo Apartments next door at 55 East 93rd—is often mistaken for it.

49. MARX BROTHERS HOME
179 East 93rd Street

Early in the twentieth century, a stage mother named Minna Schoenberg Marx raised five sons at this address and saw to it that they all entered show business at early ages. Originally named Milton, Leonard, Adolph, Julius Henry, and Herbert, Minnie's boys became much better known as Gummo, Chico, Harpo, Groucho, and Zeppo Marx. Their father, a tailor in the same Yorkville neighborhood, kept the guys nattily attired for auditions.

50. THE CORNER BOOKSTORE
1313 Madison Avenue

This charming bookshop—with a big children's section—at the corner of 93rd Street and Madison has long been a neighborhood favorite. In 1987, one of its regulars was Anne Bancroft, who starred as Helene Hanff in *84 Charing Cross Road* as a book lover who ultimately had to turn to London to find the books she needed to fuel her passion. The film documented Hanff's odd long-distance romance with a bookstore on the other side of the pond. Since the film was set in the 1950s, Madison Avenue had to be temporarily turned back to two-way traffic to make the New York scenes authentic.

51. ELAINE'S
1703 Second Avenue

Welcome to Manhattan's ultimate celebrity hangout, an unprepossessing Second Avenue bar/restaurant that owes its superstardom to its owner/overseer Elaine Kaufman, a woman who knows how to make the famous feel like family and how to make a lot of other people (especially if they don't happen to have a reservation) feel as though maybe they had better try somewhere else for dinner. Among Elaine's regulars are Gwyneth Paltrow, Ben Affleck, Jennifer Lopez, Matt Damon, Salma Hayek, Chloë Sevigny, Al Pacino, Shirley MacLaine, Warren Beatty, Mike Nichols, Diana Ross, Milos Forman, Diane Keaton, Chevy Chase, Sidney Lumet—to name a few stars of the movie crowd. For the last decade, too, the restaurant has also been the site of *Entertainment Weekly*'s East Coast answer to *Vanity Fair*'s Hollywood Academy Awards night party.

Elaine's most famous table—off to the side of the busy passageway that links the restaurant's very fashionable front room

The *Celebrity* (1998) set at Elaine's: Hank Azaria, Kenneth Branagh, Famke Janssen, Winona Ryder

·with a back dining room known as Siberia—belongs to Woody Allen. An unwritten house rule: No one—not even the biggest celebrity in the place—approaches the famous New York filmmaker's table when he's occupying it. Ever.

Woody Allen not only hangs out in Elaine's, he's always using it as a location. In *Manhattan* (1979), Elaine's is the trendy venue of the film's opening scene; in *Manhattan Murder Mystery* (1993), Diane Keaton espouses her theory that her next-door neighbor has murdered his wife at a clubby little supper with Woody Allen, Alan Alda, and Ron Rifkin; and in Allen's star-packed (Kenneth Branagh, Judy Davis, Winona Ryder, Melanie Griffith, Charlize Theron, Leonardo DiCaprio) look at *Celebrity* (1999), sooner or later everyone winds up at Elaine's.

Another Elaine's regular, director Sidney Lumet, has also immortalized the place on-screen, although only insiders will recognize it as the bustling Manhattan bistro where TV execs Faye Dunaway and William Holden find love among the Nielsen ratings in *Network* (1976). Meanwhile, for movie lovers who think they might like to have dinner at Elaine's sometime, her phone number is 212–534–8103. Good luck—and if you get in, stay away from Woody!

52. GRACIE MANSION/CARL SCHURZ PARK
East End Avenue at East 88th Street

Built in 1799, this columned clapboard Federal house has been the official residence of New York City's mayors since 1942—although the city's current mayor, billionaire Michael Bloomberg, usually spends the night at his posh townhouse on East 79th Street. Over the years, Gracie Mansion has appeared in many films—always as itself. In *The Taking of Pelham One Two Three* (1973), mayor Lee Wallace, sick with the flu, has to deal with the hijacking of a subway train from his Gracie Mansion bed; in *Ghostbusters II* (1989), the boys visit mayor David Margulies with the bad news of another kind of subterranean nightmare threatening the city; and in 1996, Al Pacino is now mayor of New York and John Cusack is his deputy and they both have to deal with big trouble at and in *City Hall,* which featured several Gracie Mansion sequences.

Movie lovers visiting Gracie Mansion will also want to take a stroll in beautiful Carl Schurz Park, which is built over a hidden section of the FDR Drive below. The park has been used by

Barry Pepper, Philip Seymour Hoffman, and Edward Norton in Carl Schurz Park for *25th Hour,* 2002

Woody Allen in *Everyone Says I Love You* (1995) and by Joan Chen in *Autumn in New York* (2000)—but it is especially photogenic in Spike Lee's *25th Hour* (2002), as the place where Edward Norton rescues a bloody wounded dog, frequently walks the same dog here, and finally gets his buddies to rough up his pretty-boy looks before he goes to jail. The beauty of the park with its gardens and Gothic tunnel provides a striking contrast to the violence and blood of the first and final scenes.

Visit www.nyc.gov/html/om/html/gracie.html.

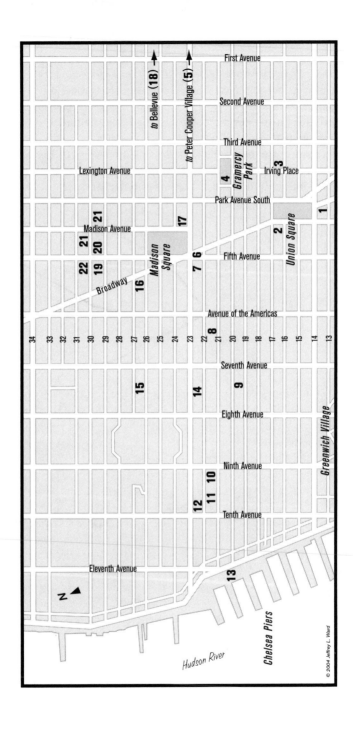

First Avenue

Second Avenue

Third Avenue

to Bellevue (18)

to Peter Cooper Village (5)

Gramercy Park

Irving Place

3

4

Lexington Avenue

Park Avenue South

Union Square

1

Madison Avenue

21

21

20

22

19

16

17

2

Broadway

Madison Square

6

7

Fifth Avenue

Avenue of the Americas

8

34 33 32 31 30 29 28 27 26 25 24 23 22 21 20 19 18 17 16 15 14 13

Seventh Avenue

15

14

9

Eighth Avenue

Ninth Avenue

11 10

12

Tenth Avenue

Greenwich Village

Eleventh Avenue

N

13

Chelsea Piers

Hudson River

© 2004 Jeffrey L. Ward

Union Square/Gramercy Park/ Chelsea: From Biograph to *Law & Order*

In 1909, when a teenaged Broadway actress named Mary Pickford decided it was time to think seriously about getting into the movie business, she hopped a Fifth Avenue bus and headed downtown toward Union Square. Her destination was the Biograph Studios, at 11 East 14th Street, where she was instantly cast in a D. W. Griffith potboiler that marked the beginning of one of the most spectacular careers in film history. If Mary hadn't been so lucky at Biograph, however, she could have continued her job search at any number of other studios—Kalem, Craftsmen, Edison, Reliance-Majestic, American Kinograph—that were headquartered in the lofts and office buildings of nearby Gramercy Park and Chelsea.

Today, these same neighborhoods provide a mixed bag of delights for the movie lover who ventures here. These include the old studio buildings of Chelsea (one of which is still used for producing TV shows), the vital new studio facility that's home to the *Law & Order* series, the 1902 high-rise on whose rooftop James Stewart and Kim Novak once spent a romantic evening (on film), two of the "factories" where the late Andy Warhol turned out underground films in the 1960s, and one of Manhattan's most exclusive—and star-studded—residential enclaves. Today's Chelsea is also the capital of gay New York—with numerous gay and lesbian bars, cafés, and shops. These days, too, the neighborhood boasts the greatest concentration of art—some two hundred galleries—in the city.

1. BIOGRAPH STUDIOS SITE
841 Broadway

The American Mutoscope and Biograph Company was the rather exotic name of one of the first motion-picture companies to mount a serious challenge to Thomas Edison's monopolistic hold on the early film industry. Biograph produced initially a better-quality image (by using larger-sized film) and enjoyed the participation of W. K. L. Dickson, a former—and the most influential—player on the team that developed motion pictures at Edison. Biograph's first studio was on the roof of the Hackett

Biograph's revolving rooftop stage atop the Hackett Carhart Building, 1896

Belle of 14th Street:
Biograph starlet
Mary Pickford

Carhart Building, a great Victorian fortress with ornate columns, pediments, and turrets that still stands on the northwest corner of Broadway and East 13th Street. Similar to the Black Maria studio that Dickson had built for Edison in West Orange, Biograph's rooftop facility was mounted on tracks and revolved with the sun. The foundations of this primitive studio are still in place atop the restored Hackett Carhart Building.

Unfortunately, the site of some of Biograph's greatest cinematic triumphs—a brownstone studio at 11 East 14th Street to which it moved in 1906—was razed in the 1960s to make way for a big boring brick apartment building. It was at the Union Square studio that D. W. Griffith directed his first film, *The Adventures of Dollie,* in 1908. Griffith went on to become the studio's top director and brought such talents as Mary Pickford, Lillian and Dorothy Gish, Blanche Sweet, Lionel Barrymore, Wallace Reid, Mabel Normand, Mae Marsh, Harry Carey, and Mack Sennett into the Biograph fold. When Griffith left the stu-

dio in 1913 for the Mutual Film Corporation, Biograph's status fell quickly, and in 1915 the company was dissolved. Many of its films survive, however, thanks both to Griffith, who saved copies of all his productions, and to the Museum of Modern Art, which acquired Griffith's collection in the mid-1930s for its then new film department.

In 1975, a plaque was dedicated by former Biograph beauties Lillian Gish and Blanche Sweet at the site of the historic townhouse studio at 11 East 14th Street. The day after the ceremony, however, the plaque mysteriously disappeared, and there have been no further efforts to put up a new one. There should be. And while we're talking about plaques, there also ought to be one at Biograph's original studio site at 841 Broadway.

2. THE FACTORY SITE
33 Union Square West

It was the best of times, it was the worst of times . . . it was the 1960s. Underground avant-garde films were the rage—especially those created by a platinum-blond NYC artist named Andy Warhol. Andy made his films—which often used stationary cameras and ranged from quickies like *Blow Job* to six-hour epics like *Sleep*—at a series of New York City studios he called "factories." Andy's first factory, which he occupied between 1963 and 1967, was at 231 East 47th Street. With its walls covered in silver Mylar, the place hosted a constant stream of drop-ins from the street, many of whom wandered in and out of whatever film Warhol and his associates happened to be shooting at the time. Just like in the old days of Hollywood, this wacky, carefree moviemaking organization also boasted its own superstars. Among them were Viva, Ultra Violet, Baby Jane Holzer, Paul America, Joe Dallesandro, and Edie Sedgwick, whose tragic, brief, fast-lane life and subsequent death of a drug overdose were documented in both the 1982 best-selling book *Edie* and in the 1983 film *Ciao! Manhattan*.

In early 1968, Warhol and company moved from their 47th Street base (which was about to be demolished for an apartment building) to the sixth floor of a ca. 1900 loft building at 33 Union Square West. Although now the walls were painted white and everything was very crisp and minimal, the moviemaking at

Factory worker: Andy Warhol with underground movie star Gerald Malanga

the new Factory was just as freewheeling as it had been uptown. Things changed radically, however, in June 1968, when a young woman named Valerie Solanis wandered into the Factory, pulled a gun, and fired it at Warhol, supposedly because he had refused to produce a screenplay she had written. The episode was the inspiration for the 1996 film *I Shot Andy Warhol,* which starred Lili Taylor—once labeled Queen of the Independent Cinema—as the crazed Solanis and Richard Harris's actor son Jared as Warhol. The film did not use the Union Square site for its Factory sequences; instead it used a loft building at 535 West 22nd Street, between Tenth and Eleventh Avenues.

In real life, Warhol survived his wounds, but from then on security at the Factory became much tighter, and the mood became more tense. Another change that took place after the shooting

Andy Warhol's 1968–1973
Factory (on right)

was that Warhol turned over most of the directorial duties to his associate, Paul Morrissey, who went on to do more commercial features such as *Flesh* (1968), *Trash* (1970), and *Heat* (1972) at the Union Square studio.

In 1973, the Factory moved again, to a building a few hundred feet across Union Square at 860 Broadway. The space was enormous, but ultimately not much filmmaking took place here, and by 1984 Warhol's enterprises, which now included the very successful *Interview* magazine, had moved into conventional offices at 22 East 33rd Street. With this move and then with Warhol's untimely death owing to complications (and possible negligence) following gall bladder surgery in 1987, the grand days of Andy Warhol movies and of the 1960s were definitely over.

3. WASHINGTON IRVING HIGH SCHOOL
40 Irving Place

A huge bust of the great American writer Washington Irving stands at the northwest corner of this big old Gramercy Park school building that bears his name. But movie lovers will be more interested in the autographed portrait of another American legend that hangs in the high school's library. Presented to her alma mater in 1986 by a small contingent of loyal fans, the portrait commemorates the most famous member of Washington Irving's Class of 1921: Lily Chauchoin. More interested in art and fashion design than in the theater during her Washington Irving days, little Miss Chauchoin nonetheless appeared in several school plays. The experience must have served her well, because two years after leaving Washington Irving she changed her name to Claudette Colbert, made her debut on the stage of the Provincetown Playhouse in Greenwich Village, and soon was acting on Broadway as well as at Paramount's Astoria film studios in Queens. Next came Hollywood, where she not only won an Academy Award in 1935 for *It Happened One Night*, opposite Clark Gable, but was one of the highest-paid people in the United States, earning $426,944 in 1938, which was the fourth highest salary in the country that year. Her age-defying beauty kept her working, mainly in the theater, well into her eighties. Her last film appearance was as Troy Donahue's mother in *Parrish* (1961); but in 1986, at the age of eighty-one, she starred with Ann-Margret in the TV miniseries *The Two Mrs. Grenvilles,* based on a novel about a high-society murder by Dominick Dunne. A longtime resident of the Caribbean island of Barbados, where she had a lavish plantation house, Colbert died on the island in 1996.

In addition to Claudette Colbert, Washington Irving High also boasts two other movie stars as former students: Sylvia Miles (Academy Award–nominated for Best Supporting Actress, both in 1969 for *Midnight Cowboy* and in 1975 for *Farewell, My Lovely*); and Whoopi Goldberg, who garnered an Academy Award nomination (for Best Actress) for her 1985 film debut in *The Color Purple* and won an Oscar as Best Supporting Actress for *Ghost* (1990). Miss Miles, who attended Washington Irving sometime in the 1940s, was Sylvia Lee at the time; Miss Goldberg, who dropped out of Washington Irving sometime in the

1960s, did so as plain-old Caryn Johnson (she had yet to encounter that burning bush in California that she says came up with her current name).

For anyone who wonders why Washington Irving produced only actresses, the answer is that the school had been an all-girls institution for most of its life. In fact, Washington Irving was the only remaining all-girls public high school in New York City up until the fall of 1986, when the board of education ruled that it had to admit boys.

4. GRAMERCY PARK
East 20th and 21st Streets between Park and Third Avenues

One of New York City's most attractive residential enclaves, Gramercy Park dates back to 1831 and, as its main attraction, boasts a locked, fenced-off private park that can be entered only by owners and tenants of the townhouses and apartments that surround it on four sides. In the last century, the legendary Amer-

John Barrymore building:
36 Gramercy Park East

Number 3 Gramercy
Park West—where
John Garfield died

.ican actor Edwin Booth spent the final years of his life in the handsome Stanford White–designed townhouse at number 16 Gramercy Park South, which was also the headquarters for the Players, the famous theatrical club that Booth helped found in 1886. Today the Players—which counts among its current and former members John and Lionel Barrymore, Irving Berlin, John and Keith Carradine, Dick Cavett, Alistair Cooke, Joseph Cotten, Walter Cronkite, Hume Cronyn, Alfred Drake, Maurice Evans, José Ferrer, Richard Gere, George Grizzard, Rex Harrison, Hal Holbrook, Raul Julia, Jack Lemmon, Garson Kanin, Charles Kuralt, Burgess Meredith, Carroll O'Connor, Sir Laurence Olivier, and Frank Sinatra—is still housed at the same landmark Gramercy Park location. Booth's former bedroom, where he died on June 7, 1893, has been kept just as it was back then, and outside in the park he is remembered with a bronze statue of him in the role of Hamlet.

No statue commemorates another show-business personality who also died here, although newspapers made quite a story of actor John Garfield's fatal heart attack, which he suffered in 1952 during a late-night visit to 3 Gramercy Park West, the townhouse of actress–turned–interior decorator Iris Whitney. Although rumor had it that Mr. Garfield died in Miss Whitney's bedroom, Garfield's biographer, Larry Swindell, in *Body and Soul: The Story of John Garfield* (Morrow, 1975), writes that the forty-year-old star expired in the guest bedroom with nothing more sensational by his side than an unfinished glass of orange

juice on the night table. A few doors down, still on the west side of the park, the gray brick apartment building at 7 (with the entrance on East 20th Street) was a former Manhattan address of Julia Roberts.

Over on the east side of the park, two bizarre apartment buildings at numbers 34 and 36 stand out and are of special interest to movie lovers. Number 34 is a mysterious turreted urban castle—with a marble-columned entrance that leads to a distinctive foyer sporting a stained-glass skylight and mosaic-tiled floor and walls. The building was the longtime home of *The Wizard of Oz*'s Wicked Witch of the West, Margaret Hamilton. Character actress Mildred Dunnock, actor John Carradine, and legendary Warner Bros. tough guy James Cagney are three other former star residents. Next door, number 36 is a Gothic white-marble affair of twelve stories guarded by statues of knights in armor. Between 1910 and 1916, John Barrymore kept an apartment in this building during the period that he appeared in his first films for the Famous Players Film Company, which conveniently had its main studio on nearby West 26th Street. Movie lovers with eagle eyes may also recognize 36 Gramercy Park East from the 1949 MGM film *East Side, West Side,* in which its exterior was used as the apartment house where Barbara Stanwyck's parents supposedly lived. (Featured in the same film was a starlet named Nancy Davis, who would become much more famous under her married name: Reagan.)

The Gramercy Park Hotel, at 52 Gramercy Park North, is easier to recognize in the 2000 film *Almost Famous* as the hotel that furnished digs for the 1970s rock group Stillwater. The hotel was also used in *The Devil's Own* (1997) and *Addicted to Love* (1997). Gramercy Park's most popular film location, however, is the National Arts Club, next door to the Player's Club at 15 Gramercy Park South. A landmark 1845 mansion, which was extensively redone in the mid-1880s by Calvert Vaux (half of the team of Olmsted and Vaux, who designed Central Park), this delightful bit of Old New York—complete with a magnificent stained-glass ceiling—was the perfect location for the glittering post-opera ball in Martin Scorsese's 1993 take on Edith Wharton's novel of upper-class life in 1870s Manhattan, *The Age of Innocence.* That same year, Woody Allen used the National Arts Club—which in real life counts not only artists and architects as

Winona Ryder and Daniel Day-Lewis at the National Arts Club on Gramercy Park South in *The Age of Innocence*

members but also a number of movie people such as Martin Scorsese, Dennis Hopper, Robert Redford, Ethan Hawke, and Uma Thurman—in *Manhattan Murder Mystery,* for a scene where Diane Keaton, while at a tony Arts Club wine tasting, sees her supposedly murdered neighbor outside in the street. For *The Thomas Crown Affair* (1999), the club was again the site of an A-list New York City event, this time a fund-raiser, at which glamorous insurance investigator René Russo confronts businessman Thomas Crown (Pierce Brosnan) about his possible involvement in a recent theft at the Metropolitan Museum. Despite conflicts of interest, the meeting turns out to be the beginning of a very beautiful friendship.

5. PETER COOPER VILLAGE
East 20th to 23rd Streets/First Avenue to FDR Drive

To accommodate the huge demand for affordable housing for servicemen returning from World War II and their soon-to-be-booming families, the Metropolitan Life Insurance Company—

with some serious tax breaks from the government—built two massive apartment complexes on the middle East Side of Manhattan. The less grand of the two—Stuyvesant Town—stands from 14th to 20th Streets between First Avenue and the FDR Drive. Movie lovers will be more interested in the somewhat posher project—Peter Cooper Village—which runs from 20th to 23rd Streets. It was here that Judy Holliday and her screen husband Aldo Ray moved (9 Peter Cooper Road) as newlyweds in George Cukor's *The Marrying Kind* (1952). Obsessed with improving their lot in life, Ray is convinced that he can make a fortune with his invention, ball-bearing sliders—which eerily turn out to be a forerunner to the Rollerblades that conquered the world some four decades later!

The 1956 boxing epic *The Harder They Fall* brought Humphrey Bogart to Peter Cooper Village, where his down-and-out sportswriter character lived at 8 Peter Cooper Road. Supposedly Bogie played with the local kids between takes. When Robert Redford dropped by the same neighborhood in 1974 to shoot *Three Days of the Condor,* he had to contend with screeching teenage female fans. Other films and TV shows that have shot at Peter Cooper and Stuyvesant Town have been *Naked City, Decoy, Kojak,* and *Mike Hammer.*

A former longtime Peter Cooper/Stuyvesant Town resident was Karl Malden, who was featured in both the stage (1947) and screen (1951) versions of Tennessee Williams's *A Streetcar Named Desire,* but who is perhaps best known as Michael Douglas's boss on the TV series *The Streets of San Francisco* and as the man who told America not to leave home without their American Express card. Playwright Arthur Miller's actress sister Joan Copeland also once resided at Peter Cooper, where she frequently entertained Miller and her then sister-in-law Marilyn Monroe.

Peter Cooper, by the way, was a nineteenth-century millionaire philanthropist who made his fortune as a glue manufacturer.

6. FLATIRON BUILDING
175 Fifth Avenue

When it went up in 1902, the three-sided, twenty-two-story Fuller Building was one of New York's most unusual-looking structures, as well as its first full-fledged skyscraper. Instantly nicknamed the Flatiron Building on account of its shape, the new architectural wonder became one of Manhattan's best-known landmarks in the early part of the twentieth century. In addition to its height and shape, the Flatiron Building was also believed to occupy one of the windiest corners in Manhattan and was thus popularly considered a prime place to catch a glimpse of a lady's ankle—or, better yet, her knee—should the wind catch her skirt at the right moment. Interestingly enough, it was this aspect of the new building and not its architecture that caught Crescent Films' camera in early 1905 when it made a risqué little docudrama entitled *The Flatiron Building on a Windy Day*. This enthusiastic description of the film from a catalogue of the time gives an idea of what turned early movie audiences on:

> This sidesplitting scene was taken January 25, 1905, when the wind was blowing a gale, and gives one a general idea of what women experience on a windy day around this noted corner. The great velocity of the wind can be plainly seen by the man-

Flatiron Building

ner in which the pedestrians are clutching at their hats and skirts and grasping at anything for support. It is at this corner where one can get a good idea of the prevailing types in hosiery and lingerie. This is the finest picture that has ever been taken at this corner, and we can safely recommend it as something exceptionally fine.

Some fifty years later, the Flatiron Building again furnished the setting for an erotic, although far more sophisticated, cinematic interlude, when James Stewart and Kim Novak find themselves in a passionate clinch atop its roof in *Bell, Book, and Candle*. "Where are we?" asks a love-dazed Stewart of the beautiful witch played by Miss Novak, who has transported them to this ultraromantic spot in the 1958 comedy about magic in modern Manhattan. "On top of the Flatiron Building," she replies. "You liked its shape, and you wanted to be on top of a tall building. We had no luck at the Empire State Building."

When star actor/director Warren Beatty came to New York to do location shooting for *Reds* in 1980, he wound up at the bottom of the Flatiron Building. Needing an early-twentieth-century backdrop for the sequence where Louise Bryant (Diane Keaton) arrives in Manhattan, Beatty found that the venerable 1902 landmark served his purposes perfectly. To shoot the scene, street and traffic lights around the building were removed, but little else had to be altered. The snow in the scene was not artificial, by the way; it was a lucky happenstance that added to the beauty of the shot. More recently, the distinctive landmark building turned up in *As Good as It Gets* (1997), as the offices of Melvin Udall's (Jack Nicholson's) publisher, and in *Spider-Man* (2002), as the *Daily Bugle* newspaper offices, where young Tobey Maguire (Spider-Man) makes a splash as the only photographer in New York able to snap pictures of the elusive superhero.

7. HASBRO TOY BUILDING
32 West 23rd Street

It was in this imposing 1892 cast-iron building—originally Stern's Dry Goods Store—that thirteen-year-old Josh Baskin had a stellar career as a creative director of the ailing MacMillan Toy

Big location: former Stern's Dry Goods building on West 23rd Street

Company. At first, since Josh looked like a thirty-something Tom Hanks, no one suspected his real age in Penny Marshall's 1988 *Big.* The building—now known as the Hasbro Toy Building—used for MacMillan Toys is in the center of Manhattan's wholesale toy district. Around the corner at 200 Fifth Avenue, the Italian Renaissance–style International Toy Center building will also be of interest to movie lovers, since it served as the offices of the *New York Globe,* which employed columnist J. J. Hunsecker (Burt Lancaster) in *Sweet Smell of Success* (1957). In the 1980s, cofounding editor of *Spy* magazine Graydon Carter is believed to have been the pen behind the rag's take-no-prisoners gossip column, which ran under the byline of J. J. Hunsecker. Today, Carter uses his own name as the editor in chief of *Vanity Fair* magazine.

8. SCHOOL OF VISUAL ARTS/KALEM FILM COMPANY SITE
131 West 21st Street

Currently home to one of the city's premier art (and film) schools, this Chelsea loft building saw a group of film pioneers set up operations here in 1907. With a director named Sidney Olcott in charge of production, the Kalem Film Company specialized in Westerns, which it shot on location across the Hudson River in the badlands of New Jersey near Fort Lee. In its heyday,

Kalem came out with over two hundred short films a year and was also noted for productions done in more exotic locations such as Florida, California, Ireland, and the Middle East. In fact, one of its greatest successes was a feature based on the life of Christ, *From the Manger to the Cross,* which was lensed in Palestine in 1911, and which featured Robert Vignola (who later became a top Hollywood director) as Judas. An even earlier Kalem success also had a biblical theme—a one-reel version of the novel *Ben Hur* in which Manhattan Beach in Brooklyn doubled as the Holy Land. Since Kalem had not acquired the motion-picture rights to Gen. Lew Wallace's book (motion-picture rights didn't even exist at the time), Kalem was sued and eventually paid the Wallace estate $25,000 in a landmark 1911 out-of-court settlement. In 1916, a financially troubled Kalem, which had continued to concentrate on short films at a time when most of the industry had switched over to features, was bought by Vitagraph and never heard from again.

9. TENTH PRECINCT
230 West 20th Street

Cinematographer William Daniels won an Academy Award for his brilliant camerawork in the 1948 film *The Naked City.* Directed by Jules Dassin, the picture was shot entirely in NYC and is considered, along with Louis de Rochemont's *The House on 92nd Street,* to be a landmark in 1940s on-location filmmaking. Among the many spots used in *The Naked City*—from Wall Street to the old Roxy Theater on Seventh Avenue at 50th Street—none was more important than the Tenth Precinct, described by the film's narrator, Mark Hellinger, as "a rather shabby building on a rather shabby street." Used both for exteriors and interiors, the Tenth Precinct was supposedly the base from which the team of detectives and cops headed by Barry Fitzgerald as Inspector Muldoon worked on solving the murder of Howard Duff's girlfriend. The murder, by the way, took place at an apartment building at 52 West 83rd Street. Why Chelsea's Tenth Precinct, some sixty blocks away from the scene of the crime, was in charge of the investigation, we are never told. But then, as we all know, "there are eight million stories in the

Inside the Tenth Precinct: Tom Pedi, Barry Fitzgerald, Don Taylor, and Howard Duff in *The Naked City,* 1948

Naked City," so nothing should surprise us. Today, the Tenth Precinct and the block it occupies—wedged between the booming restaurants and galleries of Chelsea—are anything but "shabby."

10. GENERAL THEOLOGICAL SEMINARY
175 Ninth Avenue

An oasis of nineteenth-century architecture in the middle of Chelsea, this quadrangle of handsome buildings has been home to an Episcopal seminary since 1835. Today, it is a popular location for films and TV shows that want an instant academic setting. In Gus Van Sant's 2001 feature *Finding Forrester,* the seminary's stunning refectory doubled as a college lecture hall and in *House of D* (2004), starring Robin Williams, the property's beautiful grounds and gym were used. The series *Law & Order,* based just a few blocks away at the Chelsea Piers studios, virtually treats the seminary as its back lot. Besides providing college and prep school campus locations for *L&O,* the semi-

Chelsea's secret garden:
General Theological
Seminary

nary buildings and interiors are often dressed to double as police stations, hospitals, offices, and apartments. The *Law & Order* spinoffs *Special Victims Unit* and *Criminal Intent* also shoot here on a regular basis, as does *Third Watch*. In addition, the seminary and its beautifully landscaped grounds and gardens are often booked for commercials and fashion shoots.

The gardens of the General Theological Seminary are open to the public from Monday to Friday from 12 noon to 3 p.m., and on Saturday from 11 a.m. to 3 p.m. Tours are offered in summer. Call 212-243-5150 or visit www.gts.edu.

11. ANTHONY PERKINS TOWNHOUSE
467 West 21st Street

In the 1960s and 1970s, Mr. Perkins was the live-in landlord of this Chelsea brownstone. Movie lovers will remember that the actor had his greatest success on-screen as manager of the Bates

Motel in *Psycho* (1960). In 1973, at the age of forty-one, Perkins married photographer Berinthia (Berry) Berenson, sister of actress Marisa Berenson. The two lived mainly in Los Angeles, where they had two children, Osgood (named for Perkins's famous actor father) and Elvis. In 1992, Perkins died of AIDS. On September 11, 2001, his wife perished on a flight from Boston to Los Angeles, which crashed in western Pennsylvania after being taken over by terrorists.

12. EMPIRE DINER
210 Tenth Avenue

A bit of Americana at 22nd Street and Tenth Avenue, this vintage Art Deco diner was restored in the mid-1970s and turned into a trendy watering hole long before Chelsea became the hot neighborhood it is today. A natural for photography, the Empire's shiny stainless-steel façade has been used often for commercials and print ads and stands out among various NYC landmarks in the opening of Woody Allen's *Manhattan* (1979). Recent films

Empire Diner

that have used the location have been *Igby Goes Down* (2001), where it serves as a rendezvous for Sookie (Claire Danes) and her troubled boyfriend Igby (Kieran Culkin), and *Men in Black II* (2002), where Will Smith has dinner with the young woman (Rosario Dawson) whose life he has just saved from the usual aliens. *Law & Order* has also shot here.

13. CHELSEA PIERS SPORTS AND ENTERTAINMENT COMPLEX
Eleventh Avenue between 17th and 23rd Streets

For Manhattan sports fans who would rather play than just sit and watch, this dynamic complex, which was built in a cluster of extensively refurbished piers on the Hudson River in the mid-1990s, is the answer to their prayers. Here they will find a forty-lane bowling alley, a roller rink, two ice rinks, indoor running track, rock-climbing wall, Olympic swimming pool, gymnasium, sports medicine center, and—the first of its kind in Manhattan—a massive, net-covered golf driving range with fifty-two tee-off points on four levels. Movie fans will no doubt remember the

Inside *Law & Order*: Sam Waterston and Angie Harmon on the set at Chelsea Piers

scenes in *Serendipity* (2002), where John Cusack tries to relieve the stress of his unsuccessful quest for Kate Beckinsale by slamming golf balls out toward the Hudson River.

The Chelsea Piers are also home to one of the greatest success stories in New York television history. Known as Pier 62 and taking up most of the northernmost end of the building are the production offices and soundstages—including the courtroom set and the D.A. and detectives' offices—of *Law & Order,* currently the longest-running police series in the history of television and the second longest-running drama series after *Gunsmoke.* In addition to the original *Law & Order* series, Pier 62 also is the headquarters for its spinoffs—*Law & Order: Criminal Intent*, which shoots here, and *Law & Order: Special Victims Unit,* which films in North Bergen, New Jersey.

Movie lovers who visit Chelsea Piers should make a point of checking out the third-floor gallery, which displays photos and posters of the many productions that have been done here.

Visit www.chelseapiers.com.

14. CHELSEA HOTEL
222 West 23rd Street

A 23rd Street landmark, the red-brick, iron-balconied, mansard-roofed Chelsea Hotel opened in 1884 as one of the city's first cooperative apartment houses. In 1905 it became a hotel, but throughout its history the Chelsea has catered to long-term tenants. Over the years it has been especially popular with the literati: Mark Twain, Eugene O'Neill, O. Henry, Thomas Wolfe, Tennessee Williams, Vladimir Nabokov, Brendan Behan, Arthur Miller, Dylan Thomas, and William Burroughs have all called the Chelsea home from time to time. Plaques in the lobby commemorate many of these famous former residents. Sci-fi-movie lovers will be intrigued to learn that novelist Arthur C. Clarke penned the script for *2001: A Space Odyssey* while living at the Chelsea.

It was Andy Warhol, however, who put the Chelsea on movie lovers' maps back in 1966 when he started shooting artist Brigid Berlin in her Chelsea hotel room. This footage formed the basis for *The Chelsea Girls,* the film considered by many critics to be

Chelsea Hotel

Warhol's best, and also the first of Andy's flicks to score a solid commercial success. It's therefore no surprise that the Chelsea Hotel played a featured role in the 1996 film *I Shot Andy Warhol,* which re-created the late artist's 1960s heyday. The Chelsea can also be seen on screen as one of the spots where Mickey Rourke and Kim Basinger play out their short-lived but very intense sadomasochistic relationship in Adrian Lyne's kinky *9½ Weeks* (1986).

That same year, the Chelsea also played a big role in *Sid and Nancy,* the 1986 British film, set in the 1970s, that focuses on the druggy life and times of Sex Pistols rock star Sid Vicious (played by Gary Oldman), and a year later, in an ironic bit of filmmaking coming full-circle, the hotel was featured in the low-budget film *Anna,* starring Warhol actress Sally Kirkland.

More Chelsea movies include *The House on Carroll Street* (1988); *The Professional (*aka *Léon),* where its dramatic stairwell and corridors were combined with another location on East 97th Street to create the gritty apartment building where Natalie Portman and Jean Reno both lived in Luc Besson's 1994 thriller; and *Small Time Crooks* (2000).

Visit www.hotelchelsea.com.

15. CHELSEA TELEVISION STUDIOS
221 West 26th Street

This brick barn of a building was originally headquarters for the city's Ninth Mounted Cavalry division. When the unit moved to 14th Street in 1914, pioneer film producer Adolph Zukor found the spacious armory—which came complete with a tethering ring for its former equine occupants—a great place for making movies, and he turned it into a studio for his Famous Players Film Company. Featuring "Famous Players in Famous Plays," Zukor's company relied on talent from the New York stage, and his was the first movie company to bring Broadway matinee idol John Barrymore to the screen in *An American Citizen* and *That Man from Mexico,* both of which were produced on 26th Street in 1914. Other early Famous Players names were Marguerite Clark, Hazel Dawn, May Irving, and H. B. Warner.

Famous Players' biggest star was Mary Pickford, although by

Famous Players Film Company, ca. 1915

the time Zukor scooped her up in 1913, she had already made her mark both on Broadway and in films. A clever business-woman, "Little Mary" made film-business history in 1916 when Zukor signed her to a then unprecedented two-year, $2-million-plus contract. It was also in 1916 that Zukor's Famous Players merged with Jesse Lasky and Samuel Goldwyn to form the company that eventually became Paramount Pictures. Zukor continued to use the 26th Street studios, along with various other facilities in the city, until the end of the 1910s, at which time, the Famous Players–Lasky Company consolidated their operations into one large new studio complex in Astoria, Queens.

From 1920 on, the old Famous Players studio on West 26th Street had various incarnations, but in the 1950s the place wound up back in the movie business when producer Hyman Brown bought the property, gutted it, and created two sound-stages inside. Since then, the facility, known for decades as Production-Center Studios, has seen constant movie/TV activity. Among the features that have been shot here since the 1950s are MGM's *Butterfield 8* (1960), Sidney Lumet's *Twelve Angry Men* (1957), *Long Day's Journey into Night* (1961), *The Anderson Tapes* (1971), William Friedkin's *The Night They Raided Min-sky's* (1968), *The Boys in the Band* (1970), *The French Connec-tion* (1971), Mel Brooks's *The Producers* (1967), and Francis Ford Coppola's *You're a Big Boy Now* (1967), which he pre-sented as his thesis for his Master of Fine Arts at UCLA. The stu-dio's TV hits have included Phil Silvers's *Sergeant Bilko* series, CBS's *Show of the Week*, *The Patty Duke Show, Inner Sanctum,* and episodes of Jackie Gleason's *The Honeymooners*. From the early 1970s to the late 1990s, the CBS soap opera *The Guid-ing Light* was based at the historic studio, which today as the Chelsea Television Studios is home to the *Ricki Lake* show and *Judge Hatchett*.

16. KINETOSCOPE PARLOR SITE
1155 Broadway

On April 6, 1894, the Holland Brothers' Kinetoscope Parlor opened in a storefront in a small brick building on the southwest corner of 27th Street and Broadway. A great illuminated dragon

Inside a Kinetoscope parlor, ca. 1895

with green eyes and a red tongue was suspended above the entrance and invited customers inside to see the latest bit of wizardry from Thomas Edison: a peep show–like contraption, called a Kinetoscope, which provided the public with its first glance at true motion pictures. The films lasted less than a minute and documented such simple scenes as a man sneezing, a woman dancing, or a baby being given a bath, but it wasn't the subject matter that pulled the crowds in to 1155 Broadway; it was the novelty, indeed the magic, of seeing real life captured on celluloid. The Kinetoscope parlors were an overnight sensation, and they quickly proliferated all across the country. Their moment in the sun was brief, however, for just two years later Edison unveiled his first projector, the Vitascope, and this turned movies from private peep shows into public spectacles. But the Kinetoscope parlor paved the way for films as we know them, and thus 1155 Broadway is a very important site in the history of the movies. Today, a small hotel occupies the site.

17. METROPOLITAN LIFE INSURANCE COMPANY
11 Madison Square

It was in this monumental Manhattan office building that the Vietnam vet/janitor played by William Hurt supposedly swept up and mopped marble floors in the 1981 thriller *Eyewitness*. It was also here that a Vietnamese businessman was brutally murdered at the beginning of the film, which is the incident that ultimately gets Hurt involved with TV news reporter Sigourney Weaver. The location where much of *Eyewitness* was shot is the handsome 1932 North Building of the Metropolitan Life Insurance Company. An especially dramatic architectural feature of the building is its set of four massive arcaded, golden-gated entryways—one on each corner of the block-square structure. For *Eyewitness*, director Peter Yates made extensive use of the southwest entrance, which provided an intriguing backdrop for the sequences where Ms. Weaver and her camera crew interview Hurt after the murder. The fact that Madison Square is just across the street was an added attraction of the location, since it offered an interesting space for Hurt to park his motorcycle, and the beautiful Greek temple–like building of the Appellate Division of the

Sigourney Weaver with *Eyewitness* William Hurt outside the Metropolitan Life Building, 1981

New York State Supreme Court next door was icing on the cake, further adding to *Eyewitness*'s visual appeal.

Other directors to cash in on the Metropolitan Life's cinematic assets have been Martin Scorsese, who made it Griffin Dunne's office in *After Hours* (1985); Woody Allen, who used it to represent a broadcasting network building in *Radio Days* (1986); Robert Clane, who set up Andrew McCarthy and Jonathan Silverman in business here for his 1989 black comedy *Weekend at Bernie's*; and Terry Gilliam, who made it the gilded, gated workplace for the object of street person Robin Williams's affection (Amanda Plummer) in *The Fisher King* (1991).

18. BELLEVUE HOSPITAL CENTER
First Avenue from 25th to 30th Streets

To millions of movie and TV lovers, the word "Bellevue" is synonymous with psycho ward. And no wonder: In *Miracle on 34th Street* (1947), Macy's eccentric Kris Kringle is sent to Bellevue for observation; in *The Lost Weekend* (1945), the chronic alcoholic played by Ray Milland has a very bad time of it in Bellevue's detox unit. It's also where Dracula (George Hamilton) is committed in *Love at First Bite* (1979) and where, according to a line in the script, the deranged psychiatrist played by Michael Caine in *Dressed to Kill* (1980) supposedly "did some work." Although Bellevue is best known for its psychiatric section, it is actually a vast and diverse New York City health-care facility. Tracing its beginnings to 1736, it is also the oldest general hospital on the North American continent.

Recent films that have been admitted to this famous hospital include *The Devil's Advocate* (1997), *Conspiracy Theory* (1997), *City Hall* (1998), *Meet Joe Black* (1998), *Last Days of Disco* (1998), *Autumn in New York* (2000), *Igby Goes Down* (2002), and *The Yards* (2002)—but the motion picture that best captured the scope of Bellevue's operations was undoubtedly the 1950 Universal-International film noir *The Sleeping City*. Shot totally on location at the historic hospital, the film takes us on a two-hour tour that provides insider glimpses of rarely seen areas such as the residents' dorms, the chapel, cocktail lounge, pool room, trauma ward, basement, and Victorian rooftop (where the film's dramatic climax takes place). Almost as interesting as *The Sleeping City* is the disclaimer that precedes it. It seems that when Bellevue officials saw the film—which deals with drugs, blackmail, and murder inside Bellevue—they became quite upset. In order to appease the hospital authorities and to get *The Sleeping City* into release, Universal-International had to shoot a special opening sequence in which the film's star, Richard Conte, assured the audience that what they were about to see on-screen was totally fictitious. In what then amounted to a commercial for the hospital, Conte went on to extol the virtues of the real Bellevue and wound up showing architectural renderings of the additions that hospital administrators planned to build around the haunting, original Victorian brick buildings used so effectively in *The Sleeping City*.

19. MARBLE COLLEGIATE CHURCH
1 West 29th Street/272 Fifth Avenue

One of New York's prettiest churches, this landmark 1854 neo-Gothic was the longtime base of pop preacher, the late Dr. Norman Vincent Peale, who was frequently seen on television in the 1960s and 1970s. Marble Collegiate's biggest media event, however, took place in March 2002, when Liza Minnelli, after a brush with death, a major weight loss, a possible face-lift, and a stint in rehab, got married for the fourth time to concert promoter David Gest. Despite the fact that the bride had just turned fifty-six, it was one of those weddings that little girls dream of: gorgeous ivory gown (Bob Mackie), beautiful flower-filled church (Marble Collegiate), fifteen bridesmaids . . . the works! It was also the kind of event the tabloids dream of, and Minnelli and Gest, perhaps realizing this fact, gave the U.K.'s trashy *OK!* magazine exclusive photo rights for reportedly close to $1 million. And what photos they were—from Liza and her rumored-to-be-gay husband's multiminute lizard kiss at the altar to the motley B-list wedding party—which included a white-haired Elizabeth Taylor and toy soldier–attired best man Michael Jackson. Then there were the real dinosaurs—like poor Jane Russell, gossip columnist Cindy Adams, and Gina Lollobrigida. And the stories: matron of honor Liz's delaying the ceremony by almost an hour because she had forgotten her shoes and gofers had to be sent back to her hotel to get them. But the biggest tabloid feast came seventeen months after the Marble Collegiate affair, when reports surfaced

Site of Minnelli marriage
number 4: Marble
Collegiate Church

that the Gests were splitting. These were followed by Mr. Gest's
$10 million lawsuit claiming that Liza mentally and physically
abused him, treating him like a punching bag, pummeling and
slapping him during her alleged booze-fueled rages. Even though
it took place in New York, this was the Hollywood wedding to
end all weddings, or as *Vanity Fair* writer Dominick Dunne put it,
it was "one of the great sustained camp events of the decade."

Visit www.marblechurch.org.

20. CHURCH OF THE TRANSFIGURATON
1 East 29th Street

Nicknamed the Little Church Around the Corner, this pretty little mid-eighteenth-century Episcopal Church with its lovely garden has always been popular with theater folk. Supposedly the
reason is that in 1870, a nearby church refused to bury an actor
and suggested the rites be held at "the little church around the

corner." Among the most famous former members of the congregation are Gertrude Lawrence and Edwin Booth, both of whom are remembered in stained-glass windows. A more recent show-biz connection involves the randy Samantha (Kim Cattrall) of *Sex and the City* notoriety, who fancied (and struck out with) one of the church's handsome priests, whom she dubbed "the Friar." For the series, the church converted temporarily to Roman Catholicism. The historic church—which gave shelter to runaway slaves during the Civil War era—was also the site of Susan Sarandon's funeral in *Igby Goes Down* (2001).

Visit www.littlechurch.org.

21. MARTHA WASHINGTON HOTEL/THIRTY THIRTY HOTEL
30 East 30th Street

When it opened at the beginning of the twentieth century, this small Murray Hill hotel was the Martha Washington Hotel for Women and offered safe and respectable accommodation for single women travelers and residents. It is best known to cult movie lovers, however, as the first stop in Barbara Parkins's odyssey from a small town in New England to the Big-Apple Big Time in the 1967 camp classic screen version of Jacqueline Susann's equally over-the-top novel, *Valley of the Dolls*. Today, the Martha Washington has been spiffed up for the new millennium and renamed for its unique address.

Visit www.thirtythirty-nyc.com.

22. AMERICAN ACADEMY OF DRAMATIC ARTS
120 Madison Avenue

This landmark 1905 Georgian building was designed by Stanford White for the ultra-exclusive women's club the Colony. Since 1963, however, it has been headquarters for the American Academy of Dramatic Arts, which had been based at the ANTA Theater (now the Virginia) on West 52nd Street and before that had operated out of a basement studio at Carnegie Hall. Actress Helen Hayes was very influential in orchestrating, and helping to raise the funds for, the Academy's move to Madison Avenue, and today the Academy's theater is named in honor of Miss Hayes's actress daughter, Mary MacArthur, who died of bulbar polio in 1949 when she was just nineteen years old.

Founded in 1884, the American Academy of Dramatic Arts claims to be "the oldest school of professional dramatic training in the English-speaking world." The number of pros who have studied with the institution over the years is staggering. In 2003, AADA graduate Adrian Brody won the Academy Award for Best Actor for his performance in *The Pianist*. Among the school's other big names: Lauren Bacall, Jim Backus, Conrad Bain, Anne Bancroft, John Cassavetes, Hume Cronyn, Robert Cummings, Brad Davis, Kim Cattrall, Cecil B. DeMille, William Devane, Danny DeVito, Colleen Dewhurst, Kirk Douglas, Vincent Edwards, James Farentino, Ruth Gordon, David Hartman, Florence Henderson, Judd Hirsch, Kate Jackson, John James, Jennifer Jones, Grace Kelly, Dina Merrill, Elizabeth Montgomery, Agnes Moorehead, Don Murray, William Powell, Robert Redford, Don Rickles, Thelma Ritter, Jason Robards, Eric Roberts, Edward G. Robinson, Gena Rowlands, Rosalind Russell, John Savage, John Saxon, Joseph Schildkraut, Loretta Swit, Renée Taylor, Spencer Tracy, Claire Trevor, Robert Walker, and Peter Weller.

Visit www.aada.org.

━━━━━━ **AADA HALL OF FAME QUIZ** ━━━━━━

Can you match these famous former students' names to their faces? *(See bottom of page for the answers.)*

1. Kirk Douglas
2. Agnes Moorehead
3. Jim Backus
4. Joseph Schildkraut
5. Cecil B. DeMille
6. Spencer Tracy
7. Rosalind Russell
8. Robert Redford
9. Edward G. Robinson
10. Danny DeVito
11. Grace Kelly
12. Anne Bancroft

Answers:
1 L. 2 H. 3 G. 4 K. 5 D. 6 C. 7 J. 8 I. 9 E. 10 F. 11 B. 12 A.

A

B

E

F

I

J

C

D

G

H

K

L

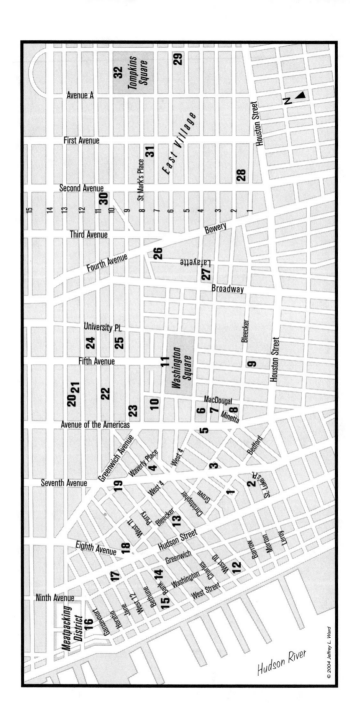

Greenwich Village: The Big Back Lot

Greenwich Village is New York City on a different scale. It is low-rise; there are lots of trees; people live in houses; you can see the sky. Needless to say, with so much going for it visually, the Village has been one of the most photographed areas of the city. This is especially true nowadays, with the resurgence of filmmaking in New York, and on practically any given day you can find a movie, television series, or commercial being shot somewhere in the Village. Quite simply, the Village is New York City's back lot—and in this chapter, movie lovers will discover many of the same Greenwich Village addresses found in directors' and location managers' notebooks—including such television classics as the *Friends* apartment building, *The Cosby Show* townhouse, and the *NYPD Blue* precinct.

Besides location-spotting, movie lovers who visit the Village will also find avant-garde cinemas, clubs, and cabarets that provided employment (both on- and offstage) to future stars during the dues-paying periods of their careers, even a secret sidewalk that has the footprints of legendary movie stars like Joan Crawford and Gloria Swanson.

1. GREENWICH VILLAGE "BACK LOT"
Bedford/Grove/Barrow/Commerce Streets

In the days when Hollywood's Paramount Studios still had its back lot, the New York section was said to have been modeled on this cluster of blocks in Greenwich Village. Indeed, wandering around this enchanting enclave of tiny townhouses, fantasy cottages, ivy-covered apartment buildings, cozy courtyards and mews, you wonder for a second whether you're really in New York or in some Hollywood art director's vision of the city. You may be further confused if you happen to have ventured onto Bedford, Grove, Barrow, or Commerce Streets on one of the many days or nights when a film crew is on the scene with trucks, trailers, lights, cameras, stars, and extras.

Directors love to shoot in this neighborhood—not only for the varied architecture, but because these little streets are easily sealed off from traffic and crowds. Major landmarks for movie lovers to look for—either on-screen or on a walking tour of NYC's own back lot—are Chumley's, a former speakeasy at 86 Bedford Street that is now a bar/restaurant and that still has no sign. Chumley's has been used as a typical NYC tavern in the features *Reds* (1981), *Wolfen* (1981), *Bright Lights, Big City*

Greenwich Village *Friends*: Matthew Perry, Jennifer Aniston, David Schwimmer, Courteney Cox, Matt LeBlanc, Lisa Kudrow

Friends apartment
building at Bedford
and Grove

(1988), Woody Allen's *Sweet and Lowdown* (1999), and *Pollock* (2000), actor-director Ed Harris's look at the short turbulent life and career of artist Jackson Pollock. Harris also used the doorway at 52 Barrow Street, which is just off Chumley's "secret" Barrow Street courtyard entrance, to represent Pollock's apartment. When art patron Peggy Guggenheim (Amy Madigan) arrives to check out the hot young artist's work and finds there's no elevator in the building, she remarks, "I don't climb up five flights of stairs." Her sixth sense tells her to climb, however, and she likes what she sees when she gets there. (In reality, this building has only two stories.)

Close by, at 38 Commerce Street, the tiny Cherry Lane Theater, founded by poet Edna St. Vincent Millay in 1924, is a famous off-Broadway playhouse and another popular back-lot location. It has doubled as the historic Provincetown Playhouse in *Reds* (1981), became a jazz club in Claude Lelouch's *Bolero* (1982), was the little theater where Gena Rowlands dreams of an off-Broadway/Times Square version of her life in Woody Allen's *Another Woman* (1988), and was once again a jazz club—called Beneath the Underdog—where Denzel Washington played trumpet in Spike Lee's *Mo' Better Blues* (1990). The Cherry Lane was also used by Tina Turner for the classic music video of her hit song "What's Love Got to Do with It?" In real life, the Cherry Lane saw James Dean perform on its stage in the 1954 off-Broadway production of *Women of Trachis*.

Just a few feet away from the Cherry Lane, the restaurant at 50 Commerce Street is another back-lot landmark. Formerly Grange Hall, it was a lunch spot for Edward Burns in *The Brothers McMullen* (1995), the comedy he also wrote and directed focusing on the lives and loves of three Irish-American brothers. A few years later, Woody Allen used it for *Anything Else* (2003); as did Martin Scorsese—not for a feature film, but rather a commercial (which he does occasionally—for big bucks, no doubt) for a French cell-phone company. Grange Hall's most recent appearance was in the final episode of *Sex and the City*. Shortly after the episode was lensed, Grange Hall shut down as well. It has since resurfaced as the Blue Mill Tavern, which is what it was for many years prior to its Grange Hall incarnation.

The most famous location on the Village back lot can be found at 90 Bedford Street, at the corner of Grove Street. It's hard to miss, especially since there are usually groups of tourists photographing this rather unprepossessing brick apartment building with a French restaurant below. Reason? It was here that four (Rachel, Monica, Chandler, and Joey) out of six New York *Friends* lived for most of the hit show's ten-year run. *Friends* fans may also recognize the Lucille Lortel Theater, just a short block away at 121 Christopher Street, as the off-Broadway house where Joey (Matt LeBlanc) once starred in a play.

Back over on Grove Street, the lovely little red house at number 12 belonged to Angela Lansbury in *The World of Henry Orient* (1964). Next door, another secret courtyard—Grove Court—conceals six small houses and a lovely garden. Closer to Bleecker Street, 26 Grove Street was where John Ritter cavorted in *Hero at Large* (1980). Around the corner, the half-timbered place with the twin-peaked roof at 102 Bedford Street was supposed to have been a trendy discothèque in *The April Fools* (1969), which starred Jack Lemmon and Catherine Deneuve. Next door, the clapboard cottage at 100 Bedford was the workshop of the sashmaker who once lived in the handsome frame house on the corner at 17 Grove Street, which was built in 1822. In 1970, Sandy Dennis and Jack Lemmon were seen scaling down the side of this historic house in *The Out-of-Towners*, whereas in 1985, Woody Allen and Mia Farrow passed by this picturesque corner in their pursuit of metropolitan happiness in *Hannah and Her Sisters*. In late 1987, Mr. Allen again turned up on Grove Street to shoot sequences for *Another Woman*.

Number 106 Bedford Street is another standard-issue New York City brick apartment house, but it may also be of interest to movie lovers, as it was here that Lawrence Selman lived. A neighborhood celebrity, this little man, whose developmental disabilities have not kept him from living a full life as an activ-

Cherry Lane Theater

ist and fund-raiser, was the subject of the 2003 Academy Award–nominated short film *The Collector of Bedford Street*. Farther down Bedford, at the corner of Morton, now occupied by a trendy Greek taverna called Snack, another back-lot local, philosopher-chef Kenny Shopsin, ran a funky love-it-or-loathe-it lunch counter called Shopsin's for decades. When the crusty restaurateur (famous for his less-than-charming counterside manner) lost his lease, filmmaker Matt Mahurin did a full-length documentary on the man and his enterprise titled *I Like Killing Flies,* which was a surprise hit at the 2004 Sundance Film Festival. (Kenny currently holds forth a few blocks away at 54 Carmine Street.)

Just around the corner from the old Shopsin's, the brownstone building at 66 Morton Street is where Kevin Anderson had a flat that he famously sublet in *The Night We Never Met* (1993); the same building housed Harrison Ford in *Working Girl* (1988) and Winona Ryder in *Autumn in New York* (2000). Back on Bedford Street, architecture buffs will find Greenwich Village's oldest house (which dates back to 1799), the brick-and-wood dwelling back at number 77. For movie lovers, however, the skinny house next door at 75 Bedford may be of more interest, since it was one of John Barrymore's early New York residences. The city's narrowest house, at just nine-and-one-half feet wide, was also home to poet Edna St. Vincent Millay.

2. ST. LUKE'S PLACE

This may well be NYC's most beautiful and most frequently photographed block. Lying between Seventh Avenue South and Hudson Street, St. Luke's Place boasts trees, old-fashioned street lamps, and fifteen elegant brick townhouses all in a row. Built in the 1850s, these Italianate beauties have been home to a number of famous New Yorkers. Mayor Jimmy Walker—whose wild and woolly life was romanticized by Bob Hope in the 1957 Paramount film *Beau James*—once lived at number 6. Playwright Sherwood Anderson occupied number 12, poet Marianne Moore had number 14, and Theodore Dreiser, whose novel *An American Tragedy* became the 1951 Paramount film *A Place in the Sun,* starring Elizabeth Taylor and Montgomery Clift, called

Cosby Show townhouse, St. Luke's Place

number 16 home. This beautiful block has also lured many film-makers. Its most famous screen appearance was in *Wait Until Dark* (1967), with the house at number 4 serving as the NYC apartment where the blind woman played by Audrey Hepburn was terrorized by a thug (Alan Arkin) who operated out of a van parked across the street in front of the playground. Part of the playground, by the way, is occupied by a public swimming pool, which movie lovers will recognize as the spot where Cathy Moriarty and Robert De Niro met up in Martin Scorsese's *Raging Bull* (1980).

Back across the street, 10 St. Luke's Place was the prime-time townhouse where Bill Cosby resided with his Huxtable TV family on *The Cosby Show*. *Ragtime* (1980) and *The Survivors*

(1983) have also used St. Luke's Place as a location, as has *Sex and the City, Law & Order,* and countless TV commercials and print ads.

3. *HESTER STREET* BLOCK
Morton Street between Seventh Avenue and Bleecker Street

Hester Street was a charming little black-and-white film about Jewish immigrants living on NYC's Lower East Side at the beginning of the century. But the film's director, Joan Micklin Silver, had a hard time finding the Lower East Side of her story in 1970s New York. The real Hester Street, having turned into a thriving commercial district of discount clothing and electronics stores, looked all wrong; whereas other parts of the historic neighborhood were too devastated even to consider. So *Hester Street* and company headed north and created their own "Lower East Side"

Hester Street on Morton Street, 1974

on a wonderfully isolated block of Morton Street that is pretty much unchanged architecturally since the early 1900s. The metamorphosis of Morton Street involved masking streetlamps and adding awnings to some of the buildings to create historically accurate storefronts. Props such as pushcarts and vintage automobiles completed the picture.

Other Village blocks that have been dressed for the movies include East 6th Street between Avenues A and B for *The Godfather* (1972) and East 11th Street between Avenues A and B for *Ragtime* (1981).

4. THE DUPLEX
61 Christopher Street

Originally across Seventh Avenue at 55 Grove Street, this legendary Village cabaret, founded in 1950, is where former unknowns like Joan Rivers, Jo Anne Worley, Rodney Dangerfield, Stiller and Meara, and Woody Allen got some of their first professional gigs. Of Woody's Duplex days it is said that when the comic couldn't get a rise out of his audience, he penciled in a mustache and started doing Groucho Marx's jokes. If they laughed, then he knew that his material needed work; if they didn't, he could blame it on the audience. Today, in its new location, the Duplex mainly features drag shows like *Dressing Room Divas,* but one old-timer who comes back periodically is Joan Rivers, who tried out many of the jokes she used in her highly successful one-woman show in London in 2002.

Visit www.theduplex.com.

5. IFC CENTER/WAVERLY THEATER SITE
323 Avenue of the Americas

"I met a boy named Frank Mills/In front of the Waverly/But, unfortunately,/I lost his address." The world heard about this Greenwich Village neighborhood movie house from the song "Frank Mills" in the legendary 1960s Broadway musical *Hair*. But, unfortunately, moviegoers didn't get to see the Waverly in Milos Forman's film version of *Hair* in 1979, because the sequence didn't make the final cut. The theater was not cut out of *Six Degrees of Separation* (1993), however, where it furnishes the background for a climactic scene in which troubled con-artist Will Smith is taken away by the police at the end of the film.

Situated at the top of the stairs of Greenwich Village's bustling West 4th Street subway station, the Waverly has always been a place where people from different parts of Manhattan, Brooklyn, Queens, and the Bronx can rendezvous fairly easily for a night at the movies. This central location may have accounted for the success of its midnight shows, which have pulled in teens from far and wide for cult classics like *The Rocky Horror Picture Show, Eraserhead*, and *Polyester*. These days, however, the Waverly, which was a church before it was converted to a movie house in 1937, is set to begin an exciting new life as the Independent Film Channel Center. This ultramodern triplex—with digital projection capabilities—hopes to be New York's premier showcase for independent films.

Visit www.ifcfilms.com.

6. JOHN BARRYMORE RESIDENCE
132 West 4th Street

John Blythe Barrymore lived on the top floor of this West 4th Street townhouse off Washington Square between 1917 and 1920. Although Barrymore had appeared in films for Adolph Zukor's Famous Players Film Company since 1913, he was still better known as a Broadway matinee idol than a movie star. Nonetheless, Barrymore's 1920 screen performance in *Dr. Jekyll and Mr. Hyde* brought him great acclaim, and his transformation from mild-mannered M.D. to monster, supposedly done without the aid of trick photography, was much discussed at the time. *Dr. Jekyll and Mr. Hyde* was made in New York at the Famous Players Studio that once stood at 130 West 56th Street.

Back in Greenwich Village, Barrymore's penthouse was lavishly appointed with gilded Chinese wallpaper, expensive European antiques, and a large roof garden. To create the latter, Barrymore brought in some thirty-five tons of topsoil and planted wisteria, cherry trees, and grapevines. This was his secret hideaway during an uncharacteristically introspective period of

John Barrymore, right, as Mr. Hyde in *Dr. Jekyll and Mr. Hyde,* 1920

his life. It is reported that Barrymore, who was known for his amorous adventures, even shunned the company of women for the first year or so that he spent in his Greenwich Village aerie. His fling with celibacy and the contemplative life did not last long, however, for he soon met and fell in love with Blanche Thomas, a very married poetess who went by the name of Michael Strange. A tempestuous courtship ensued, and in 1920 Mrs. Thomas became Mrs. Barrymore, and the couple moved to White Plains.

In the late 1980s, playwright-screenwriter (*The Addams Family* [1990], *In and Out* [1997]) Paul Rudnick lived in the Barrymore apartment, rumored to be haunted by the famous actor. Whether it was or not, it inspired Rudnick's 1991 Broadway play *I Hate Hamlet*, which told of a young actor living in a Big Apple apartment haunted by Barrymore's ghost. During the run of the show, there were no ectoplasmic incidents, but there was a newsmaking moment when the tantrum-prone Scottish star Nicol Williamson, who played Barrymore, went a little too far in a dueling scene, nicking costar Evan Handler, who walked off-stage and never returned. Today, Handler is less known for the *I Hate Hamlet* incident than for his role as Harry Goldenblatt, the lawyer Charlotte York (Kristin Davis) married and converted to Judaism for on *Sex and the City.*

Caffe Reggio

7. CAFFE REGGIO
119 MacDougal Street

The ultimate Greenwich Village coffeehouse—dark, formerly smoky, with tiny tables, background classical music punctuated by the constant whoosh of the espresso/cappuccino machine. No wonder Paul Mazursky used it as a location for his tragicomic take on early-1950s Bohemian life in *Next Stop, Greenwich Village* (1975). The same café also turns up in such other set-in-the-Village epics as *Shaft* (1971) and *Serpico* (1973), and flashes by, too, in *The Godfather, Part II* (1974), *The Next Man* (1976), and *13 Going on 30* (2004), and on episodes of *The Equalizer* and *Law & Order*. Meanwhile, movie lovers may remember another landmark Greenwich Village coffeehouse, Le Figaro Café, just down the street at the corner of Bleecker and MacDougal as the spot where ex-con Al Pacino got reacquainted with his old girlfriend Penelope Ann Miller in *Carlito's Way* (1993).

Visit www.caffereggio.com.

8. *SERPICO* HOUSE
5-7 Minetta Street

Based on a true story, *Serpico* (1973) was a hard-hitting Sidney Lumet film that starred Al Pacino as a New York City under-cover cop who tried to rectify major corruption among New York's Finest. In the film, the title character, Frank Serpico, was an offbeat guy from Brooklyn who fancied Greenwich Village life. He took courses at New York University, tried hanging out with the coffeehouse crowd, and lived in a basement pad with a tiny rear garden where he could often be found listening to opera records. The quintessential Greenwich Village apartment build-ing used for *Serpico* stands just off the Avenue of the Americas on Minetta Street. Only one block long, Minetta Street is espe-cially attractive to cinematographers because it is easy to block

Serpico's pad

off and because it curves in such a way that there's never any danger of seeing anything else—such as the nearby Avenue of the Americas—even in a long shot.

At the other end of this little block, movie lovers may also recognize the Minetta Tavern at 113 MacDougal Street as the place where attorney Brad Pitt had a get-together with the childhood friends he got acquitted of murder charges in *Sleepers* (1996), and also as an establishment called La Trattoria in *Mickey Blue Eyes* (1998). In the film the restaurant was owned by the mafia-connected James Caan, who had little in common with British auctioneer Hugh Grant other than the fact that Grant was about to marry his daughter.

9. KIM'S VIDEO III/BLEECKER ST. CINEMA SITE
144 Bleecker Street

Now home to an eclectic video store, this site was once the very eclectic Bleecker Street Cinema movie theater. Where else could Woody Allen, playing a movie lover in his 1989 *Crimes and Misdemeanors,* catch Hitchcock's little-known 1937 comedy *Mr. and Mrs. Smith* or Betty Hutton's 1943 musical *Happy Go Lucky*? And in the mid-1980s, what better cinema than this to have seen *Desperately Seeking Susan* (1985), since this is the very movie house where Aidan Quinn supposedly worked as a projectionist in Susan Seidelman's offbeat look at life in Lower Manhattan. Village history buffs may be interested in the fact that the two buildings that housed the Bleecker Street Cinema were once home to a landmark restaurant of the 1880s called Mori's.

10. *BAREFOOT IN THE PARK* HOUSE
111 Waverly Place

In the play version of Neil Simon's *Barefoot in the Park*, newly-weds Corie and Paul Bratter spend three acts coping with the perils of setting up housekeeping in pre-Yuppie Manhattan on the top floor of a brownstone in the East 40s. For the film version, however, Neil Simon and director Gene Saks decided that Greenwich Village would offer a more picturesque backdrop than the Upper East Side. Thus they transplanted the Bratters,

Jane of Washington Square: Fonda in *Barefoot in the Park*, 1967

played by Robert Redford and Jane Fonda, to a red-brick "brownstone" with a steep stoop and wrought-iron balustrades on Waverly Place, just off Washington Square Park. Other Village locations used for the film (interiors were done at Paramount Studios in Hollywood) included a Sixth Avenue deli, West 10th Street, lower Fifth Avenue, and, of course, Washington Square Park, where, toward the end of the film, we find a tipsy Robert Redford dancing . . . barefoot in the park.

11. WASHINGTON SQUARE PARK

If Greenwich Village has a center, this is it. Formerly the site of public hangings, Washington Square Park was turned into a public recreational park in the 1820s. It is distinguished by its handsome Ionic Greek Revival townhouses, some dating back to the 1830s, and by its grand Beaux Arts arch, which was erected in 1895 and which has become a symbol of Downtown Manhattan. Needless to say, the arch has turned up in many films—from *On the Town* (1949) to *Barefoot in the Park* (1966) to *When*

Harry Met Sally (1989), where it furnished the highly romantic backdrop for Meg Ryan and Billy Crystal to unromantically decide early on in the film that they can't be friends (only to become lovers in the final reel).

Since it is shared by drug dealers, students, chess players, joggers, and well-heeled denizens of the smart townhouses and apartment buildings that surround it, the park itself is a microcosm of the heady mix of humanity that makes up Greenwich Village. Films that have capitalized on its egalitarian dimension include *Searching for Bobby Fisher* (1993), which starred Laurence Fishburne as a regular at the Park's Chess Table Alley; *Kids* (1995), Larry Clark's shocking look at a gang of NYC street kids, who brutally beat up a man in the Performance Pit, while the rest of the park people look elsewhere; *Addicted to Love* (1997), where the jilted duo of Meg Ryan and Matthew Broderick take revenge on their former lovers via man-biting monkeys and perfume-spritzing kids with water pistols at the same Performance Pit; and *A Perfect Murder* (1998), where megarich Upper East Sider Michael Douglas pays $400,000 to small-time crook Viggo Mortensen, a transaction complicated by angry dogs, obtrusive Rollerbladers, a purse snatcher, and a near miss with a truck on the SW corner.

And then there's *The Heiress,* the famous 1949 Hollywood film, which starred Olivia de Havilland, Ralph Richardson, and Montgomery Clift, and was based on the Henry James novella, *Washington Square,* set at the house of Dr. James Sloper and his spinster daughter, at 16 Washington Square North. For the film, the house as well as Washington Square were created on a Hollywood back lot, but for the 1997 Jennifer Jason Leigh–Albert Finney–Ben Chaplin remake—called *Washington Square*—a real Greek Revival townhouse was used. It wasn't in New York, however, but in Union Square Park in Baltimore, Maryland, where most of the film was shot. Henry James himself lived at 1 Washington Square North, by the way, a fact that posh British art dealer Hugh Grant, in his efforts to raise the culture level of nouveau-riche Tracey Ullman in Woody Allen's *Small Time Crooks* (2000), points out. That scene *was* shot on location in Washington Square.

12. BADLANDS
388 West Street

Facing the Hudson River and its beautiful new esplanade and re-developed piers–turned–parks, Badlands is a remnant of the area's raunchier days. Currently a gay video store, Badlands was formerly a gay bar of the same name that was much in the news in 1979, when director William Friedkin used it and other nearby locations for scenes for *Cruising*. The film starred Al Pacino as an underground cop looking for a serial killer who preyed on gay victims. Many gay activists considered the film and its self-loathing gay murderer homophobic and protested the filming. One protest had a crowd of a thousand marching through the Village chanting "*Cruising* must go," after then mayor Ed Koch had refused demands that the city withdraw permits for the filming. Perhaps Friedkin should have paid more attention to the protests, since the film, if not a milestone in homophobia, was a major bomb.

13. SAMBRANCO ANTIQUES
370 Bleecker Street

In both Virginia Woolf's novel *Mrs. Dalloway* and in Michael Cunningham's book-turned-film *The Hours* (2002), which was inspired by it, flowers play an important role. The first line of Woolf's book is "Mrs. Dalloway said she would buy the flowers herself," whereas the first time we see Meryl Streep in the film, she's buying flowers for a party she's giving that day for her dying poet friend, Ed Harris. For the film, the production passed on using a real flower shop because, well, frankly, the problem with a real flower shop is the flowers! There are just too many of them and flower shops are designed to display and sell flowers—not accommodate fussy art directors, much less cameras, lighting equipment, and production crews. So, for their all-important flower shop, *The Hours* redid an antique store on Bleecker Street, which simply cleared out the antiques to the back storage area and let the production designers bring in all the right blooms.

In an intriguing bit of insider cameo casting, the woman who sells Streep the flowers in *The Hours* is the esteemed British actress Eileen Atkins, whose Virginia Woolf connections are especially impressive. She has twice portrayed Virginia Woolf on the New York stage, both in her one-woman show *A Room of One's Own* (which Atkins wrote) and in *Vita and Virginia,* a two-character play in which Atkins costarred with Vanessa Redgrave, who played Woolf's friend and one-time lover Vita Sackville-West. Furthermore, Atkins adapted *Mrs. Dalloway* for the 1997 film directed by Marleen Gorris and starring Vanessa Redgrave.

14. HB STUDIO
120 Bank Street

Based on Bank Street since 1957, this prestigious acting school was founded in 1943 by Austrian-born actor/director Herbert Berghoff. Among the many former HB students who have found show-business fame are Anne Bancroft, Candice Bergen, Matthew Broderick, Peggy Cass, Stockard Channing, Jill Clayburgh, James Coco, Robert De Niro, Faye Dunaway, Whoopi Goldberg, Judd Hirsch, Hal Holbrook, Harvey Korman, Jack Lemmon, Lorna Luft, William H. Macy, Dina Merrill, Bette Midler, Liza Minnelli, Al Pacino, Christopher Reeve, Eva Marie Saint, Lily Tomlin, and Sam Waterston.

Noted for its star teachers as well as for its famous graduates, HB counts playwright/screenwriter Horton Foote (*The Trip to Bountiful*), actors Charles Nelson Reilly, Jerry Stiller, Anne Jackson, and the late Sandy Dennis and William Hickey (*Prizzi's Honor*) as recent members of its faculty. The studio's legendary top teacher was Herbert Berghoff's wife of many years, Uta Hagen, who died in 2004. Although Hagen originated the role of Martha in Edward Albee's *Who's Afraid of Virginia Woolf?* on Broadway in 1963, Elizabeth Taylor won her second Oscar when she played the same role in the 1966 film version of the play. After many years on the stage, Miss Hagen finally made her film debut in 1972 as the Russian grandmother of those strange twin boys in *The Other*. She later appeared in featured roles in *The Boys from Brazil* (1978) and *Reversal of Fortune* (1990), in which she played the personal maid of Sunny von Bülow (Glenn Close). Hagen is best remembered, however, as one of the world's most influential acting teachers.

Visit www.hbstudio.org.

15. WESTBETH
463 West Street

Since 1970 this huge complex of brick loft buildings has provided low-cost housing for Manhattan artists. Dating back to
1896, the buildings of Westbeth—as the place is known in its
present incarnation—were originally the headquarters of the Bell
Telephone/Western Electric Laboratories, one of the most important research facilities in communications technology in the
country. Among the wonders developed here were the vacuum
tube and the condenser microphone, a dynamic duo that made
it possible to electronically amplify, as well as to record, sound.
These discoveries, in turn, paved the way for something that
Edison had wanted to do with motion pictures from the very beginning: make them talk. It was not until 1923, however, that
Western Electric scientists came up with a practical system of
synchronized sound for the movies. Offering the process—which
was dubbed Vitaphone, and which featured a sound disc that

Making movies talk: Vitaphone system at work

was synchronized with the camera—to various movie studios, Western Electric met with little interest from an industry that was content to make fabulous profits from silent films. Only one company had the foresight to realize the potential of sound: Warner Bros., which quickly signed an exclusive agreement to use the Vitaphone sound-on-disc technology for its films.

Interestingly enough, Warners didn't want Vitaphone to make its pictures talk, but rather to add background music. In this way, Warners could provide movie houses all over the country with films that had the same symphonic accompaniment and special sound effects that big-city first-run houses equipped with staff orchestras had previously offered. Thus, in Warners' first Vitaphone film, *Don Juan* (which premiered in 1926), star John Barrymore never uttered a word. The film made history because it featured a prerecorded score played by the New York Philharmonic Orchestra. It was Warner's second Vitaphone production, *The Jazz Singer,* that changed the course of motion-picture history when it opened a year later in 1927. Not only did Al Jolson

Westbeth—formerly
Bell Telephone
Laboratories

sing, he *spoke*. He didn't say very much, mind you, because *The Jazz Singer,* like *Don Juan,* was essentially a silent film that was relying on Jolson's singing to pull in audiences. But when the star insisted on ad-libbing here and there, the film's director, Alan Grosland, wound up keeping some of Jolson's patter in the picture. No one at the time had any idea of the powerful effect that Jolson's speaking, especially his now famous "You ain't heard nothin' yet," would have on motion-picture audiences. A new, intimate connection was instantly established between audience and screen actor. The sound revolution had begun, and there could be no turning back. The scientists at 463 West Street in Greenwich Village played major roles in starting the revolution.

16. MEATPACKING DISTRICT
Between West and Hudson Streets from Gansevoort to West 14th Streets

Now one of the trendiest areas in the West Village, these formerly grungy blocks were the turf of New York's wholesale meat business. In the old days, which were a mere decade ago, this same funky area was also the nighttime home to packs of transvestite prostitutes as well as some of the city's kinkiest nightspots—sex clubs, S&M and leather bars, secret after-hours spots, many of them gay, but some catering to straights as well.

For filmmakers, the meatpacking district often provided an edgy backdrop for sequences that usually involved illegal activities. Classic cases in point: *Love with the Proper Stranger* (1963), where pregnant Natalie Wood comes to the meatpacking district with Steve McQueen to see an abortionist; *Serpico* (1973), where Al Pacino, dressed as a meatpacker, stakes out an illegal payoff to the police; *Fatal Attraction* (1987), where a homicidal Glenn Close lived in a loft at 652 Hudson Street; *Goodfellas* (1990), where one of the film's many bumped-off bodies is disposed of in a deep freeze; and *The Basketball Diaries* (1995), a little-known film that starred Leonardo DiCaprio, before he was a household word, and then rock singer/Calvin Klein underwear model Marky Mark, now known as Mark Wahlberg. Based on the true story of basketball player/poet/rock

Pastis, French bistro in Meatpacking District

musician/drug addict Jim Carroll, the film featured an amusing scene where DiCaprio and Wahlberg are unloading a stolen car in the meatpacking district; while bickering over the price, the vehicle is towed away by ever-vigilant NYC traffic employees.

Today, most of the meatpackers have gone, but their former warehouses—many still sporting the overhead racks and rails once used to shift the carcasses from truck to freezer and back—have been renovated to house restaurants, clubs, and residential lofts. Recent loft-dwellers include Ed Harris, as the AIDS-afflicted poet, who lived at 675 Hudson Street in *The Hours* (2002), and Samantha Jones (Kim Cattrall), who moved into her digs at 300 Gansevoort Street in 2000, just when the neighborhood really started heating up and when *Sex and the City* started ruling the airwaves. Samantha's cool address (which actually doesn't exist) put her steps away from such fashionable spots as the ultra-exclusive SoHo House private club, happening restaurants like Spice Market and the faux-French bistro Pastis, and the chic boutiques of star designers like Stella McCartney and Alexander McQueen.

17. *SHAFT* BAR SITE
621 Hudson Street

He was a tough black private eye who got caught in the middle of a bitter battle between a Harlem gangster and a white mob. The year was 1971, and *Shaft,* which starred model-turned-actor Richard Roundtree, was one of the first of a slew of successful blaxploitation films that were big on violence, racial tension, jivey dialogue, and heavy sex. Much of the latter took place in John Shaft's classic early-1970s duplex—exposed-brick walls, louvered wooden shutters, serious shelving, leather furniture—which would have been on Jane Street across from the No Name Bar at 621 Hudson. The apartment was a set, but the No Name was a real place, and it also saw a lot of action in the film. To-day, after a stint as a deli, the former No Name is a smart little Italian restaurant called Piccolo Angelo (little angel).

18. LAUREN BACALL APARTMENT
75 Bank Street

Betty Bacall was still seventeen when she and her mother moved into this large brick apartment building at the corner of Eighth Avenue and Bank Street. With high school behind her, Betty balanced making the rounds of modeling agencies and photographers' offices with ushering for $8 a week at various Shubert theaters, as well as being a volunteer hostess at the Stage Door Canteen. All the while she hoped and waited for that big show-business break. The break was not, it turned out, her winning the rather dubious title of Miss Greenwich Village in 1942; nor was it when she landed a small part in the Broadway play *Franklin Street* later that same year (the show closed out of town). Finally, however, dame fortune showed her face when Bacall was introduced to *Harper's Bazaar* editor Nicolas de Gunzburg, who in turn introduced her to the legendary fashion editor Diana Vreeland. Bacall subsequently appeared in seven issues of *Harper's Bazaar,* but it was her cover in March 1943—showing her posing in a chic suit in front of a Red Cross blood donor office—that caught the attention of the country, including such Hollywood heavyweights as Columbia Pictures, Howard Hughes, David O.

Bacall on Bank Street

Selznick, and Howard Hawks. With firm offers from both Columbia and Hawks, it was good-bye Bank Street, hello Hollywood, as Betty Bacall decided to sign with Hawks. It was also good-bye "Betty," as Hawks quickly rechristened his discovery Lauren. Now all he needed was the right vehicle for his gorgeous new star. By the end of 1943, both the vehicle, *To Have and Have Not,* and the costar, Humphrey Bogart, had been found.

19. VILLAGE VANGUARD
178 Seventh Avenue South

Opened in a cellar on nearby Charles Street in 1934, this classic Greenwich Village night spot moved to its current location a year later and is known mainly for jazz these days. It was also used as a piano bar in Woody Allen's 2003 film *Anything Else*. Back in the early 1940s, however, cabaret acts were frequently booked at the Village Vanguard, and one of these, a group called the Revuers, saw several of its members—notably Judy Holliday, Betty

Comden, and Adolph Green—lured to the West Coast by a Hollywood talent scout. Ironically, their first Hollywood film was a 1944 Don Ameche/Carmen Miranda musical titled *Greenwich Village*. But their roles in the picture were minuscule, and before long all three performers found themselves back in the real Greenwich Village once more. Several years later, however, the Revuers had considerably better luck: Holliday became a Broadway star—via *Born Yesterday,* and went on to Hollywood film fame in *Adam's Rib* (1949) and in the 1950 screen version of her Broadway success—while Comden and Green became important screenwriters and lyricists at MGM, where they helped create such classics as *On the Town* (1949), *Singin' in the Rain* (1952), and *The Band Wagon* (1953).

Call 212-255-4037 or visit www.villagevanguard.net/frames.htm.

20. RAMBUSCH SITE
40 West 13th Street

This narrow seven-story building with the whimsical Gothic archway as its main entrance housed the offices and studios of the noted Rambusch design firm from 1898 to 1999. Specializing in stained-glass windows and in decorating the interiors of churches, the Rambusch company found a whole new outlet for its creativity and craftsmanship with the rise of the movie palace in the 1910s and 1920s. Responsible for the gilding of hundreds of theaters all over the country and the world was Harold W. Rambusch (son of the firm's founder), whose grandest achievement was the lavish interior of the now-demolished Roxy Theater at 50th Street and Seventh Avenue. Besides his work on the Roxy, Rambusch also decorated the Paramount and Loew's Kings in Brooklyn, the Beacon on Broadway in Manhattan, and the Loew's Jersey in Jersey City. Feeling that the opulent movie houses he helped create were more than just places for the public to see films, Rambusch wrote in 1929: "In our big modern movie palaces there are collected the most gorgeous rugs, furniture, and fixtures that money can produce. No kings or emperors have wandered through more luxurious surroundings. In a sense, these theaters are social safety valves in that the public can

Rambusch studios, 1987

partake of the same luxuries as the rich and use them to the same full extent." Much of that luxury and splendor was conceived at the Rambusch atelier on 13th Street.

Today Rambusch is headquartered in Jersey City and their original Greenwich Village building houses offices.

21. *AS GOOD AS IT GETS* APARTMENT
31–33 West 12th Street

Jack Nicholson was grumpy homophobic writer Melvin Udall, so set in his sick ways that he couldn't bear any change in his daily routine. Greg Kinnear was Simon, his gay artist neighbor, with an adorable little dog named Verdell, that undermined Nicholson's obsessive-compulsive serenity. In the 1997 James L. Brooks film *As Good as It Gets,* the two live in the same distinctive West Village building with fat stone façade and ornate wrought-iron marquee—and they are anything but good neighbors. Although the exterior of the apartment building was the real thing, the interiors were created on a soundstage on the Sony Pictures lot (formerly the old MGM studios) in Culver City, California. The paintings decorating Nicholson's fictional flat were from his own collection. For the role of Verdell, no less than six Brussels griffons (a relatively rare breed of canine) were used, although a pushy pup from Texas named Jill reportedly got the most screen time.

22. DUSTIN HOFFMAN RESIDENCE
16 West 11th Street

It was all coming together for Dustin Hoffman in March 1970. The years of struggling to break into the acting business—years that included being everything from a janitor to an orderly in a mental hospital—were all behind him. His overnight success as a confused college student in Mike Nichols's *The Graduate* (1967), coupled with his poignant portrayal of street person Ratso Rizzo in John Schlesinger's *Midnight Cowboy* (1969), had

Jack Nicholson/Greg Kinnear apartment building in *As Good as It Gets*

not only earned him two Academy Award nominations but had assured him of bankable superstardom. Among the fruits of Hoffman's success was an apartment in a handsome Greek Revival townhouse on a very posh block off Fifth Avenue in the Village. Here, Hoffman lived quietly and privately with his first wife, Ann. On March 6, 1970, however, all New York learned of Hoffman's address when the house next door, 18 West 11th Street, exploded and caught fire, killing one person and causing pandemonium on the block with police cars, fire engines, TV crews, newspaper reporters, and streams of gawkers. Hoffman was reportedly seen carrying paintings and at least one Tiffany lampshade out of his own house, which suffered considerable damage in the blast, before police prevented him from reentering the premises.

The blast story stayed in the papers for quite some time. At first, it was thought that the explosion had been an accident caused by a gas leak, but later it turned out that the basement of 18 West 11th Street had been used as a bomb-manufacturing center by the radical 1960s terrorist group the Weathermen, and that the accident had been caused by all the explosives on the premises. Today, a modern, oddly angled brick townhouse now occupies the site of all the commotion back in 1970, and Mr. Hoffman has long since deserted the Village for the Upper West Side.

23. VILLAGE RESTAURANT
62 West 9th Street

Today a classy French bistro called Village Restaurant, this prime piece of downtown real estate was once a gay cabaret called the Lion. In the summer of 1960, the Lion held talent contests on Thursday nights, and awarded the winner a weeklong engagement at the club plus free dinners and drinks. On one of those Thursdays, an eighteen-year-old woman from Brooklyn wowed the audience with her rendition of "A Sleepin' Bee" from Cole Porter's *House of Flowers,* and won the contest hands down. Broke at the time, the realistic young songstress was more interested in the week's worth of free meals than in the week's booking. She said later of her Lion gig, "In those days, I could be had for a baked potato." In case you haven't guessed who the winner was, it was Barbra Streisand. A portrait of the star hangs at the back of the current establishment's front dining room.

24. CINEMA VILLAGE
22 East 12th Street

At this well-known art house, the specialties are independent and foreign-language films. On-screen, Cinema Village was where a private detective snaps a photo of Richard Gere's *Unfaithful* wife, Diane Lane, and her younger lover, Olivier Martinez, as they leave the theater in Adrian Lyne's 2002 film.

Call 212-924-3363 or visit www.cinemavillage.com.

25. THE BEAUCAIRE
26 East 10th Street

A veritable high-rise Venetian palazzo—never mind the French name—this 1927 apartment building near New York University housed Richard Gere for much of the 1980s and 1990s. Among real-estate insiders, the Beaucaire was nicknamed the Richard Gere Building. These days, the reclusive Mr. Gere and his wife, Carrie Lowell, divide their time between a townhouse in another part of the Village and a classy country house in the Pound Ridge section of Westchester County. Susan Sarandon and Tim Robbins are two other star names associated with the Beaucaire.

26. PUBLIC THEATER
425 Lafayette Street

Built between 1853 and 1881 to house the Astor Library (the city's first free public library), this exotic Romanesque palazzo now houses the late producer Joseph Papp's New York Shakespeare Festival/Public Theater complex. Known for developing such landmark theatrical productions as *Hair* and *A Chorus Line,* the Public Theater and Papp discovered many talented "unknowns." One of Papp's major finds in the 1970s was the Puerto Rican–American playwright Miguel Piñero, whose greatest triumph, the gritty prison drama *Short Eyes,* premiered at the Public in 1974 and made the playwright the toast of New York. The rise and fall of the drug-addicted, ex-con playwright was documented in the 2001 film *Piñero,* which starred Benjamin Bratt (of *Law & Order* fame) and featured the real Public Theater in numerous scenes, including a famous fight where Piñero tells Papp (Mandy Patinkin) to "fuck off" after being barred from the premises.

Today, the Public lures movie lovers to those same premises with its dynamic Film at the Public presentations, featuring first-runs of foreign and U.S. films that don't get wide distribution as well as revivals and retrospectives.

Call 212-260-2400 or visit www.publictheater.org.

27. SILK BUILDING
14 East 4th Street

With Tower Records taking over the ground floor, this distinctive loft building—built in 1869 as New York's first Normal and High School—has housed some of the country's coolest celebrities over the last two decades. Among the hip and the famous who have lived at the trendy East Village address have been Cher, fellow rocker Keith Richards, pop goddess Britney Spears, actors Rob Lowe, Kelly McGillis, and Tom Cruise and Nicole Kidman in their together days.

28. ANTHOLOGY FILM ARCHIVES
32 Second Avenue

An international center for the preservation, study, and exhibition of alternative and avant-garde film and video, this vital institution was originally a division of Joseph Papp's Public Theater when it opened there in 1970. Based in the historic Second Avenue Courthouse Building since the 1980s, the center has two theaters, which feature public showings of daily programs of everything from recently restored classics—such as the 1929 backstage drama *Piccadilly,* starring Anna May Wong—to the latest videos by the likes of Erika Yeomans, Neil Ira Needleman, and Cetywa Powell. The archives is also the site of the an-

Anthology Film Archives

nual New York Underground Film Festival, currently held in March. The longtime artistic director of the center is well-known film critic and "underground" filmmaker (*The Brig*, 1964) Jonas Mekas.

For program information, call 212-505-5181 or visit www.anthologyfilmarchives.org.

29. NINTH PRECINCT
321 East 5th Street

NYPD's East Village headquarters, this police station, like its counterpart, the Tenth Precinct over in Chelsea (used for *The Naked City*), has also been immortalized on celluloid. In the 1970s, this was where a bald cop called Kojak (Telly Savalas) reported to duty (even though the show was shot in Los Angeles); and in the 1990s, the same police station became the Fifteenth Precinct for the still-running and also set in New York but shot in Hollywood series *NYPD Blue*.

30. ST.-MARKS-IN-THE-BOWERY CHURCH
10th Street and Second Avenue

One of the city's most historic houses of worship, St. Marks was established in 1799 on the former estate of New York's first governor, Peter Stuyvesant, who is buried in the churchyard. Movie lovers may recall its Georgian façade as well as its stained glass–windowed interior from Sidney Lumet's 1966 film, *The Group*. It was at St. Marks that Kay Strong, the ambitious character played by Joanna Pettet, married Harold Peterson, the "master of unproduced plays" portrayed by Larry Hagman. The film's best St. Marks scene has Lakey (Candice Bergen) arriving at the wedding in a glamorous Morgan sports car. At the end of the film, St. Marks again figures in the picture as the setting for Kay's funeral, after the stresses of climbing the corporate ladder result in her committing suicide. *The Group*'s wedding and funeral sequences were both shot by Lumet on the same day.

Two other movie weddings recently took place at this historic church: Russell Crowe tied the knot with Jennifer Connelly in *A Beautiful Mind* in 2001, although the period was the 1940s; and recently, bridesmaid Sandra Bullock was forced to walk out of a girlfriend's ceremony in *Two Weeks Notice* (2002), when her demanding Donald Trump–like boss, Hugh Grant, texts her on her cell phone, wanting her to help him pick out a suit.

31. THEATER 80 SITE
80 St. Marks Place

Now the headquarters for the off-Broadway Pearl Theatre company, back in the pre–Turner Classic Movies and pre–plasma TV era, this was the Theater 80 St. Marks, one of the city's premier revival houses. Although it no longer shows classic movies, the theater is still worth a visit, if only to check out the sidewalk, where movie lovers will find concrete slabs with the handprints, footprints, and autographs of such stars as Myrna Loy, Gloria Swanson, Alexis Smith, Ruby Keeler, Joan Blondell, and Joan Crawford. Theater 80's former owner/director Howard Otway didn't raid Grauman's Chinese in Hollywood for these treasures—they were inscribed by the stars themselves in the early

Crawford at
Theater 80,
1971

1970s in order to celebrate and publicize Otway's conversion of an off-Broadway theater into a full-fledged film-revival house.

In the late 1980s, Mr. Otway looked back with amusement on the evening that his longtime friend Joan Crawford came to the theater for her sidewalk ceremony. Playing the star to the hilt, Crawford arrived in a huge limousine, and since she was still a paid spokesperson for her late husband's company, Pepsi-Cola, she had seen that the limo was fitted with cushions that looked like giant Pepsi-Cola bottle caps. Once inside Theater 80, Miss Crawford happened to notice a young assistant drinking a Yoo-Hoo. "*What* are you doing?" she demanded of the frightened young man.

"Oh, I'm sorry," he responded. "I didn't know you were coming, Miss Crawford."

"Don't apologize," Crawford boomed. "Hide it!"

Less in character was Joan's sidewalk signing in which the legendary fussbudget ran out of cement before finishing her last name. "Let them know I don't plan ahead," she quipped.

Visit www.pearltheatre.org.

Big hair day: Drag queens in Tompkins Square Park for *Wigstock: The Movie*, 1995

32. TOMPKINS SQUARE PARK
5th to 9th Streets between Avenues A and B

Not known for its green spaces, New York's East Village surprises with this sixteen-acre park over at the beginning of Alphabet City—as the area encompassed by Avenues A, B, C, etc. is known. Laid out in the 1830s, Tompkins Square Park has the distinction of being the locale for what is said to be the first labor demonstration—by the carpenters union in 1874—in the United States. About a century later, when the East Village was the East Coast capital of hippiedom, the park was the site of happenings, be-ins, and love-ins. A few decades later, it was a trouble spot once again, when it saw homeless squatters battle the NYPD over a curfew enacted to protect the newly Yuppified area's real-estate values. When the squatters refused to move from the shantytown they had erected in the park, the police forced them out in what was a very ugly chapter in East Village history.

On a more festive note, in the 1980s and 1990s, Tompkins

Square was famous for hosting Wigstock, an annual carnival-like festival which brought out the city's most outrageous drag queens. The event was memorialized in the documentary *Wigstock: The Movie* (1995). Another film that featured the park that same year was *Die Hard with a Vengence*, notably in a scene where Bruce Willis and Samuel L. Jackson, in their quest to keep up with a maniacal bomber, try to solve the villain's latest riddle. Two years later, Tompkins Square Park is frequently seen in the Morgan Freeman–written–and–directed *Hurricane Streets* (1997), which focuses on the lives, loves, and petty crimes of a pack of East Village teenagers.

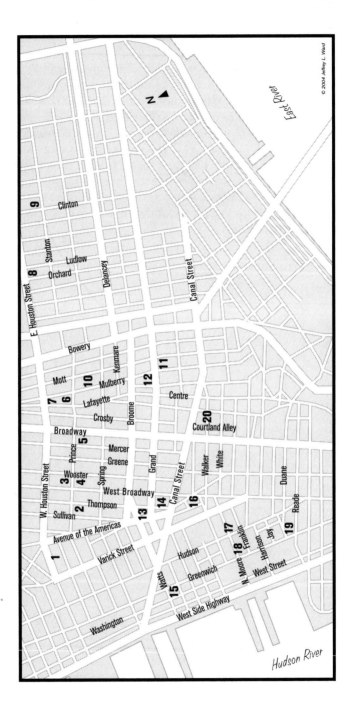

7

SoHo/TriBeCa/NoLita:
The "New" New York

In the 1980s, New York movies discovered Downtown Manhattan. Classic examples of the Downtown genre were *Desperately Seeking Susan* and *After Hours,* which showed us a Manhattan of New Wave nightclubs, Art Deco diners, trendy art galleries, and lofty living arrangements—all decidedly *below* Houston Street and with stars rarely over thirty. Edgy in the 1980s, the Downtown communities of SoHo (South of Houston Street), TriBeCa (the Triangle Below Canal Street), and NoLita (North of Little Italy) have become increasingly mainstream. That hasn't stopped their film careers, however, as they've become virtually a standard feature in even Uptown New York movies, which often have a scene or two set in a SoHo gallery, the latest NoLita restaurant, or a TriBeCa loft.

For movie lovers of all geographical persuasions, Downtown is a dream of location-spotting—from the scene of Meg Ryan's famous orgasm in *When Harry Met Sally* to the bar where the *Sex and the City* set sipped Cosmopolitans. Besides locations, Downtown now even boasts its own film festival, thanks to the efforts of local hero Robert De Niro, whose Tribeca Film Center is yet another symbol of the area's vital connection to New York filmmaking.

Downtown girls:
Rosanna Arquette
and Madonna in
*Desperately Seeking
Susan,* 1985

1. FILM FORUM
209 West Houston Street

Set on a busy block of Houston Street, usually clogged with
trucks en route to the nearby Holland Tunnel, this little movie
house reigns as the city's most important showcase for foreign,
offbeat, and often-overlooked motion pictures. In her constant
quest for the new and the noncommercial, Film Forum's longtime director, Karen Cooper, is credited with turning on New
York audiences to the German directors Werner Herzog, Wim
Wenders, and Rainer Werner Fassbinder long before they became fashionable with the mainstream. Similarly, Film Forum introduced American audiences to black-sheep Soviet filmmaker
Andrei Tarkovsky and his bizarre sci-fi visions of twentieth-
century life in *Solaris* and *Stalker*. A nonprofit operation, Film
Forum is supported by the New York State Council on the Arts,

the National Endowment for the Arts, several foundations and corporations, and, most important, by individual movie lovers who pay from $65 to $1,000 a year to become Friends of Film Forum. In return, these friends get to see all Film Forum's features at reduced rates plus additional benefits depending on the level of contribution.

Call 212-727-8110 or visit www.filmforum.com.

2. RAOUL'S
180 Prince Street

A hip little SoHo bistro, where you travel through the kitchen to reach the rear dining room, Raoul's and especially its kitchen are featured in *Addicted to Love* (1997). The film's hero, Matthew Broderick, gets a job washing dishes here in his efforts to get revenge on the restaurant's obnoxious French owner, Anton (Tchéky Karyo), who has stolen the affections of Broderick's girlfriend. In one particularly hilarious scene, Broderick unleashes an army of cockroaches the night that the *New York Times* food critic has dropped by to review the place. The critic is played by *Vanity Fair* columnist Dominick Dunne, who happens to be the father of the film's director, Griffin Dunne. Raoul's has also appeared—sans cockroaches—in *A Perfect Murder* (1998) and in Martin Scorsese's *The King of Comedy* (1983).

For reservations, call 212-966-3518.

Columnist Dominick Dunne plays a restaurant critic in *Addicted to Love* (1997), at Raoul's with Tchéky Karyo

3. LOUIS K. MEISEL GALLERY
141 Prince Street

This SoHo art gallery made its name by featuring photorealist painters in the 1970s. Just off the neighborhood's main drag, West Broadway, the Meisel establishment gained further notoriety in the late 1990s as the trendy gallery where Charlotte York (Kristin Davis) worked for several seasons in *Sex and the City.*

4. TONY SHAFRAZI GALLERY
119 Wooster Street

The Shafrazi Gallery is one of the many Downtown galleries that Downtown artist/filmmaker Julian Schnabel used for his 1996 biopic on the short blazing life and career of Jean-Michel Basquiat. Owner Tony Shafrazi, now a major player on the New York art scene, made news during his student days in 1974, when, to protest the Vietnam War, he sprayed-painted the words "Kill lies all" (*sic*) on Picasso's *Guernica,* which was on view at the Metropolitan Museum of Art at the time. Mr. Shafrazi was taken to the West 54th Street station house and was charged with criminal mischief. "I'm an artist and I wanted to tell the truth," he said at the time. The paint, it turns out, was easily removed from the masterpiece. And the incident obviously didn't hurt Mr. Shafrazi's subsequent career.

5. *GHOST* LOFT
112 Mercer Street

Demi Moore was a SoHo potter who lived, rather lavishly by struggling-artist standards, in a spacious Mercer Street loft in *Ghost* (1990). Moore's serenity was turned upside down early on in the film, when her husband, Patrick Swayze, is murdered. But she quickly comes in contact with a bizarre psychic in the person of Whoopi Goldberg, who brings Swayze very much back into her life. The loft where Demi lived and worked a wicked wheel backed by "Unchained Melody" was here in this classic nineteenth-century cast iron–columned former SoHo factory building.

6. *FRAME* MAGAZINE
270 Lafayette Street

In avant-garde filmmaker Lisa Cholodenko's story of love and drugs among Manhattan's Lipstick Lesbian crowd, *High Art* (1998), much of the action revolves around the offices of *Frame* magazine. It's an ambitious *Frame* editor (Radha Mitchell) who lures former big-time photographer Ally Sheedy back for one last photo shoot. Complications result when Sheedy seduces the editor, which does not sit well with Sheedy's cocaine-addicted German lover (Patricia Clarkson). Needless to say, Sheedy's comeback turns out to be a disaster. The magazine responsible for it all was located at this hip SoHo loft building.

7. PUCK BUILDING
295 Lafayette Street

The former home of the Victorian humor magazine *Puck,* this whimsical Romanesque brick castle at Lafayette and Houston Streets is particularly notable for the two gilded figures of Puck, a character from Shakespeare's *A Midsummer Night's Dream,*

Puck Building

that are part of the façade. Built in 1885 and handsomely restored a century later, the Puck Building is currently one of SoHo's coolest addresses. So it's no surprise that interior decorator Grace Adler (Debra Messing) had the good taste to base her design firm here in the TV series *Will & Grace*. The Puck Building was also featured in *When Harry Met Sally* (1989), as the site of the New Year's Eve party where Billy Crystal finally declares his love for Meg Ryan at the end of the film. In real life, the Puck Building's Victorian ballroom is frequently rented out for holiday parties. The SoHo landmark is also currently the site of the Outsider Art Fair held each January, displaying works primarily by untrained artists and artists who have spent time in prisons and mental institutions.

8. KATZ'S DELICATESSEN
205 East Houston Street

Even though it was fake, it was probably the most famous orgasm in the history of sex, not to mention the cinema. It was here—amid all the pastrami, salami, corned beef, brisket, and

Katz's Delicatessen

Meg Ryan and Billy Crystal at Katz's in *When Harry Met Sally*, 1989

sauerkraut—that Meg Ryan showed Billy Crystal just how easy it was for a woman to fake a climax in the film *When Harry Met Sally* (1989). Fake or not, the lady dining nearby (in fact, director Rob Reiner's mother), overhearing Meg's oohs and aahs, uttered the famous line to her waiter: "I'll have what she's having." In 2004, a stage version of the film opened in London starring Alyson Hannigan (of *Buffy the Vampire Slayer* fame) and Luke Perry (formerly of *Beverly Hills 90210*); it was largely panned by the critics, who felt even the orgasm came off better in the movie.

Katz's was also a location in *Donnie Brasco* (1997), in a scene where undercover agent Johnny Depp meets with some of his FBI colleagues. *Donnie Brasco* also gave the world another famous expression: "Fhuggedaboudit!" The phrase, as Johnny Depp/Donnie Brasco points out to an FBI colleague in the film, has different meanings: " 'Forget about it' is like if you agree with someone, you know, like 'Raquel Welch is one great piece of ass, forget about it.' But then, if you disagree, like 'A Lincoln is better than a Cadillac? Forget about it!' you know? But then, it's also like if something's the greatest thing in the world, like

Michelle Pfeiffer's *Married to the Mob* gig: Beautiful Hair Unisex Salon

mangia those peppers, 'forget about it.' But it's also like saying 'Go to hell!' too. Like, you know, like 'Hey, Paulie, you got a one-inch pecker?' and Paulie says 'Forget about it!' Sometimes it just means forget about it."

Visit www.katzdeli.com.

9. BEAUTIFUL HAIR UNISEX SALON
20 Clinton Street

Showbiz has not gone to the head of this Lower East Side barber-beauty shop. Despite the fact that this is the place where Michelle Pfeiffer wound up working after her husband was offed and she tried to start a new life in Lower Manhattan in *Married to the Mob* (1988), this unpretentious SoHo salon offers a shampoo and cut for $15.

10. OLD ST. PATRICK'S CATHEDRAL
264 Mulberry Street

Everyone knows the "new" St. Patrick's Cathedral, the massive neo-Gothic Catholic church with twin 330-foot spires that stands on Fifth Avenue between 50th and 51st Streets. Built between 1879 and 1906, it is one of the city's most impressive houses of worship. Much less well known is Old St. Patrick's Cathedral down in Little Italy, which was built in 1815, rebuilt in 1868 after a fire, and reigned as the city's premier Catholic church until its grander Midtown sibling took away its title and cachet. Now a parish church, Old St. Patrick's is an important Little Italy landmark and as such has played roles in various films set in the neighborhood. The classic, of course, is *The Godfather* (1972), where the church was used for the christening of Connie's son, at which Michael Corleone (Al Pacino) now stands as godfather after the death of his father, Vito (Marlon Brando); the scene is intercut with his enemies being brutally eliminated. The church then turns up again in *The Godfather: Part III,* when an older Michael, now a "respectable" businessman, is being presented with a high church honor. Old St. Patrick's can also be seen in *Mean Streets* (1973), Martin Scorsese's hard-edged portrait of Little Italy street life. Although much of the film was shot in Hollywood, Scorsese used St. Patrick's distinctive walled

Old St. Patrick's
Cathedral

courtyard for a private conversation between the film's stars, Robert De Niro and Harvey Keitel. *Sex and the City* has also been by.

11. MULBERRY STREET BAR
176½ Mulberry Street

Today Mulberry Street is filled with the cool bars and restaurants that are a signature of the new Little Italy. But back in the days when the neighborhood was filled with Old World bakeries, Italian social clubs, and mom-and-pop grocery stores, one of Mulberry Street's longtime landmarks was a joint called Mare Chiaro, which dated back to the turn of the last century. In the old days, the place sported oak-paneled walls, sawdust on the floor, bright overhead lights, card tables, and lots of Sinatra on the jukebox. In fact, Mare Chiaro was known as the Sinatra Bar, in honor of its most famous regular customer. Others who dropped by over the years included Ronald Reagan, Madonna, and the late George Plimpton, whose *Paris Review* editors used to meet here once a week. Needless to say, it's not surprising that this classic slice of Little Italy wound up in at least one *Godfather* film, in this case *Godfather III* (1990). It's also appeared in *The Pope of Greenwich Village* (1984), *9½ Weeks* (1986), and various episodes of *The Sopranos*. It's particularly memorable in *Donnie Brasco* (1997), as the bar where Johnny Depp as undercover FBI agent Donnie Brasco meets Mafia operative Al Pacino, who asks him to "middle" a stolen diamond ring for him. Brasco immediately recognizes that it's a "fugazy" (fake).

For movie lovers wishing to see the old Mare Chiaro, best to rent a video or DVD of one of the above films, since the bar was recently sold and has been rechristened the Mulberry Street Bar. No more sawdust on the floor, but Sinatra still rules the jukebox. Another Mulberry Street tradition that still goes on is the annual San Gennaro Festival honoring the patron saint of Naples, which turns the area into an old-fashioned Italian-American carnival every September.

Sex and the City regular: O'Neal's Grand Street

12. O'NEAL'S GRAND STREET BAR AND RESTAURANT
174 Grand Street

Better known to *Sex and the City* addicts as Scout, this was the SoHo watering hole run by Carrie and Miranda's former boyfriends Aidan and Steve. On the TV show, the drink du jour was always the vodka–cranberry juice–Triple Sec concoction known as the Cosmopolitan. Today, with *Sex and the City* now in reruns, Cosmos are on the wane and the up-and-coming cocktail is the kiwi-lime martini.

13. CAFÉ NOIR
32 Grand Street

When it comes to on-screen sex, perhaps nobody does it better than British director Adrian Lyne. Witness the intense sadomasochistic coupling of Kim Basinger and Mickey Rourke in *9½ Weeks* (1986) and the *Fatal Attraction* (1987) that brought Glenn Close and Michael Douglas together. But the assignation to end

Unfaithful hot spot

all assignations has got to be the quickie between Diane Lane and Olivier Martinez in Lyne's 2002 *Unfaithful* that took place in a stall of the ladies' room at this venerable SoHo café, while Lane was between cappuccinos with two of her unsuspecting suburban girlfriends.

Dangerous liaison: Diane Lane and Olivier Martinez in *Unfaithful*, 2002

Moondance Diner

14. MOONDANCE DINER
80 Avenue of the Americas

This funky diner on the edge of SoHo has provided on-screen employment for both Kirsten Dunst and Courteney Cox. Cox as Monica in *Friends* once worked at Moondance as a waitress, wearing Dolly Parton falsies that caught on fire, in a famous episode of the TV series. On the other hand, Dunst wears standard-issue waitress drag for her Moondance gig in *Spider-Man* (2002). An aspiring actress in the film, she is highly embarrassed when she bumps into her neighbor Tobey Maguire outside her workplace—especially since she's started dating Tobey's super-wealthy best friend Harry and doesn't want him to know about her day job. Meanwhile, Tobey is much more upset by the fact that Dunst is interested in Harry and not him. The diner is also one of the many SoHo nightspots that Griffin Dunne and Rosanna Arquette hit in Martin Scorsese's *After Hours* (1985).

Capsuto Frères

15. CAPSUTO FRÈRES
451 Washington Street

The ground floor of this many-gabled 1891 landmark building at the edge of the Holland Tunnel between SoHo and TriBeCa has been the longtime home of the fashionable, high-ceilinged French restaurant Capsuto Frères. The building has also provided trendy downtown digs for the Divine Miss Bette Midler, her buddy Barry Manilow, and fashion photographer/filmmaker (*Let's Get Lost*, 1988) Bruce Weber. On the small screen, the building and restaurant have been featured in *Law & Order*.

For reservations, call 212-966-4900.

16. AMERICAN THREAD BUILDING
260 West Broadway

Built in 1896 as the headquarters for the New York Wool Exchange, this handsome eleven-story structure facing TriBeCa Park is one of Lower Manhattan's most luxurious addresses.

Among its starry former tenants have been rock's madcap Cyndi Lauper, the late John F. Kennedy Jr., and Ingrid Bergman's model/movie-actress daughter, Isabella Rossellini. In the early 1970s, Ms. Rossellini made ends meet in Manhattan by teaching Italian classes at the American Express Language Center and at the New School.

17. HOOK AND LADDER COMPANY 8
14 North Moore Street

When *Saturday Night Live* superstars Bill Murray and Dan Aykroyd took their talents to the big screen, none of their films was ever quite as hysterical—or successful—as 1984's runaway hit *Ghostbusters*. In the film, the boys venture into the ghost-exterminating business and wind up saving Manhattan from some rather frightening ectoplasmic infestations. For their head-quarters in the film, the Number 8 Hook and Ladder firehouse

Ghostbusters'
firehouse

in TriBeCa provided the perfect location—at least for the exterior sequences. The interiors, it turns out, were all done at a firehouse in Los Angeles. Why two firehouses? For one thing *Ghostbusters,* whose principal photography was based at the Burbank (now Warner Bros.) Studios in L.A., was on a tight schedule for its location shots in New York. For another, the Moore Street firehouse is still in the business of fighting fires, whereas the firehouse used for the interiors in Los Angeles was one that had been decommissioned.

The same New York firehouse was again used for exteriors in *Ghostbusters II* (1987), which featured virtually the same cast. Number 8 Hook and Ladder was also deeply involved in the rescue efforts connected with the 9/11 catastrophe and mourned the death of its own Lt. Vincent G. Halloran in the process. A measure to rename North Moore Street between Varick and West Broadway for the late lieutenant is currently being considered by the city.

18. TRIBECA FILM CENTER
375 Greenwich Street

In the late 1980s, actor and longtime TriBeCa resident Robert De Niro was a major force behind turning a seven-story former coffee warehouse into one of New York's most exciting film centers. Not a movie house, Tribeca Film Center is a production-friendly site offering long- and short-term office space, studios, screening rooms, and other support services for companies involved in all aspects of filmmaking. Over the years, Steven Spielberg, Ron Howard, Quincy Jones, and De Niro's own Tribeca Productions have all had bases here. In 1990, a then little-known company called Miramax moved to 375 Greenwich Street, which remains its New York headquarters.

Another feature of the Tribeca Film Center is its trendy ground-floor Tribeca Grill, which opened in 1990 and boasts quite a lineup of celebrity backers—Bill Murray, Sean Penn, Christopher Walken, and Mikhail Baryshnikov among them—and regulars. Post–September 11, the Grill was one of many local restaurants that provided meals to local families and rescue workers during the aftermath of the World Trade Center attacks. It was also in the wake of that same tragedy that De Niro and his

Tribeca Film Center

associates were inspired to establish the Tribeca Film Festival, as a gesture of faith in what was then a devastated Lower Manhattan. Open to U.S. and international feature, short, and documentary films, the first festival—organized in just 120 days—took place in May 2002 and drew an audience of 150,000. The next year the numbers more than doubled, and the Tribeca Film Festival is now an important event on the world film-festival circuit. In addition to screenings and panel discussions, the festival features art exhibits and installations, concerts, and a special Drive-In series of classic American films shown outdoors on Pier 25 on the Hudson River.

For reservations at the Tribeca Grill, call 212-941-3900. For Tribeca Film Festival information, log onto www.tribecafilmfestival.org.

19. GIGINO TRATTORIA
323 Greenwich Street

In his decidedly Downtown 2000 comedy, *Dinner Rush,* director
Bob Giraldi documents both the back- and front-of-house dramas and traumas associated with the running of a hip TriBeCa
restaurant. Seemingly filmed in real time, *Dinner Rush* actually
shot for a month at a real TriBeCa restaurant, Gigino Trattoria,
which the film's executive producer Phil Suarez just happened to
own.

Visit www.giginony.com.

20. CORTLANDT ALLEY

In a city that makes movies without the luxury of studio back
lots, when an alley is needed for a mugging, gun fight, or fatal
confrontation between hero and villain, this Lower Manhattan
cul-de-sac is often called on to fill the bill. Movie lovers have
seen it in such features as *Highlander* (1986), *FX* (1986), *Crocodile Dundee* (1986), *Basquiat* (1996), *Addicted to Love* (1997),
Small Time Crooks (2000), and *In the Cut* (2003). On TV it's
been used by *The Equalizer, NYPD Blue,* and *Law & Order.*

8

Lower Manhattan/Staten Island: Old New York

The tip of Manhattan Island is the original New York—dating back to the days when the city was a small Dutch enclave called New Amsterdam. Although virtually nothing remains of the city's early-seventeenth-century beginnings, this part of New York at times has a distinct Old World feel, with its narrow streets and serious government buildings and financial institutions. Indeed, since it contains some of the city's oldest and most august landmarks, Lower Manhattan is of interest both to movie lovers and moviemakers. Ranging from Federal Hall to the New York Stock Exchange to the great lady of New York Harbor— the Statue of Liberty—many of these hallowed monuments are symbolic not just of the City of New York but of the United States of America, and over the years they have played major roles on-screen, often providing ironic counterpoint to the mood or message of the scenes in which they appear.

The city's financial heart, Lower Manhattan also abounds in modern commercial architecture, which is all part of the area's distinctive photographic potential. Sadly, two of its greatest modern landmarks are no longer here, but they are still present in spirit and on film—and whenever they appear in a pre–9/11 film, as they often do, they bring up powerful emotions.

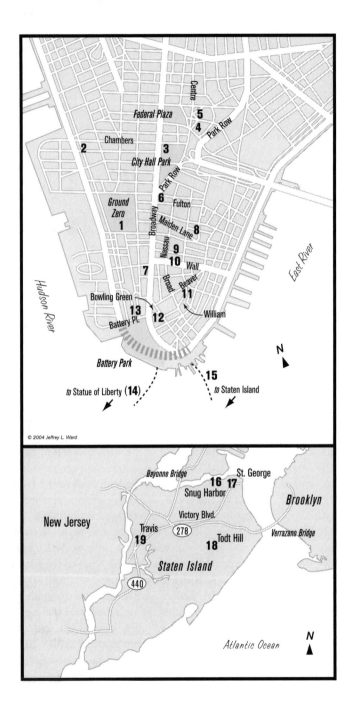

This chapter also heads across New York Harbor to that terra incognita (for most Manhattanites) called Staten Island. The borough's relative obscurity, however, has proven to be its major attraction for movie location managers, who have found that Staten Island can be a convenient and surprisingly authentic-looking stand-in for other parts of the country—from the Midwest to New England—in New York–made films.

1. GROUND ZERO
1 and 2 World Trade Plaza

Completed in 1970 and 1977, respectively, the two identical 110-story towers of the World Trade Center, at 1,350 feet each, were New York City's tallest buildings. Because of their paramount role in the city's late-twentieth-century skyline, they popped up in many made-in-NYC motion pictures during their brief lifetime. Often used to represent the ultimate New York City office building, the World Trade Center was where Cliff Robertson appeared to be an ordinary business executive in

King Kong at the World Trade Center, 1976

Three Days of the Condor (1973), although he was really a CIA baddie. It was also at the World Trade Center that Jane Fonda headed up her murdered husband's international monetary firm in *Rollover* (1982), and where Eddie Murphy and Dan Aykroyd wreaked financial ruin on the cavalier businessmen who had switched their identities in *Trading Places* (1983).

Some of the most interesting uses of the World Trade Center as a location were in fantasy films. In both *Godspell* (1973) and *The Wiz* (1978), for example, the Center's four-acre plaza provided an open-air soundstage for musical production numbers. In *Escape from New York* (1981), the rooftop of one of the towers became a tarmac where Kurt Russell landed a plane in this bizarre sci-fi film that portrayed the island of Manhattan as a maximum-security prison of the 1990s. And then, of course, there was *King Kong,* Dino De Laurentiis's monumental 1976 remake of RKO's 1933 classic ape-loses-girl love story, in which the then upstart World Trade Center won out over the tried-and-true Empire State Building for the film's star skyscraper role. Supposedly, however, Paramount's negotiations with the New York and New Jersey Port Authority, which owned and managed the World Trade Center, proved difficult, and there were moments when it looked as if the Empire State Building would get the part after all. Meanwhile, the Empire State Building was quite annoyed at being overlooked by the new *King Kong,* and its owners registered their ire by stationing men dressed as apes carrying picket signs atop the observation tower.

Unlike the original *King Kong,* which was done entirely in Hollywood with a little help from some New York process shots, De Laurentiis decided to go on location for his film's New York sequences. In addition to the dramatic production values, filming in New York promised to provide lots of publicity for a picture that was already running way over budget. The publicity began with the Hollywood–to–New York journey of the forty-foot Kong model. This involved dismantling the monster into ten pieces, which were then shipped in special vans with "King Kong" painted on them in huge letters. Press releases kept the country informed of Kong's progress.

For the actual shoot, the producers wanted five thousand extras. To fill this large order, the production company "invited" the public to the World Trade Center Plaza on the nights of June 21, 22, and 23, 1976, to take part in the excitement of moviemaking. Thousands of New Yorkers showed up and, despite brawls, trouble with the Port Authority over security, and threats of rain, *King Kong* got its crowd scenes—and its headlines. Indeed, for three days the great ape was the city's brightest star. Almost lost in all the excitement was the blond model who was making her film debut in the project as Kong's gal-pal. How did Jessica Lange enjoy shooting her first film? Best not ask Miss Lange. Since 1981, the Oscar-winning actress, supposedly embarrassed by the picture that launched her career, refuses to discuss *King Kong*.

Today the World Trade Center buildings are gone—and debate still goes on as to exactly what buildings will replace them and what memorials will be raised to them. For the moment, at least, no producer has had the bad taste to exploit the events of 9/11 in a commercial feature or television movie. One of the first films to reference the events, however, was Spike Lee's *25th Hour* (2002), which shows the New York City skyline in the opening credits with the two great beams of light which shot up into the sky for several months in 2002 to commemorate the lives lost in the tragedy. But even more moving is a haunting nighttime scene in *25th Hour*, where Barry Pepper and Philip Seymour Hoffman are alone in Pepper's Battery Park City apartment, discussing their relationship with their buddy Edward Norton, who is about to be put in prison for seven years. As they talk, earth-movers and dump trucks are constantly at work outside the window. With the exception of some small talk at the beginning of the scene, in which Pepper and Hoffman mention bin Laden and question the quality of the air ("EPA says it's fine"), no further reference is made to 9/11 or to what's going on outside the window—which makes the scene, essentially done in one long take, outside the window all the more powerful. In his subtle way, Lee acknowledges not just the complex, almost unspeakable emotions of the tragedy, but also the fact that life goes on.

Another film to acknowledge the World Trade Center horror is *September 11* (2003), which is a compilation of eleven eleven-minute films by directors from around the world: France's Claude Lelouch, Iran's Samira Makhmalbaf, Egypt's Youssef Chahine, Bosnia's Danis Tanovic, West Africa's Idrissa Quedrago, Britain's

Ken Loach, Mexico's Alejandro Gonzalez Inarritu, Israel's Amos Gitai, India's Mira Nair, America's Sean Penn, and Japan's Shohei Imamura. Some are powerful, others are not. Perhaps it was too soon.

2. STUYVESANT HIGH SCHOOL
345 Chambers Street

One of the first films to capitalize on the Internet era, *Hackers* (1995) saw high-school cyber-soldiers discover a major corporate conspiracy online and then battle the criminals behind it. The high school used for the film was this appropriately modern Battery Park City institution built in 1991. Formerly in the East Village, Stuyvesant is one of the country's top public high schools, particularly strong in science. On September 11, 2001, Stuyvesant was in the news when all of its students were evacuated safely shortly after the next-door World Trade Center was hit by two planes piloted by terrorists.

Visit www.stuy.edu.

3. TWEED COURTHOUSE
52 Chambers Street

A monument to the greed of the infamous New York political boss, William Marcy "Boss" Tweed, this extraordinary Italianate structure was built as a courthouse during the city's corrupt Tammany Hall period in the 1870s. Not only did the building take thirteen years to finish, it cost the then unbelievable sum of $14 million, most of which was skimmed off by Tweed and his cronies. (The Tammany Hall era was documented in Martin Scorsese's 2002 film *Gangs of New York*, which was shot not in New York but on a back lot in Rome.) Despite its questionable origins, the Tweed Courthouse is a spectacular space, especially the interior, where a seven-story rotunda is capped with a skylit dome, with cage elevators and two monumental cast-iron staircases adding to the drama.

For filmmakers, the Tweed building was an extremely popular location in the 1970s and 1980s, when it housed various city offices. In 1974, Joan Micklin Silver used the Tweed's grand staircases to represent the Great Hall of Ellis Island in *Hester*

Street, her comedy/drama about turn-of-the-century Jewish immigrants in New York. In 1980, Brian De Palma shot the same staircases from a different angel to create the creepy mental institution where the psychiatrist played by Michael Caine worked in *Dressed to Kill.* Two years later Sidney Lumet turned the Tweed into the Boston courthouse where much of the action of *The Verdict* takes place. Other features that shot at the Tweed include *Kramer vs. Kramer* (1979), *Turk 182* (1985), *Alphabet City* (1984), and *Angel Heart* (1987). In the 1990s, however, the building was closed down for several years for a complete renovation to turn it into offices for the New York City Department of Education. All this put the Tweed's movie career on hiatus, and it has yet to make a major comeback.

But barely a block away on the other side of Chambers Street at number 31, the stately 1911 Surrogate's Court Building—with its columned façade inspired by the Paris Opéra—has been coming on strong as another filmmaker-friendly downtown location.

Tweed Courthouse

Nicole "Catwoman" Kidman had her office here in *Batman Forever* (1995) and Keanu Reeves worked here briefly as a district attorney in *The Devil's Advocate* (1997). It can also be seen in the gory finale to Peter Medak's *Romeo Is Bleeding* (1994) as well as in *Married to the Mob* (1988), *Regarding Henry* (1991), *Conspiracy Theory* (1997), *The Last Days of Disco* (1998), and *The Cradle Will Rock* (1999).

Visit www.nyc.gov/html/dcas/html/building/man_tweed.html.

4. NEW YORK COUNTY COURTHOUSE
60 Centre Street

When a shot of this great government building, with its massive columns and dramatic stone steps, turns up in a film, it invariably signals that a courtroom scene is about to follow. It was at the New York County Courthouse that Macy's eccentric Santa Claus supposedly stood trial in 1947 in *Miracle on 34th Street*. Ten years later, Henry Fonda was a star juror in the same building in *Twelve Angry Men*. For this film, which was made entirely on location in New York, director Sidney Lumet used the courthouse's magnificent interior rotunda as well as its striking façade for several sequences.

More recently, *Legal Eagles* (1986) superstar lawyers Robert Redford and Debra Winger found themselves at 60 Centre Street, and were followed by Barbra Streisand, who had her day in court here (and also stopped traffic!) for the film *Nuts* (1987). It was also at 60 Centre Street where Charlie Sheen was put on trial for insider trading at the end of *Wall Street* (1987), and where Ray Liotta testified against his former mob buddies Robert De Niro and Paul Sorvino in *Goodfellas* (1989). In *Regarding Henry* (1991), Harrison Ford tried a case at 60 Centre Street prior to an encounter with a stray bullet, whereas new-lawyer-in-town Keanu Reeves argued his first case in Manhattan, before accepting an offer he couldn't refuse (but should have) from a diabolical Al Pacino in *The Devil's Advocate* (1997). Other films to use the courthouse include *Married to the Mob* (1988), *City Hall* (1996), and *The Hurricane* (1999).

Besides appearing in movies, the dramatic courthouse can be seen in the miniseries *Little Gloria, Happy at Last* (1985), and

Law & Order:
Chris Noth,
George Dzundza,
Michael Moriarty, and
Richard Brooks at the
New York County
Courthouse

Rage of Angels (1986), and episodes of *Kojak, Cagney and Lacey, Naked City, NYPD Blue, The Equalizer*, and, naturally, *Law & Order*.

5. CRIMINAL COURT BUILDING AND PRISON
100 Centre Street

This 1939 Art Deco monster is both a courthouse—known first-hand to many a New Yorker who's done jury duty here—and the site of the city's notorious "Tombs" prison, where alleged criminals often wind up in its holding cells. Among the latter have been such celebrated names as John Lennon's killer, Mark David Chapman, "Preppy Murderer" Robert Chambers, subway killer Bernard Goetz, rocker Sid Vicious, and rap-star/fashion de-signer/actor Sean "Puffy" Combs.

Recently the building was the inspiration—and main loca-tion—of vintage New York director Sidney Lumet's A&E series *100 Centre Street*. Although not nearly as photogenic as the neighboring New York County Courthouse at 60 Centre Street, the Criminal Courts Building has nonetheless appeared in its share of motion pictures, perhaps most notably in *Adam's Rib* (1949), which saw husband-and-wife lawyers Katharine Hepburn and Spencer Tracy spar with each other on opposite sides of a case involving Judy Holliday, who was accused of attempting to murder her husband. Another classic appearance was in *Kiss of Death* (1947), where D.A. Brian Donlevy presents a plea bargain offer to Victor Mature from his 100 Centre Street office. The building was also called on as a location for *The Paper* (1994), *Conspiracy Theory* (1997), and, again, it's a regular on *Law & Order*.

6. *WALL STREET* OFFICE
222 Broadway

A block from Wall Street, this massive office building was where young Bud Fox (Charlie Sheen) put his trust and his career in the hands of Gordon Gekko (Michael Douglas), the

Wall Street office building

unscrupulous prince of 1980s capitalism. The film was *Wall Street* (1987) and it was the definitive statement about a greedy decade that many thought would never return. How wrong they were.

7. THE *"NEW YORK SUN"* OFFICES
71 Broadway

Today in New York, there actually *is* a *New York Sun* newspaper, which started publishing in 2002 courting a conservative readership. But back in 1994, the name was up for grabs and director Ron Howard used it in *The Paper,* his hilarious look at a day in the life of a metropolitan tabloid newspaper, with Robert Duvall as editor in chief, Glenn Close as managing editor, and Michael Keaton as metro editor. The building used for the paper's headquarters was this Beaux Arts beauty. The offices of the real *New York Sun* are nearby at 102 Chambers Street.

The Paper's headquarters

8. *OFFICE KILLER* OFFICE
75 Maiden Lane

Photographer-artist Cindy Sherman made her mark as a film-maker with the 1997 black comedy *Office Killer*. It told the story of a shy little copy editor (Carol Kane) who goes on a killing spree at her office when she learns she's to be made redundant by her magazine. The office where she gets her revenge was this nondescript Downtown low-rise. Much more dramatic are the bold steel constructions by sculptor Louise Nevelson that stand in the triangular plaza across the way that bears the late artist's name. They are not seen in Sherman's film, however.

9. VITAGRAPH SITE
140 Nassau Street

In 1896, a couple of English immigrants named J. Stuart Blackton and Albert E. Smith hit upon a novel way to perk up their lack-luster vaudeville act . . . motion pictures! Aware that the Edison Company had just perfected the Vitascope projector, Smith and Blackton were among the first entrepreneurs to purchase one of these miraculous new machines. Quickly seeing that the film business was a lot more lucrative than vaudeville, the pair de-cided to switch professions. The only problem was that Edison retained exclusive control over the means of producing films: the camera. Smith, however, was a clever mechanic, and he soon fig-ured how to turn Edison's Vitascope projector into a movie cam-era. And, thus, the American Vitagraph Company was born.

Vitagraph's first office was in the twelve-story, red-brick Morse Building, which still stands at the corner of Nassau and Beekman Streets in Lower Manhattan. Vitagraph's first film, *The Burglar on the Roof*, was shot in the fall of 1897 on the roof of this same building. A makeshift affair, the sixty-second melo-drama featured Smith as cameraman, Blackton as the burglar, and a supporting cast made up of the building's janitor's wife, an office boy, and a third Vitagraph executive. According to pro-ducer/cameraman Smith, the movie cost a whopping $3.50 to make. It was an inauspicious beginning for a company that would become one of the major forces on the silent-screen scene.

Vitagraph continued to operate out of 140 Nassau Street and

Vitagraph's studio on the Morse Building roof, 1897

to shoot films on its roof for another five years. In 1903, the company's continued success—especially with its film coverage of historical events such as Teddy Roosevelt's inauguration—allowed Smith and Blackton to move to larger quarters over in Brooklyn. Today, Vitagraph's Nassau Street birthplace has been renovated and converted into apartments and offices. Few, if any, of its tenants have any idea of the building's filmmaking history. Indeed, few people except for film historians have ever heard of Vitagraph, which disappeared from the face of the earth in 1925, when it was swallowed up by an upstart company headed by a couple of brothers named Warner.

10. FEDERAL HALL NATIONAL MEMORIAL
28 Wall Street

Built as a U.S. customs house in 1842, this imposing Greek temple–like structure at the corner of Wall and Nassau Streets is now called Federal Hall because it occupies the site of our nation's first capitol. In case anyone has forgotten, New York was the

On the Town at Federal Hall: Gene Kelly, Frank Sinatra, Jules Munshin, and George Washington, 1949

capital of the United States between 1779 and 1780, and at the time its city hall building was converted into the country's first administrative headquarters and renamed Federal Hall. It was here that the Continental Congress met, and here that George Washington was sworn in as the first president of the Republic. Today, this historic event is commemorated by a statue of Washington that stands in front of Federal Hall.

Over the years, the building's dramatic façade—with its thirty-two-foot-high Doric columns and towering statue of George Washington—has provided one of New York's most popular photo opportunities for speeches, patriotic rallies, and war-bond drives. Needless to say, the site has also been used by filmmakers and has furnished a dramatic/historic backdrop for sequences in *Kiss of Death* (1947), *Force of Evil* (1948), *On the Town* (1949), *Wolfen* (1982), *Wall Street* (1987), *Godzilla* (1998), and *25th Hour* (2003). Federal Hall is especially memorable in *Kramer vs. Kramer* (1979), where its exterior and interiors were used for some of the courthouse sequences in which Meryl Streep battled Dustin Hoffman for custody of their child, and in *Ghost* (1990), as the site of Whoopi Goldberg's generous donation—prompted by ghost Patrick Swayze—of $4 million to help the homeless.

Today, besides serving as a location for Manhattan-made movies, Federal Hall is open to the public and features exhibits on the history of its site and on early New York.

Visit www.nps.gov/feha/index.htm.

11. DELMONICO'S RESTAURANT
56 Beaver Street

Opened in 1827, this is the oldest restaurant in New York—the city's original power-dining spot. Besides its history—Abraham Lincoln, Oscar Wilde, even Queen Victoria dined here—the restaurant is noted for its architecture, especially its distinctive colonnaded entrance at the top of the triangle formed by Beaver

Delmonico's restaurant

and William Streets. Over the years, the restaurant and its wood-paneled dining room with etched-glass windows have been featured in some top New York films set in the financial district. Among Delmonico's on-screen patrons have been Michael Douglas in *Wall Street* (1987), Jeremy Irons and Ron Silver (as Claus von Bülow and lawyer Alan Dershowitz) in *Reversal of Fortune* (1990), and Richard Gere in *Autumn in New York* (2000). In *The Associate* (1996), however, it's when Whoopi Goldberg is excluded from a Delmonico's power lunch that she realizes her Wall Street job is in big trouble.

Visit www.delmonicosny.com.

12. UNITED STATES CUSTOMS HOUSE
State Street and Bowling Green

One of Lower Manhattan's most impressive buildings, this 1907 Beaux Arts stunner began its life as the U.S. Customs House and is now home to federal government offices as well as the

Former U.S. Customs House, Bowling Green

National Museum of the American Indian. For filmmakers, this granite palazzo is rich in photogenic elements: a grand staircase and massive sculptures and columns mark the façade, whereas the interior boasts a magnificent muraled rotunda. A versatile location, the old Custom House has been the headquarters of the fictional Trask Corporation, where Harrison Ford worked, in *Working Girl* (1988); the Manhattan Museum of Art, where the spirit of evil emerged from a painting, in *Ghostbusters II* (1989); the Ritz Gotham Hotel, where Jim Carrey as the Riddler put on a major bash, in *Batman Forever* (1995); and the Justice Department offices, where staffer Julia Roberts was frequently visited by a paranoid Mel Gibson in *Conspiracy Theory* (1997). The venerable site has also been used in *Autumn in New York* (2000), *The Royal Tenenbaums* (2001), and *How to Lose a Guy in Ten Days* (2003).

Visit www.preserve.org/wtc/us_customs_house.htm.

13. *MIB* HEADQUARTERS
Brooklyn-Battery Tunnel Ventilator Shaft, Battery Place

Aliens are illegally immigrating to the United States—and they aren't from South America, Eastern Europe, or the Middle East. In *Men in Black* (1997), they're from Outer Space,

Men in Black headquarters—actually Brooklyn Battery Tunnel airshaft building

and they're hardly model citizens—especially since they have superhuman powers, including the ability to morph into practically anything or anyone. Lucky for Earth, we've got Tommy Lee Jones and Will Smith on the job working for a top-secret special government agency that's doing its best to fend off this wave of illegal immigration. The black-suited duo worked at this odd structure on Battery Place. In reality, it's the ventilator shaft for the nearby tunnel that links lower Manhattan with Brooklyn.

14. STATUE OF LIBERTY

Edison filmed this great American lady as early as 1896, just ten years after she made her official debut in New York Harbor, and she has been showing up on movie screens ever since. Of her undoubtedly thousands of film appearances, we nominate the following as among the all-time best: (1) *Saboteur* (1942), where Alfred Hitchcock sets the hair-raising climax of this spy thriller

Inside Miss Liberty: Robert Cummings and Norman Lloyd in Hitchcock's *Saboteur*, 1942

Ready for her close-up: Statue of Liberty, as seen in *Remo Williams—The Adventure Begins*

on the statue's crown, arm, and torch. Besides providing one of the world's most exotic locales for a fight between an all-American hero (Bob Cummings) and a Fifth Column thug (played by Norman Lloyd of *St. Elsewhere*), Miss Liberty becomes a symbolic battlefield for the struggle of Western democracy versus Axis fascism that was going on in the real world at the time; (2) *On the Town* (1949), the Statue of Liberty According to MGM, with Gene Kelly, Frank Sinatra, and Jules Munshin looking positively patriotic in their sailor suits as they sing, dance, and frolic at the base of what we're sure was Louis B. Mayer's favorite leading lady; (3) *Funny Girl* (1968), where it and the rest of New York Harbor feature big in Streisand's "Don't Rain on My Parade" production number; (4) *The Godfather, Part II* (1974), Coppola's prequel to the original *Godfather,* in which we see Vito Corleone as an innocent young boy catching sight of the statue from the ship bringing him to a new life in America; the contrast of this hopeful image versus his eventual career as a Mafia don is a powerful one; (5) *Superman* (1978), offering the most romantic close encounter with a major monument ever seen on-screen, when Superman gives Lois Lane a whole new look at Liberty late one night as part of his private flight-see of New York; (6) *Splash* (1984)—what better place than Liberty Island for a naked mermaid to make a memorable Big Apple entrance?; (7) *Remo Williams—The Adventure Begins* (1986), a dreadful film that's worth sitting through (or fast-forwarding to the last fifteen minutes of the tape or DVD) for the fight scene atop a Miss Liberty caged in scaffolding during a major spruce-up for her one-hundredth birthday bash. Most of the close-ups, however, were done in Mexico, where the film's principal photography was based; (8) *Ghostbusters II* (1989)—for the chance to see Miss Liberty come to life; and (9) *Independence Day* (1996), where she bites the dust.

After being off-limits to sightseers for security reasons post–9/11, the Statue of Liberty is open again. Tours leave Battery Park City daily and include both Liberty Island and Ellis Island. Call 212-269-5755 or visit www.circlelineferry.com.

15. STATEN ISLAND FERRY
Battery Place

The twenty-five-minute crossing from Manhattan to Staten Island aboard the venerable Staten Island Ferry is hands down the biggest bargain in New York. Providing fabulous views of New York Harbor, Ellis Island, Lower Manhattan, and the Statue of Liberty, the trip is currently *free* for pedestrians. Carrying some seventy thousand passengers a day, the ferry's real raison d'être is to shuttle commuters, most of whom live on Staten Island and work in the Financial District. On-screen, the ferry's best-known regular passenger was Melanie Griffith. In a role that revived her sagging career, Griffith was the spunky Staten Island secretary who toughed it out on Wall Street, with very little help from her monster boss, Sigourney Weaver, in Mike Nichols's *Working Girl* (1988).

A lesser-known film also featuring Staten Island Ferry commuters is *Ferry Tales,* a documentary short that eavesdrops on the early-morning conversations of women in the ferry's powder room; it was nominated for an Academy Award in 2004. A ferry bathroom also played a big role in director Jerry Schatzberg's classic look at drug addiction, *The Panic in Needle Park* (1972), when Al Pacino and girlfriend Kitty Winn are returning to Manhattan aboard the boat with a new puppy. Unable to control their craving for heroin, they shoot up inside the loo, leaving the little dog on deck. When they come out, the poor pooch winds up overboard. Other films that have used the ferry include *How to Lose a Guy in Ten Days* (2003)—Matthew McConaughey takes Kate Hudson home to his parents on Staten Island; *The Devil's Own* (1997)—Brad Pitt's Irish-American buddy Sean keeps his boat on Staten Island; *The Basketball Diaries* (1995)— the ferry takes Leonardo DiCaprio and his teammates to and from a game on Staten Island; and the prologue to Woody Allen's *Manhattan* (1979)—the ferry is part of a montage celebrating the glories of New York.

Working Girl Melanie Griffith commutes to Manhattan on the Staten Island Ferry, 1988

Offscreen, the last quarter of 2003 was not a good one for the Staten Island Ferry. On October 16, one boat in its fleet accidentally struck a concrete maintenance pier before docking at Staten Island, which resulted in the deaths of ten people and seriously injured another seventy. Also in 2003, it was believed that author/actor Spalding Gray (who in 2001 played a psychiatrist in *Kate and Leopold*), whose body washed ashore several months later, committed suicide by jumping from the ferry.

16. STATEN ISLAND BOTANICAL GARDEN
100 Richmond Terrace, Staten Island

One of Staten Island's many surprises, this magical eighty-acre enclave is a short bus ride from the Staten Island Ferry Terminal at St. George. Of its over twenty formal gardens, the star attractions include the country's only classical walled Chinese garden; a proper English garden modeled on the one at Vita Sackville-West's Sissinghurst estate; and a magnificent new Tuscan terrace with ponds, topiary, and period plantings. Indeed, so much is happening at the Staten Island Botanical Garden that it is considered the fastest-growing cultural institution in the City of New York. It's also starting to catch on with location managers—and was used extensively in *A Beautiful Mind* (2001). In the Academy Award–winning film, the little backyard building where Russell Crowe as John Nash conducted experiments, still stands on the Botanical Garden grounds. The Botanical Garden was also used in the Richard Dreyfuss series *The Education of Max Bickford*; many times by *Law & Order* and *Law & Order: Criminal Intent*; and recently by *Queer Eye for the Straight Guy*, which used the Chinese garden as a locale for one of the show's makeover men to go on a date.

For information, call 718-273-8200 or visit www.sibg.org.

17. MABEL NORMAND HOUSE
91 Tysen Street, Staten Island

These days, not too many people know who Mabel Normand was, much less where she was born. One of the greatest comedians of silent pictures, Mabel Normand was closely linked professionally and personally with the famous producer/director Mack Sennett. In her heyday, she appeared opposite superstars like Charlie Chaplin and Fatty Arbuckle, and at one point she even had her own Hollywood studio. Not bad for a Staten Island gal who started out in the world on November 9, 1892, in this sweet little corner house across from the historic Snug Harbor section of the borough. Miss Normand's eventual Hollywood success was short-lived, however. In the early 1920s a series of tragedies rocked both her emotional stability and her film career. Not only had she become addicted to drugs in the film capital, she was one of the suspects in the scandalous William Desmond Taylor murder in 1922. To make matters worse, she was implicated in another Hollywood shooting shortly thereafter, when her chauffeur was accused of killing a man with a gun that belonged to her. When she died of pneumonia and tuber-

Mabel Normand

Mabel Normand house,
Staten Island

culosis in 1930, she had not made a feature film in seven years. In 1974, her tragic life was the subject of the Broadway musical *Mack and Mabel*, which starred Queens-born Bernadette Peters (née Lazzara) as Staten Island's Mabel Normand.

18. *GODFATHER* ESTATE
110 and 120 Longfellow Road, Staten Island

Benvenuto a Casa Corleone! This cluster of handsome Tudor homes at the end of a tree-lined cul-de-sac in the fashionable Todt Hill section of Staten Island was used by director Francis Ford Coppola in 1971 to represent the Long Island estate of that nice Italian-American family that we all got to know and love in *The Godfather*. Movie lovers will remember especially the spectacular wedding sequence that was shot in the garden of 120 Longfellow.

It is interesting to note that not too far from *The Godfather* movie mansion, the real-life Mafia kingpin, Paul Castellano,

The Godfather estate, Staten Island

lived in a walled estate on Berodid Road. Castellano's name was all over the news in December 1985 when he was rubbed out at Sparks Steak House on 46th Street in Manhattan.

19. *SPLENDOR IN THE GRASS* HOUSE
4144 Victory Boulevard, Staten Island

Splendor in the Grass . . . great Hollywood movie, right? With some fine location scenes shot in the Midwest, right? Wrong—on both counts, for this classic 1960 tale of hot-blooded teenage love in late-1920s Kansas was shot completely in the New York metropolitan area. The reason for this surprising bit of location maneuvering was because the film's director, Elia Kazan, wanted to be as close as possible to New York, where his father was very ill at the time.

Of the many challenges that *Splendor in the Grass* created for its location people, none was more perplexing than finding the small-town Kansas house in which Natalie Wood's character, Deanie Loomis, lived with her family. To the rescue came Staten

Staten Island wedding: *The Godfather,* 1972

Island, which had on its underdeveloped western edge a little settlement of wood-frame homes known as Travis. The corner house at number 4144 Victory Boulevard was selected for the Loomis place, and modified slightly through the addition of a temporary staircase on one side, a bit of gingerbread trim in front, and a fresh coat of paint all over. The shooting took place between May 6 and 17, 1960, and, needless to say, it caused quite a stir in Travis—especially when Natalie Wood's handsome husband, Robert Wagner (it was their first time around), showed up one evening and gave autographs to the crowd of locals who had gathered at the location. Another "surprise" guest that same evening was a Twentieth Century–Fox starlet named Joan Collins who, according to a local newspaper report, was visiting her good friend Natalie Wood. Maybe so—but in Miss Collins's tell-all autobiography, *Past Imperfect* (Simon & Schuster, 1984), she indicates that she had been secretly living with Miss Wood's co-star, Warren Beatty, at the time. Miss Collins goes on to tell of Mr. Beatty's lovemaking prowess as well as of the abortion that

Staten Island sweethearts: Natalie Wood and Warren Beatty in *Splendor in the Grass*, 1961

she had at his insistence in Newark, New Jersey, during the *Splendor* shooting.

Today, the little house at 4144 Victory Boulevard is still standing, but the community of Travis, with its new condo developments, could no longer double for pre-Depression Kansas.

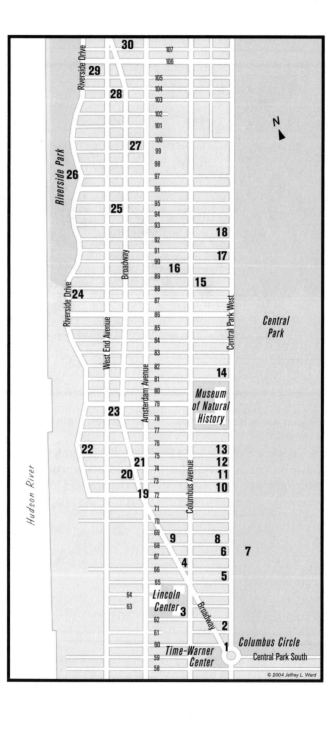

9

The Upper West Side: Rebel Territory

Just as there is the East Coast and the West Coast, there is the Upper East Side and the Upper West Side. And despite the fact that there's only Central Park, rather than a whole country, separating these two Manhattan neighborhoods, they are often as different in outlook and spirit as New York is from California. Whereas the East Side has a reputation for being the bastion of establishment Manhattan, the West Side has been noted for its individuality, its liberal politics, its cultural pursuits. Granted, the West Side has lost some of its brashness and originality through decades of gentrification and Yuppiefication, but old-timers, proud of the way things used to be, are hanging on to their traditions and trying hard to keep their neighborhood unique. Classic Upper West Siders from the world of show business include rebels like Lauren Bacall, Barbra Streisand, Mia Farrow, William Hurt, Cicely Tyson, Bruce Willis, Alec Baldwin, Robert Duvall, Mick Jagger, Kevin Bacon, Teri Garr, Dustin Hoffman, Christopher Walken, Faye Dunaway, Michael J. Fox, John Lennon, Yoko Ono, Madonna, Sean Penn, and the greatest rebel of them all—James Dean.

Almost as intriguing as the stars who have called the Upper West Side home are the extraordinary buildings that many of them have occupied. Landmarks of Art Deco, Beaux Arts, or Gothic Revival architecture, the great celebrity apartment buildings of Central Park West and Broadway stun with their style and their diversity. Ultimately, diversity is what the Upper West Side is all about—and that includes cultural diversity. Witness the West Side location of Lincoln Center, New York's "acropolis of the performing arts," home to opera, symphony, ballet, theater, and, of special interest to movie lovers, one of the country's most important cinema events—the New York Film Festival, held every autumn.

1. COLUMBUS CIRCLE

While traffic circles are commonplace in European cities such as London, Paris, and Rome—Manhattan, with its grid-straight street setup, has precious few. Arguably the most notable is Co-

Columbus Circle, 1953: Judy Holliday and Heywood Hale Broun in *It Should Happen to You*

Columbus Circle, 2004:
Trump International
Hotel and Tower

lumbus Circle, which was named for the oft-disputed "discoverer" of America, who is remembered here with a statue rising from a central fountain. Like Times Square, this impressive intersection—which marks the convergence of Central Park South, Central Park West, Eighth Avenue, and Broadway—has had several distinct incarnations in the last fifty years. In the late 1940s and early 1950s, for example, Columbus Circle had a formal, Old World feel, edged at the time mainly by low-rise buildings, with Central Park an integral part of the picture. To see it as it was then, *On the Town* (1949) has a lovely Columbus Circle sequence, but the film that documents it best is George Cukor's 1954 *It Should Happen to You,* where unsuccessful actress Judy Holliday takes one last shot at fame by putting her name— Gladys Glover—on a vacant Columbus Circle billboard. Especially memorable is the scene with Holliday and a young Peter Lawford—the Hugh Grant of his era—circling and recircling

Columbus Circle in Lawford's white Jaguar convertible to check out the sign. Are you in Manhattan—or Rome?

In the 1960s, Columbus Circle started looking considerably less European, as dramatic new buildings such as the white marble Huntington Hartford Museum, the New York Coliseum, and the forty-four-story Gulf + Western Building (where Paramount Pictures, then part of the G+W conglomerate, was headquartered) radically altered its profile. In the mid-1970s, this new Columbus Circle was an important location for Martin Scorsese's *Taxi Driver* (1976), as the site of a big political rally during which the sociopath ex-Marine played by Robert De Niro attempts to assassinate New York's mayor. Two years later, the site was again used for a shooting, this time in thriller *Eyes of Laura Mars,* where Faye Dunaway played a photographer stalked by a killer.

Cut to 2004. Paramount, now part of a different conglomerate—Viacom—has moved to Times Square; the former Gulf + Western Building now belongs to Donald Trump, who spent many millions glitzing it into Trump International Hotel and Tower; and the old New York Coliseum has been razed and is now home to the dazzling twin eighty-story skyscrapers of Time Warner Center, which encompasses the luxurious Mandarin Oriental Hotel, an upscale dining-shopping-entertainment center, the New York studios of CNN, and the new East Coast headquarters for another legendary old Hollywood studio, Warner Bros. Now all the place needs is a good movie. Stay tuned.

2. MAYFLOWER HOTEL
15 Central Park West

Once a little funky, now rather posh, the Mayflower has traditionally attracted writers (it's a favorite of transgendered British travel writer Jan Morris), musicians (Lincoln Center is just a block away), and long-stay guests (its rooms used to be relatively inexpensive and many had kitchenettes). In the last category was Jack Nicholson, who in *Wolf* (1994) checked into the Mayflower after being downgraded by his publishing company and cuckolded by his wife, Kate Nelligan. Things pick up for Jack after a bizarre encounter with a wolf makes him a force to be reckoned with.

Visit www.mayflowerhotel.com.

3. LINCOLN CENTER
Columbus Avenue from 62nd to 66th Streets

Home to opera, ballet, symphonic music, and theater, the Lincoln Center for the Performing Arts is one of the largest and most impressive complexes of its kind in the world. What many people have forgotten is that Manhattan's arts acropolis stands on land that was once a neighborhood of dreary brick tenement buildings. In 1961, before they were torn down to make way for Lincoln Center, these old West Side blocks had a brief fling with show business when they were called on to furnish the realistic locales for some of the scenes in United Artists' *West Side Story*. Later, filmmaking would return to the area in a big way once Lincoln Center made its debut as a dramatic—and camera-ready—New York City landmark.

Especially photogenic is Lincoln Center's main plaza, which clusters the New York State Theater, the Metropolitan Opera House, and Avery Fisher Hall around a black-marble fountain. Movie lovers may remember the tour of a then still-new Lincoln Center given by Lee Remick, who worked here as a guide in *No Way to Treat a Lady* (1968), where she points out to her group the Henry Moore sculptures in the reflecting pool and the thirty-

Arts acropolis: Lincoln Center, 1987

foot-high Chagalls in the Metropolitan Opera House lobby, which the great artist helped install. A few years later, Det. Frank Serpico (Al Pacino) indulged in his taste for things cultural with a night at the ballet at Lincoln Center in Sidney Lumet's *Serpico* (1972). More recently, Lincoln Center doubled for the Dorothy Chandler Pavilion in L.A. for the Academy Awards ceremony in *In & Out* (1997), where an Oscar winner accidentally "outs" his closeted gay former teacher (Kevin Kline). Ironically, the Dorothy Chandler Pavilion in L.A. doubled for Lincoln Center in the late Herbert Ross's saga of two dancers (Shirley MacLaine and Anne Bancroft) in *The Turning Point* (1977).

Of all of Lincoln Center's locations, arguably its famous fountain has been used most—in films such as *Ghostbusters* (1984), *Moonstruck* (1987), and recently *Sweet Home Alabama* (2002), where New York City's first lady-mayor, a rather snobbish Candice Bergen, while officiating at a red-carpet gala, gets the unwelcome news that her son is engaged to a cheap Southern fashion designer (Reese Witherspoon). By far the fountain's most memorable screen appearance, however, was in Mel Brooks's outrageous 1967 comedy, *The Producers*. In the Lincoln Center sequence, Zero Mostel is trying to convince Gene Wilder that there's big money to be made in producing a bound-to-flop Broadway musical called *Springtime for Hitler*. When Wilder finally says yes to Mostel's cockamamie scheme, all the lights of the Metropolitan Opera House come up full, the fountain starts going crazy, and fireworks finish off the fantasy.

Serious movie lovers will also be interested in two Lincoln Center buildings beyond the main plaza area. The first is the New York Public Library and Museum of Performing Arts at 111 Amsterdam Avenue. Here, on the third floor, the Billy Rose Theater Collection is one of the country's major research facilities for theater, radio, television, and film. The other Lincoln Center building that draws movie lovers is Alice Tully Hall, which every September–October hosts most of the presentations of the Film Society of Lincoln Center's prestigious New York Film Festival (Avery Fisher Hall is used for the festival's opening and closing nights).

Credited with staging the U.S. premieres of some of the world's most important films, the New York Film Festival is where New Yorkers first got to see Ján Kadár's *The Shop on Main Street* (1965), Gillo Pontecorvo's *The Battle of Algiers* (1965), Eric Rohmer's *My Night at Maud's* (1969), Bernardo Bertolucci's *The Conformist* (1970), Bob Rafelson's *Five Easy Pieces* (1970), Louis Malle's *Murmur of the Heart* (1971), Peter Bogdanovich's *The Last Picture Show* (1971), Luis Buñuel's *The Discreet Charm of the Bourgeoisie* (1972), Rainer Werner Fassbinder's *The Bitter Tears of Petra von Kant* (1973), Martin Scorsese's *Mean Streets* (1973), François Truffaut's *Day for Night* (1973), Wim Wenders's *The American Friend* (1977), Truffaut's *The Last Metro* (1980), Werner Herzog's *Fitzcarraldo* (1982), Lawrence Kasdan's *The Big Chill* (1983), Akira Kurosawa's *Ran* (1985), Maximilian Schell's *Marlene* (1986), Francis Ford Coppola's *Peggy Sue Got Married* (1986), John Boorman's *Hope and Glory* (1987), Yurek Bogayevicz's *Anna* (1987), Mike Leigh's *Secrets and Lies* (1996), Ang Lee's *The Ice Storm* (1997), Pedro Almodovar's *All About My Mother* (1999), and Lars von Trier's *Dancer in the Dark* (2000).

For information on the New York Film Festival as well as on the New Directors/New Films festival (March–April), which Lincoln Center cosponsors with the Museum of Modern Art, write Film Society of Lincoln Center, 70 Lincoln Center Plaza, New York, NY 10023-6595, or log onto www.filmlinc.com.

4. ABC CAMPUS
West 66th/67th Streets

Part of the Disney empire, the American Broadcasting Company has taken over so much of West 66th and 67th Streets from Central Park West to West End Avenue that the corridor has become known as the network's "campus." TV fans may be interested in checking out the following campus addresses: 47 West 66th Street—where *World News Tonight* originates; 56 West 66th Street—longtime home of the soap opera *One Life to Live*; 77 West 66th Street—ABC headquarters; 7 Lincoln Square—*Live with Regis and Kelly!*; 320 West 66th Street—*All My Children* and *The View*; and 30 West 67th Street: *Millionaire*. ABC's highest-visibility facility, however, is its Times Square Studios, with huge windows at Seventh Avenue and 43rd Street, where *Good Morning America* and *20/20* overlook Times Square and vice versa (see Chapter 3, item 8).

5. *GHOSTBUSTERS* BUILDING
55 Central Park West

New Yorkers often have to put up with a lot for the privilege of living in the Big Apple. Exorbitant rents, ancient plumbing, roaches, noise—but nobody had it quite as bad as Sigourney Weaver when she resided on Central Park West in the 1984 film *Ghostbusters*. Terror dogs! Lecherous arm chairs! Leaping eggs! Evil refrigerators! Who ya gonna call? For Sigourney's *Ghostbusters* building, a real Central Park West apartment house (whose celebrity residents have included designer Calvin Klein

Ghostbusters Harold Ramis, Dan Aykroyd, and Bill Murray on Central Park West, 1984

and actress Marsha Mason) was used for many exteriors, but the exotic pre-Columbian temple that appeared to be on the roof of 55 Central Park West was created—for long shots—by matte artist Matthew Yuricich. Meanwhile, for medium shots a fifteen-foot model of the temple was used; and for close-ups with actors, a full-scale temple complex was built at the Burbank (now Warner Bros.) Studios on the West Coast. For the scene where the street caves in at the end of the film, parts of the sequence were done in New York at 55 Central Park West, while others were lensed at the Columbia (now Warner Bros.) Ranch in Burbank, California, where the façade of the New York apartment building was reconstructed, along with a hydraulically controlled collapsing street! Ultimately the whole sequence was put together in the editing room.

This Central Park West address, it turns out, was not the *Ghostbusters* company's first choice for an apartment building. They really wanted to use 1 Fifth Avenue—both for its Art Deco architecture and its proximity to Washington Square—but 1 Fifth's co-op board nixed the plan.

6. HOTEL DES ARTISTES
1 West 67th Street

Originally built to house painters and sculptors, this beautiful 1918 building—with studios that feature double-height windows and wonderful light—quickly began to draw artistic residents from other fields. One of these was America's hottest male movie star, Rudolph Valentino, who rented a bachelor pad at Des Artistes in 1922, even though he was married to his second wife, Natacha Rambova, at the time. Actually, he was only sort of married to Miss Rambova, because his divorce from his first wife, Jean Acker, would not be final in California until the following year. Like many movie people at the time, Valentino had tried to get around California's tough divorce laws by wedding Natacha in Mexico. Upon their return to California, however, there was an uproar that resulted in Valentino's being charged with bigamy and having to spend a night in jail. Fed up with Hollywood's provincialism and also with his studio (Paramount) for offering him little help with his legal difficulties, Valentino and Natacha escaped to New York. Not wanting to risk any more trouble with the authorities or with the press, however, Valentino moved into Des Artistes alone. This wasn't too much of a hardship, though, because Natacha resided with an aunt who lived on the same West 67th Street block. Also, by the following year Valentino's divorce had gone through, and both Valentinos were able to live together legally at Des Artistes. It was during his Des Artistes period that Valentino also settled his differences with Paramount and went on to make his two New York pictures, *Monsieur Beaucaire* and *A Sainted Devil,* at the Astoria Studios in Queens. But by 1924, Valentino was working and living in Hollywood once again, and by 1925, his marriage to Natacha was on the rocks.

Besides Valentino, Des Artistes also counts among its famous former and current residents artist Norman Rockwell, dancer

Hotel des Artistes

The Valentinos in New
York: Rudolph and wife
Natacha Rambova

Isadora Duncan, novelist Fannie Hurst, playwright/performer
Noël Coward, Algonquin Round Table wit Alexander Woollcott,
former New York City mayor and sometime newscaster John
Lindsay, and actors Richard Thomas and Joel Grey.

Taking over much of the ground floor of the Hotel des
Artistes is the elegant Café des Artistes—noted for its naughty
murals by erstwhile resident Howard Chandler Christy. The
restaurant was featured in Louis Malle's groundbreaking two-
character (Wallace Shawn and André Gregory) *My Dinner with
André* (1981). It was also used in the Richard Benjamin–directed
farce *The Money Pit* (1986), and it is at this chic café that Diane
Keaton, Bette Midler, and Goldie Hawn have a nostalgic lunch
after attending a college friend's funeral in *The First Wives Club*
(1996).

Visit www.cafedesartistesnyc.com.

At Tavern on the Green: Joseph Cotten and Ethel Barrymore in *Portrait of Jennie*, 1948

7. TAVERN ON THE GREEN
Central Park West at 67th Street

The Land of Oz is alive and well in Central Park at Tavern on the Green. A sheepfold in the 1870s, the building became a restaurant in the 1930s, but it wasn't until Warner LeRoy (1935–2001) got his hands on the place in 1974 that Tavern on the Green became one of the city's most dazzling dining rooms. With strong Hollywood roots—LeRoy's father was director/producer Mervyn LeRoy (*The Wizard of Oz*); his mother, Doris, was Harry Warner's daughter—Warner LeRoy gave Tavern on the Green the total Tinseltown treatment, redoing it with brass, glass, mirrors, crystal chandeliers, and pastel-painted plaster of Paris. Most opulent of the various dining rooms is the Crystal Room, a great glass pavilion that looks out on gardens—and, at night, trees strung with fairy lights—backed by Central Park. Movie lovers may remember the scene in *Ghostbusters* (1984) where Rick Moranis, pursued by a red-eyed, fang-toothed "terror dog," pounds on the glass wall of the Crystal Room desperately trying to get the attention of the diners on the other side. In true New York fashion, everyone in the restaurant keeps right on eating, trying their best not to notice the horror show going on outside.

In 1989, the restaurant was especially popular with Woody Allen, who dined here alfresco with his mother (who kvetches about the table) in the "Oedipus Wrecks" sequence of *New York Stories* and inside with Alan Alda in *Crimes and Misdemeanors.* Tavern on the Green is also where James Caan, as the novelist in Stephen King's *Misery* (1990), celebrated his latest best seller—though he would have little to celebrate once he met up with Kathy Bates. And speaking of celebrations, Bette Midler, who had given up her illegitimate daughter to be raised by her wealthy father in *Stella* (1990), stood outside and watched the young woman get married in the Tavern's Terrace Room in this remake of the 1937 Barbara Stanwyck classic *Stella Dallas.* Meanwhile, to see what the place was like in its pre–Warner LeRoy days, movie lovers should check out another classic—David O. Selznick's 1948 *Portrait of Jennie*, which shows Joseph Cotten and Ethel Barrymore having cocktails here.

Visit www.tavernonthegreen.com.

8. JAMES DEAN APARTMENT
19 West 68th Street

"Across the room on the shoulder-high shelf that ran the width and length of the entire room were empty beer cans, an open peanut butter jar, an album cover of *Romeo and Juliet,* a baseball bat, a hot plate, a bunch of dried leaves stuck in a Maxwell House can, several sheets of music and a bust of Jimmy gazing down upon a new chrome music stand." That's how (in David Dalton's *James Dean: The Mutant King,* St. Martin's, 1975) an actress friend of his described the tiny twelve-by-twelve room—with bathroom down the hall—that was James Dean's Upper West Side home before he went off to Hollywood in 1954 to shoot his first major film, *East of Eden.* Despite the fact that he was heading for the big time, Jimmy Dean held on to his minuscule New York City pad, and stayed there in January 1955 when he returned to the city after having wrapped *Eden* as well as a couple of television shows on the West Coast. It was to have been a happy reunion with the city he loved—a time to see old friends, visit old hangouts, and revel in his newfound success. It turned out to be anything but. Throughout the visit, Jimmy's behavior was extremely erratic. He was edgy, ill at ease, often nasty. Some friends accused him of having "gone Hollywood." Others felt he was strung out on drugs. There was a particularly unpleasant episode with his former girlfriend, Barbara Glenn, when she broke the news to Jimmy that she had gotten engaged during his absence from the city. At first he took it well, and even had dinner with Barbara and her fiancé. But the next day, he pleaded with her to come by his apartment for a talk. There, he opened up a suitcase full of cash and ordered her to help herself to the stash, since she had lent him money during his starving-actor days. When she refused the money and insisted that it was all over between them, Jimmy got hysterical, screamed at

James Dean's
West Side digs

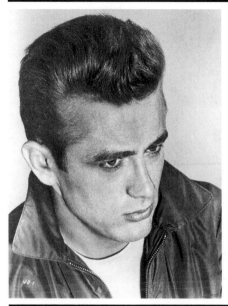

West Side rebel:
James Dean

her, and threw wads of money at her as she left the apartment. His last words were: "And when I die, it'll be your fault!"

Jimmy left New York soon thereafter, never to see the city or his West 68th Street digs again. The car crash that ended his life and burgeoning career lay just nine months ahead of him. Today, a half century later, the little building with the bow windows that James Dean called home still stands off Central Park West on 68th Street. Ironically, Dean's last NYC address is just five blocks away from his first, which was a room at the West Side YMCA at 5 West 63rd Street, where he stayed when he landed in the Big Apple in the fall of 1951.

9. MAYA SCHAPER CHEESE AND ANTIQUES
106 West 69th Street

Nora Ephron wrote and directed this cyber version of Ernst Lubitsch's 1939 Jimmy Stewart–Margaret Sullavan comedy *The Shop Around the Corner* (1939). The story of two people who don't get along in the workplace but are much more compatible

Maya Schaper Cheese and Antiques (Meg Ryan's *You've Got Mail* bookstore)

as secret pen pals, the film was remade a decade later as the MGM musical *In the Good Old Summertime* with Judy Garland and Van Johnson. Enter Ephron a half century later with *You've Got Mail* (1998), a slick take on the classic tale that has Meg Ryan as the owner of an eccentric Upper West Side bookstore threatened by the latest branch of a mega-book emporium chain, which Tom Hanks is opening across the street from her. In the Ephron version, Meg and Tom are not only secret e-mail buddies but they each have other significant others. Meg's little bookstore was actually this well-known West Side establishment that deals not in books but in the odd combo of cheese and antiques.

10. THE DAKOTA
1 West 72nd Street

In 1884, the *New York Daily Graphic* called it "one of the most perfect apartment houses in the world." Besides offering the most lavish apartments that New Yorkers had ever encountered, the Dakota also provided some of the best views in town. "Every prominent landmark in the landscape can be discerned from this location," the *Daily Graphic* gushed on, "and the great buildings of the lower city are as prominently marked as if the sightseer were floating over the island in a balloon."

Today, some 120 years later, the Dakota still has fabulous apartments and drop-dead views. It also boasts one of the most remarkable tenant rosters of any building in the country. Among the Dakota's most famous former and current residents are Lauren Bacall, Judy Holliday, Zachary Scott, Teresa Wright, Robert Ryan, Marian Mercer, Rex Reed, Kent Smith, William Inge, John Frankenheimer, Jack Palance, Roberta Flack, Fannie Hurst, Rudolf Nureyev, John Madden, Judy Garland, Gwen Verdon, José Ferrer and Rosemary Clooney, Eric Portman, Warner LeRoy, John Lennon and Yoko Ono, Gilda Radner, Connie Chung, and a mild-mannered gentleman whose real name was William Henry Pratt, but whom movie lovers know as Boris Karloff.

The Dakota

Stories of the Dakota's star tenants abound. Boris Karloff, for example, evidently felt very unloved every Halloween, because the kids in the building were too afraid of his horror-film image to take any of the trick-or-treat candy he left outside his door. Another legend of the Dakota, reported by Stephen Birmingham in *Life at the Dakota* (Random House, 1979), is the saga of Lauren Bacall's air conditioners. Since the building has landmark status, the New York Landmarks Commission must give its blessing to any renovations planned by Dakota tenants. When Bacall wanted to knock out some exterior bricks to install through-the-wall air-conditioning units, she asked a fellow tenant who was familiar with the workings of the Landmarks Commission to plead her case before the commissioner. When the official found out just who wanted permission to install the air conditioners, he hinted that he would prefer to see the legendary actress in person. A meeting was arranged at Miss Bacall's apartment at cocktail time. Bacall, whose standard Dakota drag consisted of slacks and an old sweater, pulled out all the stops and received the city

Trouble at the Dakota: Ruth Gordon, Sidney Blackmer, and Mia Farrow in *Rosemary's Baby,* 1968

official in full Hollywood-star attire. It was a charming cocktail hour, everyone got along beautifully, and Bacall was permitted to knock down all the bricks she wished.

Then there were the Lennons. Not all Dakota residents were thrilled, it seems, to have John and Yoko as neighbors—especially since their presence meant a constant pack of photographers lurking around the building waiting to get a photo of the famous couple. Nor were the Dakota's telephone operators back in those days pleased with the fact that they would have to handle a good thirty calls a day from fans asking to be put through to the famous former Beatle and/or his wife. Needless to say, the whole building was saddened and horrified by Lennon's murder outside the Dakota on December 8, 1980.

At the time of the murder, many Americans were already familiar with the Dakota because of the famous thriller, *Rosemary's Baby*, which had been shot there twelve years earlier. Movie lovers may also remember the Dakota from its appearance in Twentieth Century–Fox's 1949 film *House of Strangers*, which starred Edward G. Robinson, Richard Conte, and Susan Hayward. More recently it housed Tom Cruise in the psychological thriller *Vanilla Sky* (2001).

11. THE LANGHAM
135 Central Park West

Built in 1905, this Central Park West château has furnished luxurious living space to Cyril Ritchard, Lee Strasberg, Merv Griffin, Carly Simon, Maureen O'Sullivan, and Mia Farrow (Miss O'Sullivan's daughter). When Woody Allen starred both Mia and her mom in his 1986 *Hannah and Her Sisters,* he added a bit of Central Park West cinéma vérité by featuring Farrow's Langham apartment in the film as well. Mia's eleven-room flat was a rental, by the way—and in the 1990s, she and her many children reportedly had to move out when the rent skyrocketed from a modest $2,300 to $8,000 per month. Back on-screen, the Langham was where Susan Saint James had to contend with a very suave Eastern European count named Dracula (George Hamilton) in *Love at First Bite* (1979).

12. SAN REMO APARTMENTS
145-146 Central Park West

A longtime favorite address of celebrities, this massive Central Park West landmark has been home at various times to Dustin Hoffman, Mary Tyler Moore, Raquel Welch, Bruce Willis, Demi Moore, Steve Martin, Donald Sutherland, Paul Simon, Barry Manilow, Elaine May, Tony Randall, Robert Stigwood, Harold Arlen, and Diane Keaton. When rock star Madonna (she had yet to reinvent herself as model mother and children's book author) tried to buy a $1.2 million co-op apartment in the San Remo in July 1985, Diane Keaton was the lone member of the prestigious building's co-op board who did not reject the singer's application. The others, it seemed, felt Madonna's flamboyant lifestyle—which had included nude layouts in *Playboy* and *Penthouse* as well as a hot-tempered actor fiancé named Sean Penn—would bring unwanted publicity to the San Remo's elegant classical entryways. Expecting trouble with the board, Madonna showed up for her personal appearance dressed in a basic black dress accessorized with a single strand of pearls and two gold crucifixes (she had yet to discover the Kabbalah) around her neck. But neither God nor Diane Keaton were enough to get Madonna into the San Remo. She had better luck down the street at 65 Central Park West, where she and Sean ultimately wound up living.

On a sadder note, the San Remo is where the legendary screen goddess of the 1940s, Rita Hayworth, lived out the last years of her life in the apartment of her daughter by Aly Khan, Princess Yasmin Khan. A victim of Alzheimer's disease, Miss Hayworth—installed in a suite that tried to duplicate the furnishings of her Beverly Hills home—had nurses round the clock. The single rose that arrived every day up until her death in 1987 was a gift of her *Gilda* costar and longtime friend, Glenn Ford.

13. THE KENILWORTH
151 Central Park West

Notable for its massive columned entryway, the Kenilworth was completed in 1908. For many years, the movies' most famous Sherlock Holmes, Basil Rathbone, resided here. Old-time Central Park Westers recall with amusement seeing Rathbone walking in Central

The Kenilworth

Park with his friend Boris Karloff, who lived three blocks away in the Dakota. Needless to say, it's not every day that you run into Sherlock Holmes on a stroll with Frankenstein! Other Kenilworth tenants of note have been actors Keir Dullea and Michael Douglas.

14. THE BERESFORD
211 Central Park West/1 and 7 West 81st Street

A building so vast it has three different addresses, the magnificent Beresford is where Rock Hudson had his six-room home away from Hollywood. After the star died of AIDS in October 1985, most of the contents of his Beresford apartment were auctioned off at the William Doyle Galleries in New York, bringing prices that far exceeded the auction house's expectations. Among the items that fans fought over were a silverplated box inscribed "Dynasty, 100th episode," which brought $900; a needlepoint

The Beresford

rug made by Rock ($2,100); a Steinway piano ($6,875); and the footstool that five-foot, four-inch Elizabeth Taylor used to reach the six-foot, five-inch actor's Beresford bathroom sink ($1,400).

Other famous former Beresford tenants: John McEnroe and Tatum O'Neal, Mike Nichols and Diane Sawyer, Calvin Klein, Beverly Sills, Isaac Stern, Meryl Streep, Peter Jennings, Helen Gurley Brown, Tony Randall, Miramax cochairman Bob Weinstein, and Jerry Seinfeld. Supposedly, when the comedian renovated his spacious duplex apartment, the project took several years, which did not delight his neighbors and resulted in strict new renovation rules being set by the building's famously fussy co-op board. These allow a maximum of ten days for the demolition and no more than ninety for the heavy work. The same board was less successful when it fought to stop the American Museum of Natural History from erecting its new planetarium across the street—it seems they didn't like its design and were also concerned about noise. The board was also unable to block a statue honoring Alfred Nobel—of the famous Nobel Prize—on West 81st Street; they were worried it would attract too many tourists.

15. *KISSING JESSICA STEIN* APARTMENT
61 West 88th Street

In *Kissing Jessica Stein* (2001), the writing-acting team of Jennifer Westfeldt and Heather Juergensen broke new ground with their poignant, funny look at lesbian love in the city. Westfeldt's sexually unsettled title character seemingly has everything: good job, great friends, supportive family, and fabulous digs in a brownstone—with a spiral staircase no less—on the Upper West Side. The only thing lacking in Jessica's life is romance. After a string of failed relationships with men, Jessica answers a "woman seeking woman" ad and everything changes—for a while.

Kissing Jessica Stein
brownstone

16. CLAREMONT RIDING ACADEMY
175 West 89th Street

This four-story horse barn on West 89th Street saw a lot of action in the 1981 thriller *Eyewitness,* when William Hurt foiled his would-be murderer by letting loose scores of horses in the middle of the Upper West Side. Dating back to 1889, the Claremont Riding Academy has taught riding to the Kennedy kids, the Lawfords, and the children of Diana Ross; it has also rented mounts for romantic rides through Central Park to such celebrities as Jacqueline Onassis and writer-editor Michael Korda. In addition to *Eyewitness,* movie lovers may also recognize Claremont as the stable from which a band of *Hair* hippies stole their ponies for the "Sodomy" production number in the 1979 Milos Forman film.

Call 212-724-5100.

17. THE ELDORADO
300 Central Park West

Lying between 90th and 91st Streets, this twin-towered 1930s apartment building is about as far north as you can go on Central Park West and still claim a fashionable address. Among the stars who have had such claims are Faye Dunaway, Roddy McDowall, Richard Dreyfuss, Carrie Fisher, Bianca Jagger, Martin Balsam, Tuesday Weld, Michael J. Fox and Tracy Pollan, and Phil Donahue and Marlo Thomas. One celebrity who couldn't wangle an Eldorado apartment, however, was Lena Horne, who reports that she and her late husband, Lennie Hayton, who was Jewish, were once denied a spot in the building. In her autobiography, *Lena* (Doubleday, 1965), she writes of her Eldorado experience: "We were caught in three different kinds of prejudice—against Negroes, against Jews, and against mixed marriages. I don't know which of these the management was responding to, but the Eldorado, on Central Park West, refused us an apartment. At the time it was owned by a Negro, Bishop C. M. ('Daddy') Grace."

18. THE ARDSLEY
320 Central Park West

Designed by Emery Roth, the same architect who did the San Remo down the street, the Art Deco Ardsley is where Barbra Streisand lived (first with, later without, husband Elliott Gould) throughout the second half of the 1960s. When, in late 1969, Ms. Streisand tried moving across Central Park to posher digs in a cooperative at 1021 Park Avenue, she was turned down by the building's board of directors. The building has also been home to actresses Dianne Wiest and Swoosie Kurtz.

19. NEEDLE PARK
Broadway at 72nd and 73rd Streets

Al Pacino's first starring role was in this raw little 1971 film about the ravages of drugs—specifically heroin—in the Big Apple. The film was Jerry Schatzberg's *The Panic in Needle Park,*

Needle Park, 2004

and its major location was this formerly grungy little park that pricks Broadway and 72nd Street. Once a hangout for addicts and pushers, Needle Park, officially Verdi Square (a statue of composer Giuseppe Verdi stands at its center), has been considerably spiffed up in the last few years as part of the ongoing Yuppification of the Upper West Side and the extensive renovation of the subway station on the same spot. The film made a star out of Pacino. Alas, the same cannot be said of his *Needle Park* costar Kitty Winn, who also got rave reviews and was judged Best Actress at the 1971 Cannes Film Festival, but who disappeared from the screen by the end of the decade.

20. THE ANSONIA
2107–2109 Broadway

Loaded with towers, mansard roofs, ornate balconies, balustrades, and bay windows, the Ansonia is easily Broadway's most opulent, if not its most beautiful, structure. When it opened in 1903, this extraordinary sixteen-story Beaux Arts building provided tenants with such luxuries as electric stoves, hot and cold filtered water, freezers, a pneumatic-tube system to deliver messages, and even an early form of central air-conditioning. The building also had incredibly thick walls, installed to protect against fire, which meant that Ansonia suites were among the most soundproof in the city. For this reason, it is said, many famous musicians took up residence in the building, including Enrico Caruso, Lauritz Melchior, Igor Stravinsky, Arturo Toscanini, Ezio Pinza, and Lily Pons. Besides their musical careers, Pinza and Pons both appeared in the 1947 film *Carnegie Hall,* as well as in various other Hollywood films. Another legendary film personality who once lived at the Ansonia is Billie Burke of *The Wizard of Oz* and *Topper* fame. During her Ansonia days, she was married to the great theatrical impresario Florenz Ziegfeld, who lived with Miss Burke on one floor of the building and supposedly kept a mistress in an identical apartment on another!

In addition to its famous residents, the Ansonia has been a star in its own right on numerous occasions. In the 1975 film *The Sunshine Boys,* it was Walter Matthau's Manhattan apartment house. That same year the building also served as the location for a dramatic sequence in *Three Days of the Condor* that finds

Beaux Arts beauty:
The Ansonia

Robert Redford narrowly escaping being gunned down in the Ansonia's alleyway. The Ansonia surprisingly winds up in the 1989 French film *Life and Nothing But,* which deals with people looking for their loved ones after World War I. In the film a French war widow doesn't find her husband's body on the battlefields of Verdun but she does meet an officer with whom she has a relationship. She ultimately leaves France sans officer and toward the end of the film she is seen reading a letter from him in an apartment in the Ansonia. In the thriller *Single White Female* (1992), Bridget Fonda is getting over a bad-news boyfriend when she takes in a roommate (Jennifer Jason Leigh) in her Ansonia flat. More bad news! And recently, Brittany Murphy had a funky red suite at the Ansonia, which was filled with the guitars of her late rock-star dad in *Uptown Girls* (2003).

The Ansonia was also the spot where a now-famous singer and movie star got her big break in show business. The star was Bette Midler, who became the toast of New York when she sang, danced, and clowned at the Continental Baths, a gay spa that once occupied the Ansonia's basement and whose cabaret room enjoyed a brief vogue among both gay and straight New Yorkers in the early 1970s. The Continental Baths were replaced by Plato's Retreat, a hedonistic heterosexual follow-up that Spike Lee re-created in *Summer of Sam* (1999) for a scene where John Leguizamo and movie wife Mira Sorvino behave dreadfully, signaling the disintegration of their marriage.

Today the Continental Baths and Plato's Retreat are history, but a gloriously restored Ansonia is one of the Upper West Side's brightest stars.

21. BEACON THEATER
2124 Broadway

Its architect, Walter W. Ahlschlager, was the same man responsible for designing the legendary Roxy Theater, which stood at Seventh Avenue and 50th Street. This was no coincidence, since the Beacon Theater was originally conceived as one of a citywide chain of smaller Roxy theaters, all under the direction of Samuel L. ("Roxy") Rothapfel, the entrepreneur who aside from giving New York City some of its most famous movie palaces also gave the world the name "Roxy." Roxy's chain of theaters never got off the ground, however, because by the late 1920s he had started working for William Fox, who wanted him to concentrate on Fox's own enormous national network of movie houses.

Since Roxy had gone over to Fox while the Beacon was under construction, it never opened with his name on it, but when it debuted in 1929 as Warner's Beacon, the theater was still essentially the house that Roxy wanted built, and it reflected his grandiose taste and style. Its ornate lobby, for example, had a rotunda that was a scaled-down version of the one that Ahlschlager had designed for the original Roxy's grand foyer. Today, that lobby remains pretty much intact, as does its auditorium, which dazzles with glorious murals, a huge Art Deco chandelier, colossal gilded statues flanking the proscenium, and a fully playable Wurlitzer organ. Films haven't been shown in the fabulous old movie palace since 1974, but the space has been beautifully restored and now reigns as a popular venue for soul, rap, R&B, and rock concerts.

22. *DEATH WISH* APARTMENT
33 Riverside Drive

Despite his posh Riverside Drive address, Charles Bronson could not isolate himself from the dangers and violence that were a frightening reality in New York City—especially in the crime-ridden 1970s. When businessman Bronson's wife is murdered and his daughter raped by three intruders, Bronson not only gets angry, he gets even by waging his own personal one-man war against Manhattan's mugger population. The controversial film tapped into the helplessness felt by many Americans in the face of urban crime as well as their seething anger. A big box-office hit, *Death Wish* (1974) spawned four sequels.

23. APTHORP APARTMENTS
2207 Broadway

With its iron gates, its monumental tunnel-like entrances, and its impressive interior courtyard, the Apthorp is one of the city's most dramatic, and most frequently photographed, apartment buildings. In *Heartburn* (1986), when Meryl Streep escapes from her marital problems in Washington, she finds refuge in her fa-

Courtyard classic: The Apthorp

ther's Apthorp apartment in New York. (In real life, *Heartburn*'s author, Nora Ephron, is a former Apthorp resident.) The Apthorp also turns up in *Network* (1976) as the love nest shared by TV execs William Holden and Faye Dunaway. On the other hand, in *Eyewitness* (1981) it is a TV newscaster (Sigourney Weaver) who resides in the landmark 1908 building. Other Apthorp feature-film credits include *The Cotton Club* (1984), where mobster "Dutch" Schultz keeps his moll, Diane Lane, in grand style at the Apthorp; as well as *The Changeling* (1978), *The Money Pit* (1986), and *When Harry Met Sally* (1989).

In real life, the Apthorp's tenant roster has boasted Lena Horne, Rosie O'Donnell, Conan O'Brien, Steve Kroft, Cyndi Lauper, and Kate Nelligan. All apartments in the building look out over the magnificent courtyard.

24. *WILL & GRACE* APARTMENT
155 Riverside Drive

Since 1998, Will Truman and Grace Adler have shared a stylish apartment with a terrace overlooking the Hudson in this building on leafy Riverside Drive. Truman is a successful lawyer, who

Upper West Siders: Debra Messing and Eric McCormack of TV's *Will & Grace*

Will & Grace
apartment building

happens to be gay, and Adler is a much in-demand interior decorator, who happens to be straight. Together they share not only
a wonderful friendship, unencumbered by sex, but a pretty successful TV series—*Will & Grace*—as well. Granted, Grace did
move out for a season, when she married Harry Connick Jr. in
2002, but the marriage didn't last and by 2003 she was back on
Riverside Drive. Also residing at number 155 is their struggling
actor friend Jack McFarland (Sean Hayes).

25. POMANDER WALK
260–266 West 95th Street

One of the Upper West Side's best-kept secrets, this tiny Tudor
village tucked between Broadway and West End Avenue was
built in 1921 to resemble the set of a hit play of the era called
Pomander Walk. Among the showbiz people who have lived in
Pomander Walk's cottages are Humphrey Bogart, Rosalind Russell, and Lillian and Dorothy Gish. In 1986 Woody Allen let film
audiences see this enchanting Manhattan hideaway in *Hannah*

Cottage colony:
Pomander Walk

and Her Sisters. While Sam Waterston has no trouble escorting Dianne Wiest and Carrie Fisher through this private compound, movie lovers who visit Pomander Walk should be aware that its steel gates are often locked. Even so, a peek through the bars is still quite satisfying. In 2004, a two-bedroom Pomander Walk cottage sold for $840,000.

26. RIVERSIDE PARK PLAYGROUND
96th Street at Riverside Drive

For five nights during the long hot summer of 1978, Riverside Park's 96th Street playground saw more filmmaking than residents of the apartment buildings across the way ever wished to see again. The film was Walter Hill's cult classic *Warriors,* which depicted the freaky òdyssey of a Brooklyn street gang fighting its way across Manhattan to its home turf on the other side of the East River. For the opening sequence of *Warriors,* close to a thousand dress extras were recruited to play the delegates to a massive convocation of all the street gangs in New York. Since the Screen Actors Guild permits nonunion actors to be hired to fill in crowd scenes that require over eighty-five people, the bulk of the extras were recruited from the streets, lured to the shoot by the promise of $30 plus two box lunches a night. At first it was fun, but as the nights wore on, the glamour of filmmaking wore thin for some of the background players (a number of whom, it turned out, were gang members in real life!). There were food fights, fist fights, and cases of disappearing actors, disappearing costumes, and disappearing equipment. When it looked as if *Warriors* might have a real gang war on its hands, the producers tried raffling off color television sets to calm everyone down. To add to the nightmare, the apartment dwellers across the park—angered by the noise and bright lights, which, on some nights, didn't let up until five in the morning—often interrupted the shooting with jeers and protests. Sometimes things go better on a back lot.

When director, star, and producer Barbra Streisand hit Riverside Drive in the mid-1990s for a night scene in her *The Mirror*

Panic in Riverside Park: *Warriors*, 1978

Has Two Faces (1996), supposedly the neighbors again were not pleased with the noise, lights, and commotion. Reportedly, too, La Streisand, wearing her director's hat, had her own noise issues, what with all the airplanes making their final approach to nearby La Guardia Airport. In fact, she is said to have had a production assistant contact the airport to get them to change the evening's flight path to accommodate her shoot. Request denied.

Other films to use the park, supposedly without major incident, were the first *Death Wish* (1974), which saw a revenge-bent Charles Bronson zap his first mugger there, and *Small Time Crooks* (2000).

27. METRO THEATER
Broadway and 99th Street

This jewel of a neighborhood movie house was called the Midtown when it opened "uptown" on Broadway and 99th Street in 1933. Over the years it has featured everything from second-runs to porn to Japanese films to revivals. Now restored and twinned, the Metro is currently showing first-run films. The theater's glazed terra-cotta Art Deco façade has been officially landmarked, and its neon marquee is a beauty, too. No wonder Woody Allen used the Metro as a location in *Hannah and Her Sisters* (1986).

Call 212–222-1200.

28. HUMPHREY BOGART HOUSE
245 West 103rd Street

This unimpressive four-story row house on the Upper West Side is where movie idol Humphrey DeForest Bogart was born in 1899, and where he lived off and on until he was in his early twenties. His father, Dr. Belmont DeForest Bogart, a respected surgeon, had his office on the ground floor, his mother, Maude Humphrey Bogart, was a magazine illustrator, and often worked out of a studio on the third floor, where little Humphrey also had his bedroom. Completing the family portrait were Humphrey's two sisters.

Unlike many of the tough-guy characters he would later play

on screen, Humphrey Bogart enjoyed a pleasant childhood on what was then a very upper-middle-class Upper West Side. Sent to fashionable private schools, the young Bogart attended Trinity School at 91st Street and Amsterdam Avenue from 1913 to 1917, where his best subject was religion. He then went to Andover in Massachusetts, as his father had done before him. Unlike his father, however, young Bogart was expelled for disciplinary problems. After that, he joined the Navy, and upon returning to New York and to 245 West 103rd Street, drifted into the theater. It wasn't until Bogie was in his mid-twenties and starting to get small parts on stage that he finally left home and moved downtown to 43 East 25th Street. There he lived with actress Helen Menken, who became the first of the three wives he had prior to marrying Lauren Bacall in 1945.

By 1933, the elder Bogarts had left the family home as well. Owing to financial problems brought on by the Depression, they were forced to sell the house on 103rd Street and move to a small rental apartment in Tudor City. Soon, however, they would have nothing to worry about financially, because in 1936 their son would play a gangster in a film called *The Petrified Forest*, and he would become one of Hollywood's biggest stars. Today, the Upper West Side home where that star got his start in the world still stands.

29. MARION DAVIES MANSION
331 Riverside Drive

In 1918 fifty-five-year-old William Randolph Hearst got serious about turning his twenty-year-old showgirl mistress, Marion Davies, into a full-fledged movie star. Not only did Hearst establish Cosmopolitan Studios to produce Miss Davies's films, he moved Marion, her mother, her sisters, and various other family members into an opulent French château at the corner of Riverside Drive and 105th Street. Hearst saw to it that Marion's new abode was nothing less than a palace fit for a movie queen—especially since the queen would frequently be receiving the press on the premises. Marion's interviews were usually scheduled to take place in her private sitting room, which was decorated with a marble fountain and statues of cupids. Bejeweled and coiffed, the young star would appear in a shimmery pink or white negligee if the reporter were a woman, or turn up in a chic suit if he were a man. Everything was very carefully controlled and mapped out and, unlike Orson Welles's fictionalized version of the Hearst–Davies relationship in his 1941 film *Citizen Kane*, Hearst's plot to make his mistress a star ultimately was a stunning success. Her first features, while pulling in mixed reviews from the non-Hearst press, were popular with the public, and Marion Davies had developed into a fine screen comedian by the early 1920s. It was also at this time that Hearst decided that the future of feature films lay in Hollywood and so, just as quickly as he had moved Marion and family to Riverside Drive, he whisked them off to California, where he found them equally palatial quarters on Lexington Road in Beverly Hills.

Today, Marion's former Manhattan mansion belongs to a Buddhist sect, and movie lovers who visit the site will find a huge statue of Shinran-Shonin, the founder of the sect, looming in front of the shrine next door.

At home on Riverside Drive: Marion Davies

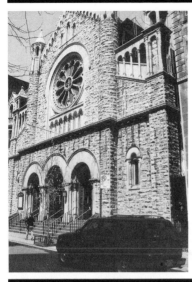

Keeping the Faith: Church of the Ascension

30. CHURCH OF THE ASCENSION
221 West 107th Street

Actor Edward Norton directed and starred in *Keeping the Faith* (2000), a romantic comedy that followed the complications of two boyhood friends in love with the same woman, another childhood friend who comes back into their adult lives. Further complicating the triangle is the fact that Norton is a Catholic priest and his best friend (Ben Stiller) is a rabbi. For the film, Norton reportedly chose the Church of the Ascension, which was also used in *Big Night* (1995), not just for its beautiful Gothic interior, but because it was in a working-class, mostly Latino neighborhood, which fit with his conception of his character as someone working closely with different ethnic groups and trying to make positive changes in the community. For Ben Stiller's temple, director Norton went with the B'nai Jeshrun Synagogue, twenty blocks south at 267 West 86th Street. Norton is said to have particularly liked its exotic Byzantine/Romanesque interior, fashionable for well-to-do temples, when it was built back in 1918.

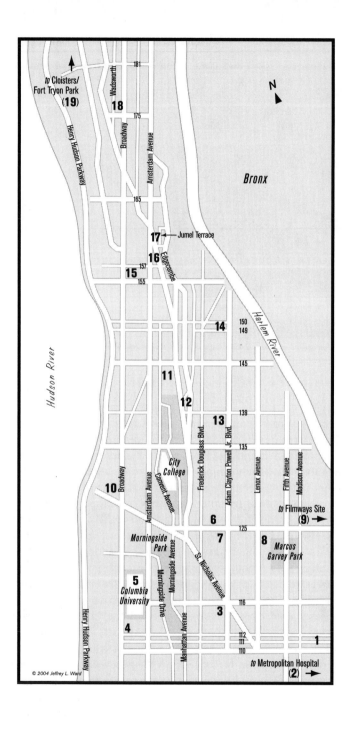

to Cloisters/
Fort Tryon Park
(19)

Wadsworth

181

18

Broadway

175

Amsterdam Avenue

Henry Hudson Parkway

N

Bronx

165

17 — Jumel Terrace

16

Edgecombe

15   157

155

Harlem River

14   150
      149

145

11

12

139

13

Frederick Douglass Blvd.

Adam Clayton Powell Jr. Blvd.

Lenox Avenue

Fifth Avenue

Madison Avenue

135

City
College

Hudson River

10   Broadway

Amsterdam Avenue

Convent Avenue

to Filmways Site
(9) →

6

125

7

8   Marcus
     Garvey Park

Morningside
Park

St. Nicholas Avenue

5
Columbia
University

Morningside Drive

Morningside Avenue

116

3

4

Manhattan Avenue

112
111
110

1

Henry Hudson Parkway

to Metropolitan Hospital
(2) →

© 2004 Jeffrey L. Ward

Harlem/Washington Heights: Uptown Renaissance

For years Harlem was written off as a crime-ridden ghetto by many white New Yorkers who had never experienced its grand boulevards, handsome brownstones, hilly streets, and proud spirit. Today, however, the whole city is looking at this fabled African-American enclave with fresh eyes as it emerges as one of the hottest neighborhoods in New York City—with a fresh influx of black and white homesteaders as well as a burgeoning number of new restaurants, clubs, shops, theaters, and museums.

What's going on in Harlem is being called a renaissance. For old-timers, it is reminiscent of that glorious era in the 1920s and 1930s, when Harlem was the undisputed capital of African-American culture in America. Known then as the Harlem Renaissance, this vital period in Harlem's history was marked by music, poetry, theater, and some of New York's liveliest nightclubs and speakeasies. It was a time, too, when most of the country's best-known African-American entertainers—Paul Robeson, Bill "Bojangles" Robinson, Ethel Waters, Duke Ellington—lived in Harlem, and since they all made significant contributions to America's film history, today their former homes and apartment buildings are high on the list of Harlem must-sees for movie lovers.

Harlem and nearby Washington Heights also preserve some of New York City's most historic movie theaters, including one built in 1913 that is considered to be the first movie palace in the City of New York. Although it's still packing people in, it's no longer showing movies; it's now a Baptist church. Another Harlem theater still going strong is the legendary Apollo, which since the 1930s has hosted the biggest names in the entertainment world. Today it is a symbol of the grand old and the dynamic new Harlem. In the words of the Harlem Chamber of Commerce, "You haven't done this town till you've done it Uptown!"

1. P.S. 101
141 East 111th Street

Based on the real story of an East Harlem music teacher who tries to bring a serious music program to her neighborhood's budget-challenged schools, the 1999 film *Music of the Heart* starred Meryl Streep as the crusading Roberta Guaspari-Tzavaras. The main location used for the film was this East Harlem public school. The Streep film, directed by Wes Craven, best known for his *Scream* and *Nightmare on Elm Street* horror flicks, was not the first to tell the teacher's tale; it was also the basis for the 1995 documentary *Small Wonders*, which was nominated for an Academy Award.

2. METROPOLITAN HOSPITAL CENTER
1901 First Avenue

The Hospital's hospital . . . Metropolitan was the principal location for the 1971 black comedy that fleshed out our worst fears about the medical profession. Paddy Chayefsky won an Academy Award for his screenplay, and George C. Scott received an Oscar nomination for his performance as a hospital honcho in this made-in-Manhattan masterpiece. *The Pope of Greenwich Village* (1984) and *Donnie Brasco* (1997) were two other New York films that used Metropolitan Hospital as a location.

3. FIRST CORINTHIAN BAPTIST CHURCH
1212 Adam Clayton Powell Jr. Boulevard

Now a church, this exuberant tile-faced building with its façade of columns and arches also marks a milestone in the history of moviegoing in New York: When it made its debut as the Regent Theater in 1913, this was the city's very first *deluxe* theater built expressly for the showing of motion pictures. Before that, movies were presented either in narrow storefront nickelodeons or in vaudeville theaters. The owners of the Regent, however, were banking on the fact that audiences were ready for something new—and better—and so, when the Regent opened, everything in the house was designed to make the experience of going to the movies a truly special event. The Regent featured its own eight-piece orchestra, a separate string trio, the city's first movie-house pipe organ, uniformed ushers, printed programs, and a special screen with black borders that made the picture seem brighter and clearer. Unfortunately, even all of these innovations did not provide enough incentive to fill the new theater, especially since

Regent Theater, 1948

it was all the way up on 116th Street and Seventh Avenue, where the locals—who were mostly of German, Irish, and Jewish origin at the time—still felt that their money went further at the neighborhood vaudeville houses, where they got a show *and* a movie. Thus, two months after opening, the Regent was in big trouble.

To its rescue came a man named Samuel L. Rothapfel, who, having had quite a bit of success managing a movie house in Milwaukee, was hired to fix the Regent. First off, Rothapfel moved the projector from the balcony down to the orchestra floor, which provided a sharper, brighter image on the screen. Next he gave the screen its own special curtain to add drama to the film presentation. Rothapfel's most important innovation, however, had to do with the music. While house orchestras often played during the film portion of a vaudeville show, little attempt was made by the conductor to have the music fit what was going on up on the screen. Rothapfel changed all that by carefully choosing the music and programming it to match the action and mood of the film. In doing this, he added a new dimension to the experience of seeing a film. He also turned around the fortunes of the Regent—and the age of the movie palace had begun.

After his success with the Regent, Rothapfel moved downtown to the Strand, the Rialto, the Rivoli, and his ultimate triumph, the theater that bore his nickname: the Roxy. Whereas all these other theaters have since been demolished, the historic building where Roxy began his New York career in 1913 still stands, reborn as a Baptist church. Hallelujah!

4. TOM'S RESTAURANT
2880 Broadway

Seinfeld fans will instantly recognize this funky diner with the neon sign at the corner of Broadway and 112th Street. It's where Jerry, Kramer, Elaine, and George hung out for eight TV seasons from 1990 to 1998—despite the fact that this neighborhood spot was some twenty-one blocks north of Jerry's apartment building at 129 West 81st Street. But there's more to the story—or rather the geography—because the exterior used for Jerry's Upper West Side apartment building was actually off Wilshire Boulevard in downtown Los Angeles. Since *Seinfeld* was shot in

Seinfeld lucheonette: Tom's Restaurant

Los Angeles, that made sense—as did having a movie-set version of Tom's Restaurant on the soundstage of the CBS Studio Center in Studio City, where the show was filmed. Back in New York, Tom's boasts such *Seinfeld* memorabilia as a signed poster from the cast and a portrait of Kramer.

Call 212-864-6137.

5. COLUMBIA UNIVERSITY
Broadway to Morningside Drive from 112th to 123rd Streets

Barbra Streisand and Jeff Bridges taught English literature here in *The Mirror Has Two Faces* (1996); Woody Allen's field was creative writing in *Husbands and Wives* (1992), whereas for Julia Roberts, it was art history, and the campus stood in for Wellesley College in the 1950s in *Mona Lisa Smile* (2003). Other Columbia University star connections have been William Hurt, who performed some very questionable experiments with human

Ivy League Manhattan: Columbia University

subjects in *Altered States* (1980), and Sigourney Weaver, who did research in the University's Biological Sciences Department in *Tadpole* (2002), whereas Weaver's buddies Bill Murray, Dan Aykroyd, and Harold Ramis also did research here two decades earlier—but lost their funding so they had to go into business for themselves as *Ghostbusters* (1982). And it was on a field trip to Columbia with his high school classmates from Queens that Tobey Maguire got that fateful spider bite that turned him into *Spider-Man* (2002).

These are but a few of the many films that have shot sequences at this New York City Ivy League institution, whose main Morningside Heights campus encompasses many blocks and dates back to the 1890s. Besides being a popular location for filmmakers, Columbia has a well-respected film department in its School of the Arts, which has turned out the likes of writer/director Daniel Algrant (*Naked in New York*, 1994), director Kimberly Peirce (*Boys Don't Cry*, 1999, which won Hillary Swank a Best Actress Oscar), writer/director Nicole Holofcener (*Lovely and Amazing*, 2001), and screenwriters Sabrina Dhawan (*Mon-*

soon Wedding, 2001) and Simon Kinberg (*Mr. and Mrs. Smith,* 2005). Besides its famous and up-and-coming graduates, Columbia's film school can boast a number of industry names who have taught master classes here, with Milos Forman, David Mamet, and Martin Scorsese heading the list.

Visit www.columbia.edu.

6. APOLLO THEATER
253 West 125th Street

One of America's most important show-business shrines, the Apollo has hosted practically every major black performing artist of the twentieth century on its stage at some point during its seventy-year-plus history. Bessie Smith, Billie Holiday, Duke Ellington, Ella Fitzgerald, Louis Armstrong, Pearl Bailey, Aretha Franklin, Ray Charles, James Brown, Dionne Warwick, the Supremes, and the Jackson Five have all played the Apollo, and the list could go on and on. It is said that when a teenaged Elvis Presley came to New York for the first time, the one place he

Denzel Washington as *Malcolm X*, outside the Apollo

wanted to see was the Apollo. A decade later, the same story would be told of the Beatles on their first trip to America.

The building that houses the Apollo was built in 1913 as Hurting and Seaman's New Theater, which presented burlesque and vaudeville to a Harlem that was then predominantly white. Twenty years later Harlem was a very different community when entrepreneur Frank Schiffman took over the theater and started showcasing black entertainers on their home ground as well as relying on black audiences to fill the Apollo's seats. This was very different from a number of other fashionable Harlem nightspots (such as the famed Cotton Club), which featured black acts on their stages but refused to allow locals in the audience.

Three years after the Apollo opened, a white reporter for the *New York World Telegram* published the following account of a firsthand visit to what many people at that time considered a very exotic place:

> The Apollo is a sort of uptown Met dedicated to furious jazz, coffee-colored chorus girls and grinning, drawling comedians . . . the first stand and last jump-off for the large caravanserai of Harlem entertainers. . . . The theater stands behind a gaudy neon sign on West 125th Street, between a haberdashery and a leather-goods store. The sidewalk outside is a favored location for old men lugging sandwich signs and pitchmen unloading razor blades and patent medicines. You buy your ticket at a sidewalk booth (from fifteen cents mornings to a fifty-cent top Wednesday and Saturday nights) and enter through a narrow lobby lined with bathroom tiles, glistening mirrors and photographs of such Harlem idols as Ethel Waters and Louis Armstrong, all affectionately inscribed to the Apollo. At the candy counter you can buy chocolate bars and peanuts, but no gum. That is to protect the seats. In the lobby, three or four colored boys generally are waiting for their dates to show up.

Whereas Harlem's whites-only clubs eventually moved downtown (the Cotton Club relocated to Broadway and 48th Street in the late 1930s) or closed down, the Apollo continued to flourish through the 1960s. By the 1970s, however, when America's color barriers and complexes had been somewhat broken down through the civil rights movement, and when many black entertainers found that they could make better money in the mainstream, the Apollo fell upon hard times. During this period, it can be seen in the opening frames of the 1973 film *Across 110th Street,* when a Cadillac loaded with black mobsters and Italian mafia pass the theater, where the Miracles and Junior Walker and the All Stars are appearing at the time. Despite its brush with the movies, by 1976 the theater, no longer able to book top talent and no longer able to fill seats, closed down.

In today's hot new Harlem, however, that is no longer the case. Refurbished and reopened in the 1980s and refurbished yet again in 2002, the Apollo is one of the city's most exciting venues, hosting big-name acts like Patti LaBelle, Vanessa Williams, and B. B. King; big-time filmmakers like Spike Lee, who shot scenes for *Malcolm X* (1992) here; Broadway-style musicals; TV specials; the syndicated TV show *Showtime at the Apollo*; and the famous Amateur Night, currently every Wednesday at 7:30 p.m.

For information on what's on at the Apollo as well as on guided tours and tickets for Showtime at the Apollo, *call 212-531-5301 or visit www.apollotheater.com.*

7. OSCAR MICHEAUX FILM CORPORATION SITE
200 West 125th Street

An electronics store now marks the spot where one of the country's most prolific and ingenious independent filmmakers of the 1920s and 1930s once had his headquarters. Unknown to most white and many African Americans, Oscar Micheaux was a black man from the Midwest who came to Harlem in the early 1920s and specialized in producing "race films." These featured all-black casts playing the roles—handsome heroes, glamorous heroines, villainous gangsters—that they were denied in mainstream movies at the time. Literally a one-man film industry, Micheaux wrote, directed, produced, and promoted the majority of his pictures and was successful in getting them distributed not only in Europe but also in the U.S. South, where he convinced many white theater owners of the profits to be made from setting up special matinee showings of his features for African-American audiences.

With a few exceptions, Micheaux's movies rarely dealt with the important social and economic issues that confronted his race. Instead, he produced highly commercial black versions of the same formula stories that spelled success for Hollywood. Typical Micheaux titles were *Daughter of the Congo,* a 1930 swashbuckler that had a dashing black cavalry officer rescuing a wealthy Negro girl lost in the wilds of Africa, and *Underworld* (1936), a standard 1930s gangster yarn in which both the good guys *and* the bad guys were black. Even Micheaux's stars were marketed with Hollywood counterparts in mind: suave Lorenzo Tucker, for example, was the Black Valentino, sultry Ethel Moses was the Negro Harlow, sexy Bee Freeman was the Sepia Mae West, and Slick Chester, who often played gangsters, was the Colored Cagney. These stars, by the way, were usually light-skinned, and Micheaux is sometimes criticized today for the unreal black world that his films created. But this criticism is offset by films like *The Exile* (1931), which dealt with the sensitive issue of a black man who falls in love with a woman he thinks is white, and *God's Stepchildren* (1937), which focused on the perils of trying to pass for white

A scene from Oscar Micheaux's *Underworld,* 1936

The building that
housed the
headquarters of Oscar
Micheaux Film
Corporation

in a racist society. Ultimately, Micheaux was not a philosopher but
a filmmaker, and his films provided black audiences of the 1920s
and 1930s with positive self-images at a time when the major studios systematically kept people of color in their place on-screen by
casting them as maids, mammies, butlers, and shoeshine boys.

8. LENOX LOUNGE
288 Lenox Avenue

A legendary Harlem jazz club, the Lenox Lounge debuted in
1939 and over the years has welcomed greats like Billie Holiday,
Miles Davis, and John Coltrane to its Zebra Room performance
space. Restored to its original Art Deco splendor in 1999, the
Lenox Lounge is a major player on the contemporary Harlem
nightlife front. A hangout for Malcom X in the 1950s and
1960s, the Lenox was used as a location for Spike Lee's 1992
chronicle of the controversial African-American leader's short

Harlem hot spot: Lenox Lounge

life. The club also turned up in the 2000 version of *Shaft*, based on the 1972 film of the same name, directed by Gordon Parks and one of the first mainstream movies to star an African American (Richard Roundtree) as a private detective. While the original *Shaft* spawned the popular blaxploitation genre of the 1970s, the 2000 film, directed and coscripted by John Singleton, is a much more sophisticated piece; Shaft (Samuel L. Jackson), now a former police officer, deals not only with fighting crime but with the social and racial issues involved in that struggle.

For reservations at the Lenox Lounge, call 212-427-0253 or visit www.lenoxlounge.com.

9. FILMWAYS SITE
Second Avenue and 127th Street

Though now a vast parking lot, a barn of a building once stood on the southwest corner of 127th Street and Second Avenue and reigned for two decades as one of New York City's most active movie studios. Among the many features that were done at Filmways (which had been a city transit garage before it was made a studio) during the 1960s and 1970s were *Murder Incorporated* (1960), *Splendor in the Grass* (1961), *The Brotherhood* (1968), *Klute* (1971), *The Godfather* (1972), *The Taking of Pelham One Two Three* (1973), *Annie Hall* (1977), and *Manhattan* (1979). Filmways also saw a number of TV series lensed on its soundstages, the most famous of these being *The Defenders, The Nurses,* and *The Blue Men.* When the studio closed in the early 1980s, one of the reasons was supposedly because the neighborhood had become too dangerous. Fortunately, by then the city had a number of new production facilities such as the reborn Astoria Studios to fill the void caused by Filmways' demise.

Across the street from the Filmways building, another famous movie studio once stood. Also a conversion, Cosmopolitan Studios was created in 1918 out of a former nightclub on the east side of Second Avenue at 127th Street. The man behind the makeover was William Randolph Hearst, who at the time was obsessed with turning his showgirl protégée Marion Davies into a movie star. In typical Hearstian fashion, the famous newspaper man/movie mogul spared no expense in order to make Cosmopolitan one of the top studios in town. His ultimate extravagance was the special five-piece string orchestra that he hired to play popular melodies in or-

William Randolph Hearst's Cosmopolitian Studios

der to keep Miss Davies in a pleasant frame of mind between takes. The group was nicknamed the Marion Davies Orchestra, and Marion is said to have used them throughout her career.

10. THE COTTON CLUB
656 West 125th Street

The inspiration for Francis Ford Coppola's 1984 film *The Cotton Club,* the real thing opened at 142nd Street and Lenox Avenue in 1923 and was considered a white sanctuary, meaning it featured black entertainers but refused to allow African Americans in the audience. Supposedly even the great composer W. C. Handy was not allowed in, despite the fact that his music was emanating from inside. Known for its light-skinned, "Tall, Tan, and Terrific" chorus girls and its orchestras led by Duke Ellington and Cab Calloway, the Cotton Club held forth on 142nd Street until the Depression, which devastated Harlem. The club hoped for better business down on West 48th Street in the slightly more cheerful Times Square area, but this was a short-lived venture. The current Cotton Club, housed in a cool little Deco building beneath the West Side Highway, is another story. Opened in 1978, when the new Harlem was just starting to emerge, it is still going strong, although it is better known these days for its weekend gospel brunches than for its big-name entertainers.

For reservations, call 212-663-7980 or visit www.cottonclub-newyork.com.

The current
Cotton Club

The Royal Tenenbaums' Harlem home

11. TENENBAUM MANSION
339 Convent Avenue

In the film *The Royal Tenenbaums* (2001), the overachieving yet dysfunctional Tenenbaum family—matriarch Anjelica Huston, kids Gwyneth Paltrow, Luke Wilson, and Ben Stiller—supposedly lived on Archer Avenue in the Bronx at an address which doesn't exist. The very real Victorian mansion used for the picture, however, is this distinctive turreted number in the historic Hamilton Heights section of Harlem. The film's director, Wes Anderson, who used to draw fantasy mansions when he was growing up in Texas, knew the kind of house he wanted for the film and finally found it in Harlem. At the time the place appeared to be abandoned and needed a major redo, but it turned out that a new owner was just about to renovate the property. Anderson and an undisclosed sum of money from his Disney backers were able to convince the owner to put off his renovations and rent the house to *The Royal Tenenbaums* for six months. In addition to having the storybook quality that Anderson wanted for his film, the location had the additional advantage of being situated on a corner, which made it a cinematographer's dream, since corner buildings are much easier to shoot.

12. ETHEL WATERS RESIDENCE
580 St. Nicholas Avenue

Throughout most of the 1920s and on into the 1930s, Harlem not only presented a place for African Americans to find decent housing in a country that usually denied it to them, it also promised intellectual stimulation and creative fulfillment. Popularly known as the Harlem Renaissance, the flourishing of African-American culture that took place in Harlem in the 1920s and 1930s was marked by large numbers of talented writers, poets, artists, and performers flocking to Upper Manhattan. One of the major centers of the Harlem Renaissance was a posh apartment house at 580 St. Nicholas Avenue in the fashionable Sugar Hill district. Known simply as "Five eighty" to the in-crowd, the building boasted many celebrity tenants during its heyday, but none more famous than Ethel Waters, considered the first black woman to win star billing both on the stage and in the movies. Of her films, *Cabin in the Sky* (1943), *Stage Door Canteen* (1943), *Pinky* (1949), and *The Member of the Wedding* (1952) are the most memorable. Miss Waters was also a star of early television, playing the title role in the *Beulah* series during its first two seasons, from 1950 to 1952.

13. STRIVER'S ROW
West 138th and 139th Streets
between Seventh and Eighth Avenues

Built in 1891, these smart tree-shaded row houses were among then-white Harlem's most desirable addresses. When the whites moved away in the early twentieth century and African Americans started settling in the area, these same houses now attracted some of the community's most successful and affluent black residents. Hence, the nickname Striver's Row. Among them were the composers W. C. Handy and Eubie Blake, and theater entrepreneur Noble Sissle. When Spike Lee made his provocative film *Jungle Fever* (1991), which dealt with an interracial love affair between a middle-class African-American man (Wesley Snipes) and an Italian-American secretary (Annabella Sciorra) from Brooklyn, he had Snipes living in a Striver's Row flat.

14. DUNBAR APARTMENTS
2588 Adam Clayton Powell Jr. Boulevard

This cluster of six six-story walk-up apartment buildings between West 149th and 150th streets was built in the late 1920s by John D. Rockefeller as the country's first large cooperative-apartment complex for blacks. Named for the African-American poet Paul Laurence Dunbar (1872–1906), the Dunbar offered courtyards and gardens, published its own gossipy newsletter, and housed some of Harlem's toniest citizens. Among those who enjoyed Dunbar luxuries were the dynamic NAACP leader W. E. B. DuBois, poet Countee Cullen, newspaperman Asa Philip Randolph, and explorer Matt Henson, who was part of Admiral Perry's North Pole expedition and the first Westerner to set foot at the Pole.

The world of show business was represented at the Dunbar by the famed leading man and operatic basso Paul Robeson, stage and movie character actor Leigh Whipper, violinist-composer Clarence Cameron White, and the illustrious musical performer

Harlem star Bill "Bojangles" Robinson with Shirley Temple in *The Little Colonel,* 1935

Bill "Bojangles" Robinson, who sang and tap-danced in many major films throughout the 1930s and is especially remembered for his screen appearances with Shirley Temple. In addition to performing with the child star in *The Little Colonel* (1935), *The Littlest Rebel* (1935), *Rebecca of Sunnybrook Farm* (1938), and *Just Around the Corner* (1939), Robinson also choreographed Temple's 1936 film *Dimples*. In 1943, Twentieth Century–Fox's all-black film, *Stormy Weather,* not only starred Robinson but was based loosely on his career in show business.

Today the Dunbar Apartments, after having fallen into disrepair during the 1960s and 1970s, have been renovated and are now playing a role in the current second Harlem Renaissance.

15. AUDUBON BALLROOM SITE
3940 Broadway

The Audubon Ballroom was an important social and political center for Harlem from the 1930s to the 1960s. Housed on the second floor of a historic Fox theater that opened in 1912, the ballroom was famous for its Mardi Gras Festival, a highlight of the Harlem social calendar, where a King and Queen of Harlem were crowned every year. Important labor union meetings and political rallies were held here as well. At one of these, a rally of the Organization of Afro-American Unity, which took place on February 21, 1965, Black Muslim leader Malcolm X was assassinated. After that incident, the ballroom was closed down, despite protests by the community. When Spike Lee made his film *Malcolm X* in 1991, he used this exact location, which at the time still stood abandoned. Another film to feature the abandoned Audubon Ballroom was Susan Seidelman's ode to Downtown Manhattan, *Desperately Seeking Susan* (1985), in which designer Santo Loquasto turned it into the film's fictional Magic Club, where bored suburban housewife Rosanna Arquette gets a job as a magician's assistant.

Today, again pointing to Harlem's impressive comeback, the famous ballroom has been refurbished, and the site has been redesigned as a mixed-use complex—anchored by the biomedical research facility of New York–Presbyterian Medical Center, which now owns it—with shops, restaurants, the Harlem-Heights Historical Society, and the home of the new Malcolm X

The Audubon Ballroom, 2004

Memorial Museum. There is currently a life-size statue of the great leader in the Broadway lobby of the building. Also incorporated in the site is the historic terra-cotta façade of the original Fox theater.

For Malcolm X museum information, visit www.themalcolmx museum.org.

16. DUKE ELLINGTON RESIDENCE
935 St. Nicholas Avenue

A plaque at the entrance to this Harlem Gothic apartment building indicates that it has been declared a National Historic Landmark because Edward Kennedy "Duke" Ellington once lived here. Ellington resided in apartment 4A of the building from 1939 to 1961, and for much of the time his lady friend Beatrice Ellis lived there too. More often known as Evie Ellington, even though Ms. Ellis was never officially married to the Duke, she was still with him when they moved downtown to West End Avenue in the early 1960s. By that time, however, they saw little of each other, since Duke was constantly on the road and Evie had become reclusive in her later years.

Although known principally as a musician, composer, and band leader, Ellington was connected with motion pictures throughout his career. As a performer, Duke and his band appeared in a number of films in the 1930s and 1940s, including *Murder at the Vanities* (1934), with Mae West in *Belle of the Nineties* (1934), and *Cabin in the Sky* (1943). In addition, Ellington wrote music for the Marx Brothers' *A Day at the Races* (1936), and did complete scores for *Anatomy of a Murder* (1959), *Paris Blues* (1960), *Assault on a Queen* (1964), and *Change of Mind* (1968). His *Paris Blues* score received an Academy Award nomination. Of Ellington, Orson Welles is reported to have said that, next to himself, Duke was the only genius he had ever known.

Ellington died of lung cancer in 1974 and was buried at Woodlawn Cemetery in the Bronx, beside his parents. When his life partner Evie died (also of lung cancer) two years later, she was laid to rest in the same plot. The site of Duke and Evie's Harlem apartment—where they shared their happiest years together—was given landmark status that same year.

Duke Ellington residence

Going Hollywood: Duke Ellington and orchestra arrive in L.A. to shoot
Belle of the Nineties at Paramount with Mae West

17. PAUL ROBESON HOUSE
16 Jumel Terrace

One of Harlem's many lovely surprises, Jumel Terrace preserves a clutch of handsome townhouses on a small cobbled street. Tourists come here mainly to visit the historic Morris-Jumel Mansion, a columned Georgian residence dating back to 1765, which sits on a grassy hill on the east side of Jumel Terrace. Movie lovers will be more interested in the townhouse at number 16, however, because it was the last Harlem home of the great African-American actor Paul Robeson. In addition to his stage triumphs—notably in Shakespeare's *Othello* and in Eugene O'Neill's *All God's Chillun Got Wings* and *The Emperor Jones*—Robeson will always be remembered for his screen performances in *The Emperor Jones* (1933) and as Joe in Universal's 1936 film version of *Show Boat*, in which he sings "Ol' Man River."

Robeson is also remembered for his leftist political views, which got him into no end of trouble with the infamous Mc-

Paul Robeson
residence
(second from left)
on Jumel Terrace

Carthy committee and the U.S. State Department in the late 1940s and well into the 1950s. Through it all, Robeson remained true to his country—even when the State Department revoked his passport in 1950 and refused to allow him to travel

King of Harlem:
Paul Robeson in
The Emperor Jones, 1933

out of the United States. When he finally got his passport back eight years later, he went on to spend several years in Europe and the USSR. He returned to the United States in the early 1960s and moved into 16 Jumel Terrace, where he lived as a virtual recluse until failing health forced him to take up residence with a sister in Philadelphia. He died there in 1976.

From 1939 to 1941, Robeson lived not far from Jumel Terrace at 555 Edgecombe Avenue. One of Harlem's grandest apartment buildings, 555 Edgecombe Avenue has been declared the Robeson Home National Historic Landmark.

18. UNITED CHURCH
Broadway and 175th Street

This spectacular neo-Assyrian fortress at the northeast corner of Broadway and 175th Street was called "the apogee of the movie palace" when it debuted on February 22, 1930, as Loew's 175th Street Theater. Designed by Thomas W. Lamb, the 175th Street featured an interior that looked like a great gaudy Hindu temple.

Reverend Ike's United Church, formerly Loew's 175th Street Theater

Inside Loew's 175th Street

One of Loew's five Wonder theaters (so called because each had a huge Robert Morton Wonder organ), the 175th Street joined the Paradise in the Bronx, the Kings in Brooklyn, the Valencia in Queens, and the Jersey across the Hudson in Jersey City as the final jewel in the crown formed by Loew's most sumptuous New York metropolitan-area movie palaces. Today the Wonder organ is still going strong on 175th Street—not as part of any film presentation, but to back up the religious services. For many years, the church's star preacher was the controversial minister and radio personality known as Reverend Ike.

19. THE CLOISTERS/FORT TRYON PARK
Margaret Corbin Road, off Ft. Washington Avenue

A hilly green enclave above the Hudson River at the far northern end of Manhattan Island, Fort Tryon Park encompasses sixty-two acres that were formerly part of an estate that belonged to the financier John D. Rockefeller. The highlights of the park are its gardens—laid out by Frederick Law Olmsted of Central

Park fame—and the Cloisters. The latter is a cluster of sections of French and Spanish medieval buildings that were imported and creatively reassembled here in the 1930s. An annex to the Metropolitan Museum of Art, the Cloisters display the museum's extensive collection of medieval tapestries, paintings, sculptures, and architectural antiques. With their authentic medieval look, the Cloisters would undoubtedly have been used by early East Coast filmmakers as background for the swashbuckling and historical epics that were produced in Fort Lee, New Jersey, at the beginning of the last century. But by the time the Cloisters were erected, that kind of filmmaking was being done only on the back lots of Hollywood.

Still, the Cloisters have provided an atmospheric location for a number of films. One of the earliest of these was David O. Selznick's *Portrait of Jennie* (1948), where they are used to represent the convent that the mysterious title character played by Jennifer Jones winds up in at the end of the film. Perhaps the film that has used the site most extensively was Al Pacino's *Looking*

Al Pacino and company take on Shakespeare at the Cloisters in *Looking for Richard*, 1996

Natascha McElhone and Brad Pitt share a romantic moment at the Cloisters in *The Devil's Own*, 1997

for Richard (1996), which documented a group of actors (Pacino, Kevin Spacey, Estelle Parsons, Alec Baldwin, and Winona Ryder among them) workshopping Shakespeare's *Richard III*. The film starts in a rehearsal studio but as the actors become increasingly involved in their roles, Pacino takes them to far more Shakespearean surroundings: the Cloisters. Movie lovers may also remember the Cloisters and Fort Tryon Park from *Coogan's Bluff* (1968), as the setting for a love scene between Clint Eastwood and Susan Clark as well as for the film's final motorcycle chase. More recently, *The Devil's Own* (1997) used the Cloisters for a dramatic rendezvous between IRA operatives Brad Pitt and Natascha McElhone; as their New York caper is falling apart, their attraction for each other is intensifying.

Visit www.metmuseum.org.

Brooklyn: Hometown of the Stars

Mae West, Mickey Rooney, Rita Hayworth, Barbra Streisand, Mary Tyler Moore, Danny Kaye, Susan Hayward, Lena Horne, Harvey Keitel, Gregory Hines, Woody Allen, George Gershwin, Irving Thalberg, Veronica Lake, Clara Bow, Mel Brooks—the list of megastars who hail from Brooklyn would make a sizable who's who of the entertainment industry. This chapter's itinerary takes in the actual sites where many of Brooklyn's illustrious natives were born and raised and also visits such star Brooklyn neighborhoods as Flatbush, with its leafy streets and landmark mansions, one of which starred in the film *Sophie's Choice*; Bensonhurst, land of *Saturday Night Fever*; Fort Greene, used by Spike Lee; Coney Island, an inspiration to filmmakers from the 1890s to the present day; and Brooklyn Heights, whose ivy-covered townhouses, landmark churches, and knockout views of the Lower Manhattan skyline across the harbor have made it a favorite location for New York movies.

Other discoveries awaiting movie lovers in Brooklyn are the site of the legendary Vitagraph Studios, a major force in the film industry at the turn of the century and still being used for television productions; New York City's newest movie studio, within the historic Brooklyn Navy Yard; Erasmus Hall High, boasting

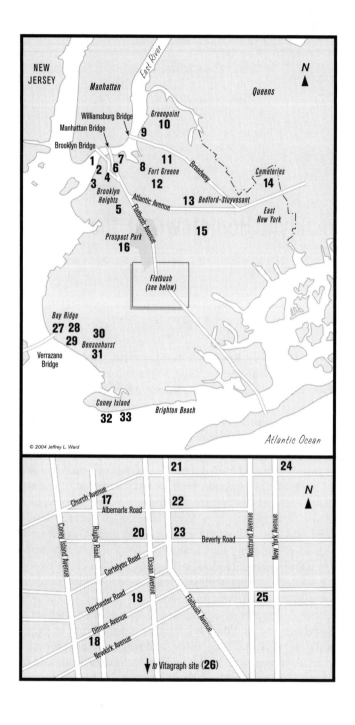

NEW
JERSEY

Manhattan

Queens

East River

Williamsburg Bridge
Manhattan Bridge

Greenpoint

Brooklyn Bridge

9

10

1
2   6   7

11

Cemeteries

4

8   *Fort Greene*

14

3

12

*Brooklyn
Heights*

Atlantic Avenue

13 *Bedford-Stuyvesant*

5

*East
New York*

Flatbush Avenue

15

Prospect Park

16

*Flatbush
(see below)*

Bay Ridge

27 28

30

29

Bensonhurst

31

*Verrazano
Bridge*

Coney Island

Brighton Beach

32   33

Atlantic Ocean

© 2004 Jeffrey L. Ward

21

24

N

Church Avenue

17

Albemarle Road

22

Coney Island Avenue

Rugby Road

20

23

Beverly Road

Nostrand Avenue

New York Avenue

Cortelyou Road

Ocean Avenue

Dorchester Road **19**

25

Ditmas Avenue

18

Flatbush Avenue

Newkirk Avenue

↓ *to* Vitagraph site (**26**)

an impressive pedigree (it was founded in 1887), dazzling architecture, and stellar alumni; and Cypress Hills Cemetery, where fans can pay their respects to Miss Mae West, who, despite her fifty years in Hollywood, never forgot her Brooklyn roots, which is true of the best of Brooklynites and is perhaps the secret of their success: They always remember where they came from—and therefore always know who they are.

1. BROOKLYN BRIDGE

Joan Peers walked across it hand in hand with Henry Wadsworth in Rouben Mamoulian's 1929 *Applause* and exclaims: "Even Brooklyn looks pretty!"; Fredric March and Carole Lombard sailed under it in *Nothing Sacred* (1937); F. Scott Fitzgerald wrote about it in *Brooklyn Bridge* (1940)—a script he did for a Columbia film that was never produced; Johnny Weissmuller dove off it in *Tarzan's New York Adventure* (1944); Gene Kelly, Frank Sinatra, and Jules Munshin danced over it in *On the Town* (1949); Superman flew Lois Lane alongside it in *Superman*

Brooklyn Bridge, 1880s

(1978); Sidney Lumet covered it with yellow linoleum so that Diana Ross, Michael Jackson, and a cast of hundreds could "Ease on Down the Road" across it in *The Wiz* (1978); Meryl Streep, Kevin Kline, and Peter MacNicol drank champagne atop it in *Sophie's Choice* (1982); a dazed Bruce Willis weaved in and out of traffic on it aboard a hospital gurney and angered motorists no end in *Hudson Hawk* (1991); tanks rolled across it in a terrorist-threatened New York City under martial law in *The Siege* (1998); Hugh Jackman followed Liev Schreiber across it in 1876 (while it was still being built) and wound up in twenty-first-century Manhattan in *Kate and Leopold* (2001); and there have been hundreds more films that have taken advantage of this architectural wonder of Gothic arches and spiderweb steel cables—which took seventeen years, 1867 to 1883, to build—linking Lower Manhattan with Brooklyn.

Arguably one of the most memorable film sequences featuring the Brooklyn Bridge is in the 1978 disco-docudrama *Saturday Night Fever,* when, toward the end of the movie, the youth played by John Travolta has finally gotten up the nerve to leave his provincial Brooklyn neighborhood to try his luck in near-but-oh-so-far Manhattan. Travolta's crossing the Brooklyn Bridge is a poignant, pivotal moment in the film—a rite of passage. Whereas the Verrazano-Narrows Bridge was the scene of the immature, dangerous games of Travolta and his friends earlier in the story, the Brooklyn Bridge—older, more substantial, and leading to Manhattan rather than Staten Island—comes to represent the challenge of moving on, growing up. Quite clearly, at least in the movies, this is not just another pretty bridge.

2. BROOKLYN HEIGHTS PROMENADE

The dramatic view of the Brooklyn Bridge, Lower Manhattan, New York Harbor, and the Statue of Liberty that can be seen from the Brooklyn Heights Promenade may well be NYC's ultimate photo opportunity. Built in 1951 to protect Brooklyn Heights residents from the sight and some of the sounds of the Brooklyn-Queens Expressway, which runs beneath it, this paved esplanade—with its trees, shrubs, and park benches—quickly became one of the most popular spots in the neighborhood for strollers, joggers, romantic couples . . . and filmmakers. Indeed, sometimes it seems as though directors deliberately house a major character in Brooklyn Heights just so they can feature a scene set on the promenade. A case in point: *Three Days of the Condor*, where, because Faye Dunaway happens to live in Brooklyn Heights, Robert Redford (whom she happens to be hiding in her apartment) is able to have a dramatic promenade confrontation with bad-guy Cliff Robertson. Other features in recent years that have also used the promenade to add to the drama—and often the romance—of a scene or two are: *Moonstruck* (1987), *She's Gotta Have It* (1986), *Prizzi's Honor* (1985), *Luna* (1979), *Saturday Night Fever* (1978), *The Sentinel* (1977), and *Sweet November* (1968). And let's not forget the *Patty Duke Show,* which was filmed in Manhattan, set in Brooklyn Heights, and showed off the promenade during its opening credits for several primetime television seasons in the 1960s. In addition to its TV and film appearances, the promenade is constantly used for print ads and fashion photography.

3. *PRIZZI'S HONOR* MANSION
3 Pierrepont Place

The late William Hickey, New York actor and acting teacher extraordinaire, was nominated for an Academy Award in 1986 for his portrayal of the dying Mafia chieftain, Don Corrado, in John Huston's *Prizzi's Honor*. In the film, the fabulous brick palazzo with magnificent gardens that was Don Corrado's home and headquarters was actually a landmark Brooklyn Heights mansion built in 1857 for a wealthy local named Abiel Abbot Low. Low's son, Seth, went on to be mayor of Brooklyn, president of Columbia College, and eventually mayor of New York, after Brooklyn and the other boroughs were consolidated into the City of New York in the 1890s. Little did Mr. Low know that his handsome family home would one day be in the hands of the underworld.

Another *Prizzi's Honor* location—standing just across the street from the Pierrepont Place palazzo—is the apartment building at 57 Montague Street. It was here that Jack Nicholson had that pad with the great view of the Brooklyn Bridge.

Prizzi's Honor Brooklyn
Heights mansion

4. *THE SENTINEL* BUILDING
10 Montague Terrace

It looks like an idyllic place to live, this beautiful Brooklyn
Heights brick building with its wrought-iron gate, lush front
garden, and elegant stained-glass entryway. But in the 1977
supernatural thriller *The Sentinel,* Cristina Raines found anything but peace and quiet when she rented an apartment here.
For, unbeknownst to her, she had entered the gates of hell, and
for the rest of the film she battled all manner of ghosts and
ghouls as neighbors. The real-estate agent who got Miss Raines
into this otherworldy mess was none other than the great MGM
beauty Ava Gardner (1922–1990), playing one of the many
cameo roles, along with a stint on the TV series *Knots Landing,*
that kept her more or less active for the last decades of her
career.

Regina Taylor reads Pee Wee Love at Gowanus Housing Projects in Spike Lee's *Clockers*, 1995

5. GOWANUS HOUSING PROJECTS
Hoyt and Wycoff Streets, Boerum Hill

Brooklyn-raised Spike Lee (his family moved here from Atlanta when he was an infant) shoots as much as he can in his favorite borough and his 1995 film version of Richard Price's novel *Clockers* was no exception. The Price novel, which tracked the lives of round-the-clock drug runners ("Clockers"), was originally set in New Jersey and Martin Scorsese was to have directed it. But Scorsese, who opted to direct *Casino* instead, wound up producing *Clockers* and giving it to Lee to direct. Rather than venture across the Hudson, Lee stayed in familiar territory and set the film in these basic Boerum Hill low-income housing projects, which became the Nelson Mandela Houses in the film. The projects' green wide-open spaces—originally designed for the pleasure of the residents—provided the clockers with an ideal locale for their complex, multistep drug-peddling operations.

Brooklyn Paramount, ca. 1930

6. PARAMOUNT THEATER SITE
385 Flatbush Avenue Extension

The sweeping marquee that once wrapped around Flatbush and DeKalb Avenues is gone, as are the two nine-story-high neon signs that told all of Brooklyn that this was the fabled Paramount Theater. With 4,126 seats, the Brooklyn Paramount reigned as the borough's biggest movie palace from 1928—when it opened with Nancy Carroll starring in *Manhattan Cocktail*—to 1962, when its last picture show was *Hatari* with John Wayne. Designed by Rapp and Rapp, the architectural firm responsible for the Paramount Theater on Times Square, the Brooklyn Paramount was just as famous for its Paramount-Publix stage shows as for its films. Early in the theater's history, a chorus girl named Ginger Rogers leapt successfully from the Paramount stage-show circuit to Broadway and eventually to the Paramount Studios in Astoria.

By the time the 1950s rolled around, the once-lavish stage shows at the Paramount had given way to rock-and-roll extravaganzas. By that time, too, Long Island University had acquired the office building that towered over the Paramount, and in 1962, when the theater shut down permanently, LIU turned the massive auditorium—with its mighty Wurlitzer organ and its star-studded ceiling—into a gymnasium. It's still that today.

7. DUMBO
Washington and Front Streets

Among film people in New York City, DUMBO is not a famous Walt Disney cartoon elephant but rather refers to Down Under the Manhattan Bridge Overpass. When filmmakers want a glamorous, romantic background for a Brooklyn-set film, they head to the Brooklyn Heights Promenade, but when they want a bit of grime, grit, old warehouses and factory buildings along with a spectacular riverfront view, they shoot at DUMBO. Often used for commercials (one art director brought in tons of sand to turn a DUMBO street into a desert for a car advert) as well as TV series like *The Sopranos, Third Watch,* and *Law & Order,* the area has welcomed such features films as *The Siege* (1998), *Stay* (2004), and *The Forgotten* (2004). Indeed, DUMBO had become so inundated with film crews that some residents felt that things were getting out of hand—what with overzealous production assistants trying to keep residents from entering their lofts and ruining a take, not to mention the guy who racked up over $400 in parking tickets and towing charges because of covered parking signs and unsympathetic NYPD towing crews. Because of all the neighborhood discontent, in early 2004 DUMBO was put on a "Hot List" by the Mayor's Office of Film, Theater, and Broadcasting—the city agency that issues permits for location shoots. Hot List status means that, for the moment at least, DUMBO is off-limits to moviemakers—but not to movie lovers, who may want to wander down there and see what all the fuss is about.

8. STEINER STUDIOS
15 Washington Avenue, Brooklyn Navy Yard

The Brooklyn Navy Yard dates back to 1801, when the U.S. Navy took over an already thriving Brooklyn port and turned it into a military base, which served the country from the War of 1812 through the Civil War and the two world wars. It reached its high point during World War II, when some seventy thousand people worked here. In the midst of that war, Alfred Hitchcock used the Brooklyn Navy Yard as an important location in his scary look at Axis terrorists at work in the United States, *Saboteur* (1942); in the film, the Fifth Columnists plan to blow up the USS *Alaska* in the yard, but Robert Cummings saves the day. After the war, Hollywood returned to the navy yard when director Stanley Donen used it as the point of embarkation for Frank Sinatra, Gene Kelly, and Jules Munshin for their whirlwind musical adventure as sailors on leave in New York in *On the Town* (1949).

Abandoned by the navy in the early 1970s, the yard has been redeveloped as a 265-acre industrial park. For movie lovers, the most exciting tenant here is Steiner Studios, a brand-new, built-from-the-ground-up film studio that debuted in 2004 with 170,000 square feet of soundstages plus postproduction facilities, a screening room, and the pièce de résistance—New York's only back lot, since most of the old navy yard's historic buildings are still standing, some dating back to Civil War times, and can easily be adapted for background work.

Visit www.steinerstudios.com.

9. WILLIAMSBURG BRIDGE

Its neighbor to the south, the Brooklyn Bridge, made history when it opened in 1883. Not only was the Brooklyn Bridge an architectural and engineering marvel, it was a thing of extraordinary beauty. On the other hand, the Williamsburg Bridge, when it came along in 1903, was just another bridge—and not a very pretty one at that, looking more "propped up" than suspended. If it was noted for anything, it had the dubious distinction of opening up the Williamsburg section of Brooklyn to the impoverished masses of the Lower East Side.

Over the years, unlike the glamorous and photogenic Brooklyn Bridge, the lowly Williamsburg span has inspired few filmmakers. Indeed, when it has been used cinematically, it has usually been as a location for films that emphasize the gritty downside of New York City's mystique. A classic case in point is

Williamsburg Bridge as seen in *The Naked City,* 1948

the 1979 film *Last Exit to Brooklyn,* which told of drugs, drag queens, and abuse in 1950s Brooklyn and made extensive use of the bridge's pedestrian walkway. In 1950, another edgy film, *The Sleeping City,* focused on drugs and murder at a major metropolitan hospital and starred Richard Conte as an undercover cop posing as a doctor at the hospital. In the film, the park at the foot of the Williamsburg Bridge furnishes the gloomy backdrop for a number of secret meetings that Conte has throughout the film.

Perhaps *The Sleeping City*'s director, George Sherman, remembered the Williamsburg Bridge from the landmark New York film noir two years earlier that also used it as a location—Jules Dassin's *The Naked City.* This time the Williamsburg Bridge provides a cold, erector-set-like setting for a confrontation between the police and the killer at the end of the film. The killer, needless to say, loses the battle, and winds up falling to his death in the East River. More recently, in Sidney Lumet's look at corruption in the New York Police Department, *Serpico* (1974), the Williamsburg Bridge again turns up. Here, when street-smart

Italian-American cop Frank Serpico (Al Pacino) leaves his Brooklyn home for a new life in a Greenwich Village apartment, he drives into the city in a battered Dodge and takes the Williamsburg Bridge. Clearly the Brooklyn Bridge and even the Manhattan Bridge would have been much too glamorous for this character, this car, this film.

Of the Williamsburg Bridge's film appearances, its most dramatic may well have been in a 1914 silent called *Fighting Death,* in which daredevil movie hero Rodman Law and a young actress both jump from one of its parapets and parachute into the East River. Both performers, it turns out, actually did the stunt, and caused quite a bit of commotion among passersby and motorists who thought that they were witnessing a double suicide. However, as the *New York Times* reported in its February 6, 1914, edition, "the shouts, shrieks and yells which greeted the double jump stopped for a moment when it was seen that the two had parachuted . . . and as the two struck the water, the breathless crowd on the bridge noticed a tug cruising near them with motion picture cameras aboard." Just another day of Manhattan moviemaking.

Recently the Williamsburg Bridge emerged from a major makeover, since in the early 1990s, the dangerously deteriorating century-old structure was found to be a real-life disaster film waiting to happen.

10. MAE WEST BIRTHPLACE?
184 Franklin Street

One thing is certain, she was definitely from Brooklyn. Just where in Brooklyn is another story. Indeed, Ridgewood, Bushwick, Flatbush, and Greenpoint have all claimed Mae West as their own. Perhaps not wanting to disappoint any of her fellow Brooklynites, Mae offers no help in her autobiography, *Goodness Had Nothing to Do with It* (Prentice Hall, 1959), where all she has to say on the subject of her birthplace is: "I was born on a respectable street in Brooklyn." In addition to the question of where, there is also the question of *when.* Mae claimed that she came into the world in 1893—but there are those who have calculated the year to be more like 1887. And just who was her father? Mae's stories had John Patrick West being everything from

Brooklyn bombshell: Mae West

a prizefighter to a detective to a medical doctor. In reality, it seems, Mr. West ran a livery stable in Brooklyn. Which brings us back to where. This exotic Gothic "fortress" on Franklin Street between Java and India streets in Greenpoint is frequently said to be Mae's birthplace.

Tracy Camilla Johns
and Tommy
Redmond Hicks in
Fort Greene Park in
Spike Lee's *She's
Gotta Have It,* 1986

11. FORT GREENE PARK
DeKalb to Myrtle Avenue/Washington Park to St. Edwards Street

Spike Lee's 1986 film *She's Gotta Have It,* a politically not quite correct, but very funny look at a beautiful African-American woman with a very healthy libido, put the writer-director on the movie map. For the film, Brooklynite Lee shot extensively in this historic little park, originally laid out in 1860, south of the old Brooklyn Navy Yard and east of Brooklyn Heights. Although not on the East River, the park offers fine views of the waterfront from its hilltop. For history buffs, a 150-foot column remembers some twelve thousand American prisoners of war who died on British ships anchored near the Navy Yard during the Revolutionary War. An underground crypt, not open to the public, holds their remains.

Visit www.fortgreenepark.org.

12. PRATT INSTITUTE
Between DeKalb and Willoughby
Avenues/Classon Avenue to Hall Street

The unlikely setting for a landmark in pornographic cinema was the library of the Pratt Institute, a prestigious school of art, architecture, and engineering, which was founded in 1887. In the infamous film *Debbie Does Dallas* (1978), the title character (played by Bambi Woods), who dreams of becoming a Dallas Cowboys cheerleader, uses the library stacks for things other than scholarly research. At the time of the shoot, Pratt officials thought they were making their premises available for a respectable film. In 2001, *Debbie Does Dallas* was turned into a play, which was a hit at the New York Fringe Festival but which didn't fare so well when it opened off-Broadway a year later.

Visit www.pratt.edu.

13. LENA HORNE HOUSE
189 Chauncey Street

She made history in 1941 when she became the first black woman to be signed to a long-term contract by a major Hollywood studio. Before that, African-American performers freelanced in Hollywood, picking up jobs as they came along at whatever studio happened to be casting maids, butlers, bootblacks, etc., in the less-enlightened times and movies of the 1920s and 1930s. But Lena Horne changed all that with her MGM contract—or so she had hoped. As it turned out, Lena was usually featured on-screen as an exotic lead singer in a production number that could easily be cut from the film when it played in the South.

Lena Horne was born in Brooklyn and spent the first seven years of her life in her paternal grandparents' three-story brownstone on Chauncey Street in the Bedford-Stuyvesant district. Because her parents separated not long after her birth, Lena spent her formative years growing up under the strong influence of her grandmother, Cora Calhoun Horne. A vigorous civil rights activist and a stalwart member of the black bourgeoisie,

Cora Horne taught her granddaughter to be polite to the less-advantaged white families that lived in the neighborhood, but refused to allow her to play with any children—white or black—whose behavior and language did not meet her high standards.

Lena's life on Chauncey Street was filled with cultural opportunities. While Cora often took the child along to her many club meetings, Lena's grandfather exposed her to museums, theater, and movies. Indeed, all that Lena missed were her parents. Occasionally she would be visited by her father, who had shunned middle-class respectability for the freewheeling life of a Harlem gambling man. Less often, her mother, who was a sometime actress and who didn't get along with Grandmother Horne, would arrange to see Lena away from Chauncey Street.

Lena's life took an abrupt turn when she was seven years old and her mother decided that it was time to have her daughter live with her. Thus began a long period of instability that had Lena moving all over the South and the Midwest. Sometimes she would live with her mother; other times, when her mother was pursuing her theatrical career, Lena would be put up with relatives or family friends. Eventually, when her mother realized that

Still standing: Lena Horne house (on left)

Lena in Hollywood: *Stormy Weather,* 1943

she couldn't provide a proper home for her daughter, Lena, now in her early teens, returned to the house on Chauncey Street.

Unfortunately, Lena's grandparents died within three months of each other a year or so after her return, and she was uprooted once again. Lena's next home was with a woman-friend of her grandmother's. As it turned out, the woman was a very kind lady who encouraged Lena in dance and theater. A few years later, she wound up auditioning for the chorus of the famous Harlem night spot the Cotton Club. She got the job, and suddenly a whole new life began.

Like her old life, however, show business would also involve frequent uprootings and the same loneliness. In her autobiography, *Lena* (Doubleday, 1965), Miss Horne speaks movingly of her lifelong affection for her grandparents' Brooklyn brownstone: "The Brooklyn house was coming, I suppose, to symbolize normalcy and stability to me. I felt I belonged there and all through my life—until my father finally sold it a few years ago—the existence of that house, the knowledge that it was there, unchanged, was a comfort to me."

Attention, Lena Horne: It's still there.

14. CYPRESS HILLS CEMETERY
833 Jamaica Avenue

One of the many cemeteries that are clustered along the border between northern Brooklyn and southern Queens, Cypress Hills is a vast hilly enclave of trees, flowering shrubs, and graves that range from traditional headstones to architecturally exotic mausoleums to small stone slabs embossed with Chinese characters. Toward the back of the property, near the Queens border, stands a huge white-granite building with stained-glass windows and a dramatic columned entryway. This is the Cypress Hills Abbey mausoleum, and inside, off to the right, along aisle EE, movie lovers will discover a whole wall of crypts that bear the name West. At the bottom of the stack is John E. West, 1900–1964; above him are John West, 1862–1935; Beverly West, 1898–1982;

Cypress Hills Abbey
Mausoleum, housing
Mae West's crypt

Matilda West, 1875–1930; and, at the very top, one of Brooklyn's most illustrious native daughters, the legendary Mae West, 1893–1980. Reportedly, when Mae was first interred in the abbey, she had been put in the number-three slot. Once her will was read, however, it became quite clear that Mae would not settle for anything less than top billing, and Cypress Hills saw that her wishes were carried out.

Besides Mae, Cypress Hills Abbey also houses the crypt of comic character-actor Victor Moore (1876–1962), baseball great Jackie Robinson (1919–1972), and prizefighter James J. ("Gentleman Jim") Corbett (1866–1933). While best known for his boxing exploits, Corbett occupies a unique position in motion-picture history because in 1894 he signed an exclusive deal with the Kinetoscope Exchange Company (the company that marketed Edison's Kinetoscope motion-picture viewing device) to appear in filmed fight sequences *only* for that company. In so doing, Corbett was the first performer to sign a motion-picture-star contract.

In 2003, it was discovered that the ashes of the famous African-American performer and songwriter ("Memories of You") James Hubert "Eubie" Blake (1883–1983) were interred here in an unmarked grave. In February 2004, a proper marker was put in place and the intersection where it is located renamed Eubie Blake Corner. Blake's life was celebrated in the Broadway musical *Eubie* (1978), which starred the late Gregory Hines as the great man.

For movie lovers who don't go to the cemetery, they can catch it in the last reel of *Spider-Man* (2002), as the location of the funeral of Tobey Maguire's Aunt May (Rosemary Harris).

15. BARBRA STREISAND BIRTHPLACE
457 Schenectady Avenue

In the early 1940s, the Brooklyn phone directory listed Emmanuel Streisand as living in this six-story brick apartment building not far from Kings County Hospital. Streisand was an English teacher married to Diana Rosen, the daughter of a Brooklyn cantor who also worked in the garment district. The couple had a son, Sheldon, born in 1935, and a daughter, Barbara, who came into the world in 1942. Less than a year later, Mr. Streisand died and Mrs. Streisand left Schenectady Avenue and moved herself and her two kids into her parents' home in nearby Williamsburg.

16. PROSPECT PARK

One of Brooklyn's greatest treasures, Prospect Park provides the borough with 345 acres of streams and ponds, green lawns and gardens. Designed by Frederick Law Olmsted and Calvert Vaux—the same team responsible for Manhattan's Central Park—Prospect Park was completed in 1874, some twenty-four years before the independent City of Brooklyn would become part of the City of New York.

Movie lovers, especially, will be interested in the park's Celebrity Path, which wraps around an enchanting lake over by the Japanese Garden. Brooklyn's answer to Hollywood's star-studded Walk of Fame sidewalk, the Celebrity Path honors the talents of artists, performers, and athletes who were born or who flourished in Brooklyn. Among the stars who are remembered here with their names inscribed on stepping-stones around the lake are F. Murray Abraham, Joey Adams, Woody Allen, Lauren Bacall, Gene Barry, Eubie Blake, Joe Bologna, Clara Bow, Mel Brooks, Eddie Cantor, Betty Comden, Tony Danza, Dom De-Luise, Richard Dreyfuss, Harvey Fierstein, Vincent Gardenia, George Gershwin, Jack Gilford, Jackie Gleason, Louis Gossett Jr., Elliott Gould, Buddy Hackett, Moss Hart, Susan Hayward, Rita Hayworth, Gregory Hines, Celeste Holm, Lena Horne, Edward Everett Horton, Harry Houdini, Anne Jackson, Lainie Kazan, Danny Kaye, Harvey Keitel, Alan King, Carole King, Tony Lo Bianco, Anne Meara, Arthur Miller, Mary Tyler Moore, Zero Mostel, Rosie Perez, Martha Raye, Mickey Rooney, Jackie Robinson, Phil Silvers, Neil Simon, Jimmy Smits, Paul Sorvino, Barbara Stanwyck, Connie Stevens, Barbra Streisand, Gene Tierney, Marisa Tomei, John Turturro, Brenda Vaccaro, Ben Vereen, Eli Wallach, Mae West, and Shelley Winters.

Harder to find, but also a must for movie lovers visiting the park, is the tiny, fenced-off Quaker cemetery at the center of the property (best reached from the 16th Street and Prospect Park Southwest entrance). A private burial ground that dates back to 1849 (some twenty-five years before Prospect Park was built), this is a peaceful preserve of green hills, big trees, and ancient gravestones. One of the newer memorials, on the slope to the right of the main gate (which is always locked), marks the grave of Montgomery Clift, who was buried here in 1966. Although Clift's funeral was held at the Episcopal Church of St. James in Manhattan, he rests in Prospect Park because his mother, Sunny Clift, had become enamored of the Quaker religion in her later years. Clift's simple headstone, by the way, was designed by John Benson, the same artist responsible for John F. Kennedy's at Arlington National Cemetery in Virginia.

Visit www.prospectpark.org.

17. *SOPHIE'S CHOICE* HOUSE
101 Rugby Road

They painted this distinctive Queen Anne–style Victorian mansion shocking pink for the 1980s film based on William Styron's 1970s novel about 1940s Brooklyn, *Sophie's Choice*. As Yetta

Sophie's Choice house, Flatbush

Mary Pickford
house, Flatbush

Zimmerman's Brooklyn boardinghouse, this "Pink Palace" was where a young writer from the South named Stingo (Peter Mac-Nicol) first lived in New York, and where he slowly discovered the dark secrets of his fellow tenants Sophie (Meryl Streep) and Nathan (Kevin Kline). The Pink Palace, actually a private house on a magnificent residential block of Flatbush, was repainted gray once the film crew had gotten all their shots.

18. MARY PICKFORD HOUSE
1320 Ditmas Avenue

According to local legend, this handsome half-timbered Tudor house was built for Mary Pickford by the executives of the Flatbush-based Vitagraph Company so that their new star would have a luxurious Brooklyn bungalow near the studios. The same story goes on to say that Miss Pickford never moved into this Brooklyn house because Vitagraph moved to Hollywood before the place was finished.

To set the record somewhat straight, Vitagraph never *moved* to Hollywood; it did set up studios there, but these were always in addition to its Brooklyn operations. Also, Miss Pickford was *never* a Vitagraph artist, although in the spring of 1916 it looked as if she might become one. Shopping around for a new studio at the time, Miss Pickford was in serious negotiations with Vitagraph's head, Albert E. Smith, when a very minor incident—detailed in Terry Ramsaye's *A Million and One Nights* (Simon & Schuster, 1926)—

occurred to nix the whole proposition. It seems that during a final meeting between Mary and Smith, there had been much small talk about the new baby that had just been born to Smith and his wife. When at the end of the meeting, Pickford and Vitagraph had still not come to terms, Mary, fully expecting another meeting, kept everything cordial by asking when she might see Smith's new baby. To this, Smith, more interested in contracts than in babies, answered: "Just as soon as we get this business signed up and out of the way." Not appreciating Smith's crass sense of priorities, the ever-so-proper Miss Pickford came back with, "If that's it, I'll never see the baby," and kissed Vitagraph good-bye.

It wasn't a bad move on Mary's part, as it turned out, because six weeks later she signed a new contract with the studio she had just left, Adolph Zukor's Famous Players. It was quite a contract for 1916: Mary would get more than a million dollars over a two-year period—plus an extra $300,000 when her pictures earned out. In addition, her name was to be the only one featured in any advertisements for her films, and the type size of her name had to be larger than the title of the movie. She would also receive her own exclusive studio plus script, cast, and directorial approval. Needless to say, Mary never moved to Ditmas Avenue in Flatbush.

Helen Morgan house, Flatbush

Helen Morgan in
Applause, 1929

19. HELEN MORGAN HOUSE
466 East 18th Street

Ann Blyth starred in this singer's tragic life story in the 1957 Warner Bros. film *The Helen Morgan Story*. The same year, Polly Bergen won an Emmy portraying the same singer in the TV special also called *The Helen Morgan Story*. Born on a farm in Illinois in 1900, Helen Morgan became the 1920s' most famous torch singer, appearing both on the stage—often in the *Ziegfeld Follies*—and in early talking pictures. Her greatest triumph on screen was in Rouben Mamoulian's 1929, made-in-Astoria musical *Applause,* in which she sang "What I Wouldn't Do for That Man." Miss Morgan also appeared as Julie in two screen versions of Jerome Kern's *Show Boat,* a 1929 part-talking production that now is lost, as well as the much more famous 1936 Universal extravaganza that also starred Irene Dunne, Allan Jones, Paul Robeson, and Hattie McDaniel. In 1941, Helen Morgan died of cirrhosis of the liver brought on by years of alcoholism. In the 1920s and 1930s, she called this barny 1899 Flatbush Victorian house home.

20. BUCKINGHAM COURT
726 Ocean Avenue

It's all very Hollywood—the tapestry-brick façade, the bay windows and ornate iron grilles, the gabled and tiled roofs. Add a few palm trees and it could almost be the set for a Raymond Chandler murder mystery. Actually, back in 1913, when the exotic Buckingham Court apartments were built at 726 Ocean Avenue, fantasy played a rather major role in Flatbush life—what with the Vitagraph studios churning out "eighty-seven miles of film a year" down on Elm Street. In those days, many of Vitagraph's actors, technicians, and executives lived in Flatbush, and it seems that Buckingham Court was an extremely popular address with the Vitagraph crowd. Indeed, the building's exotic architecture may well have been an attempt by developers to cater

A-list accommodations:
Buckingham Court

to the theatrical tastes of the Flatbush film colony. Locals say that Douglas Fairbanks, Mary Pickford, Fatty Arbuckle, and Norma and Constance Talmadge all once lived at Buckingham Court. In the cases of Pickford, Fairbanks, and Arbuckle, this would seem highly unlikely, since none of them ever worked for Vitagraph. On the other hand, it is quite possible that the Talmadge sisters did reside at Buckingham Court—along with their forceful stage mother, Peg, and their other sister, Natalie, who made some films in the 1910s but never became a star. Today the building is popular with the many West Indian immigrants who live in this section of Brooklyn.

21. ERASMUS HALL HIGH SCHOOL
911 Flatbush Avenue

Founded in 1787, Erasmus Hall High School is the oldest secondary school in New York State, and the second oldest in the United States. Among the many famous Brooklynites educated within its hallowed halls are lyricist Betty Comden, record-

Erasmus Hall High School

STREISAND, BARBARA
Freshman   Chorus,   1,   2;   Choral
Club, 2-4.   Class of '59 graduate

company executive Clive Davis, chess star Bobby Fischer, *Oprah!* editor-in-chief Amy Gross, interviewer Larry King, comedian Gabriel Kaplan, diva Beverly Sills, singer/actress Stephanie Mills, novelist Mickey Spillane, and songwriter/performer Neil Diamond. And then there are the motion picture folk: Jeff Chandler (Ira Grossel during his Erasmus days), Susan Hayward (Edythe Marrener), Barbara Stanwyck (Ruby Stevens), Barbra Streisand, Jane Cowl, Aline MacMahon, Eli Wallach, and Norma and Constance Talmadge. Movie lovers may remember, too, a famous fictional Erasmus student. Her name was Phoebe, and in her brief appearance at the end of *All About Eve* (1950), we find her coveting Broadway star Eve Harrington's Sarah Siddons Award, as the Eve Harrington–Margo Channing cycle is about to go round once again.

Today's Erasmus Hall is a very different place from the time when most of the people listed above were students there.

Reflecting the changes in the ethnic makeup of Flatbush, the student body is now largely black and Asian. The historic institution has changed in other ways as well, notably with its bold plan to turn the campus into a series of small high schools, each with a different specialty. The first of these, STAR (Science, Technology, and Research) Academy at Erasmus Hall, debuted in 2003.

22. ALBEMARLE THEATER
973 Flatbush Avenue

Just like the old Stanley Theater in Jersey City, Brooklyn's 2,700-seat Albemarle movie palace later served as a Kingdom Hall for the Jehovah's Witnesses. Among the renovations made to this historic 1920 theater, with its French Empire façade and enormous lobby, has been the installation of a baptismal font in the basement.

23. LOEW'S KINGS THEATER
1049 Flatbush Avenue

With two enormous lobbies, a 3,609-seat auditorium lavished with sculpted columns, magnificent murals, velvet draperies, and gilded ceilings, Loew's Kings brought the splendors of the French Renaissance to Flatbush Avenue. Designed by the Chicago firm of Rapp and Rapp and decorated by Harold W. Rambusch of New York, the Kings opened on September 7, 1929, with a "part-talkie" called *Evangeline,* starring Dolores del Rio, who showed up in person for the glamorous event. Also on the bill was a stage show that featured the revue *Frills and Fancies,* Wesley Eddy and his Kings of Syncopation, plus the Chester Hale Girls "direct from the Capitol Theater" (Loew's famous first-run house on Times Square). In addition to the luxuries the theater provided its patrons, it treated its staff pretty well, too, offering them such perks as a gym and basketball court in the basement.

Like many movie palaces, Loew's Kings started losing its luster—and its customers—during the 1960s. Nonetheless, the place somehow managed to hang on until 1977, when it finally went out of business. Since then, the theater has been frequently in the local news, as various groups with different agendas try to

Splendor on Flatbush Avenue: Loew's Kings Theater

figure out what to do with the massive old palazzo. In 2000, it looked as though a group headed by Magic Johnson was going to turn it into a twelve-screen multiplex—but that never happened. There are now plans to turn the theater into a cultural center for the area's Caribbean community.

While waiting for that to happen, movie lovers can see the theater in Jim Jarmusch's taxi-driver odyssey *Night on Earth* (1992) as well as in Barry Levinson's gripping drama of teenage revenge *Sleepers* (1996).

24. SUSAN HAYWARD BIRTHPLACE
3507 Church Avenue

The daughter of a transit worker, the woman whom the world knew as Susan Hayward was born Edythe Marrener on June 30, 1918. This three-story brick apartment on a commercial block in Flatbush was her first home. Hayward's most famous screen roles were as the alcoholic singer Lillian Roth in *I'll Cry Tomorrow* (1955) and as a B-girl who winds up on death row in *I Want to Live* (1958), which won her an Academy Award. She died of a brain tumor in 1975.

Brooklyn-born Susan
Hayward arriving at
La Guardia, 1952

25. BARBRA STREISAND PROJECTS
3102 Newkirk Avenue

A great brick jungle of aging post–World War II apartment
houses rises between Newkirk and Foster, Nostrand and New
York Avenues, in the center of Flabush. Today these projects offer housing to low-income, mostly Afro-Caribbean families. Fifty
years ago these same buildings housed many of Flatbush's once
large Jewish middle class. One family that resided here in the
early 1950s was that of Louis Kind, his wife, Diana, and their
child, Rosalind. Also sharing the Kind apartment were Diana's
son and daughter from her first marriage, Sheldon and Barbara
Streisand. By all accounts, it was not an idyllic situation—especially for little Barbara, who had to contend with a stepfather
who is said to have referred to his baby daughter and his ten-
year-old stepdaughter as Beauty and the Beast. At the same time,
it seems that Barbara referred to Mr. Kind as "a used car salesman or something," when in reality he was a real-estate agent. In

Barbra Streisand's
childhood home,
Flatbush

any event, Kind didn't last too long on Newkirk Avenue. He moved out in 1953 and never came back.

Meanwhile, Barbara appears to have had a fairly uneventful adolescence. She spent a lot of time watching television on a neighbor's seven-inch set; she also babysat, worked as a cashier at a nearby Chinese restaurant, ushered at the Loew's Kings movie house on Flatbush Avenue, and attended Erasmus High School, where she won a medal in Spanish, sang in the chorus, and graduated in 1959 with a 93 percent average. After that, she went to Manhattan because she wanted to become an actress. To pay for acting lessons, she started singing in clubs . . . and, well, we all know the rest.

26. J. C. STUDIOS/VITAGRAPH STUDIOS SITE
1268 East 14th Street

On the edge of Flatbush, this is one of New York's most historic, albeit least-known television studios. From 1984 to 1987, *The Cosby Show* was taped here, and for a long time it was also home to the soap opera *Another World*. Today, it hosts the venerable soap *As the World Turns*. The history of this facility—currently called J. C. Studios—goes way beyond television, however. In 1903, a young and prosperous film company called Vitagraph established its main studio here and on the adjacent property now occupied by the Orthodox Jewish high school at 1277 East 14th Street. Today, with the exception of the studio's modern front-office structure, the rest of the compound—including all the buildings of the Yeshiva next door—dates back to the Vitagraph era.

Vitagraph was a studio of famous firsts. In 1907, for example, Vitagraph was the first motion-picture company to put an actress under contract. Her name was Florence Turner, but to movie audiences of the day she was simply the Vitagraph Girl. Miss Turner costarred with the screen's first matinee idol, Maurice Costello, who set an important precedent for the film industry by refusing to help build sets or paint scenery, activities actors in early films were often called upon by their producers to do.

The greatest star in Vitagraph's firmament was Brooklyn's own Norma Talmadge. Norma was a teenager when she made her first appearance before the Vitagraph cameras rather unexpectedly in 1910. On a visit to the studio with her mother, Norma saw her idol, the aforementioned Florence Turner, and rushed up to meet her. As it turned out, Miss Turner was shooting a scene—which Norma ruined. By 1913, Florence Turner had left Vitagraph, and Norma Talmadge had taken over as queen of the lot. Other famous Vitagraph players of the 1910s were the heavyweight (three hundred pounds!) comic John Bunny, whose career came to a sudden end when he suffered a

Vitagraph's Brooklyn studios

Vitagraph superstar:
Norma Talmadge

fatal heart attack in 1915, and Anita Stewart, who made headlines in 1917 when she signed on with an upstart producer
named Louis B. Mayer before her Vitagraph contract had run
out. Vitagraph sued, and won, in a landmark case that established for many years the power of producers over their stars.
Less well known during their Vitagraph days were Leon Trotsky,
the Russian revolutionary, and Rudolph Valentino, the superstar,
both of whom worked as $5-a-day extras at the Brooklyn studio
long before they became famous.

By the mid-1920s, Vitagraph, which now had studios in Hollywood as well as Brooklyn, was having serious financial difficulties. Unlike many of its competitors, the Vitagraph Company
had not developed its own chain of theaters, and ultimately it
had trouble booking its features into first-run houses. Thus,
when Warner Bros. offered to buy the studio from its cofounder,
Albert E. Smith, in 1925, Smith had no choice but to sell. After

the sale, Warners held on to the Flatbush facility, and modified it for their new Vitaphone sound system. In addition to carrying out a number of important Vitaphone experiments, Warners also produced short subjects with New York talent at its Brooklyn plant. By 1939, however, there was little actual filming going on at the old Vitagraph lot, and Warners sold off much of the property (the part that's now the Yeshiva) to Technicolor. Then, in 1952, NBC acquired the rest of the studio and equipped it for color-television broadcasting. Among the famous early color "Spectaculars" that came live from Brooklyn was the 1955 production of *Peter Pan* that starred Mary Martin. Today, the studio is privately owned, and television is still here. Granted, things are a lot quieter than in the old days when Vitagraph had twenty-nine directors and hundreds of actors working simultaneously, but the fact that this historic show-business site is still in show business is good news. Viva Vitagraph!

Saturday Night Fever
house, Bay Ridge

27. *SATURDAY NIGHT FEVER* HOUSE
221 79th Street

John Travolta took the country by storm in 1978 with his dead-on portrayal of a callow/callous Brooklyn teenager named Tony Manero in Robert Stigwood's *Saturday Night Fever*. Based on a 1976 piece in *New York* magazine by writer Nick Cohn called "The Tribal Rites of the New Saturday Night," the film shot a lot of scenes on location in Brooklyn. For the Manero family abode, this Bay Ridge bungalow got the nod. In the film, as we all remember, John Travolta/Tony Manero worked in a paint store by day and was king of the disco floor at night. In between, he spent a lot of time at home on 79th Street blow-drying his hair, posing in front of his bedroom mirror, and at the dinner table (which was in the kitchen) coming out with some of the foulest four-letter language ever to burst forth from the Dolbys.

28. SPECTRUM
802 64th Street (at Eighth Avenue)

In the 1970s this Bay Ridge boîte was called Odyssey and had its fifteen minutes of fame as the location for many of the disco sequences in the 1977 film *Saturday Night Fever*. Today, with its flashing dance floor, laser lighting effects, and pulsing music, it is still in business as a gay dance club called Spectrum. Outside the club, if you look up Eighth Avenue, you'll see the towering Verrazano-Narrows Bridge off in the distance. Connecting Brooklyn with Staten Island, this dramatic span also played an important role in *Saturday Night Fever* as the bridge where Travolta and his drunken Bay Ridge buddies climbed, clowned, and tempted fate.

29. CLARA BOW HOUSE
857 73rd Street

She was the ultimate flapper and clinched her film fame in the 1927 Hollywood feature *It*, through which she became known forever after as "the It Girl." Whatever "it" was that Clara Bow had, it didn't last long. A combination of nervous breakdowns and sex scandals—including a story of how she had "entertained" the entire starting lineup of the University of Southern California football team—quickly shook the flimsy foundations of her film career. Then talking pictures came along and finished her off entirely.

Born in Brooklyn in 1905, Miss Bow spent most of her adolescence on the second floor of this modest wood-frame house which still stands across from McKinley Park in the Bay Ridge section of the borough. Her father was a waiter and her mother, plagued with the same emotional problems that would later afflict her daughter, died while Clara was in her early teens. At the age of sixteen, Clara managed to escape her dreary Bay Ridge existence when she won a movie-magazine beauty contest. The prize: a small role in a Hollywood film. On the West Coast, Paramount biggie B. P. Schulberg took a liking to the Brooklyn teenager, and Clara's brief fling with fame is often thought to have been the result of her fling with Schulberg.

Bay Ridge beauty: "It" Girl Clara Bow

Today, the "It" thing is having a renaissance, with celebrities like Gwyneth Paltrow being given über-It status by *Vanity Fair* magazine and even international party boys like Fabian Basabe, romantically linked with First Daughter Barbara Bush in 2004, being labeled the new "It Kid" by the *New York Observer*. But arguably the ultimate It Girls are the Hilton Sisters—Paris and Nicky—who hark back to Clara Bow with their famous partying and, in the case of Paris, infamous X-rated antics, e.g., her sex video that got a lot of play on the Internet.

30. BENSONHURST ELEVATED RAILWAY
Stillwell Avenue to New Utrecht Avenue

In 1968, Peter Yates directed what was considered the definitive car chase in the Steve McQueen thriller *Bullitt*. But three years later director William Friedkin topped Yates with the chase at the climax of *The French Connection*—and he did so without the hills and valleys of San Francisco to add to the drama. Instead, it happened right here in the unprepossessing Bensonhurst section of Brooklyn under the shadows of the hulking Bensonhurst Elevated Railway. It reportedly took Friedkin five weeks to shoot the scene, which covered some thirty blocks from Bay 50th Street Station at Stillwell Avenue to the 62nd Street Station at New Utrecht Avenue.

31. NEW UTRECHT HIGH SCHOOL
Sixteenth Avenue and 79th Street

Fans of vintage TV shows may recognize this Bensonhurst high school from the credit roll of the 1970s hit series *Welcome Back, Kotter,* which Brooklyn-born comic Gabriel Kaplan created and starred in. Kaplan never attended New Utrecht High, however; he was an Erasmus grad and is said to have based *Kotter* on his Erasmus days. To further complicate matters, the name of the school in the series was neither New Utrecht nor Erasmus, but the created-for-television James Buchanan. Things were different in the old days: New Utrecht got to use its own name when it played a featured role in MGM's 1947 *It Happened in Brooklyn*. In the film, New Utrecht High is where returning World War II vet Frank Sinatra solves his postwar housing problem by moving into the basement of the school. Sharing his pad is the school's janitor, Jimmy Durante. Welcome back, Frankie.

32. CONEY ISLAND

In the days when newsreels informed America's moviegoing public of what was happening in the country and the world, summers would always bring the standard newsreel puff piece telling of record-breaking weekend crowds jockeying for a place in the Coney Island sunshine. Accessible by public transportation, this three-mile-long strip of Brooklyn beach was for many New Yorkers the easiest and least expensive way to escape the horrors of summer in the city. And in the days before air-conditioning, New York summers were pretty horrendous.

Besides its beaches, Coney Island offered vast bathhouses with sports facilities, a boardwalk, penny arcades, side shows, all sorts of food stalls and cafés, and several totally self-contained amusement parks. In its heyday, there was nowhere on earth quite like Coney Island; it was the world's biggest carnival.

Harold Lloyd at Coney Island in *Speedy,* 1928

Uptown Girls Dakota Fanning and Brittany Murphy at Coney Island, 2003

When the movies came along in the 1890s, Coney Island was already well established as America's capital of fun and fantasy. Therefore it is not surprising that early filmmakers were attracted to this magical and infinitely photographable island. Indeed, in 1896, the year that movies were first projected onto screens in front of an audience, one of the titles that the Edison Manufacturing Company offered to its exhibitors was called *Sea Waves at Coney Island.* That same year Edison also produced a twenty-nine-second film called *Shooting the Chutes,* which documented a particularly thrilling Coney Island ride of the day. More chilling than thrilling was Edison's 1903 Coney Island shocker *The Electrocution of an Elephant,* which captured on film the execution of Topsy, an elephant employed to help build Luna Park but who had killed three men, including a drunken spectator who fed her a cigarette. (Supposedly this was not Edison's first execution—he had been publicly killing, but not filming, dogs and cats with AC power to show that his company's DC power was more effective and less dangerous.)

On November 3, 1899, Coney Island was the site of an important event in the history of the American cinema—when the American Mutoscope and Biograph Company filmed a prizefight between two boxers named Jim Jeffries and Tom Sharkey. To capture the event, which took place at night in the Coney Island Athletic Club, Biograph suspended some four hundred lights above the ring. This turned out to be the first time that a film had been successfully made with artificial light. The fighters were not too thrilled about their history-making bout, however, because the heat from all the lamps was intolerable. Between rounds, they had to be shielded by umbrellas and fanned by their seconds in order to complete the match.

The famous Edison director Edwin S. Porter also helped make film history at Coney Island. In 1903, his *Rube and Mandy at Coney Island* starred two leading vaudeville comics in an amusing ten-minute-long romp around Coney. Not as significant as some of his story films, *Rube and Mandy* is nonetheless a valuable, and wonderfully photographed, documentary on turn-of-the-century life. More of a landmark is Porter's 1904 *Fighting the Flames at Coney Island,* which captured a mock fire at a resort hotel and took an important step in bringing staged spectacles to the screen. Also important is the director's 1905 *Coney Island at Night.* Just three minutes long, this beautiful little film was a brilliant experiment in night photography.

More made–at–Coney Island film history: In 1908, the Kalem film company used Manhattan Beach (adjacent to Coney Island) to stage the chariot race for a very low-budget, highly condensed version of *Ben Hur.* Since Kalem had not secured the screen rights for the popular novel on which it had based its little film, the company was sued by the estate of author Gen. Lew Wallace, and wound up settling out of court for $25,000. From then on, screen rights became a force to be reckoned with in the movie business.

Dissolve to 1912, and a film called *Cohen at Coney Island,* produced by a newly formed company called Keystone, which planned to specialize in comedies. Directing as well as acting in the film was one of the new company's founders, Mack Sennett. *Cohen at Coney Island,* as it turns out, was the first in a long line of Keystone comedies, some of which featured Sennett's legendary Bathing Beauties frolicking in the Coney Island surf long before they got their feet wet in the Pacific. Ironically, four years after Sennett had used Coney Island for his first independent picture, one of his company's greatest stars, Roscoe "Fatty" Arbuckle, left Keystone to set up his own production company. Among the first films Arbuckle directed and starred in for his new company was *Fatty at Coney Island*!

The Coney Island movies went on and on. In 1925, Adolphe Menjou took a hair-raising roller-coaster ride at Coney Island in *The King on Main Street*. The innovative camera work for the sequence was that of James Wong Howe, who would become one of the industry's leading cinematographers, earning Academy Awards for *The Rose Tattoo* (1955) and *Hud* (1963). In 1928, when Harold Lloyd, the bespectacled comic who made most of his films in Hollywood, came to New York to shoot *Speedy,* he couldn't pass up Coney Island as a location. In *Speedy*'s Coney Island interlude, we see Lloyd and his girlfriend riding the air-

Alice Mann, Fatty Arbuckle, and Buster Keaton in *Fatty at Coney Island*, 1917

planes of Luna Park and the famous mechanical racehorses of Steeplechase Park (where, by the way, Cary Grant worked as a stiltwalker). Today, both of these amusement parks are gone, but film historians in the 1980s found a very good print of Lloyd's film—with Czech subtitles!—providing another rare glimpse of a lost world.

In the 1930s the movies started to talk. This meant that increasingly they were made on soundstages or on back lots, where noise could be carefully controlled. It also meant that almost all feature-film production moved to Hollywood. Thus, when we see Claudette Colbert and Ray Milland riding the Cyclone in *The Gilded Lily* (1935), it's thanks to the wonders of rear projection; and when we get Betty Grable, George Montgomery, Cesar Romero, and Phil Silvers starring in *Coney Island* in 1943, we also get a lot of the back lot at Twentieth Century–Fox in Los Angeles.

By the end of the 1940s, however, things had started to change again. Lighter, more sophisticated cameras and sound equipment that had been developed during the war meant that movies could come back outdoors again. Once this started happening, movies also started coming back to New York, and occasionally to Coney Island. In 1953, Morris Engel did *The Little Fugitive,* a low-budget independent film about a little boy who mistakenly thinks he has killed his brother and who spends a day at Coney Island trying to run away from his fear. The film was shot entirely on location, and was one of the features that helped to reestablish New York as a moviemaking town.

And then, of course, there's Woody Allen, whose career is very much in the tradition of pioneer New York directors like Morris Engel—and who came to Coney Island in 1977 to shoot part of *Annie Hall.* In the film, Alvy Singer's childhood home is under Coney Island's famous Cyclone roller coaster. Despite the fact that precious little of vintage Coney Island survives today, Allen found his Cyclone as well as some antique bumper cars and successfully managed to evoke the feeling of the place in the 1940s. And speaking of success, *Annie Hall,* shot entirely in New York, won the Academy Award for the best film of 1977, as well as two additional Oscars for Woody's script and direction. Once again, Coney Island had played a role in the saga of filmmaking in New York.

That saga has continued with Brooklyn by the sea featured

in *Little Odessa* (1994), *The Object of My Affection* (1998), *Pi* (1998), *He Got Game* (1998), *Mickey Blue Eyes* (1999), *Requiem for a Dream* (2000), *Angels in America* (2003), and *Uptown Girls* (2003), in which the teacup ride takes on special significance for both Brittany Murphy and her precocious eight-year-old charge (Dakota Fanning). Meanwhile, movie lovers who visit the old Coney Island will find the place revitalized, the Cyclone and Wonder Wheel restored, Nathan's doing land-office business in perhaps the world's most famous hot dogs, and taking a cue from Disneyland, daily fireworks displays.

Visit www.coneyisland.com.

33. *REQUIEM FOR A DREAM* APARTMENT
3152 Brighton 6th Street, Brighton Beach

Actress Ellen Burstyn received an Academy Award nomination for her role as the lonely, pill- and junk-food/junk-TV-addicted widow Sarah Goldfarb in *Requiem for a Dream* (2000), director Darren Aronofsky's freaky portrayal of an American nightmare

Jared Leto on Coney Island boardwalk in *Requiem for a Dream*, 2000

in Brighton Beach, Brooklyn. Besides her own demons, Sarah has a son (Jared Leto) hooked on street drugs. Shot entirely in Brighton Beach and adjacent Coney Island, the film captures the weird beauty (a jetty view of the enormous beach and dazzling sea), but more often the loneliness (the deserted Cyclone roller coaster in winter, looking like a great hulking dinosaur skeleton) of these Brooklyn neighborhoods. Especially memorable in the film is Sarah's big brick boardwalk-facing apartment building, where yentas with lawn chairs vie for prime places in the sun out front. Proud of the twenty-five pounds she's lost (thanks to speed) in hopes of getting on a trash TV show, Sarah exclaims to her son: "Did you see who had the best seat? I'm somebody now, Harry."

Queens: The Return of the Movies

Two decades ago, the borough of Queens was the site of one of the most important developments in New York film history: the renovation and reopening of the Astoria Studios. Representing the renaissance of feature-filmmaking in New York, this reborn 1920 studio was soon joined by another important Queens moviemaking complex—Silvercup Studios—which has been home not just to feature films but TV hits like *Sex and the City* and *The Sopranos*. If all this wasn't exciting enough, Queens in 1988 saw the debut of the American Museum of the Moving Image, the country's first museum devoted exclusively to the art and industry of filmmaking.

For those who can tear themselves away from this exciting Queens museum, the borough has other attractions—from the longtime home of the great jazzman and sometime film star Louis Armstrong (now a museum) to the place where commercial television was launched to the community of Bayside, which in the early part of the last century was a movie colony where New York moguls and stars spent their summers. These days, Bayside is a quiet little suburban community—but who knows, with the comeback of Astoria, perhaps Bayside will regain its former cachet? And it's a lot closer than the Hamptons.

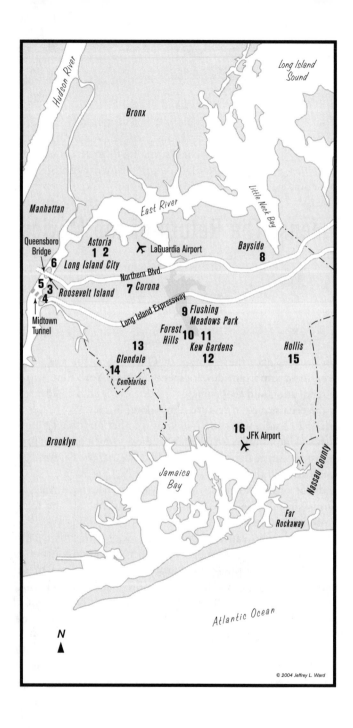

Long Island
Sound

Hudson River

Bronx

East River

Manhattan

Little Neck Bay

Queensboro
Bridge

Astoria
1 2 ✈ LaGuardia Airport

Bayside
8

6 Long Island City

Northern Blvd.

5 3 Roosevelt Island

7 Corona

4

Midtown
Tunnel

Long Island Expressway

9 Flushing
Meadows Park

Forest
Hills **10 11**

13 Kew Gardens

Glendale **12**

Hollis
15

14

Cemeteries

Brooklyn

16 JFK Airport ✈

Jamaica
Bay

Nassau County

Far
Rockaway

Atlantic Ocean

N
▲

1. KAUFMAN ASTORIA STUDIOS
34-12 36th Street

Of all the links that modern New York has with its proud moviemaking past, this great studio today stands as one of the most visible and most vital. The Astoria Studios were founded in 1920 by Jesse Lasky and Adolph Zukor in order to centralize the production facilities of their Famous Players–Lasky Corporation (known as Paramount Pictures by 1927), which at the time had studios scattered all over New York. Throughout the 1920s and well into the 1930s, Astoria would reign as the most important film studio on the East Coast.

Known as the Big House to the old-timers who worked there, the original studio encompassed thirteen acres of an industrial area of Queens that had been opened up by the building of the 59th Street Bridge in 1909 and the elevated subway in 1917. As befitted a proper movie factory, Astoria had a dramatic columned entrance, a huge main stage as well as numerous

Astoria's back lot, dressed for *The Battle of Paris*, 1929

smaller ones, a back lot, scene shop, and commissary, not to mention lavish suites and dressing rooms for its stars.

Among those stars were such legends as Gloria Swanson, who disliked Hollywood's provincialism and who in 1923 decreed to her Paramount bosses that she would work only at Astoria. Since Swanson was the biggest thing in pictures at the time, she got her way—as well as the most glamorous star quarters on the lot, where her enormous closetsful of shoes were the talk of New York.

Another legendary Astoria star of the 1920s was the screen's ultimate male sex symbol, Rudolph Valentino, who made *Monsieur Beaucaire* and *A Sainted Devil* at Astoria in 1924 so that he could have more artistic control over his films than the Hollywood studio system permitted. When the news broke that Rudy was coming East, it is said that Astoria real-estate agents were deluged with women seeking apartments near where their idol would be working.

Last tango in Astoria:
Rudolph Valentino in
A Sainted Devil, 1924

Besides Valentino and Swanson, other notable names from Astoria's silent era were Billie Burke, May McAvoy, Richard Barthelmess, Elsie Ferguson, Wallace Reid, Nita Naldi, Louise Brooks, Bessie Love, Adolphe Menjou, Bebe Daniels, Richard Dix, Thomas Meighan, Rod La Rocque, W. C. Fields, Gilda Gray, and William Powell. Among the studio's top directors were Allan Dwan, Robert Vignola, Sidney Olcott, as well as D. W. Griffith, who in 1924 had run into financial difficulties as an independent producer and had made a deal with Adolph Zukor to work at Astoria. Griffith's first Astoria production, *Sally of the Sawdust,* introduced W. C. Fields to movie audiences.

The year 1927 marked the end of Astoria's silent era, and indeed looked like the end of Astoria as well, since Paramount's production head, B. P. Schulberg, had managed to convince the studio's top brass to close their Queens operation and center all feature production in California. Schulberg hadn't counted on the impact of the talkies, however, and when it looked as though they were around to stay, Paramount reopened Astoria in 1928 to capitalize on Broadway plays and Broadway actors. The great names of Astoria's talkie days include: the Marx Brothers, who did *The Cocoanuts* and *Animal Crackers* at Astoria in 1929 and 1930, respectively; Tallulah Bankhead, noted more for her milk baths than for the quality of her films; Ginger Rogers, who made her screen debut with brown hair and the line "Cigarette me, big boy!"; Claudette Colbert, who filmed many of her pictures both in English and in French; Nancy Carroll, considered to be the first star created by the talkies; and Clive Brook, the first Sherlock Holmes of the sound era.

Despite Astoria's sound revival, by 1932 Paramount was having financial difficulties on both coasts. Facing bankruptcy, it therefore again decided to shoot all of its features in Hollywood. It was at this time, too, that one of the company's creditors, the Western Electric Company, took charge of Astoria and changed its name to Eastern Services Studios. With its new management and new name, Astoria remained a major filmmaking facility on the East Coast and still kept strong ties with Paramount, as is evidenced by the fact that Paramount's newsreel division—"the Eyes and Ears of the World"—continued to be based here. During the 1930s, Astoria/Eastern Services Studios specialized in short subjects, and many of these brought to the screen such New York–based talents as George Burns and Gracie Allen, Jack Benny, Milton Berle, Bob Hope, and Danny Kaye. In the 1930s Astoria was often used for projects that Hollywood wouldn't touch, such as *The Emperor Jones* (1933), which starred the great black actor Paul Robeson. Finally, Astoria in the 1930s was where many promising New York performers made their screen tests. Among this group of Hollywood hopefuls was Fred Astaire. Of his Astoria test, the West Coast casting people noted: "Can't act. Slightly bald. Can dance a little."

By the late 1930s, activity at Astoria had slowed down considerably, and Hollywood was definitely the motion-picture capital of the nation and of the world. With World War II, however, Astoria suddenly found itself back in action in a big way, when it was taken over by the U.S. Army and turned into the U.S. Signal Corps Photographic Center for the production of training and propaganda films. After the war, the army stayed on at Astoria and shot, among many projects, its television series *The Big Picture.*

In 1971, the army got out of the motion-picture business, and for the next few years the future of Astoria was dicey. Although the government gave the studio to the City University of New York in 1973, plans to turn it into a college campus and/or a film school were never realized. Indeed, by the mid-1970s it looked as if the property would have to be turned back over to the federal government, which might then have auctioned it off as surplus real estate, thus spelling the end of Astoria as a film studio. Seeing its historic significance and its potential role in the resurgence of filmmaking that was taking place in the city at the time, a group of New York film people formed a foundation in 1976 that not only managed to get the Astoria Studios declared a National Historic Landmark, but that also got the facility restored and back in operation.

Today's Astoria Studios—further expanded and modernized in 1983 and renamed Kaufman Astoria Studios by real-estate developer George S. Kaufman—boasts the country's largest soundstage outside Hollywood, plus six smaller stages (a brand-new one just added in 2004), and a recording studio big enough for a symphony orchestra. In addition, there are scenery rooms,

Rudolph Valentino and cast of *Monsieur Beaucaire* lunching in Astoria
Studios commissary, 1924

equipment-rental operations, production offices, health club, tennis court, bank, and commissary (which is open to the public). Today's KAS also boasts *The Wiz* (1978), *All That Jazz* (1979), *Going in Style* (1979), *Arthur* (1981), *Fort Apache, the Bronx* (1981), *Wolfen* (1981), *The World According to Garp* (1982), *The Verdict* (1982), *Daniel* (1983), *The Money Pit* (1986), *Brighton Beach Memoirs* (1986), *Ishtar* (1987), *Radio Days* (1987), *The Secret of My Success* (1987), *The Glass Menagerie* (1987), *Orphans* (1987), *September* (1987), *Presumed Innocent* (1990), *Alice* (1990), *Scenes from a Mall* (1991), *Scent of a Woman* (1992), *Shadows and Fog* (1992), *Glengarry Glen Ross* (1992), *The Age of Innocence* (1993), *Carlito's Way* (1993), *The Preacher's Wife* (1996), *Ransom* (1996), *The First Wives Club* (1996), *The Devil's Own* (1997), *The Devil's Advocate* (1997), *Great Expectations* (1998), *A Perfect Murder* (1998), *Cruel Intentions* (1999), *Man on the Moon* (1999), *Hollywood Ending* (2002), and *The Stepford Wives* (2004). All of these films were produced wholly or partially at Astoria. As for television, the studio has been home to *The Cosby Show, Sesame Street, 100 Centre Street,* and *Whoopi,* to name a few. With so much production, KAS is currently expanding. Those pioneers Jesse Lasky and Adolph Zukor must be quite proud, wherever they are.

Visit www.kaufmanastoria.com. For information on the Studio Café, call 718-392-5600.

2. AMERICAN MUSEUM OF THE MOVING IMAGE
35th Avenue at 36th Street

While there are no tours of Kaufman Astoria Studios for the general public, movie lovers who venture out to Queens to see the studios can get an insider's view of the history and technology of moviemaking at the American Museum of the Moving Image, which opened in 1988 in a former studio building on the Astoria lot. The nation's first museum dedicated solely to the art and artifice of film, television, video, and digital media, AMMI ex-

Mae West working the concessions stand at "Tut's Fever," fantasy movie house created by artists Red Grooms and Lysiane Luong for the American Museum of the Moving Image, Astoria

hibits historic and contemporary props, set models and sketches, posters, lobby cards, annotated scripts, production photos, and equipment. This is a place where movie lovers can marvel at everything from the earliest Edison camera to Valentino's French court costumes for *Monsieur Beaucaire* (shot next door) to the desk used by Tom Brokaw on *NBC News Tonight*.

AMMI does more than just display movie and TV memorabilia, however; it has a number of hands-on exhibits that focus on editing, animation, and sound effects. These include computer-based interactive experiences as well as a working soundstage where visitors can shoot their own scenes.

A 200-seat movie theater and three screening rooms are also part of the AMMI picture, presenting adventurous programs of silents, classic and contemporary sound films, plus avant-garde film, video, and digital art. Special mini-festivals focus on famous directors like Bernardo Bertolucci, Stephen Frears, and Lars Von Trier as well as on esoteric themes like the evolution of widescreen cinema. All in all, over four hundred films are screened here every year, with many featuring personal appearances by filmmakers and actors involved with the productions.

For program information, call 718-784-0077, or visit www.ammi.org.

3. SILVERCUP STUDIOS
42-22 22nd Street

Further evidence of the dramatic rise of film production in New York, the former Silvercup Bakery in Long Island City (whose trademark sign can still be seen across the East River from Manhattan) was turned into a movie studio in 1983. Originally specializing in commercials and music videos (Madonna, Britney Spears, Janet Jackson, Bon Jovi, Billy Joel, Cyndi Lauper, and Billy Idol have all shot here), Silvercup studios currently has thirteen soundstages within its enormous three-block-long building plus five drive-in studios. The studios' most famous recent tenants have been the HBO TV series *Sex and the City* and *The Sopranos*.

On the feature front, Silvercup has provided studio space for such made–in–New York films as *Broadway Danny Rose* (1984), *Garbo Talks* (1984), *Romancing the Stone* (1984), *Com-*

Silvercup sirens
(clockwise, from top):
Sex and the City stars
Sarah Jessica Parker,
Cynthia Nixon,
Kim Cattrall, and
Kristin Davis

promising Positions (1985), *The Purple Rose of Cairo* (1985), *Heartbreak House* (1985), *Highlander* (1986), *Street Smart* (1986), *Three Men and a Baby* (1987), *Crocodile Dundee II* (1988), *Working Girl* (1988), *When Harry Met Sally* (1989), *Do the Right Thing* (1989), *Black Rain* (1989), *Sea of Love* (1989), *Bird on a Wire* (1990), *Godfather III* (1990), *First Knight* (1995), *Sabrina* (1995), *Ransom* (1996), *City Hall* (1996), *Extreme Measures* (1996), *Addicted to Love* (1997), *Men in Black* (1997), *Private Parts* (1997), *Mickey Blue Eyes* (1999), *Music of the Heart* (1999), *Stuart Little 2* (2002), *Mr. Deeds* (2002), *Changing Lanes* (2002), and *Two Weeks Notice* (2002).

With its continuing success, Silvercup is now expanding with an adjacent two-million-square-foot mixed-use complex of retail stores, residences, and, naturally, more studios and production facilities. For the project, which covers six and a half acres just south of the Queensboro/59th Street Bridge, Silvercup has engaged world-class British architect Richard Rogers.

Visit www.silvercupstudios.com.

4. QUEENS MIDTOWN TUNNEL

Tunnels are not particularly photogenic, and this underground link between Queens and Manhattan has never been one of the city's major locations—especially since there are so many great-looking bridges to shoot. A few exceptions have been *The Boys in the Band* (1970), one of the country's first mainstream gay films, which has one of the main characters driving through the Midtown Tunnel from Long Island for the birthday party from hell, around which the story revolves. The artery was also used in *The Devil's Own* (1997), but it was another 1997 film that permanently put the Queens Midtown Tunnel on movie lovers' maps. The film was *Men in Black* and its tunnel scene features MIB agents Tommy Lee Jones and Will Smith chasing extraterrestrials in a 1987 Ford LTD that makes anything ever driven by Batman or James Bond look positively primitive. Facing impossible traffic (a frequent occurrence in the Midtown Tunnel), the Men-in-Blackmobile levitates and flies above the congestion and straight through the toll booth. The ultimate E-Z Pass!

5. QUEENSBORO/59TH STREET BRIDGE
Queens Plaza to 59th Street in Manhattan

With its crown-topped finials and intricate steel webbing, this distinctive 1909 structure was a longtime staple for Hollywood art directors. Whenever they wished to portray a particularly grand Upper East Side apartment—such as Rosalind Russell's in *The Velvet Touch* (1948), Barbara Stanwick's in *Sorry, Wrong Number* (1949), and playboy Frank Sinatra's in *The Tender Trap* (1955)—it invariably looked out at the Queensboro Bridge. Particularly beautiful at night, the bridge—despite its name—became the signature image for Woody Allen's homage to Manhattan in his 1979 film of the same name, both on screen and on the poster. Far earlier, the gritty Hollywood film *Dead End* (1937) used the bridge to join the two worlds of Depression-era New York—the poor living in grubby, four-story tenements in the shadow of the bridge and the glamorous society types residing well above the squalor in their posh penthouse towers with views of the bridge in all its glory.

In the last decade, the Queensboro Bridge has continued to be glamorous in such films as *The Mirror Has Two Faces* (1996), *The Last Days of Disco* (1998), *Celebrity* (1998), and *Two Weeks Notice* (2002). It's also provided additional drama in various action films. In *Donnie Brasco* (1997), for example, there's a long tracking shot with Johnny Depp driving over the East River while his passenger Al Pacino waxes philosophical on the art of the hit. In *Conspiracy Theory* (1997), the bridge is the scene of a car switch whereby Mel Gibson with Julia Roberts in tow foils his pursuers. Perhaps most memorable is the bridge sequence in *New Jack City* (1991), when drug lord Wesley Snipes and a partner-in-crime dangle a dude who owes them money by his heels from the bridge; when he doesn't pay up, they drop him into the drink.

On a less violent note, the bridge has a big moment in a very different sort of film, French director Jacques Perrin's Oscar-nominated documentary on the long-distance voyages of migratory birds, *Winged Migration* (2001). In the film, Canada geese, for whom the East River is along their migratory path, fly under the magnificent span as they head to warmer climes for the winter.

6. ROOSEVELT ISLAND TRAM/ROOSEVELT ISLAND

This skinny 147-acre island lies in the East River off Midtown Manhattan and Western Queens. Technically part of the borough of Manhattan, but linked to Queens by a small bridge, it was for many years called Welfare Island, because of the various hospitals and sanitariums that were once located here. In the 1970s, work began to turn the island into a bold new city within New York City. Today the renamed Roosevelt Island is a quieter, pedestrian-freindly alternative to both Manhattan and Queens. Not terribly interesting to filmmakers, Roosevelt nonetheless has one attraction that is unique to the metropolitan area—an aerial tramway, inaugurated in 1976, that takes passengers on a magical amusement park–like ride between Manhattan and the island.

For directors of action-adventure films, the tram was an irresistible new toy. Some of the tram's star appearances include the Sylvester Stallone–Billy Dee Williams thriller *Nighthawks* (1981), where terrorists hijack the tram, holding hostages until their demands are met; *Die Hard with a Vengence* (1995), where Bruce Willis jumps impossibly from the Queensboro Bridge to the tram and then onto a barge below in his stunt-filled pursuit of a mad bomber (Jeremy Irons); and in *Spider-Man* (2002), where the villainous Willem Dafoe knocks a tram-full of children off its pulleys, leaving it dangling over the East River until we-all-know-who saves the day.

Fans of the film *The Professional* (1994) may also remember a much gentler tram sequence in an otherwise unrelentingly violent film. In the final scene of the picture, we see twelve-year-old Natalie Portman crossing the East River aboard the tram, as she abandons her fledgling life of crime for a more conventional existence at an orphanage called the Spencer School on Roosevelt Island. Just three hundred feet from Manhattan, her new world seems many many miles away in spirit. It is the one hopeful image in the film.

7. LOUIS ARMSTRONG MUSEUM
34-56 107th Street, Corona

From 1943 until his death in 1971, Louis Daniel Armstrong lived in this attractive red-brick home in Corona, Queens. Known primarily for his superstar trumpeting, "Satchmo" also appeared in some two dozen motion pictures, beginning with

Louis Armstrong house, now a museum

Pennies from Heaven in 1936 and ending with *Hello, Dolly!* in 1969. Today, Armstrong's former Queens home, a National Historic Landmark, is one of New York City's newest museums. Opened to the public in late 2003, the Louis Armstrong Museum allows visitors to see the house exactly as it was when Armstrong and his wife, Lucille, lived here. Highlights of the property are Armstrong's private den, the couple's spectacular bathroom with gold fixtures, a classic 1960s turquoise kitchen, and all sorts of memorabilia from paintings by Armstrong's friend Tony Bennett to Armstrong's gold-plated trumpets, scrapbooks, and photographs.

For information on opening times and prices, call 718-478-8274 or visit www.satchmo.net.

8. FLUSHING MEADOW PARK

Much of it was a garbage dump before it was filled in, graded, and built upon for the 1939 New York World's Fair. While some fair visitors enjoyed riding in shiny new Lincolns along the Ford Motor Company's half-mile elevated highway of the future, and while others marveled at the artificial thunder and lightning generated inside the General Electric pavilion, everyone agreed that the most impressive wonder at Flushing Meadow was on view at the Radio Corporation of America Building: television!

It was in RCA's pavilion—designed to resemble an Art Deco radio tube—that television made its official commercial debut. The five- and nine-inch TV sets on display were not just for looking; they were authentic production models that RCA hoped soon to market all over the country. At the same time, NBC (RCA's network) would be providing several hours of scheduled television programming every day, and soon CBS, not to be outdone, would follow suit.

But while TV was a big hit with the masses at Flushing Meadow, it was not a hit with the buying public. Not only did the price tags on those first models—between $199.50 and $600—amount to big bucks for a small screen at the tail end of the Depression, there was also the increasingly disturbing world situation, which meant that Americans had other things on their

Alien-busters Tommy Lee Jones and Will Smith at work in Flushing Meadow Park in *Men in Black*, 1997

minds besides television. In fact, by 1941 there were only ten thousand TV sets in the entire country, and once the United States entered the war at the end of that same year, all television production as well as commercial broadcasts had been discontinued. When the war ended, however, the story of television would be a very different one. What happened at Flushing Meadow in 1939 was just a sneak preview.

For TV lovers who visit Flushing Meadow Park, little remains of the 1939 World's Fair except the old New York City Building, which is now the Queens Museum. Its main attraction is a wonderful scale model of New York's five boroughs, which was built for the 1964 World's Fair and is continually updated to reflect the architectural changes in the city. Other vestiges of the 1964 Fair at Flushing Meadow are the 140-foot Unisphere globe—the fair's symbol, which can be seen from both the Long Island Expressway and the Grand Central Parkway. Also hard to miss from the highways skirting Flushing Meadow Park are the futuristic towers of the New York State Pavilion. Adding a surreal dimension to the skyline, they wound up, appropriately, as part of Munchkinland in Sidney Lumet's 1978 fantasy musical, *The Wiz*.

Those same towers as well as the 1964 Unisphere can also be seen in *Men in Black* (1997), as the preferred point of entry for the extraterrestrial aliens overrunning the planet in the fantasy comedy produced by Steven Spielberg. *Men in Black* also has great shots of flying saucers hovering over nearby Shea Stadium and then crashing into the Unisphere, as the aliens try to make a fast exit from Earth.

9. BAYSIDE

Enjoying a prized position on Little Neck Bay, the community of Bayside in northeastern Queens was a fashionable spot for wealthy New Yorkers to have summer estates in the last decades of the nineteenth century. Close to the nerve center of Manhattan, yet delightfully peaceful and rural, Bayside was an especially convenient location for people whose businesses didn't allow them the luxury of being too far from the city. When the twenti-

Baysider Nancy Carroll
with Richard Arlen in
Wayward, 1932

eth century rolled around, it wasn't long before a whole new group of wealthy, hardworking New Yorkers—the stars and executives of the burgeoning motion-picture industry—discovered the many charms of the Bayside summer, and during the 1910s and 1920s they turned the little Queens community into what may have been the world's first movie colony. Long before Malibu . . . there was Bayside!

One of the grandest of the Bayside film colony's summer places was that which producer Joseph Schenck and his movie-star wife, Norma Talmadge, rented from publisher John Ridenour. Ensconced in their hideaway on Little Neck Bay, the Schencks frequently hosted weekend parties that had some of the brightest stars of the era sunning, sailing, and playing croquet. The Schenck compound, it seems, was also a popular spot for celebrity weddings. In 1920, screenwriters Anita Loos and John Emerson tied the knot in Joe and Norma's Bayside garden, and a year later Norma's sister, Natalie, married the famous comedian Buster Keaton there as well. Today the historic property has been seriously subdivided, but the main house with its enormous driveway can still be seen off 222nd Street between Corbett Road and Second Place. The guest house—number 35–45 222nd Street—was used by Gloria Swanson in the summer of 1923 when she was making her transition from Hollywood movie queen to Astoria film star.

Around the corner from the Schencks', W. C. Fields supposedly spent several summers in the split-level frame house at 35–25 223rd Street. Only the back of the place can be seen from the street; the front, which had direct access to the beach and the bay in W. C. Fields's day, is now separated from the shoreline by the Cross Island Parkway.

Movie lovers *can* get a good look, however, at the handsome turreted mansion that was the longtime Bayside home of boxer James "Gentleman Jim" Corbett at 221–04 Corbett Road. Remembered for inventing the left hook and for defeating John L. Sullivan in a famous match in 1892, Corbett was also the first celebrity to sign an exclusive contract to appear in motion pictures. The year was 1894—and the company was the Kinetoscope Exhibition Company, one of the firms involved in marketing Edison's Kinetoscope motion-picture viewing devices.

Not far from the Corbett property, at 215th Place and 32nd

Avenue, one of the most famous stars of the silent screen had Bayside's most spectacular estate. The owner of the property was Pearl White, queen of the cliff-hanger serials in the 1910s, who is still remembered as the star of the legendary *The Perils of Pauline*. According to one Bayside old-timer, however, in person Pearl cut quite a different figure from the embattled heroine she portrayed on-screen. He remembered often seeing the star passing by in a great chauffeur-driven motorcar. If the railroad gates happened to be down at the Bell Avenue crossing, Miss White would simply have her chauffeur drive through them, knowing full well the railroad would bill her for the repairs!

Pearl eventually gave up Bayside and the United States for a château and a continued life of luxury in France. Meanwhile, theater critic John Golden, for whom Broadway's Golden Theater is named, bought Miss White's estate and eventually bequeathed the property to the city to be turned into a public park upon his death. Today, Golden's wishes have been followed and the former Pearl White/John Golden estate is now John Golden Park. The main house is gone, but the grounds—with gardens, walkways, park benches, playing fields, and old-fashioned street lamps—make this one of the prettiest spots in Bayside.

Farther afield, character actress May Robson—noted for playing society matrons in many movies, but who was nominated for an Academy Award in 1933 for her performance as the bag-lady-like Apple Annie in Frank Capra's *Lady for a Day*—lived at

Joseph
Schenck/Norma
Talmadge
Bayside "cottage"

42–34 209th Street. Across the way, at 43–25 209th Street, Duncan "The Cisco Kid" Renaldo was in residence until his death in 1980. Farther along 209th Street, the Dutch Colonial mansion at number 42–46 was, in the late 1920s, briefly home to a beautiful, frequently forgotten star of the early talkies, Nancy Carroll. In her second film, *Abie's Irish Rose* (1928), originally made as a silent and then turned into a "part-talkie," Carroll was the first woman to sing in a commercial feature film. While many careers were ruined by the talkies, Miss Carroll was considered the first actress to have been made a star thanks to the new medium.

Nancy Carroll shot her first films at Paramount Studios in nearby Astoria but, by 1932, she and most of Paramount's other East Coast stars had packed their suitcases and steamer trunks and had taken off for Hollywood, where feature films would be based for the next couple of decades. The 1930s also saw the end of Bayside as a film colony, and soon the exclusive community on Little Neck Bay was swallowed up by Greater New York and became just another suburb. Meanwhile, out on the West Coast, Malibu was starting to become very popular.

The Bayside Historical Society periodically gives walking tours that take in some of the town's more interesting properties. For information, call 718-352-1548.

10. WESTSIDE TENNIS CLUB
1 Tennis Place, Forest Hills

Established in 1802 and one of the country's most exclusive tennis clubs, this was the site of the prestigious U.S. Open from 1915 until the event moved to the newly built USTA National Center in Flushing Meadow Park in 1978. For movie lovers, the tennis match that may interest them most is a Davis Club trial between the United States and Australia that took place here in 1950, long shots of which were used to represent a match in Hitchcock's classic *Strangers on a Train,* where tennis player Farley Granger plays against time, while two police officers are waiting to pick him up for supposedly murdering his estranged wife. The film was based on one of Patricia Highsmith's first novels; another book of Highsmith's, *The Talented Mr. Ripley,* would have two

Playing against time:
Farley Granger at Forest
Hills in *Strangers on a
Train,* 1950

screen incarnations: *Purple Noon* (1961), a French film directed by René Clement that starred Alain Delon, and Anthony Minghella's 1999 feature that used the novel's actual title and starred Matt Damon as Tom Ripley. Highsmith's sequel to her first Mr. Ripley, *Ripley's Game,* also inspired two big-screen versions: German avant-garde director Wim Wenders's *The American Friend* (1977) and Liliana Cavani's 2002 film, which used the original title of the novel and starred John Malkovich.

Back in Forest Hills, the classy Westside Tennis Club—which has thirty-eight courts, eight of which are grass—also pops up in *The Royal Tenenbaums* (1999), for a sequence with Luke Wilson as the former professional tennis player Tenenbaum son.

11. WILL ROGERS HOUSE
124 81st Avenue

In the early 1920s, actor/humorist Will Rogers lived with his family in this stately Tudor mansion in Kew Gardens. At the time Rogers was often a headliner in the Ziegfeld Follies on Broadway. By the end of the decade, however, he would have great success in talking pictures and would move permanently to the West Coast, where he wound up living on a vast ranch near the Pacific Ocean. Today, his L.A. estate has become the Will Rogers State Park and is a popular attraction for locals and tourists. Meanwhile, the world has forgotten that Rogers once lived in Queens.

12. CHARLIE CHAPLIN HOUSE
105 Mowbray Place

Although Chaplin made most of his feature films on the West Coast, at his own studio on La Brea Avenue in Hollywood, the great silent-picture star is said to have acquired this modest Kew Gardens brick bungalow in 1919 to use when his business as producer, writer, and star brought him east.

13. *ALL IN THE FAMILY* BLOCK
89-66 to 89-88 Cooper Avenue

ABC had backed two separate pilots of *All in the Family*, but in each case had dropped the project. Ultimately, a television series in which the main character was a raving bigot was just too con-

All in the Family block, Glendale

troversial for American TV audiences in 1969—despite the fact that the British series on which *All in the Family* was based (*Till Death Do Us Part*) had been extremely successful in the United Kingdom. Indeed, when Norman Lear finally got CBS to take a chance on the project, it was with little enthusiasm that the network put the show on the air. Much to everyone's surprise, *All in the Family* was an instant hit, and it spawned a rash of sitcoms that dealt with formerly taboo-on-TV subjects like race, abortion, premarital sex, homosexuality, and impotence. *All in the Family* also gave birth to the phenomenon of the spinoff, which started when Edith Bunker's cousin Maude segued into her own eponymous series, and was followed by the Bunkers' African-American neighbors becoming the prime-time *Jeffersons*—not to mention Maude's maid, who went off to have her own *Good Times*.

Although the series was taped in California, *All in the Family* supposedly took place in a conservative neighborhood in Queens. For the show's credit roll, a real block of middle-class wood-frame houses on Cooper Avenue between Woodhaven Boulevard and 88th Street in Glendale, Queens, was used. The home that was supposedly Archie and Edith's is thought to have been number 89–70 Cooper Avenue. Besides the notoriety that the block gained from its weekly appearances on network TV, it also found itself in some grizzly newspaper headlines in October 1972, when a woman living at number 89–88 Cooper Avenue shot her three children and then turned the gun on herself.

14. MACPELAH CEMETERY
82–30 Cypress Hills Street

The great star of this cemetery is the Incredible Houdini (born Ehrich Weiss), whose grave just beyond Macpelah's main gate is distinguished by a large marble monument topped by a bust of the famous showman. While the world remembers Harry Houdini for his escape artistry and his feats of magic, it has forgotten that, in the late 1910s and early 1920s, Houdini also appeared in a series of swashbuckling, daredevil adventure films that exploited his acrobatic skills and his special-effects expertise. The first of these film projects was a fifteen-part serial called

Grave of escape artist Harry
Houdini (born Ehrich Weiss),
Macpelah Cemetery

The Master Mystery, which Houdini made in 1918 for Octagon
Films at their studio in Yonkers, New York. From there, Houdini
went to Hollywood, and starred in two features for Paramount–Artcraft Pictures, *The Grim Game* (1919) and *Terror Island* (1920), and he soon became more interested in making
movies than in doing live performances. So interested that, in
1921, he formed the New York–based Houdini Picture Corporation which, for its first film, came out with *The Man from Beyond* (1922), featuring Houdini as producer, writer, editor, and
star. It also featured a hair-raising sequence, filmed on location at
Niagara Falls, and the movie met with critical and box-office
success. A year later, however, Houdini didn't fare quite as well
with *Haldane of the Secret Service,* in which the fiftyish escape
artist–turned–movie actor couldn't cut the mustard as a romantic lead. The film failed, and Houdini returned to the stage.

Houdini died of a ruptured appendix suffered in October
1926 while he was performing at the Garrick Theater in Detroit.
The theatrics surrounding his funeral and burial in New York

Spanish Colonial Queens: Loew's Valencia, Hollis

were reminiscent of those that had attended Valentino's death just two months earlier. And like Valentino's grave at the Hollywood Memorial Cemetery on the West Coast (which continues to draw fans and cultists to this day), Houdini's tomb at the Macpelah Cemetery in Queens has also seen its share of bizarre visitors over the years. Many of these are spiritualists who come to the Houdini crypt annually on Halloween to commemorate the many séances held by Houdini's widow to try to contact her husband after his death. Unfortunately, vandals have also visited the Houdini grave from time to time, and on various occasions have made off with the great magician/movie star's bust.

15. TABERNACLE OF PRAYER
16511 Jamaica Avenue

Today the discarded crutches of those who have been healed here hang beneath the two-story vaulted ceiling in the lobby of what is now the Tabernacle of Prayer. Before being born again as a house of worship, this Hollis, Queens, landmark was, from 1929 to 1977, the Loew's Valencia movie house. A dazzling mix of

Spanish Colonial and pre-Columbian architecture and decor, the Valencia had an auditorium that gave moviegoers the illusion that they were in a lushly planted patio under a moonlit sky. These days, many of the nude statues that adorned this fantasy patio have been given wings to make them more in keeping with the Valencia's present incarnation.

16. JOHN F. KENNEDY INTERNATIONAL AIRPORT
Jamaica

In the post-9/11 world, filming at major U.S. airports is extremely difficult, if not impossible. Before the tragedy, however, numerous films featured sequences at JFK—from *The Marrying Kind* (1952), when the airport was called Idlewild, to *Dog Day Afternoon* (1975), where the final showdown with the Al Pacino–led bank-robbing kidnappers takes place on the tarmac. Other pre 9/11 films that have JFK moments are *The Gang Who Couldn't Shoot Straight* (1971), *Addicted to Love* (1997), *The*

Tom Hanks and Leonardo DiCaprio in the pedestrian tunnel of Eero Saarinen–designed TWA terminal at JFK airport in *Catch Me If You Can*, 2002

Last Days of Disco (1998), and *Music of the Heart* (1999). One exception to the post-9/11 embargo on filming was *Catch Me If You Can* (2002), which used the striking Eero Saarinen–designed former Trans World Airlines terminal for the final scene where con man Frank Abaganale Jr. (Leonardo DiCaprio), impersonating an airline pilot, meets his FBI agent nemesis (Tom Hanks) in one of the terminal's distinctive tubular pedestrian tunnels. One of the reasons the film was able to shoot at the terminal was that TWA went out of business in October 2001, and abandoned its landmark JFK base at the same time. Current plans call for the sleek terminal, which opened in 1962, to be restored and redeveloped by the booming budget carrier Jet Blue.

The Bronx and Beyond: Final Stops

Like Brooklyn, the Bronx is noted for the many stars who were born here. Among them: Jennifer Lopez, James Caan, Tony Curtis, Carl Reiner, June Allyson, Anne Bancroft, Carroll O'Connor, Sal Mineo, and director Stanley Kubrick. Besides stars, the borough was also once noted for its movie studios. Perhaps the most important of these was the uptown branch of Biograph, whose large facility at 175th Street and Prospect Avenue dated back to 1905, and which, in its later years as Gold Medal Studios, was used both for feature films (*On the Waterfront, A Streetcar Named Desire, The Fugitive Kind*) and television productions (*Car 54, Where Are You?*). Then, too, there was Edison's Bronx facility, which went up in 1908 at Decatur Avenue and Oliver Place, and also hosted during the 1950s and 1960s a number of important TV series (*Man Against Crime, You Are There,* and *I Spy*) and film projects (*The Wrong Man, The Last Angry Man,* and *The Hustler*). Both studios are gone now, but another famous Bronx movie landmark, Loew's Paradise Theater, still stands and if all goes well will be restored and reopened soon.

North of the Bronx—in Westchester, Putnam, and Rockland counties—movie lovers will find areas that traditionally have provided instant small-town and/or rural locations for New

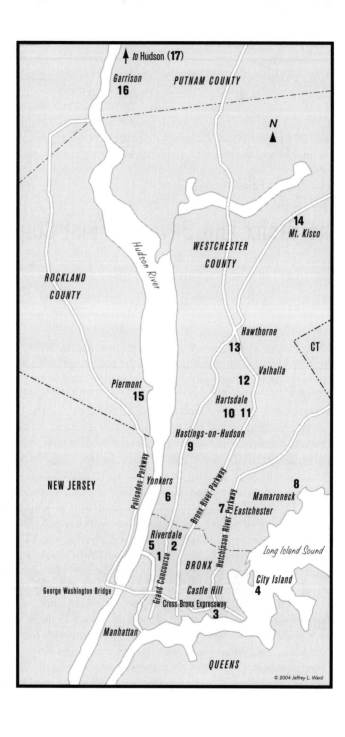

to Hudson (**17**)

Garrison
16

PUTNAM COUNTY

N

14
Mt. Kisco

WESTCHESTER
COUNTY

Hudson River

ROCKLAND
COUNTY

Hawthorne
13

CT

Valhalla
12

Piermont
15

Hartsdale
10 11

Hastings-on-Hudson
9

Palisades Parkway

NEW JERSEY

Yonkers
6

Bronx River Parkway

8
Mamaroneck

7 Eastchester

Hutchinson River Parkway

Riverdale
5   2
1

Long Island Sound

BRONX

George Washington Bridge

Grand Concourse

Castle Hill

City Island
4

Cross Bronx Expressway
3

Manhattan

QUEENS

© 2004 Jeffrey L. Ward

York film crews. But perhaps the greatest attractions awaiting movie lovers north of New York City are the superstar cemeteries of Westchester Country, where a surprising number of legends are buried—from the pop singer Aaliyah to classic screen queens Joan Crawford and Judy Garland. Neither depressing nor morbid, these beautiful, peaceful, dignified enclaves are a pleasure to visit and provide a fitting finale to the careers of some of the movie world's brightest stars.

1. LOEW'S PARADISE
2417 Grand Concourse

For the first half of the twentieth century, the Bronx's Grand Concourse was one of the most glamorous boulevards in the five boroughs. Often compared to the Champs-Élysées in Paris, this fabulous thoroughfare was divided by elegant islands and edged with stately apartment buildings. Mention the Grand Concourse today to anyone who grew up in the Bronx in the 1940s or 1950s, and they'll undoubtedly wax rhapsodic about

Paradise on the Grand Concourse: inside Loew's theater

this grand old main street, and they'll invariably go on to talk about its crown jewel—Loew's Paradise Theater. They won't have too much to say about the theater's exterior, because the Paradise had a rather conservative Italianate façade and a simple flat marquee, since Grand Concourse zoning laws forbade projecting marquees as well as big vertical signs. But just wait until they get to the inside!

The interior of this famous 1929 movie house was an extravaganza of baroque balconies and balustrades, columns and cornices, intricately sculpted niches that showcased exact copies of classical statues. To finish off the fantasy, the Paradise had a deep-blue ceiling where white puffy clouds drifted by and stars twinkled. A night at the Paradise was just about the closest anybody could get to heaven—certainly in the Bronx. The Paradise's atmospheric special effects as well as its overall design were the work of John Eberson, known among movie palace historians as the Father of the Atmospheric Theater. Besides being spectacular, Eberson's designs were amazingly cost-efficient, since the smooth-plaster ceilings of his houses were much less expensive to build than the ornate, chandelier-hung affairs that were customary in nonatmospheric theaters.

So it was a sad day both for the Bronx and for movie lovers when this great theater was twinned in 1974 and its lobby statuary painted blue. But that was just the beginning of the bad news. Two years later, the Paradise was triplexed, and in 1981 it was quadded. It closed down entirely in the early 1990s and its future looked grim—but a development group subsequently bought it, de-quadded it, and embarked on an exciting major restoration program to bring the theater back to its former glory as a concert and general entertainment venue. The project was never completed, however; the building changed hands once more, but now all work seems to have stopped, despite the fact that 3,800 brand-new seats are waiting to be installed. Hopefully, there's a happy Hollywood ending out there somewhere; otherwise, welcome to Paradise Lost.

2. FORDHAM UNIVERSITY
441 East Fordham Road, Bronx

This prestigious Jesuit institution was founded in 1841—and with its green lawns, spreading trees, and stately brick-and-stone buildings, Fordham's eighty-five-acre campus is one of the Bronx's loveliest sights. University records indicate that it was used in 1943 as the idyllic academic locale for the Pat O'Brien–Ruth Warrick biopic *The Iron Major,* based on the true story of a disabled World War I vet who became a famous football coach. Fordham was also the campus where gambling-addicted professor James Caan lectured in *The Gambler* (1974), where schizophrenic mathematician Russell Crowe advanced the science of abstract economics in *A Beautiful Mind* (2001), and where Liam Neeson, as controversial guru Alfred Kinsey, investigated the taboo subject of sex in puritanical 1940s America in *Kinsey* (2004). Frequently used to represent famous universities in other parts of the city and country, Fordham has doubled for Harvard in *Love Story* (1970), Georgetown in *The Exorcist* (1973), and Columbia in *Quiz Show* (1994).

Visit www.fordham.edu.

3. CASA LOPEZ
2210 Blackrock Avenue, Castle Hill, Bronx

Latina superstar Jennifer Lynn Lopez was born in the Bronx in 1970 of Newyorican parents. Proud of her Puerto Rican roots and her Bronx hometown, Lopez acknowledged both in her debut album *On the 6's,* which referenced her forays into Manhattan on the number 6 subway train and then in her 2002 hit song and video "Jenny from the Block," in honor of her middle-class Castle Hill Bronx neighborhood. Lopez attended local schools, eight years at the all-girls Holy Family Catholic elementary school, across the street from her house, before moving to Preston High School. As a young girl, she also studied with the esteemed Ballet Hispanico and eventually went on to dance with the Fly Girls on TV's *In Living Color* before hitting it big as a singer.

Lopez's move into acting was equally smooth. After some small roles, she won praise for her portrayal of the murdered Mexican singer Selena in the 1997 film of the same name. A year later she proved she was not a flash in the pan when she held her own opposite George Clooney in Stephen Soderbergh's *Out of Sight*. But her off-screen exploits have kept her in the news for reasons other than her talents. These include two divorces, being arrested with her on-again/off-again boyfriend Sean "Puffy" Combs, her disastrous on-again/off-again romance and engagement to Ben Affleck, not to mention their equally disastrous 2003 film *Gigli*, which is considered one of the worst films ever made, and recently her quickie marriage to Puerto Rican singing star Marc Anthony. There have also been rumors of serious diva behavior, even though Lopez, who travels with one of Hollywood's largest entourages, claims she's still "Jenny from the Block."

Meanwhile, her childhood home, where her room was on the

A long way from the block: Jennifer Lopez in *Maid in Manhattan*, 2003

Jennifer Lopez's childhood home, Castle Hill

second floor, still sits on Blackrock Avenue in Castle Hill. It had a brush with immortality in 2003, however, when some errant Fourth of July fireworks landed on the roof and almost burned the place down. The Guyanese family that purchased the house from the Lopezes in 1999 has since restored it.

4. *LONG DAY'S JOURNEY INTO NIGHT* HOUSE
21 Tier Street, City Island

Katharine Hepburn didn't want to play the part, and producer Ely Landau had to make two trips to Hollywood to convince her that she was both right for it and up to the rigors of doing Mary Tyrone in the 1962 film version of Eugene O'Neill's play *Long Day's Journey into Night*. And if Landau and director Sidney Lumet had had their way, Hepburn's costar in the film would not have been Sir Ralph Richardson, who wound up being cast, but rather Hepburn's longtime very close friend Spencer Tracy. But Tracy would have nothing of the $25,000 that Landau was offering to pay him to perform in the very low-budget movie.

"Look, Kate's the lunatic," Tracy is reported to have said to

Long Day's Journey into Night house, City Island

Landau and Lumet in Charles Higham's *Kate* (Norton, 1975). "She's the one who goes off and appears at Stratford in Shakespeare. I don't believe in that nonsense—I'm a movie actor. She's always doing these things for no money! Here you are with twenty-five thousand each for *Long Day's Journey*—crazy! I read it last night, and it's the best play I ever read. If you offered me this part for five hundred thousand and somebody else offered me another part for five hundred thousand, I'd take this!" But $500,000 was out of the question, and Hepburn wound up doing the film without Tracy.

Long Day's Journey into Night, which literally documents a *long* day in the life of the Tyrone family, whose problems range from alcoholism to drug addiction, takes place entirely at their Connecticut waterfront estate. Instead of going on location all the way up to Connecticut, Lumet and Landau found an ideal *Long Day's Journey* house on City Island, that delightfully remote, New England–like community in the Bronx that's linked via causeway to the rest of the borough. Needless to say, City Island was a lot closer than Connecticut to the Production Center Studios on West 26th Street in Manhattan, where the film's interiors were lensed. It was also a lot less expensive. Today, the

Long Day's Journey property, with its turreted mansion, distinctive gazebo, and low stone fences appears to have changed little since the early 1960s when the film was done. The pristine view across Eastchester Bay is another story, however, now that condo colonies have sprouted up on the other side. To do *Long Day's Journey* today, a producer just might have to go to Connecticut after all—or even farther.

5. JOSEPH P. KENNEDY ESTATE
5040 Independence Avenue, Riverdale

From 1926 to 1929, a very important film producer lived in this big white house at the corner of Independence Avenue and 252nd Street in the exclusive Bronx residential enclave of Riverdale. Although he is better known as the financier father of a U.S. president, two senators, and various other famous children among his brood of eight, Joseph P. Kennedy was in the film

Joseph P. Kennedy fiasco: *Queen Kelly,* with Gloria Swanson and Walter Byron, 1929

business in a big way in the 1920s. In fact, one of the reasons he moved his family from Boston to the Bronx in 1926 was so that he could head up Film Booking Offices of America (FBO), the production company he had just purchased.

Kennedy's FBO was definitely not a major studio and produced schlock titles like *The Dude Cowboy* and *Hot Hooves*. The company made money, however, and for Kennedy it was a foot in the door of a business that he found both seductive and lucrative. By 1929 Kennedy had acquired the Keith-Albee-Orpheum theater chain, and eventually he used his equity in this company to mastermind the merger deal that created RKO.

It was also during the late 1920s that Kennedy became professionally as well as emotionally involved with a great star of the era, Gloria Swanson. Taking a page from William Randolph Hearst's book, Kennedy served as executive producer on Swanson's films, just as Hearst did on the films of his mistress, Marion Davies. At the height of their affair, Kennedy is said to have made so many long-distance phone calls to Swanson that he had the largest private long-distance phone bill in America in 1929. Despite his attentiveness to his movie-star mistress, Kennedy was responsible for Swanson's greatest failure, a picture called *Queen Kelly*. Directed by Erich von Stroheim, the film ran so over budget and was so long that the project was shelved. (A reconstructed version has since been exhibited at film festivals and in art houses.) Then, not long after the *Queen Kelly* disaster, Swanson, who lost around $1 million of her own money on *Queen Kelly,* was also shelved by her producer/lover. By that time, Kennedy, who had somehow managed to make $5 million in the film business, had moved from Riverdale to an even grander estate in Bronxville, New York. Throughout his Hollywood/Swanson phase, Kennedy continued to be married to Rose Fitzgerald Kennedy.

6. YONKERS TRAIN STATION
Buena Vista Avenue at Dock Street, Yonkers

Whether it's Garbo watching Vronsky leave her life forever in *Anna Karenina* (1935) or Robert Donat saying good-bye in the Swiss Alps to Greer Garson in *Goodbye, Mr. Chips* (1939) or

Far from Heaven: Yonkers train station

Celia Johnson saying good-bye to Trevor Howard after their short love affair in *Brief Encounter* (1945) or Jennifer Jones running after the train that is taking her fiancé Robert Walker off to war (and death) in *Since You Went Away* (1944)—there's nothing like a train-station scene to heighten the drama, the emotion, and often the finality of a cinematic farewell. Often a combination of the trackside embrace, the train pulling away, slowly at first, usually swirled in steam, and then gaining speed, leaving one character anchored in their shared past, while the other goes off to another life. Back it all up with the right score—and there won't be a dry eye in the house.

In recent film history, no train-station farewell is more poignant than the classic one between Julianne Moore and Dennis Haysbert in Todd Haynes's *Far from Heaven* (2002). Knowing that their unconsummated interracial romance has no future—especially in late-1950s small-town America—they still have a few final trackside moments to wallow in what could have been. As the train pulls away, we see Moore still trying to hold on to the moment, as the Elmer Bernstein score soars. Then, accepting the finality of their situation, she turns and walks away. For this archetypal scene, Haynes made downtown Yonkers's train station look like a 1950s movie set thanks to the expertise of art director Peter Rogness, production designer Mark Friedberg, and a fleet of bright-colored vintage 1950s cars.

Meanwhile, *Far from Heaven* worked more magic in Yonkers, when the production turned the town's post office at 79–81 Main Street into the film's police station, where earlier in the film Moore bails out her alcoholic, sexually confused husband (Dennis Quaid).

7. *GARP* RESIDENCE
2 Brassie Road, Eastchester

Of all the crazy things that went on at this big white colonial house where Robin Williams faced the absurdities of life as T. S. Garp in the 1982 screen adaptation of John Irving's best-selling novel *The World According to Garp,* the craziest was when a small plane crashed into its side. While many of the exteriors of *The World According to Garp* were shot at this real house in Eastchester, New York, for that airplane sequence a mock-up of the side of the house was built at a private airport in Lincoln Park, New Jersey, where the "crash" was carefully controlled. Meanwhile, the interiors of the house were done on a soundstage at Kaufman Astoria Studios in Queens. Sometimes it takes a lot of houses to make a place a home—especially in the movies.

8. D. W. GRIFFITH STUDIO SITE
Orienta Point, Mamaroneck

In 1919, D. W. Griffith was at the height of his wealth, his fame, his power—and his hubris. It was the year that Griffith had joined with Mary Pickford, Charles Chaplin, and Douglas Fairbanks to form the revolutionary United Artists Corporation, which gave its star founders control over both the production and distribution of their films. It was also the year that Griffith decided to leave Hollywood and set up his own studio back east. The place Griffith chose for his operation was the former estate of Standard Oil/Florida real-estate millionaire Henry Flagler,

D. W. Griffith's Mamaroneck movie studio, ca. 1920

which occupied a secluded spit of land jutting out into the Long Island Sound near Mamaroneck. Besides making films here, Griffith planned to live on the estate, too—a situation which many felt fulfilled the Southern-born director's fantasies of being master of the plantation. Others who knew Griffith well also pointed out that the seclusion of Orienta Point would enable him to carry on his various romantic liaisons with young actresses far away from the prying New York press.

Griffith's first major film at his grand Mamaroneck estate-studio was *Way Down East* (1920), which was a big hit. Other ventures, such as *Dream Street* (1921), in which Griffith pioneered synchronized sound some six years before Warners released its first Vitaphone picture, were less successful. As for *Dream Street*'s sound system, Griffith became its biggest critic and discontinued its use immediately after the picture opened. In fact, Griffith eventually became one of the industry's most vocal anti-talkie spokesmen: "It puts us back to Babel," he once told

Made in Mamaroneck: D. W. Griffith directs *Orphans of the Storm*, 1921

Lillian Gish. "Do you realize how few people in the world speak English? If we make pictures that talk, we can't send them around the world. That's suicide."

Next to *Way Down East*, Griffith's most important film from his Mamaroneck period was *Orphans of the Storm* (1921). For this epic story of the French Revolution, enormous sets depicting eighteenth-century Paris were constructed at Mamaroneck—and Griffith deliberately scheduled the filming of major crowd scenes for weekends in order to use as many of the locals as extras as possible. After *Orphans of the Storm*, however, it was all down-hill for the great director, and by 1924 he was forced to abandon independent producing, signing on with Paramount to do pictures at Astoria. That same year, Griffith put his Mamaroneck estate up for sale, and in early 1925 a developer bought most of the property for the purpose of subdividing it.

Today all of the Griffith and Flagler buildings on Orienta Point are gone, and the property—once the site of the French Revolution—is now part of an exclusive, gated community.

9. WESTCHESTER HILLS CEMETERY
400 Saw Mill River Road, Hastings-on-Hudson

One of Westchester County's star cemeteries, Westchester Hills is a small Jewish burial ground that will intrigue movie lovers from the moment they drive inside. Just beyond the entrance, two large columned mausoleums stand across from each other, one on either side of the roadway. The one on the left belongs to the great showman Billy Rose, whose famous Manhattan nightclub, the Diamond Horseshoe, was immortalized in the 1945 Betty Grable–Dick Haymes musical, *Billy Rose's Diamond Horseshoe.* The mausoleum on the right is that of the Gershwin family, and contains the crypts of the immortal composer-lyricist brothers, George and Ira Gershwin, whose music graced such movies as *Delicious* (1931), *Girl Crazy* (1932), *Shall We Dance?* (1937), and *A Damsel in Distress* (1937). Although George Gershwin died in 1937 at the age of thirty-eight, his melodies have continued to inspire films and filmmakers such as Woody Allen, who relied exclusively on Gershwin for the score of *Manhattan.*

Up the road from the Gershwins, a large headstone bears the family name of Tuvim. While this name probably doesn't mean much to many movie lovers, a glance down at one of the smaller individual markers, will reveal that Judy Holliday (born Judith Tuvim) is buried here. Judy's first screen appearance was in a small role in Twentieth Century–Fox's musical *Greenwich Village,* in 1944, but it was her Broadway performance in 1946 as Billie Dawn, the lovable no-so-dumb blonde of *Born Yesterday,* that made her a star and that ultimately wound up bringing her an Academy Award for her performance in the film version in 1950. (Judy had stiff competition that year, by the way: She was up against Bette Davis in *All About Eve* and Gloria Swanson in *Sunset Boulevard.*) Judy Holliday, "Beloved Mother, Dear Daughter," died in 1965 of cancer at the age of forty-three.

Another star whose light faded prematurely was John Garfield, who was not quite forty when he died in 1952 of an apparent heart attack at the Gramercy Park apartment of a lady friend. Born Julius Garfinkle on the Lower East Side, Garfield lies toward the back of the Westchester Hills property, across the road from a large mausoleum that bears the name Silver. Garfield, "Beloved Husband and Father," became a big film star in the 1940s, but ran into trouble in the early 1950s when he was blacklisted for refusing to tell the House Un-American Activities Committee the names of his Hollywood friends who were suspected of being Communists.

The grave of director/producer Robert Rossen lies not too far from Garfield's (up the hill and off to the right where the road ends in a small traffic circle). It was Rossen who directed Garfield in his 1947 hit *Body and Soul*. Like Garfield, Rossen also refused to name names to HUAC in 1951, and his career ground to a halt. Two years later, however, Rossen went back before the committee and ratted on fifty of his colleagues. Although he made films afterward—including *The Hustler* in 1964—Rossen is said to have gone to his grave a haunted man. He died in 1966.

Finally, off to the left of Rossen's stone, movie lovers will find Lee and Paula Strasberg, the couple who founded the Actors Studio and who influenced the craft and careers of acting greats from James Dean to Marlon Brando to Marilyn Monroe. Paula Strasberg (1909–1966) was Marilyn Monroe's personal acting coach for many years, and is said to have driven many of Marilyn's directors crazy with the "private" directions she gave on the set to the insecure star. On the other hand, Lee Strasberg (1901–1982), in his later years, managed to practice in front of the cameras what he had been teaching from behind the scenes

George Gershwin
mausoleum,
Westchester Hills
Cemetery

for so long, when he appeared in—and won an Academy Award nomination for—*The Godfather, Part II,* in 1974. Strasberg then went on to act in other films, including 1979's *Boardwalk* and *Going in Style.* His tombstone is easy to miss, since it is in the shape of a rock and blends right in with the terrain of Westchester Hills.

The cemetery is open from 9 a.m. to 4 p.m. Sunday through Friday; closed on Saturdays.

10. FERNCLIFF CEMETERY
Secor Road, Hartsdale

It's about as far from Hollywood as anyone can get, this pastoral, very East Coast enclave of rolling hills, green lawns, and big shady trees that lies a few miles north of the town of Hartsdale, New York. The surprise is that two of Hollywood's all-time biggest stars are buried here—Judy Garland and Joan Crawford—both of whom got their start at the same studio: MGM. Who would have thought that they would wind up together in Westchester?

Actually, if Sid Luft, Garland's third husband and the father of two of her three children, had had his way, Judy would not have been buried at Ferncliff. Feeling that Hollywood—the town that had made her a star—was her real home, Luft had wanted Judy to be interred there. But Mickey Deans, Judy's fifth and final husband, as well as Liza Minnelli, her eldest daughter, felt that Judy would have preferred an East Coast cemetery because, according to them, she had never been fond of California. Since Deans had custody of Judy's body, and since Liza was handling the funeral arrangements, Sid couldn't argue.

At the time of Judy's death in 1969, Mickey Deans had plans for an elaborate tomb to be dedicated to the memory of his legendary wife of six months. Since the wing at Ferncliff that would house this memorial was still being built (and Deans didn't have the $37,500 to cover the cost of the crypt at the time), Judy was first put in a temporary vault. Deans had hoped to raise the needed money from Judy's friends and fans, but by November 1970, almost a year and a half after his wife's death, he still

Ferncliff legend:
Judy Garland

hadn't managed to pull it off. It was then that Liza stepped in and had her mother placed in a permanent and very simple wall crypt, which says only, "Judy Garland, 1922–1969." Movie lovers who visit Judy will find her on the second floor in the new wing of Ferncliff's main mausoleum (Unit 9, Alcove HH, Crypt 31). There is usually some kind of floral tribute in front of her beige marble slab, which is at floor level.

Downstairs in the old wing of the same building, movie lovers will find Joan Crawford in Unit 8, Alcove E, where her ashes rest in a vault next to that of her fourth and last husband, Pepsi-Cola executive Alfred N. Steele. The inscription is again very simple, just, "Joan Crawford, 1908–1977." Joan's fans may chuckle at these dates, however, because their idol was always notorious for lying about her age, and it seems that at Ferncliff she managed to pull off one final fib. At the latest, Joan was born in 1904, and according to one Hollywood contemporary who knew Joan when, it was really closer to 1901!

Besides Crawford and Garland, Hollywood is further represented at Ferncliff by Basil Rathbone (buried in the cemetery's smaller Shrine of Memories mausoleum), Ona Munson (who played Belle Watling in *Gone With the Wind*), Harold Arlen (who wrote Judy's "Over the Rainbow"), legendary director-screenwriter Preston Sturges (*The Lady Eve, Sullivan's Travels, The Great McGinty, The Palm Beach Story*), and silent-screen idol Richard Barthelmess (whom Lillian Gish described as "the most beautiful man who ever went before a camera"). More

Ferncliff names of note include the pop singer and fledgling film star Aaliyah (Haughton), who died in a plane crash in 2001 and whose crypt is in the main mausoleum (Unit 11, Alcove BBB, Crypt 114). As well as James Baldwin, Ed Sullivan, Jerome Kern, Richard Rodgers, Paul Robeson, Moss Hart, Elsa Maxwell, Connie Boswell, Diana Sands, Malcolm X, Sherman Billingsley, "Toots" Shore, Jackie "Moms" Mabley, Thelonius Monk, Adolph Caesar, and Sigmund Romberg. Welcome to Forest Lawn East!

Ferncliff is two miles north of Hartsdale on Route 9W. At Secor Road, turn left and continue for 1½ miles until you reach the driveway for the main mausoleum, which is off to the right. Ferncliff is open from 9 a.m. to 5 p.m. daily. Visit www.ferncliffcemetery.com.

11. HARTSDALE CANINE CEMETERY
75 North Central Avenue, Hartsdale

The oldest pet cemetery in the United States, Hartsdale Canine has buried some seventy thousand dogs and cats—as well as several hundred birds, fish, and at least one lion cub—since it opened in 1896. Among its dearly departed doggies are celebrity pets like Mariah Carey's cat Clarence, who joined Diana Ross's German shepherd Lady, Kate Smith's Freckles, George Raft's Ruggles, and Gene Krupa's Jerk and Susie. Dancer Irene Castle, actress Gloria (*Summer Stock*) DeHaven, 1950s TV queen Dagmar, radio host Barry Gray, band leader Xavier Cugat, and cosmetics empress Elizabeth Arden have also used Hartsdale's "complete interment services" over the years. Those services include transporting the animal to the cemetery, annual flower care, endowment plans for perpetual care—plus a wide assortment of burial vaults, headstones, and satin-lined caskets. Recently, cremation became another option available at Hartsdale. The most bizarre option of all, however, which around 150 people have chosen, is to be buried on the property next to one's pet.

In addition to the pets of the famous that populate Hartsdale Canine, the cemetery also has buried several animals who were celebrities in their own right. Vintage TV viewers may remember

Hartsdale Canine
Cemetery entrance

a winsome basset hound named Morgan, who appeared on the
tube with Perry Como, Jackie Gleason, Arthur Godfrey, and
Steve Allen in the 1950s, as well as on-screen opposite Dean
Martin and Jerry Lewis in *Living It Up* (1954). Morgan is at
Hartsdale, along with Boots, a 1940s canine film star credited
with helping to raise $9 million worth of war bonds during
World War II. When Boots died, his Hartsdale graveside service
received national media attention.

The cemetery and office are open Monday to Saturday from 8 a.m.
to 4:30 p.m., and on Sunday from 9:30 a.m. to 3:30 p.m. The staff
is very helpful in pointing out who's where. Visit www.petcem.com.

12. KENSICO CEMETERY
Lakeview Avenue, Valhalla

Gloriously landscaped, studded with splendid monuments and
mausoleums, Kensico is one of the most beautiful cemeteries in
the country. For movie lovers the main reason to visit here is to
pay one's respects to the multitalented Danny Kaye, born David
Daniel Kaminski in 1913, who died in 1987. A lovely memorial
bench marks the spot where Kaye and his longtime wife Sylvia
Fine—who wrote many of his songs and much of his material—
are buried not far from the cemetery entrance in Section 28,

across from Mineola Lake. After dropping out of school at age thirteen, Kaye started his career as a busboy/comic on the Borscht Circuit in the nearby Catskill Mountains. He later went on to great acclaim in vaudeville, nightclubs, and eventually Broadway, which led to a contract with Samuel Goldwyn in Hollywood in 1943. There he starred in such hits as *The Secret Life of Walter Mitty* (1947), *The Inspector General* (1949), *The Court Jester* (1956), and, perhaps his most memorable performance, in the title role of *Hans Christian Andersen* (1952).

Another Hollywood great here at Kensico is the enchanting Billie Burke, who will always be remembered as *The Wizard of Oz*'s Glinda, Good Witch of the North. Miss Burke also played Cosmo Topper's scatterbrained wife in the *Topper* series as well as a host of leading and character roles in films from the 1930s to the 1950s. Prior to her career in the talkies, Miss Burke was a popular Broadway performer, and in 1914 she married the legendary producer Florenz Ziegfeld (1868–1932), who managed her career until his death in 1932. At Kensico, Miss Burke, who died in 1970 at the age of eighty-five, is buried next to Ziegfeld

Danny Kaye, 1947

under a huge weeping willow tree at the end of Powhatan Avenue. The bronze statue of the dancing woman nearby is not Billie Burke, but her circus-performer mother, Blanche Betty Burke, who is interred here as well.

Four other notables at Kensico will please movie lovers. Not far from the Burke–Ziegfeld graves (at the intersection of Powhatan and Ossipee Avenues) lies the tomb of Thomas F. Dorsey Jr. (1915–1956). Dorsey's headstone is embossed with a trombone, musical notes, and the inscription: "The Sentimental Gentleman." A few steps away, novelist Ayn Rand (*The Fountainhead* . . . Gary Cooper, Patricia Neal—remember?) is buried. Farther afield, a large Russian Orthodox cross marks the plot where Russian-born composer Sergei Rachmaninoff (1873–1943) and his wife, Natalie, lie. Movie lovers who pass by may hear the notes of Rachmaninoff's *Variations on a Theme of Paganini,* which figured prominently in MGM's 1953 film, *The Story of Three Loves.* Finally, over in Sharon Gardens off Sharon Drive, the grave of screenwriter Paddy Chayefsky (1923–1981), who won Academy Awards for *Marty* (1955), *The Hospital* (1971), and *Network* (1976), can be found in the Community of Rye Synagogue section.

The Kensico Cemetery is open daily from 8:30 a.m. to 4:30 p.m.; the Sharon Gardens section is closed on Saturdays. The office provides a guide map to celebrity graves. Visit www.kensico.org.

13. GATE OF HEAVEN CEMETERY
Stevens Avenue, Hawthorne

Yet another of Westchester's superstar cemeteries, Gate of Heaven is the final resting place for some of New York's most famous Roman Catholics. Among those buried here are former New York City mayor Jimmy Walker, *What's My Line* alums Fred Allen and Dorothy Kilgallen, baseball great Babe Ruth, and movie stars James Cagney and Sal Mineo. The Gate of Heaven office staff will provide visitors with a map showing who's where.

Gate of Heaven is open daily from 8 a.m. to 5 p.m.

Ragtime house, Mount Kisco

14. *RAGTIME* HOUSE
81 Main Street, Mount Kisco

Although it was set in turn-of-the-century New York, *Ragtime* was shot largely in and around London. One American location that director Milos Forman did use (for both exteriors and interiors) in his 1980 film was this handsome hilltopping Victorian mansion in Mount Kisco. According to *Ragtime*'s art director, Patrizia von Brandenstein, she scouted hundreds of locations before coming up with this one.

The house lies along Route 133 just east of Sand Street.

15. *PURPLE ROSE OF CAIRO* TOWN
Piermont

When Woody Allen passed through the tiny Hudson River village of Piermont, New York, in the fall of 1983, the local paper called it a miracle. Not because Allen had chosen the place as the principal location for his film, *The Purple Rose of Cairo*, but because the film company had magically turned Piermont's clock back over half a century. The man behind the miracle was Stuart Wurtzel, the film's production designer, who dressed Piermont's

Main Street with false fronts, vintage signs, and antique cars to make it look just like a middle-American small town in the 1930s.

While movie lovers who visit Piermont may recognize some of the buildings on Main Street from *The Purple Rose of Cairo,* they will find one landmark missing: the Jewel movie theater, which played a major role in this story about a woman (Mia Farrow) who escapes the dreary realities of her small-town life by literally entering into the fantasy world of a film playing at the local movie house. The Jewel, it turns out, is now a parking lot. The Jewel, it also turns out, had been a parking lot before *The Purple Rose of Cairo* crew came to town and built a 1930s movie-house façade on the site. At the time it was all happening, Piermont locals watched with amazement as their town was transformed and then immortalized by Allen's cameras. It was an exciting ten days and nights. And then, practically as quickly as it began, the company wrapped its Piermont location, tore down the Jewel movie house and the other façades on Main Street, hauled away the vintage props and the antique cars, and Woody

Piermont locals see their town transformed for Woody Allen's *The Purple Rose of Cairo,* 1984

Allen and company picked up and disappeared, leaving Piermont pretty much as it had been before they came. In many ways, it wasn't unlike the ending of *The Purple Rose of Cairo*, where the film at the Jewel winds up its run, moves on to another theater in another town, and leaves Mia Farrow back in the real world again.

16. *HELLO, DOLLY!* VILLAGE
Garrison's Landing

In June 1968, the cast and crew of *Hello, Dolly!* descended upon the tiny village of Garrison's Landing, which lies on the east bank of the Hudson River, just across from West Point. To turn 1960s Garrison's Landing into 1890s Yonkers, Twentieth Century–Fox had spent weeks and used some thousand gallons of paint, six thousand pieces of lumber, three hundred truckloads of earth, and a hundred thousand square feet of lawn. The cost of the operation, which also involved transporting the *Dolly* company to New York from Los Angeles, where the principal photography was being done at Fox Studios on Pico Boulevard, was no object because this was a *big* picture, with a *big* director (Gene Kelly), based on a *big* Broadway hit, and featuring the decade's *biggest* star: Barbra Streisand.

There was also *big* trouble on the set between Miss Streisand and her leading man, Walter Matthau. And on one hot, humid, mosquito-swarming afternoon in Garrison's Landing, there erupted a battle that Mr. Matthau describes in Shaun Considine's *Barbra Streisand: The Woman, the Myth, the Music* (Delacorte Press, 1985) as follows:

> If the elements were not enough, Barbra kept asking Gene [Kelly] whether he didn't think it would be better if I did this on this line, and that on the other, et cetera, et cetera—and I told her to stop directing the fucking picture, which she took exception to, and there was a blowup in which I also told her she was a pipsqueak who didn't have the talent of a butterfly's fart. To which she replied I was jealous because I wasn't as good as she was. I'm not the most diplomatic man in the world, and we began a slanging match like a couple of kids

Hello, Dolly! at Garrison's Landing train station, 1968

from the ghetto. I think Gene thought one of us was going to die of apoplexy or something, or that I'd belt her, or maybe she'd scratch my eyes out—or worse, that we'd walk off, leaving twenty million dollars' worth of movie to go down the drain.

Today, anyone visiting Garrison's Landing will find it hard to imagine the above scene having taken place in this green, peaceful spot with its glorious views of the Hudson River. Besides the charm of the setting, movie lovers who visit Garrison's Landing will also find various vestiges of the *Hello, Dolly!* shoot. Most notable is the pretty white gazebo with the weathervane on top that is the centerpiece of the village's waterfront park, both of which were built for the film. (Actually, the gazebo is a replica of the Fox original, which had rotted so badly in the 1970s that it had to be replaced.) Not far from the gazebo, a barbershop advertises ten-cent haircuts and five-cent shaves. On closer inspection, the place turns out to be a façade. However, the solid three-story building with the big veranda around the corner is for real, housing an art studio and offices. If it looks familiar, that's because it served as Horace Vandergelder's grocery store in *Dolly*. Today its glass doors are still embossed with a large *V* and the name Vandergelder. Meanwhile, the little train station that Dolly used to go from Yonkers down to Manhattan is now a theater. But in the late 1960s, it was a working station. Supposedly, when its sign was changed from Garrison's Landing to Yonkers for the film, it confused quite a few commuters.

17. *ODDS AGAINST TOMORROW* TOWN
Hudson

This Hudson River port town with a population of 7,452 was the first city chartered after the signing of the Declaration of Independence, making it the first city chartered in the newly formed United States of America. Today Hudson is recovering

Downtown Hudson, as seen in *Odds Against Tomorrow*, 1959

from decades of stagnation and is currently a fashionable spot for New York City dwellers to have second homes. The community also has a thriving antiques scene, with numerous shops and boutiques dotting its downtown. In the late 1950s, Hudson had a brief fling with fame when director Robert Wise brought his film crew here along with stars Harry Belafonte, Robert Ryan, and Ed Begley (senior) for the thriller *Odds Against Tomorrow* (1959), tracing the above trio's plans to rob a bank in an unnamed small town, which happened to be Hudson. The bank they target—a distinctive neo-classical building—is still standing at Sixth and Warren Street. The town's main square, Warren Street (long before it was lined with antiques stores), and the Hudson River–fronting promenade also figured prominently in the film, whose plot was complicated by the fact that the Robert Ryan character was a racist and Belafonte was African American.

Index

p. iii Theatre Historical Society of America, Elmhurst, Ill./Michael R. Miller collection.

1. New Jersey: In the Beginning

Museum of Modern Art/Film Stills Archive; U.S. Department of the Interior National Park Service, Edison Historical Site; Library of Congress; Theatre Historical Society of America, Elmhurst, Ill./Michael R. Miller collection; Marc Wanamaker/Bison Archives; Marc Wanamaker/Bison Archives; Richard Alleman (RA); Tom Hanlon; Tom Hanlon; Tom Hanlon; RA; Patterson Museum; Marc Wanamaker/Bison Archives; Patterson Museum; RA; Photofest

2. Midtown Manhattan: Archetypal NYC

Theatre Historical Society of America, Elmhurst, Ill./Terry Hegelson collection; Marc Wanamaker/Bison Archives; Marc Wanamaker/Bison Archives; RA; RA; Courtesy Academy of Motion Picture Arts & Sciences; RA; RA; Courtesy Academy of Motion Picture Arts & Sciences; Algonquin Hotel; Kenneth Kneitel collection; Marc Wanamaker/Bison Archives; Museum of Modern Art/Film Stills Archive; Museum of Modern Art/Film Stills Archive; RA; RA; RA; Marc Wanamaker/Bison Archives; RA; Marc Wanamaker/Bison Archives; Westin Plaza; Marc Wanamaker/Bison Archives; Carnegie Hall; Marc Wanamaker/Bison Archives

3. Broadway: That's Entertainment!

Marc Wanamaker/Bison Archives; RA; Boneau/Bryan-Brown; RA; Theatre Historical Society of America, Elmhurst, Ill./Michael R. Miller collection; RA; Playbill; Photofest; Playbill; Marc Wanamaker/Bison Archives; Playbill; RA; Museum of Modern Art/Film Stills Archive; RA; Playbill; Museum of Modern Art/Film Stills Archive; RA; Theatre Historical Society of America, Elmhurst, Ill./Michael R. Miller collection; RA; Marc Wanamaker/Bison Archives; RA

4. The Upper East Side: Beverly Hills East

RA; RA; Photofest; Marc Wanamaker/Bison Archives; RA; Museum of Modern Art/Film Stills Archive; RA; Courtesy Academy of Motion Picture Arts & Sciences; Marc Wanamaker/Bison Archives; Museum of Modern Art/Film Stills Archive; RA; Kenneth Kneitel collection; Photofest; RA; RA; Courtesy Academy of Motion Picture Arts & Sciences; RA; Photofest; Marc Wanamaker/Bison Archives; Courtesy Academy of Motion Picture Arts & Sciences; RA; Museum of Modern Art/Film Stills Archive; Museum of Modern Art/Film Stills Archive; Mitchell-Manning-Vatter Associates; Mitchell-Manning-Vatter Associates; RA; RA; Ken Peters, courtesy Cooper-Hewitt National Design Museum; Museum of Modern Art/Film Stills Archive; Courtesy Academy of Motion Picture Arts & Sciences; Courtesy Academy of Motion Picture Arts & Sciences

5. Union Square/Gramercy Park/Chelsea: From Biograph to *Law & Order*

Marc Wanamaker/Bison Archives; Museum of Modern Art/Film Stills Archive; Museum of Modern Art/Film Stills Archive; RA; RA; RA; Courtesy Academy of Motion Picture Arts & Sciences; Marc Wanamaker/Bison Archives; RA; Marc Wanamaker/Bison Archives; RA; RA; Photofest; RA; Marc Wanamaker/Bison Archives; Marc Wanamaker/Bison Archives; Museum of Modern Art/Film Stills Archive; RA; American Academy of Dramatic Arts

6. Greenwich Village: The Big Back Lot

Photofest; RA; RA; RA; Joan Micklin Silver; Marc Wanamaker/Bison Archives; RA; RA; Marc Wanamaker/Bison Archives; Marc Wanamaker/Bison Archives; RA; RA; RA; RA; RA; RA; Howard Ottway Zodiac Photographers; Courtesy Academy of Motion Picture Arts & Sciences

7. SoHo/TriBeCa/NoLita: The "New" New York

Photofest; Andy Schwartz/Photofest; RA; RA; Courtesy Academy of Motion Picture Arts & Sciences; RA; RA; RA; RA; Photofest; RA; RA; RA; RA

8. Lower Manhattan/Staten Island: Old New York

Marc Wanamaker/Bison Archives; RA; Photofest; RA; RA; Marc Wanamaker/Bison Archives; Marc Wanamaker/Bison Archives; RA; RA; RA; Museum of Modern Art/Film Stills Archive; Marc Wanamaker/Bison Archives; Courtesy Academy of Motion Picture Arts & Sciences; Courtesy Academy of Motion Picture Arts & Sciences; RA; RA; Marc Wanamaker/Bison Archives; Courtesy Academy of Motion Picture Arts & Sciences

9. The Upper West Side: Rebel Territory

Courtesy Academy of Motion Picture Arts & Sciences; RA; RA; Marc Wanamaker/Bison Archives; RA; Museum of Modern Art/Film Stills Archive; Museum of Modern Art/Film Stills Archive; RA; Museum of Modern Art/Film Stills Archive; RA; RA; Museum of Modern Art/Film Stills Archive; RA; RA; RA; RA; RA; RA; Photofest; RA; RA; Marc Wanamaker/Bison Archives; Museum of Modern Art/Film Stills Archive; RA

10. Harlem/Washington Heights: Uptown Renaissance

Theatre Historical Society of America, Elmhurst, Ill./Michael R. Miller collection; RA; RA; Photofest; Museum of Modern Art/Film Stills Archive; RA; RA; Marc Wanamaker/Bison Archives; RA; RA; Museum of Modern Art/Film Stills Archive; RA; RA; Courtesy Academy of Motion Picture Arts & Sciences; RA; Museum of Modern Art/Film Stills Archive; RA; Theatre Historical Society of America, Elmhurst, Ill./Michael R. Miller collection; Courtesy Academy of Motion Picture Arts & Sciences; Photofest

11. Brooklyn: Hometown of the Stars

Brooklyn Bridge Centennial Committee; RA; Courtesy Academy of Motion Picture Arts & Sciences; Theatre Historical Society of America, Elmhurst, Ill./Michael R. Miller collection; Marc Wanamaker/Bison Archives; Museum of Modern Art/Film Stills Archive; Photofest; RA; Museum of Modern Art/Film Stills Archives; RA; RA; RA; RA; Museum of Modern Art/Film

Stills Archives; RA; RA; Erasmus Hall High School; Theatre Historical Society of America, Elmhurst, Ill./Michael R. Miller collection; Museum of Modern Art/Film Stills Archive; RA; Marc Wanamaker/Bison Archives; Museum of Modern Art/Film Stills Archive; RA; Museum of Modern Art/Film Stills Archive; Museum of Modern Art/Film Stills Archive; Photofest; Courtesy Academy of Motion Picture Arts & Sciences; Courtesy Academy of Motion Picture Arts & Sciences

12. Queens: The Return of the Movies

American Museum of the Moving Image; Museum of Modern Art/Film Stills Archive; American Museum of the Moving Image; American Museum of the Moving Image; Photofest; RA; Photofest; Bayside Historical Society; Bayside Historical Society; Springer/Photofest; RA; RA; Theatre Historical Society of America, Elmhurst, Ill./Michael R. Miller collection; Courtesy Academy of Motion Picture Arts & Sciences

13. The Bronx and Beyond: Final Stops

Theatre Historical Society of America, Elmhurst, Ill./Michael R. Miller collection; Photofest; RA; RA; Museum of Modern Art/Film Stills Archive; RA; Museum of Modern Art/Film Stills Archive; RA; Martin J. Walsh; RA; Photofest; RA; Sally Savage; Museum of Modern Art/Film Stills Archive; Courtesy Academy of Motion Picture Arts & Sciences

ABOUT THE AUTHOR

RICHARD ALLEMAN, a longtime contributing editor at *Travel + Leisure* magazine, is a former travel editor of *Vogue*, where he is still a regular contributor on travel and entertainment. An actor who has appeared in a number of films and TV shows, including *Sex and the City* and *Law & Order*, he lives and works in New York.